# Histories of international legal theories in Japan

Manchester University Press

MELLAND SCHILL PERSPECTIVES ON INTERNATIONAL LAW

*General editors*
Jean d'Aspremont
Iain Scobbie
Sufyan Droubi

Building on the history of Melland Schill Classics and Melland Schill Studies at Manchester University Press, Melland Schill Perspectives on International Law was established to reflect the diversity of international legal scholarship worldwide. This inclusive, accessible series aims to offer a platform for scholars from different regions who adopt innovative approaches to new and old topics.

Melland Schill Perspectives on International Law is founded on the idea that every international legal issue should be debated from various and, at times, incommensurable perspectives. Though there is a great deal of diversity in international legal debates and practice, this diversity is often obfuscated by prevailing Euro-centric and positivist narratives, which not only creates difficulties for non-Western scholars to be heard but hinders the development of different approaches.

To buy or to find out more about the books currently available in this series, please go to: https://manchesteruniversitypress.co.uk/series/melland-schill-perspectives-on-international-law/

# Histories of international legal theories in Japan

## From dialogue to conversation

Edited by Maiko Meguro and Yota Negishi

Manchester University Press

Published by Manchester University Press
Oxford Road, Manchester, M13 9PL

www.manchesteruniversitypress.co.uk

British Library Cataloguing-in-Publication Data
A catalogue record for this book is available from the British Library

ISBN 978 1 5261 7494 9 hardback

First published 2026



EU authorised representative for GPSR:
Easy Access System Europe, Mustamäe tee 50, 10621 Tallinn, Estonia
gpsr.requests@easproject.com

Typeset
by Deanta Global Publishing Services, Chennai, India

# Contents

# Contributors

## FUKUSHIMA Ryoshi (福島涼史)

**Affiliation:** *Faculty of Law, Otemon Gakuin University*
Ryoshi Fukushima is Associate Professor at Otemon Gakuin University. He holds an MA (2000) and a PhD (2006) from Kyoto University, Graduate School of Human and Environmental Studies, where his doctoral thesis examined just war theories and their theoretical backgrounds. He also earned a PhD (2013) from Osaka University, Graduate School of Law, with a doctoral thesis on the public law theory of Carl Schmitt. He served as a Lecturer at Siebold University of Nagasaki from 2010 to 2014 and has been Associate Professor since 2014. His research interests encompass the intersection of international law theory, just war doctrine and constitutional public law theory, particularly examining how German legal philosophy influenced Japanese international legal scholarship during the interwar period.

## KAKU Shun (郭舜)

**Affiliation:** *Faculty of Law, Waseda University*
Shun Kaku is Professor of Legal Philosophy at the Faculty of Law, Waseda University. He previously served as a Research Associate at the University of Tokyo and Associate Professor of Legal Philosophy at Hokkaido University and has held various research positions, including Visiting Fellow at the Lauterpacht Centre for International Law, University of Cambridge, Visiting Researcher at the Max Planck Institute for Comparative Public Law and International Law and Special Research Fellow of the Alexander von Humboldt Foundation. He is a member of the Executive Committee of the Japanese Association of Legal Philosophy. His research ranges from general issues in analytical and normative jurisprudence to questions concerning the concept and moral foundations of international law and the relationship between international and domestic legal systems. He is the author

of *Reclaiming the Philosophy of International Law* (2022, in Japanese), which won the JALP prize 2024, and a co-editor of *The Enterprise of Legal Philosophy* (2025, in Japanese).

## KANETAKE Machiko (金武真智子)

**Affiliation:** *Amsterdam Law School, University of Amsterdam; TMC Asser Instituut*
Machiko Kanetake is Professor of International Law and Security Governance at the University of Amsterdam and Academic Director of the TMC Asser Instituut. She received her PhD from Kyoto University and LLM from the London School of Economics. Previously, she served as a Postdoctoral Researcher and Lecturer at the University of Amsterdam (2011–2014), Hauser Visiting Doctoral Researcher at New York University School of Law (2010–2011), Visiting Fellow at Harvard Law School's Human Rights Program (2014–2015) and Visiting Fellow at King's College London (2015). She serves on the Editorial Board of the *Leiden Journal of International Law*. For her 2018 article on domestic courts' engagement with UN treaty bodies published in ICLQ, she received the G. J. Wiarda Prize 2019.

## KODERA Satoshi (小寺智史)

**Affiliation:** *Faculty of Law, Seinan Gakuin University*
Satoshi Kodera is Professor at the Faculty of Law, Seinan Gakuin University, Fukuoka, Japan. His research focuses on public international law, international economic law, international law of development and the psychology of international law. He is co-author of *The Introduction to WTO and FTA Law*, 2nd edition (Horitsu Bunkasha, 2021, in Japanese). His diverse publications include studies on special and differential treatment in the free trade system in *Public Policy Review*, vol. 20(4) (2024), on flexibility of norms in international labour law in *The Journal of International Law and Policy*, vol. 121(1) (2022, in Japanese) and on critical streams in French international law doctrine in *Yearbook of World Law*, No. 40 (2021, in Japanese).

## MEGURO Maiko (目黒麻生子)

**Affiliation:** *Amsterdam Law School, University of Amsterdam*
Maiko Meguro is Research Fellow at the Amsterdam Centre for International Law, University of Amsterdam, and Lead Coordinator and Senior Policy

Analyst of the OECD. Her expertise includes legal theory, trade law, law and technology, climate change and interdisciplinary approaches to international law. Her career spans policy-making and legal scholarship. She served as Japan's senior negotiator and co-chair of the G7 Digital and Tech Ministerial Working Group. At Japan's Ministry of Economy, Trade and Industry and the Digital Agency, she was Head of Division, leading international data governance negotiations and frameworks for Data Free Flow with Trust, while representing Japan in G7/G20, OECD, United Nations and other international forums. She previously worked as Legal Officer at the European Commission's DG CONNECT. Her publications appear in various journals, including the *Leiden Journal of International Law* and the *American Journal of International Law*. She has contributed to publications by Oxford University Press and Edward Elgar.

## MORITA Akio (森田章夫)

**Affiliation:** *Faculty of Law, Hosei University*
Akio Morita is Professor of International Law at the Faculty of Law, Hosei University, holding a Doctor of Law degree from the Postgraduate Course of Law and Politics, University of Tokyo. His academic career began at the Faculty of Law, Tokyo Metropolitan University, before he assumed his current position. He has served as Visiting Fellow at the Lauterpacht Centre for International Law, University of Cambridge, and NILOS (The Netherlands Institute for the Law of the Sea), Utrecht University. He serves as a Council member of several academic societies, including the Japanese Society of International Law, the Japanese Association of World Law and the Japan Association of International Economic Law. He has been a member of the Associate Editors of the *Japanese Yearbook of International Law*.

## NEGISHI Yota (根岸陽太)

**Affiliation:** *Seinan Gakuin University*
Yota Negishi is Professor of Public International Law at Seinan Gakuin University, Fukuoka, Japan. He holds an LLM and a PhD from Waseda University in Tokyo. He conducted research on comparative public law and international law as a Doctoral and Postdoctoral Research Fellow of the Japan Society for the Promotion of Science (2013–2017). He stayed as a Visiting Scholar at the Max Planck Institute for Comparative Public Law and International Law in Heidelberg (2014–2017). His monograph *Conventionality Control of Domestic Law: Constitutionalised International*

*Adjudication and Internationalised Constitutional Adjudication* was published by Nomos in 2021. His contributions appear in publications by Cambridge University Press and distinguished journals, including the *European Journal of International Law*. He was granted the sixth IKUSHI Prize, established by the Japan Society for the Promotion of Science with the endowment from Emperor Akihito.

## NISHI Taira (西平等)

**Affiliation:** *Faculty of Law, Kansai University*
Taira Nishi is Professor of International Law at Kansai University, Osaka. He graduated from the Faculty of Law at Tokyo University in 1995 and earned his LLM (1997) and PhD (2018) in law from Tokyo University. He served as Research Fellow at the Institute for Social Sciences, University of Tokyo (2000–2003), and Guest Researcher at the Max-Planck-Institut für europäische Rechtsgeschichte (2001–2002). He has taught international law at Kansai University as a Lecturer (2004–2006), Associate Professor (2006–2013) and Professor (2013–present). His monograph on the genealogy of international political science was published by Nagoya University Press in 2018 (in Japanese). His English publications focus on legal protection structures and methodological debates in international law scholarship.

## OGURI Hirofumi (小栗寛史)

**Affiliation:** *Keio University Law School*
Hirofumi Oguri is Associate Professor of International Law at Keio University Law School. He obtained his PhD from Kyushu University in 2018, with a dissertation on the structure and development of consensual theory in the history of international law, revisiting Lassa Oppenheim's common consent theory (in Japanese). Previously, he served as a Visiting Researcher at the Max Planck Institute for Comparative Public Law and International Law, a Visiting Researcher at the University of Vienna, Faculty of Law, and a Lecturer (2020–2023) and Associate Professor (2023–2025) at the Okayama University. His research interests lie in the history of international law, with a particular focus on the development of European Law of Nations in the nineteenth century and its reception in East Asia, including Japan. His recent publications in English include 'Inseparable Pairs for Modernising Japan? Japanese Ministry of Foreign Affairs and Academia, 1880–1914'; in P. Allorant et al. (eds), *Relations internationales et droit(s)/ Law(s) and International Relations* (Pedone, 2024).

## TAKATA Hinako (髙田陽奈子)

**Affiliation:** *Osaka School of International Public Policy (OSIPP), Osaka University*

Hinako Takata is Associate Professor of Public International Law at Osaka University. She earned her PhD from Kyoto University in 2019. Her research focuses on the interactions between human rights treaty organs – the European Court of Human Rights, the Inter-American Court of Human Rights and the UN Human Rights Committee – and state organs such as parliaments, courts, administrative organs and national human rights institutions. She has developed original theoretical frameworks, including the separation of powers in a globalised democratic society, two-tiered bounded deliberative democracy and inter-state organ norms. Her forthcoming monograph, *Pluralising Actors and Norms in Human Rights Treaties: Beyond Monolithic States* (Hart Publishing), synthesises these ideas. Her work has appeared in leading journals such as *Human Rights Law Review*, *Global Constitutionalism* and the *German Law Journal*, as well as in the *Max Planck Encyclopedia of International Law* (Oxford University Press, online edition).

## TOYODA Tetsuya (豊田哲也)

**Affiliation:** *Akita International University*

Tetsuya Toyoda, Professor of International Law at Akita International University, obtained a DEA from the Université of Paris-II in 1997. After working at the Japanese Ministry of Foreign Affairs (1994–2000), he started to teach at Akita International University in 2007. Fellow at the Woodrow Wilson International Center for Scholars (2013–2014) and Visiting Scholar at the University of Buckingham (2018–2019), he authored *Theory and Politics of the Law of Nations: Political Bias in International Law Discourse of Seven German Court Councilors in the Seventeenth and Eighteenth Centuries* (Martinus Nijhoff, 2011) and articles in English, Japanese and French, including 'Exclusive Legal Personality of States in East Asia and the Legacy of Bandung Pragmatism', *Indonesian Journal of International Law*, vol. 21(2) and 'Universality and Peculiarity of the Concept of Exclusive Territoriality – The Linearization of Borders and Territorial Sovereignty in East Asia Since the Late 19th Century', *Japanese Yearbook of International Law*, vol. 66, both in 2023.

## WANI Kentaro (和仁健太郎)

**Affiliation:** *Osaka School of International Public Policy (OSIPP), Osaka University*
Kentaro Wani is Professor of Public International Law at Osaka University. He holds an LLB from Sophia University (1999), an MA (2001) and a PhD (2007) from the University of Tokyo. He joined Osaka University in October 2010 as Associate Professor and has served as Professor since August 2021. His research interests encompass the law of armed conflict, the use of force in international law, the law of the sea and the history of international law. His principal publications include the monograph *Neutrality in International Law: From the Sixteenth Century to 1945* (Routledge, 2017), articles on the law of the sea and the legal status of international straits in times of armed conflict in the *Japanese Yearbook of International Law*, vol. 61 (2019) and on the status of rebels in non-international armed conflict in *Changing Actors in International Law* (Brill, 2020).

## YAMASHITA Tomoko (山下朋子)

**Affiliation:** *Associate Professor of International Economic Law, Osaka Metropolitan University*
Tomoko Yamashita is an Associate Professor at Osaka Metropolitan University. She holds a PhD (2015), an LLM (2009) and an LLB (2007) from Kobe University, Japan, complemented by a Master complémentaire en droit international (2012) from the Université Libre de Bruxelles, Belgium. Dr Yamashita's research is grounded in the theoretical foundations of customary international law, particularly in the context of diplomatic protection. Her scholarship has evolved to focus on the protection of individuals through the law of state responsibility, bridging classical and contemporary international legal challenges. Before her current appointment, she served at Aichi Prefectural University (2017–2025). Her key English-language publications include chapters in the edited volumes *International Organizations, Non-State Actors, and the Formation of Customary International Law* (Manchester University Press, 2020) and *Human Rights and Power in Times of Globalisation* (Brill Nijhoff, 2018).

# Introduction

This book intends to present two issues: the first is a genealogy of Japanese international legal theory, tracing the theoretical themes and academic struggles of thirteen scholars situated in their respective historical contexts. By so doing, it illustrates one national tradition in international law. The second is to invite readers to experiment with, or practise in the face of an academic current that seeks to construct common ground in international law in the post-critical era.

In the face of increasing visibility of hierarchy and gaps in international law, the current state of international legal scholarship is often broadly presented as oscillating between doctrinal approaches that embrace pragmatic resignation and overconfidence in inherent commonalities based on a vision of a better future through dialogue across different traditions and cultures. The former is based on the view that, regardless of its Eurocentric pedigree, for international law to function, the common foundation currently envisaged must continue to be logically and institutionally assumed. The latter continues to actively address perceived gaps in the reconstruction of such common ground by borrowing various methodologies and frameworks from adjacent disciplines. This book does not choose resignation in the post-critical era, nor does it overestimate commonality as academic work from an international law perspective in the non-Western tradition. In our daily lives as international lawyers, we have seen the differences between the assumptions of international law and our traditions.

The central theme of this volume is the mode of inter-traditional communication and its implementation in international law. The mode of inter-traditional communication that it seeks is not 'dialogue'. Instead, it invites the readers to join the 'conversation'. While conversation can sometimes be used interchangeably with dialogue, for the sake of this book, they are defined as two different modes of communication.

While many contemporary international lawyers are well aware of the naive triumphalism of Western civilisation underlying beliefs in universalism, scholarship keeps returning to the project of creating a universal base as the next step after the multi-perspectivist productions that advertised how diverse the world still is. For example, collecting and consolidating the histories of international law (turn to history), studying and comparing modern legal systems and finding common elements (turn to comparatism) and turning to the universal truth status of scientific theories or evidence (turn to empiricism). While seeking a common foundation is inevitable for making sense of international law, previous studies repeatedly contended that there is an obvious lack of non-Western experience in international legal theories.[1] While the scholarly discourses often experience extreme oscillation between over-denial and over-affirmation of universality, what must be acknowledged is that the discipline is still left without the framework and methodology to redefine the foundation of what makes international law 'inter-national'.[2]

In this Introduction, the authors particularly focus on the mode of communication between different legal traditions.[3] We consider the dominant mode of communication to be in the form of *dialogue* – embedded in the epistemological and empirical lens that we apply in the daily practice of international law. The mode of dialogue is, in our view, framed by 'commensurability thinking' based on the ontological hierarchy that reproduces and strengthens the existing structures that scholars are meant to overcome through the attempt at communication. The following will define 'dialogue' and 'conversation' as modes of communication across different legal traditions within international law: whereas 'dialogue' seeks to reach a common truth through the confrontation of different positions, 'conversation' prioritises the continuation of exchange without demanding commensurable outcomes. It will also explain how the mode of dialogue persists in the existing efforts to reconstruct the common ground of international law and

1 Luis Eslava and Sundhya Pahuja, 'Between Resistance and Reform: TWAIL and the Universality of International Law' (2011) 3 *Trade, Law and Development* 103; Martti Koskenniemi, 'Histories of International Law: Dealing with Eurocentrism' (2011) *Rechtsgeschichte* 19; B. S. Chimni, 'The Past, Present and Future of International Law: A Critical Third World Approach' (2007) 8(2) *Melbourne Journal of International Law* 499; Karin Mickelson, 'Rhetoric and Rage: Third World Voices in International Legal Discourse' (1998) 16(2) *Wisconsin International Law Journal* 353; Karin Mickelson, 'Taking Stock of TWAIL Histories' (2008) 10 *International Community Law Review* 355; Makau Mutua, 'What Is TWAIL?' (2004) 94 *Proceedings of the ASIL Ann. Meeting* 31; Sundhya Pahuja, *Decolonising International Law: Development, Economic Growth and the Politics of Universality* (2011); Anne Orford, *International Law and its Others* (Cambridge University Press 2009).

2 MEGURO Maiko, 'Appraisal of Diversity in International Law: A Note on Self-Serving Biases and Interdisciplinarity' in P. Westerman, K. Gorobets and A. Hadjigeorgiou (eds), *Philosophical (De)Constructions of International Law* (Edward Elgar Publishing 2021).

3 The authors are aware that the presentation of 'Western' and 'non-Western' traditions is also another construction that serves the purpose of the discourse they are making.

is deeply rooted in the fundamental structure of international law as law and discipline. After delineating the issue of dialogue, the authors propose a new mode of communication, *conversation* based on the thoughts of Tatsuo Inoue, whose focus is to continue conversations among parties. In order to continue 'conversation', Inoue argues that the focus should always be on the manner necessary for parties to continue conversations. In this view, seeking commensurable outcomes, or even expecting that parties will understand one another in the end, is counterproductive for communication.

## Quest for commonalities: the trap of commensurability in theoretical and empirical inquiry in international legal discourse

International legal scholars have, in recent years, increasingly grappled with multi-perspectivism in international law, questioning what international law *is* and *should be*. It follows decades of critical examination of the remaining gaps in the ways international law is adopted and applied. This recognition fuelled a series of scholarly quests for new means to appreciate the diversity that remains in international law and to redefine its commonalities, which is tied to the ambition to achieve genuine communication across the legal traditions, to better integrate the inclusive and overarching foundation of international law and to re-establish the authority of international law. In doing so, international legal scholarship has borrowed frameworks and methods from various other disciplines and has created major interdisciplinary trends: the turn to history, the turn to comparatism and the turn to empiricism. While one of the main themes of this book is to propose a new mode of communication, 'conversation' to cross-cultural aspects under international law, this section explains why the various existing methods are not sufficient to start with. In the following, we will revisit these 'turns' in light of their underlying communicative mode of 'dialogue' and seek to elucidate the trap of commensurability thinking.[4]

The notion of dialogue has received a great deal of attention as scholarship grapples with multiple perspectives, pluralism, global constitutional concepts and interactions among related disciplines. In particular, the notion is widely used across international law, constitutional law and various

4 The term 'commensurability thinking' is used by d'Aspremont as assuming 'permanent comparability between all legal artefacts, legal institutions, legal practices, and interpretations thereof falling under the purview of the comparativist project, irrespective of their location and time'. For this book, we reconstructed the notion as building upon the nature of discipline as law. See Jean d'Aspremont, 'Comparativism and Colonizing Thinking in International Law' (2019) 57 *Canadian Yearbook of International Law* 89–112.

branches of law in rephrasing referring, borrowing, citing judgments, decisions, reasonings, thoughts and other relevant knowledge from 'other' institutions such as foreign law,[5] other branches of law[6] or other disciplines[7]. Engaging with comparative law itself can also be called dialogue.[8] It should also be noted that there is increasing direct interaction among legal scholars and professionals across regions in person or otherwise. The 'dialogue' metaphor conveys an image of 'inclusive and mutual' engagement where all participants are entitled and empowered to speak. The image provides much appeal. Yet, from the perspective defended in this book, the dialogue is problematic both empirically and epistemologically. Namely, even as traffic in ideas is growing more than at any time in history, much of it remains one-way for the discipline of law.[9]

Even when focusing on diverse perspectives, much of this international law research ultimately boils down to finding commonalities among the various legal perspectives that can be summarised as international law. This is inevitable as long as international law advocates as 'law'. The modes of legal reasoning and various modes of thinking that make international law a jurisprudence are patterned after national laws that have a body of law. Furthermore, 'the very notion of 'a legal system' implies that a legal order is in some significant sense a 'unity', '(t)he whole of jurisprudence, indeed, is in a sense an explanation of this assumption'.[10] It is true that international law is situated in a different context from domestic law, and we must bear in mind that not all of it can be spoken of by analogy. Yet, at least insofar as international law is treated as 'law', this means that the 'unity'

5 For example, Tara Leigh Grove, 'The International Judicial Dialogue: When Domestic Constitutional Courts Join the Conversation' (2001) 114 *Harvard Law Review* 2049; Lee Epstein and Jack Knight, 'Constitutional Borrowing and Nonborrowing' (2003) *International Journal of Constitutional Law* 196; Christopher McCrudden, 'Common Law of Human Rights? Transnational Judicial Conversations on Constitutional Rights' (2000) 20 *Oxford Journal of Legal Studies* 499.

6 For example, Anne-Marie Slaughter, 'A Global Community of Courts' (2003) 44 *Harvard International Law Journal* 191; Melissa Waters, 'Mediating Norms and Identity: The Role of Transnational Judicial Dialogue in Creating and Enforcing International Law' 93 *Georgetown Law Journal* (2005).

7 For example, Marcílio Toscano Franca Filho, 'Westphalia: A Paradigm? A Dialogue Between Law, Art and Philosophy of Science' (2007) 8 *German Law Journal* 955.

8 Sujit Choudhry, 'Globalization in Search of Justification: Toward a Theory of Comparative Constitutional Interpretation' (1999) 74 *Indiana Law Journal* 3, 836.

9 Generally, on this point, see, for example, David S. Law and Chang Wen-Chang, 'The Limits of Global Judicial Dialogue' (2011) 86 *Washington Law Review* 523, especially, 528–525.

10 Julius Stones, *Legal Systems and Lawyers' Reasonings* (Stanford University Press 1964) 1.

of international law as a system requirement is continuously reproduced through the practice of judges, scholars and other legal practitioners who have received common specialised training in the patterns of legal reasoning and legal knowledge. The edited volume argues that this structural bias towards unity shapes the current mode of communication among different legal traditions within the discipline of international law (termed 'dialogue' in this edited volume) in a way that recognises and seeks to overcome the gaps, rather than respecting them as they are.

Another fundamental issue is that the vocabulary, techniques, understandings and value standards that define the patterns of professional thought and practice in international law continue to be Eurocentric, and it will not change. It is deeply integrated into the identity of international law. That is, the criteria for determining what is and is not appropriate for the current 'academic framework of international law' are Eurocentric. Even if one tries to overcome Eurocentrism, the gap between the centre and the periphery is the distance between the identity of international law itself and the periphery. The more eager they are to engage in dialogue with the periphery, the more the process of integration of heresy into orthodoxy advances. Of course, through the tireless efforts of critical thinkers and a growing understanding of Eurocentrism, self-reflexive pluralist and multiculturalist tendencies have become a trend in Western academia. The problem, however, is that these works inevitably involve the act of comparing, which rests on the assumption of comparability and commensurability.[11] Will the result of these efforts of reconciliations not be a reproduction of past Eurocentric patterns?

It is precisely this question that the editors and the authors who participated in the project of this volume – a systematic presentation of Japan's international legal tradition – faced. Even if one speaks of an 'international law' tradition tied to the periphery – to Japan's own context – it is necessary to adopt a common cognitive framework of international law and relevant concepts of international law (even though that is the problem) in order to write content that can be accepted as reliable expert knowledge in the field by the readers, or to put it simply, for the reader to understand the book's content in relation to international law. In doing so, we must accept that there are indigenous elements in our tradition of 'international law' (which are written and practised in Japanese) missed and uncaptured by such frameworks, concepts and argumentative patterns tied to them. Nevertheless, this is a necessary and bitter task in order to begin the new

11 d'Aspremont, 'Comparativism and Colonizing Thinking in International Law' (n 4).

mode of communication called 'conversation', which we present with other legal traditions.

*Turn to history* is one of the most common ways to critically unearth alternative paths and semantic causalities to the official story among the major interdisciplinary trends to facilitate communication among different clans and traditions. It has been a recurring and symbolic trend in international legal scholarship.[12] History is a defining feature of a discipline. A discipline of law is built upon pedigree, which is a defining framework of semantics and disciplinary continuity. Engaging with the history of international law is not only about changing how we perceive the past, but also how it determines the present.[13] The history of international law is the linchpin of the discipline of international law, which continues to define the way to understand what international law *is* and *should be*.

Yet, there is persistent criticism that the disciplinary history is an expression of Euro-expansionism,[14] since a vast majority of markers, periodisation and causal sequencing to give shape to the history of international law are Western events, legal thoughts and other key publications.[15] These critics revealed that the learning and training of international law is an adopting process to the pattern of building thoughts, reasons, logic and arguments that are rooted in European traditions. The past decades witnessed the surging number of scholarly works on the thread of multi-perspectivism, moving away from 'grand Eurocentric narratives and toward global, micro, and subaltern histories; a renewed interest in socio-historical accounts of the

12 Craven illustrates how the historisation of international law at the end of the eighteenth century contributed to the formation of 'European International Law' in addition to new 'Third World' trends of turning to history. See Matthew Craven, 'Theorizing the Turn to History in International Law' in Anne Orford and Florian Hoffmann (eds), *The Oxford Handbook of the Theory of International Law* (Oxford University Press 2016).

13 Orford writes, 'the past, far from being gone, is constantly being retrieved as a source or rationalisation of present obligation'. See Anne Orford, 'On International Legal Method' (2013) 1 *London Review of International Law* 175.

14 Martti Koskenniemi, *Gentle Civilizer of Nations* (Cambridge University Press 2004); David W. Kennedy, 'International Law and the Nineteenth Century: History of an Illusion' (1996) 65 *Nordic Journal of International Law* 385.

15 Martti Koskenniemi, 'Histories of International Law: Significance and Problems for a Critical View' (2013) 27 *Temple International and Comparative Law Journal* 215; A. Claire Cutler, 'Critical Reflections on the Westphalian Assumptions of International Law and Organization: A Crisis of Legitimacy' (2001) 27 *Review of International Studies* 133; Jean d'Aspremont, 'Critical Histories of International Law and the Repression of Disciplinary Imagination' (2019) 7 *London Review of International Law* 89, 4.

profession'.[16] However, some also point out that such repeated criticism has yet to renew the historical markers, periodisation and causal sequencing against which they meant to counter. d'Aspremont aptly states, '(h)istorical critique has merely been a matter of 'applying' differently the very categories around which mainstream historical narratives are articulated, critical histories often being reduced to a variant of the linear disciplinary histories with which they are engaged'[17]. Yet the question was also raised whether we could actually reproduce a new version of history by renewing markers, periodisation and causal sequencing without losing the continuity and integrity of the field. Koskenniemi has illustrated how a critical historian would face difficulty in writing a professionally credible version of history, even in making a critique of Eurocentrism, since all the intellectual language, frameworks and other key notions in making professional discussion in the field are all 'European'.[18]

The structure of this volume cannot be fundamentally immune to such criticism. However, it must also be clarified that Japanese international law has, in some respects, been defined by its defence against Western colonialism, its confrontation with Western powers in the inter-war period and the Second World War, its desire for an independent line against the Western-centric world structure and its distance from the West. Drawing upon the fact that the relationship between Japan and international law (scholarship) has been contoured by the tensions between Western modernity and the country's own 'context', the edited volume emphasises that the historical context is a key determinant of the thoughts in Japanese traditions of international law. The chapters on respective Japanese thinkers are placed to analyse how Japanese traditions of international law developed in the light of the following periodisation: (1) the initial stage: acceptance of international law; (2) the inter-war period; (3) during the war; (4) the post-war period (from 1945 to the 1970s); (5) from the 1970s to the end of the Cold War; and (6) from the end of the Cold War to the present.

For example, the chapter on SENGA Tsurutaro (the chapter by Toyoda) illustrates how Senga theoretically defended positivism from the viewpoint of protecting Japan's sovereignty against civilisation-oriented Eurocentrism at the dawn of Japan's international legal scholarship. TABATA Shigejiro (the chapter by Kanetake), in his early days, critically examined the principle

16 Thomas Skouteris, 'The Turn to History in International Law' *Oxford Bibliographies* https://doi.org/10.1093/OBO/9780199796953-0154

17 Jean d'Aspremont, 'Critical Histories of International Law' 19 (n 15).

18 Koskenniemi, 'Histories of International Law: Significance and Problems for a Critical View' 222–224.

of equality developed by Western scholars to function as a 'regulative principle of international society' during the Second World. In the same book, his argument justified 'the Greater East Asia Co-Prosperity Sphere' promoted by Japanese militarism as the sphere of 'cooperative internationalism', and the argument remained in his post-war writings as a legal order based upon a 'large space' (*kōiki*), which is a general idea in his theory. His contemporary, YASUI Kaoru (discussed in the chapter by Yamashita), is also another figure who contributed to the notion of the Greater East Asia Co-Prosperity Sphere by drawing inspiration from critics of Western liberal democracy, such as Hans Morgenthau, E. H. Carr and Carl Schmitt.

The anti-positivist, then activist, stance of SOGAWA Takeo (the chapter by Nishi) was also built around the sharp contestation with YOKOTA Kisaburo over the US–Japan Security Treaty. Yokota (the chapter by Tanaka), on the other hand, took a purely legalistic position that could be called the Japanese Kelsen, and his consistent pragmatic interpretation of the UN Charter, the Japanese Constitution, and the Japan–US Security Treaty helped Japan to accept the reality of the Cold War regime in which it was forced to become involved. Even in the twenty-first century, ONUMA Yasuaki (the chapter by Kaku) and KOTERA Akira (the chapter by Meguro), who had been long-time colleagues at the University of Tokyo, were academically at odds with each other in various debates about the function of international law, the role of international courts and how Japanese 'peripheral' lawyers should strategically engage with international law. Underlying the controversy, too, was a common theme of what non-Western international lawyers should do in light of the Eurocentric reality.

The chapters in this volume also discuss how Japanese scholars have defined themselves as peripheral in the context of the conflict that Japan is still only a 'black sheep', despite its successful adaptation to the current international system and international law, and how, in facing the Western-led discipline, these scholars more or less fostered their unique legal thoughts and standpoints.

*Turn to comparatism* is another novel trend in international legal scholarship to find the common framework among the different legal systems within the international community in this context. This Introduction, for the reason explained earlier, refrains from facile comparatism. However, it must also be recognised that behind the development of the Japanese tradition of international legal theory has been an awareness of the gap between Japan and the West. And for the authors of this book, too, when discussing the Japanese tradition in relation to international law, they cannot help but find there the problem of the gap between legitimate international law and us – that is, comparison.

While the results of major works in comparative international law so far have been relatively modest, concerns are already common in the field of comparative legal studies. As LaGrand aptly states, there is always the risk that engaging with other traditions would result in 'an act of totalisation that neutralises the other'.[19] A similar warning has been issued by Frankenburg that seeking and comparing with other perspectives has the dimension of a self-confirming exercise of unity and divergence according to the underlying ideologies.[20] All these warnings again pertain to the very standard that frames the disciplinary boundaries, namely, what is *relevant* for comparing. When two or more legal traditions are compared in relation to, within or for the purpose of international law, the said discipline's epistemological limits also determine the very lens of observation in defining the relevant 'otherness' to be considered and the irrelevant 'exoticism' to be disregarded.

There appears to be no clear methodological response to address or mitigate these concerns in comparative international law. However, the ambition of this field at this moment may not be so high either. Roberts et al. explain that the field of comparative international law is purported to penetrate international law's 'aspirations to universality and uniformity' by contextualising its study in the series of attempts to emphasise the local, national and regional approaches regarding the tradition and practice of international law.[21] In defining the field of comparative international law, the authors distinguished the field from the study on fragmentation by highlighting 'it focuses largely on *similarities and differences* between national or regional actors in their approaches to international law'.[22] Roberts later stated in her monograph that there is not really an 'invisible college of international lawyers' as Schachter claims, but that there is more a divided college composed of 'different national communities of international lawyers' who construct 'their understandings of international law in ways that [challenge] the field's claim to universality'.[23] Overall, she concludes that 'taking an intellectually

19 Pierre Legrand, 'The Same and the Different' in Pierre Legrand and Roderick Munday (eds), *Comparative Legal Studies: Traditions and Transitions* (Cambridge University Press 2003) 300.

20 Gunter Frankenberg, 'Critical Comparisons: Re-Thinking Comparative Law' (1986) 26 *Harvard International Law Journal* 422.

21 Anthea Roberts, Paul B. Stephan, Pierre-Hugues Verdier and Mila Versteeg, 'Comparative International Law: Framing the Field' (2017) 109 *American Journal of International Law* 467.

22 Ibid 469.

23 Robert compared the practices of the five permanent member states of the United Nations Security Council regarding the educational profiles of universities, university hiring processes, trans-border student flows, publication links with practice and

honest look ... means acknowledging in a pluralist – or realist – way that there may not be just one universal way of understanding and applying international law'.[24]

Japanese scholars can also be considered members of such a community of nations. For example, Kotera had the vision that there is no one universal way to understand and apply international law, and that both frontier and mainstream jurists should co-construct an understanding of the 'universality' of international law through practice, reflecting individual circumstances through interpretation. On the other hand, YAMAMOTO (the chapter by Morita) is internationally known as one of the scholars who systematically organised and theorised the concept of 'international administrative law'.[25] In this book, Yamamoto is the only jurist who does not bring Japan's regional characteristics into his research, and his stance differs from that of Kotera, who is also a doctrinal jurist but has a strong frontier perspective and strategic intent based on that perspective.

The assumption that international law, being law, cannot escape the assumption of certain universality is embedded in the expertise and professional ethics of international legal scholars. From the perspective defended in this paper, this pattern of thinking is what creates the epistemological problem of excluding what is not commensurable, or failing to recognise what is not commensurable, in an attempt to address the problems in ways that are comfortable as law when relying on turns to methodologies such as history or comparatism. This is what is called here the 'trap of commensurability'.

MOGAMI Toshiki (the chapter by Negishi), described as 'one of those in the histories of Japanese international legal theories, who clearly and consciously set out his normative position' should be mentioned here. While being less active in the West than Onuma, he is a scholar who, like Onuma, has developed his arguments from a deconstruction of international law. His theory is still a work in progress, but as a Christian, critical thinker and non-Westerner, his 'awaken-normative realist' perspective may provide an exquisitely nuanced narrative of international law in the context of Russia's invasion of Ukraine. Mogami, who states 'we must live the "post-Ukraine" not without, but with, Russia', insists on shelving normative judgments other than excluding those who are not commensurable within the

textbooks published in these countries. See Anthea Roberts, *Is International Law International?* (Oxford University Press 2017) 312–325.

24 Ibid 22.

25 For example, when Kingsbury et al. proclaimed the emergence of global administrative law, Yamamoto was introduced as the major prior work in the field. See Benedict Kingsbury, Nico Krisch and Richard B. Stewart, 'The Emergence of Global Administrative Law' (2005) 68 *Law and Contemporary Problems* 15.

framework of international law, and works on the process of correcting the flaws in the system with an eye to the reality of the double standard in which Western nations justify their own violence by using international law.

The previous critical studies on comparative law indicate that ideas are consumed by comparison during the 'dialogue' type communication with other ideologies and cultural traditions. The degree of exhaustion is more intense the further away from the orthodoxy, as the frame of discipline is defined by orthodoxy. This theory by Mogami may eventually represent one theoretical consequence of the 'conversation' considered in the next section.

*Turn to empiricism* is also driven by a similar desire to reintegrate the foundations of international law. Instead of the belief that the authority of law is given ('a dogma') or derived from the accordance with the fundamental values (a moral), some international lawyers attempt to overcome the eroding formalistic foundation of law by demonstrating the conditions under which international law actually produces effects based on a scientific approach.[26] A new realist lawyer, Greg Shaffer, called the latest wave of this trend the 'empirical turn in international legal scholarship'.[27] They defined the scope of the empirical turn as 'midrange theorizing concerning the conditions under which international law (IL) is formed and those under which it has effects in different contexts, aiming to explain variation'.[28] The empirical turn introduces international legal scholarship to the development and testing of explanatory hypotheses about the role of international law, often transplanting the existing social science theories, such as realist, rationalist, institutionalist, constructivist, sociological, law and society theories.[29] By so doing, it is meant to provide the picture of the operative mechanism behind the law, on which the scholars seek to build a firmer ground of legal 'science'.

While the original intention is to transplant a social scientific basis to strengthen the authority of international law, the turn to empiricism is

26 The focus on law's functioning from a social science standpoint is not new for legal studies. Max Weber, for example, emphasised sociological perspectives to explain law's functioning not from a normative but from a causal standpoint. For international law, the stocktaking by Abebe et al. stated, 'scholars have argued that international law should be studied using a "scientific" approach'. See Daniel Abebe, Adam Chilton and Tom Ginsburg, 'The Social Science Approach to International Law' (2021) 22 *Chinese Journal of International Law* 1, 23.

27 Gregory Shaffer and Tom Ginsburg, 'The Empirical Turn in International Legal Scholarship' (2012) 106 *American Journal of International Law* 1.

28 Ibid 1.

29 For the stocktaking of the approach, ibid 6–7. See also Karen J. Alter 'Visions of International Law: An Interdisciplinary Retrospective' (2020) 33 *Leiden Journal of International Law* 837.

said to suffer from an existential scepticism as a branch of legal study, as well as criticism of its disciplinary status as science. The first criticism is that it would simply strip off the law's normative dimension ('ought') and disaggregate law into a set of descriptive functions.[30] This criticism does not readily concern the inquiry of the current chapter. The second claim is what directly concerns the issue, namely, there is a flaw or potential flaw in the current framework of empiricism for the purpose of identifying the diversity and re-integrating the foundation of international law. One of the most common criticisms of the empirical turn, or interdisciplinary approach in this perspective, is that these studies are actually not testing but producing an explanatory construction.[31] It is mainly caused by the flaws of original disciplines that scholars have borrowed – namely, these studies often lack a causal explanation, are characterised by spontaneous and arbitrary ways of collecting evidence and lack the framework to evaluate evidence.[32] All thus end up applying assumptions of respective theories in the alleged observation. The assumptions – such as that the way states should behave, a rational individual should behave or an increased number of NGOs should bring about – all function as filters in collecting and evaluating empirical facts. In other words, empirical facts are *produced*, rather than collected, through the standards that pre-exist in the minds of international lawyers.[33]

It is no exaggeration to say that reliance on social science, not to say empirical studies, is still heresy in Japanese academic circles today. Moreover, interdisciplinary study in social science in the Japanese tradition of international law has always developed around Marxism.[34] For example, MATSUI Yoshihiro (the chapter by Kodera) developed the tradition of international law as a social science in Japan. His perspective of international law is also rooted in Marxism, a lens that has probably allowed him to incorporate analysis on the socioeconomic foundations of international law

30 See, in general, ONUMA Yasuaki, 'International Law in and with International Politics: The Function of International Law in International Society' (2003) 14 *European Journal of International Law* 105; also, Simon Chesterman, 'Herding Schrodinger's Cats: The Limits of the Social Science Approach to International Law' (2021) 22 *Chinese Journal of International Law* 49, 51–55.

31 For example, Oona A. Hathaway and Ariel N. Lavinbuk, 'Rationalism and Revisionism in International Law' (2006) 119 *Harvard Law Review* 1404; Andrew Moravcsik 'Bringing Constructivist Integration Theory Out of the Clouds: Has it Landed Yet?' (2001) 2(2) *European Union Politics* 226.

32 A proposed solution to these problems is to turn to experimental and behavioural insights. For example, Anne van Aaken 'Experimental Insights for International Legal Theory' (2019) 30 *European Journal of International Law* 1237; Harlan Grant Cohen and Timothy Meyer (eds), *International Law as Behavior* (Cambridge University Press 2021).

33 MEGURO, 'Appraisal of Diversity in International Law' (n 2).

34 See Chapter 10 by KODERA Satoshi in this book.

and to actively situate non-state actors behind the veil of the state within international law. Due to the Marxist orientation of the Japanese interdisciplinary tradition, the influence of the various methodological revolutions in the past decades does not seem to have had much of an impact in Japan. However, all international law scholars, whether in the position of observer or observed, should keep in mind the risks of commensurability thinking underlying the disguise of science in empirical approaches. As with the turns to history and comparatism, the empirical turn thus illustrates that the quest for commonalities, however methodologically refined, remains caught in the epistemological structure that presupposes what ought to be examined. It is this shared predicament that calls for a different mode of communication.

## Conversations with the incommensurable

### *From dialogue to conversation*

To avoid the aforementioned trap of commensurability in comparing international legal histories and theories, this section explores a new approach: assuming the incommensurable therein. In a nutshell, our approach shifts emphasis from *dialogue* (*Taiwa*: 対話) to *conversation* (*Kaiwa*: 会話). These two concepts are etymologically differentiated as Japanese philosopher NOE Keiichi explains in his commentary on the Japanese translation of Richard Rorty's *Philosophy and the Mirror of Nature*.[35] According to Noe, dialogue is the Greek-rooted concept *διάλογος*, implying the duel between different *logos* seeking to reach the truth. In contrast, conversation, originating from the Latin word *conversari*, simply puts prime importance on maintaining open and friendly personal relationships, thereby enabling *conviviality* (*Kyosei*: 共生) with heterogeneous people.[36]

Noe draws inspiration for the concept of conviviality from Japanese legal philosopher INOUE Tatsuo's masterpiece titled *Manner of Kyosei: Justice as Conversation*.[37] In envisioning a liberal type of *Kyosei* in the manner of ordinary human conversation, Inoue refers to Michael Oakeshott's two social models:[38] setting apart from the communicatively substantive community

35 TANI Tōru, 'Japanese Phenomenology' in Bret W. Davis (ed.), *The Oxford Handbook of Japanese Philosophy* (Oxford University Press 2020) 631–648.

36 NOE Keiichi, 'Epilogue' in the translation of Richard Rorty, *Philosophy and the Mirror of Nature* (Sangyo Tosyo 1993) 487–488. See also, USUI Mikoto, 'A Socio-Philosophical Perspective on Our *Kyosei Science(s)*' (2012) 2 *Journal of Kyosei Studies* 9–19, 12–13.

37 INOUE Tatsuo, *Manner of Kyosei: Justice as Conversation* (*Kyosei no Saho: Kaiwa to shite no Seigi*) (Keiso Shobo, New and Improved Edition 2021).

38 Michael Oakeshott, *Rationalism in Politics and Other Essays* (Methuen 1962) 197–199.

of *universitas*, Inoue seeks a formal social union of *societas* by stipulating the twofold 'decorum' not to end conversations, namely *reciprocal recognition* and *respectful care*.[39] First, a conversation ceases by losing its reciprocity when the division of roles between speakers and audiences occurs – a speaker either compels audiences to remain silent or abandons their responsibility to speak to them.[40] The decorum of reciprocal recognition does not demand the exchange of roles for finishing a dialogical goal, as communication theories do, but rather the *aufheben* of these roles for continuing conversations in equality.[41]

Rorty's *Philosophy and the Mirror of Nature*, another inspirational source for Noe, also owes a debt to Michael Oakeshott's distinction between *universitas* and *societas* to struggle against the epistemological 'assumption that all contributions to a given discourse are commensurable'.[42] In contrast to the desire for truth in epistemology, for Rorty, hermeneutical conversations embrace the desire for *edification* (corresponding to *Bildung* in the Gadamerian terminology) 'to reinterpret our familiar surroundings in the unfamiliar terms of our new inventions'.[43] As rephrased in *Science as Solidarity*, the conversational attempt at edification brings about the result where '[b]eliefs suggested by another individual or another culture must be tested by trying to weave them together with beliefs which we already have'.[44] Since the phenomenon of continually reweaving a web of beliefs necessarily involves a first-person plural perspective blurring the traditional distinction between subjectivity and objectivity, Rorty substitutes the latter with the intersubjective idea of *unforced agreement*.[45] Rorty's position is labelled ethnocentrism by himself, but he convincingly rejects the imputation of relativism by claiming that we must 'simply ... work by our own lights' because 'there are no other lights to work by'.[46]

The shift of emphasis from dialogue to conversation also occurs in social science, especially global international relations. A sophisticated theory is offered by Karin Fierke and Vivienne Jabri, who identify the intertwined

39 INOUE 256–257 (n 37).
40 Ibid.
41 Ibid 257–258.
42 Richard Rorty, *Philosophy and the Mirror of Nature* (Princeton University Press 1979) 316–318.
43 Ibid 360.
44 Ibid.
45 Richard Rorty, 'Science as Solidarity' in John S Nelson, Allan Megill and Deirdre N McCloskey (eds), *The Rhetoric of the Human Sciences* (University of Wisconsin Press 1987) 38–52, 43.
46 Ibid 44.

triangle elements of conversations to depart from the ideal type of dialogues: first, *normative ethos* that '[c]onversations aren't won and lost but involve a more open-ended exchange that is receptive to difference and by which difference is continuously transformed'; second, *constitutive* ontology/epistemology that '[f]ar from a static exchange between a priori identities, conversation shapes and reshapes difference and being along the way'; and third, *globality* in that 'difference is constituted within relationships and belongs to a relational whole'.[47] In formulating the first and third legs, Fierke and Jabri are indebted to Lily Ling, who developed the notion of *epistemic compassion* on the image of *bodhisattva Guanyin*. Like the Buddhist metaphor's thousand arms and eyes, epistemic compassion tends towards Others by learning from them while stemming from one body politic.[48] Rephrasing it with the wording of NISHIDA Kitaro (Japanese leading philosopher of the Kyoto School),[49] Ling envisions that our *world-of-worlds* (*Sekaiteki Sekai*: 世界的世界) as a totality is still affirmed by epistemic compassion embracing a thousand ways of knowing and being.[50] Fierke and Jabri's second limb complements Ling's observation on the Part–Total relationality, which 'is itself constitutive of global conversation and is reproduced and constituted in turn by such conversations as these occur in situated practices'.[51]

### *Conversation with the incommensurable in international law*

The idea of conversation can be applied to the field of international law. In the final chapter of *From Apology to Utopia*, Koskenniemi illustrates 'the process of conversation' as a way of critical practice and imposes the following two conditions for it: 'the solution must be arrived at through an open (uncoerced) discussion of the alternative material justifications; two, the critical process must continue and put that rival justification – as it will now have become part of dominant consciousness – to future criticism'.[52]

47 Karin M. Fierke and Vivienne Jabri, 'Global Conversations: Relationality, Embodiment and Power in the Move Towards a Global IR' (2019) 8 *Global Constitutionalism* 506–535, 524.

48 Lily H. M. Ling, 'Postcolonial-Feminism: Transformative Possibilities in Thought and Action, Heart and Soul' (2016) 19 *Postcolonial Studies* 478–480, 479.

49 For a critical analysis of Nishida's concept of world-of-worlds, see Yoko Arisaka, 'The Controversial Cultural Identity of Japanese Philosophy' in Bret W. Davis (ed.), *The Oxford Handbook of Japanese Philosophy* (Oxford University Press 2020) 755–780.

50 Lily H. M. Ling, 'Three-ness: Healing World Politics with Epistemic Compassion' (2019) 39 *Politics* 35–49, 36, fn 2.

51 Fierke and Jabri 524 (n 47).

52 Martti Koskenniemi, *From Apology to Utopia: The Structure of International Legal Argument, Reissue with a New Epilogue* (Cambridge University Press 2006) 545.

By explicitly citing Rorty's theory of conversation, Koskenniemi regards the conditions of openness and continuity of conversation as the bases for the institutional ideal of a 'conversant culture'.[53] While he mentions the practical application of conversation, Koskenniemi does not go into any further depth about its potential role in international law. The editors thus set the threefold *decorum* of conversations with the incommensurable for international legal histories and theories by underpinning the philosophical and social science theories with the genealogy of hermeneutics.[54]

First, conversations with the incommensurable bracket the *objective–universal* foundation for the scientific truth of international law. Oscar Schachter famously coined the concept of *invisible college*, 'the professional community of international lawyers [...], though dispersed throughout the world and engaged in diverse occupations, [...] dedicated to a common intellectual enterprise'.[55] To consolidate the disciplinary distinctiveness of international law, constantly *historicising* and *theorising* their argumentations 'constitute the core business of international lawyers in the many capacities with which they intervene in the problems of the world'.[56] As evinced by a recent empirical analysis, however, the discourse of international law has mainly been influenced by a small and tight-knit community of iconic intellectuals composed of white men from the developed world.[57] To avoid a naive universalist objectivism merely camouflaging particular hegemonic interests, conversations in international legal history and theory acknowledge the stance of *perspectivism*: knowledge is never absolute but always biased and based on one's personal interpretation of reality.[58] It does not mean, however, that our approach lapses into nihilism or solipsism;

53 Ibid 546.

54 Alexandra Kemmerer, 'Sources in the Meta-Theory of International Law: Hermeneutical Conversations' in Samantha Besson and Jean d'Aspremont (eds), *The Oxford Handbook on the Sources of International Law* (Oxford University Press 2017) 469–490, 487.

55 Oscar Schachter, 'The Invisible College of International Lawyers' (1977–8) 72 *Northwestern University Law Review* 217–226.

56 Jean d'Aspremont, '[Introduction] International Law, Theory and History: Ordering Through Distinctions' in Jean d'Aspremont (ed.), *The History and Theory of International Law*, vol. I: *Historicizing the Theory of International Law* and vol. II: *Theorizing the Histories of International Law* (Edward Elgar 2020).

57 Luiza Leão Soares Pereira and Niccolò Rid, 'Mapping the "Invisible College of International Lawyers" Through Obituaries' (2021) 34 *Leiden Journal of International Law* 67–91.

58 Andrea Bianchi, *International Law Theories: An Inquiry into Different Ways of Thinking* (Oxford University Press 2016) 17–18 (referring to Friedrich Nietzsche's perspectivism).

rather, bracketing the objective truth permits the existence of multiple first-person plural perspectives.[59]

Second, conversations with the incommensurable, therefore, entail the plurality of *subjective-relative* perspectives based on our own lived experiences of international lawyers.[60] According to a hermeneutical account of law(yering), the encounter between lawyers and clients usually begins not with a written legal text but rather an unwritten, 'face-to-face' conversation, in which the emerging relationship has a set of 'affective' components.[61] This embodied critique also brings international lawyers 'face-to-face' with 'emotional' dispositions as well as historical practices, attitudes and habits, all of which have become part of the discipline's background.[62] Affective or emotional elements expressed in words and behavioural modes are one of the vital portions of conversations, providing clues to illuminating 'historically embedded and embodied relations of power that shape who can speak and who is silenced or heard'.[63] Silence of the unspeakable, which has been regarded as a deliberate and conscious act of defiance in the dominant communicative theory, is thereby salvaged in our approach as 'a consequence of externally and internally imposed force'.[64] Embodied sensibility in conversations is not just a subjective characteristic of particular individuals but is fostered through 'the complicated relationship between the projects of individuals and their simultaneous participation in the dynamic, multiple, and contested collective endeavor'.[65]

59 Anne Peters, 'Multiperspectivism in and on International Law (The Introduction to the symposium on "South and East Asian Perspectives on International Law")', *Völkerrechtsblog*, posted on 15 January 2019; *Ignacio de la Rasilla del Moral, International Law and History: Modern Interfaces* (Cambridge University Press 2021) Chapter 11.

60 Husserliana (hereinafter Hua) VI: *Die Krisis der europäischen Wissenschaften und die transzendentale Phänomenologie* (1954) 158–159.

61 Julian Webb, 'On Encountering Life and Learning With/out the Text: Reflections on Bańkowski and Del Mar' in Zenon Bańkowski and Maksymilian Del Mar (eds), *The Moral Imagination and the Legal Life: Beyond Text in Legal Education* (Ashgate 2016) 65–84.

62 Sahib Singh, 'Koskenniemi's Images of the International Lawyer' (2016) 29 *Leiden Journal of International Law* 699–726, 726 referring to Martti Koskenniemi, *The Gentle Civilizer of Nations: The Rise and Fall of International Law 1870–1960* (Cambridge University Press 2001) 7 ('[i]nternational law is also a terrain of fear and ambition, fantasy and desire, conflict and utopia, and a host of other aspects of the phenomenological lives of its practitioners').

63 Fierke and Jabri 509, 523 (n 47).

64 Ibid 516–517, 523 citing Edward Said, *Culture and Imperialism* (Chatto and Windus 1993) 278

65 Andrew Lang and Susan Marks, 'People with Projects: Writing the Lives of International Lawyers' (2013) 27 *Temple International & Comparative Law Journal*

Third, conversations with the incommensurable ingrains afresh the scientific foundation of international law in the *intersubjective–correlational* constitution of worlds.[66] It is noticeable in this direction that Roberts' idea of *divisible college*,[67] opposing Schachter's invisible college, situates international legal argumentations in a certain number of we-ness (first-person plural perspective) or 'localizable standpoint'.[68] Nonetheless, the plurality of first-person plural perspectives does not simply show the boundaries of fragmented colleges of international lawyers, which have mutually distinctive but commensurable histories and theories. In fact, Roberts focused on academies and textbooks in the five permanent members of the UN Security Council, assuming their commensurability for comparative analysis.[69] At the same time, Roberts carefully notes that 'nor do I focus on the experiences and approaches of international lawyers from states that are less powerful and privileged than the permanent members' and that her 'project would be improved if other observers broadened it to look at more states, deepened it by delving into greater detail within particular states, and historicized it by examining continuities and change over time'.[70] Rephrasing it for the present purpose, multi-we-ness rather reveals the limits of a certain historicised–theorised community, dividing it from the *un(der)-historicised–theorised* domain.[71] In other words, a collective of international lawyers inevitably closes the collective self by *including* as *normality* particular histories and theories; at the same time, something other-than-self that could be otherwise historicised or theorised is *excluded* as *exception* (*ex-ceptio*: 'precisely through this exclusion, it is included as *archè* and foundation').[72] This point is captured by Lauri Mälksoo: 'a number of fragmented colleges, epistemic communities, speaking each a different language or at least dialect of the same language, and thinking they are "predominant" while being

437–453 (emphasis in the original text). See also, Yota Negishi, 'The Phenomenological Embodiment of International Lawyers: Gazing at People Living "In This Corner of the Beautiful World"' in Makoto Seta and Yota Negishi (eds), *International Law for Constructive Resistance: A Festschrift in Honor of Professor Toshiki Mogami* (file with the author).

66 Hua VI 158–159.

67 Roberts Chapter 1 (n 23).

68 Martti Koskenniemi, 'The Case for Comparative International Law' (2009) 20 *Finnish Yearbook of International Law* 1

69 Roberts 5–6 (n 23).

70 Ibid.

71 Hans Lindahl, *Fault Lines of Globalization: Legal Order and the Politics of A-Legality* (Oxford University Press 2013).

72 Giorgio Agamben, *Homo Sacer: Sovereign Power and Bare Life*, translated by D. Heller-Roazen (Stanford University Press 1998) 21–22.

relatively ignorant about the others'.[73] Conversation with the incommensurability therefore exposes the asymmetrical structure of inclusive exclusion, in which the histories and theories of a collective self of international lawyers are 'co-constituted' with others whose lived experiences are captured in the *un(der)-historicised-theorised* realm.[74]

## A call for conversation from Japan

### *Micro (personal) and macro (periodical) histories of international legal theories in Japan*

While systematic European scholarship on Japanese international law remains notably scarce – with Zachmann's *Völkerrechtsdenken und Außenpolitik in Japan, 1919–1960* (2013)[75] standing as a rare exception – this very scarcity reveals the asymmetrical nature of current academic engagement. The 'conversation' this volume advocates, premised on accepting the incommensurable and prioritising the continuation of relationships rather than seeking common ground, fundamentally differs from 'dialogue' with its inherent epistemological force of objectifying the analysed. The current situation exemplifies this problem: systematic self-representation from Japan remains largely absent even though Western scholars like Zachmann – exceptionally – to engage with Japanese work directly from others' perspectives. By presenting Japanese international legal theorists through Japanese perspectives, this volume offers Japan's long-overdue 'proposal' in what should be a reciprocal exchange. While perspectives may remain

73 Lauri Mälksoo, 'International Legal Theory in Russia: A Civilizational Perspective, or: Can Individuals Be Subjects of International Law?' in Florian Hoffmann and Anne Orford (eds), *The Oxford Handbook on the Theory of International Law* (Oxford University Press 2016) 257–275, 273.

74 For the concept of co-constitution between international lawyers and the discipline, see Gleider Hernández, '*E Pluribus Unum?* A Divisible College? Reflections on the International Legal Profession' (2018) 29 *European Journal of International Law* 1003–1022, 1021–1022. See also Jean d'Aspremont and Sahib Singh, 'Introduction: Concepts for International Law: Contributions to Disciplinary Thought' in Jean d'Aspremont and Sahib Singh (eds), *Concepts for International Law: Contributions to Disciplinary Thought* (Edward Elgar 2019) 1–24, 16 (citing Martin Heidegger, *The Basic Problems of Phenomenology*, translated by Albert Hofstadter (Indiana University Press 1988) 169–170).

75 Urs Matthias Zachmann, *Völkerrechtsdenken und Außenpolitik in Japan, 1919–1960* (Nomos 2013). Zachmann, trained in both law and Japanese studies, offers a comprehensive European analysis of Japanese international legal thought to date, though his work necessarily approaches its subject from an external position in analysis.

incommensurable, the existence of works like Zachmann's suggests that the publication of this volume takes a necessary step towards genuine bilateral 'conversation' – not because we seek agreement or commensurability, but because both sides can begin to speak from their own standpoints, enabling the continuous relationship that defines conversation rather than dialogue.

To cultivate a culture of conversation about the incommensurable in international legal histories and theories, the edition focuses on the lived experiences of international lawyers in Japan. The relationship between Japan and international law (scholarship) has been contoured by the tensions between Western modernity and the country's own context. In the expansion of modern international law centred around Europe, Japan has been positioned as a semi-periphery 'encountering' the great powers.[76] In this sense, Japan has the lived experiences of being 'in-between' in international politics, situated between the European world of the coloniser and its outside world of the colonised.[77]

In spite of the semi-peripheral position, Japanese international law scholars contributed to the groundwork for the consolidation of knowledge production in international law.[78] Although there are countries that have trained their own international law scholarship over generations comparable to the Western one in a long history, Japanese international legal scholarship has occupied a special position among them due to its long – more than one hundred years – history.[79] The Japanese Society of International Law (JSIL) was established in 1897, which is the oldest academic society in Japan in the field of jurisprudence and was about ten years earlier than the founding of the American Society of International Law (ASIL). The JSIL's periodic

76 AKASHI Kinji, 'Japan–Europe' in Bardo Fassbender and Anne Peters (eds), *The Oxford Handbook of the History of International Law* (Oxford University Press 2012)

77 IKEDA Josuke, 'Japanese Vision of International Society A Historical Exploration' in SHIMIU Kosuke, IKEDA Josuke, KAMINO Tomoya and SATO Shiro (eds), *Is There A Japanese IR? Seeking an Academic Bridge Through Japan's History of International Relations* (Afrasian Centre for Peace and Development Studies, Ryukoku University 2008) 5–28.

78 Andrew Cobbing, 'Shaping a New Profession: Japanese Encounters with International Law, c. 1600–1900' in Marcus M Payk and Kim Christian Priemel (eds), *Crafting the International Order: Practitioners and Practices of International Law since c.1800* (Oxford University Press 2021) 21–47.

79 AKASHI Kinshi, '"External Transmission" of Japanese International Legal Scholarship for 100 Years: With Special Reference to Activities of Publishing European Literature' in Japan Society of International Law (ed.), *Law and Politics in the International Society* (Sanseido 2001) (in Japanese).

journal was born as the third international law journal in the world, after France (1874) and Belgium (1899).

Since a huge number of international law scholars have contributed to shaping Japanese international law scholarship, it is extremely difficult to select the candidates to introduce to the world. To open the possibility of conversation with the incommensurable described above, this edition focuses on thirteen prominent figures whose unique theories merit introduction on a global scale. To narrow down the candidate theorists, the editors established the following two interrelated principles.

The first principle is to focus on scholars who have developed an *epistemic or cognitive* framework that considers their historical, political, social or personal contexts. As the starting point, the editors reaffirmed our awareness of the problems facing Japanese international law in the contemporary era. The problem is the tendency to avoid discussing the concept of law and the normative positions one holds. In Japan, as discussions reflecting on the Second World War came to a close, there was a noticeable trend towards refraining from delving into the substance of international legal norms themselves: consciously or unconsciously, international legal scholars have tended to specialise in legal positivism, which posits the value neutrality of international law.[80] To borrow AKASHI Kinji's expression, there is still a 'negative international legal consciousness' that considers only the positive legal norms directly related to the individual and subdivided areas to be sufficient.[81] In contrast, the eminent scholars who are featured in the edition did not stop at individual research on positive law, but went on to construct theories that delved into the level of epistemology that made them possible.

The second principle is to unearth *the otherness or alterity* that has been buried in the mainstream of Japanese international law and brushed aside. As noted above, legal positivism, a methodological doctrine for constructing a unified legal system without omissions by eliminating non-legal elements, has long dominated the centre of international law in Japan. This book does not intend to deny the important role that legal positivism has played in Japanese international legal scholarship. In fact, the book introduces international legal scholars who shaped the era by advancing legal positivism at an extraordinary level compared with other legal positivists. However,

80 ONUMA Yasuaki, 'Law and Politics in the International Society: Beyond the Curse of "Legal Positivism" in International Legal Scholarship and "Realism" in International Political Science' in Japan Society of International Law (ed.), *Law and Politics in the International Society* (Sanseido 2001) (in Japanese).

81 AKASHI Kinji, *Invisible 'International Law': Possibilities of Hobbes, Leibniz and Rousseau* (*Fukashi no 'Kokusaiho': Hobbs, Leibniz, Rousseau no Kanosei*) (Keio University Press 2019) 7–8.

behind the sweeping influence of legal positivism, it must be acknowledged that there are different streams of scholars who engage in the work of theories to elucidate the politics of positivism or the risks of 'intentional retreat' from theories and sources. The alternatives to legal positivism build theoretical frameworks to resist political and ideological contestation under the veil of neutrality of law. To be sure, it does not mean their theoretical attempts are to radically relativise international law. By contrast, these theoretical endeavours aim to identify the truly universal law applicable to all actors in the world. In this vein, their attempt should be understood as building scaffolding for conversation among different traditions of international legal scholarship.[82]

Three caveats should be considered when selecting scholars. First, just because other scholars do not fulfil the two principles above does not mean that they have not made great contributions to Japanese international law. Other excellent scholars who also practise international law at centres such as the ICJ, the ILC and treaty organs are not featured in principle. In fact, they tended to adopt legal positivism, which has an affinity to their own practice and had opportunities to disseminate their own ideas independently due to their prestige. The exception is TANAKA Kotaro, who was theoretically a minority in advancing the concept of world law derived from the natural law tradition. Since countless other scholars have made significant contributions, it is also possible to address their unique theories in a follow-up to this project.

Second, this volume does not include the non-Japanese influencers on international law in Japan. As a possible candidate, one can probably mention Thomas Baty, the legal adviser to Japan's Ministry of Foreign Affairs during the inter-war period. However, it is unclear whether his traditional state-centric doctrines, implied in *International Law in Twilight*, have been theorised in relation to his experiences with Japanese diplomacy or academia. It does not mean that the editors underestimate Baty's and others' non-Japanese theoretical contributions to Japanese academia. In the sequel to this project, research should be deepened into conversations between Japanese scholars and scholars from overseas.[83]

82 Anne Peters, 'International Legal Scholarship under Challenge' in Jean d'Aspremont, Tarcisio Gazzini, André Nollkaemper and Wouter Werner (eds), *International Law as a Profession* (Cambridge University Press 2017)

83 As an example, Urs Matthias Zachmann, 'The Reception and Use of International Law in Modern Japan, 1853–1945' (2014) 37 *Zeitschrift für Japanrecht/Journal of Japanese Law* 109–137.

Third, another point that this book lacks is that it does not include any female theorists. As with global trends,[84] the male-dominated tendency remained deeply rooted in the world of international law in Japan. It is easy to assume that such a male-dominated situation has imposed a significant handicap on female researchers in their education and in the formation of their theories of international law. Among them, HIROSE Kazuko's sociology of international law is exceptional in relation to the interests of this book. In her writings, she presents a unique theoretical framework in which conflict resolution is discussed from the perspective of behavioural systems theory and legal systems theory. Since her major works have already been published in the global language, we prioritised promoting conversation by introducing works that have not been translated into English. In recent years, Japanese female researchers have made great strides, contributing significantly to both theory and practice.[85] In order to bridge the gender gap in international legal theory, it is necessary for future research to continue conversations based on the theories of female international legal researchers.

To help understand the development of Japanese international law scholarship, the editors present a macro-history of international legal theories in the country, divided into six periods.[86] (1) At the outset, Japanese scholars energetically absorbed and accumulated the information and knowledge concerning international law beyond the barriers of language and culture, so that Japan could be recognised as a member of the international society; (2) such efforts enabled some talented scholars to elaborate 'original' theories mixing Western perspectives and Japanese experiences. (3) Subsequently, the originality of the Japanese context in theories was excessively emphasised to derogate from Western modernity in the Second World War period, which resulted in the collapse of the Empire. (4) Japanese international legal

84 ILC, *Seven Women in Seventy Years: A Roundtable Discussion on Achieving Gender Parity* at the International Law Commission.

85 For example, there are also female researchers who have accumulated such outstanding research that they are invited to give lectures at the Hague Academy. Mariko Kawano, 'The Role of Judicial Procedures in the Process of the Pacific Settlement of International Disputes' (2009) 346 *Recueil des cours*; Atsuko Kanehara, 'Reassessment of the Acts of the State in the Law of State Responsibility – Non-State Actors' (2019) 399 *Recueil des cours*.

86 For a previous attempt to divide the periodisation of Japanese international legal scholarship, see Yasuaki Onuma, '"Japanese International Law" in the Prewar Period: Perspectives on the Teaching and Research of International Law in Prewar Japan' (1986) 29 *Japanese Annual of International Law* 23–47; '"Japanese International Law" in the Postwar Period: Perspectives on the Teaching and Research of International Law in Postwar Japan' (1986) 33 *Japanese Annual of International Law* 25–53.

scholars, therefore, reflect the failure of solipsist theories and embarked on a new chapter by reviewing the structure of modern international law. (5) Following this attempt, they furthermore elucidated the dynamic transformation of the structure from modern to contemporary international law, and (6) eventually sought to establish innovative theories that embraced relativist perspectives but never abandoned the pursuit of universality.

Having reviewed this history, it is not appropriate to argue that each period is separated from the others. Rather, the tasks imposed on Japanese international legal scholars have gradually changed depending on the situation which Japan has faced in relation to the world. Such a categorisation of historiography into different periods can be labelled an 'idealist intellectual' approach, as it divides the past into a succession of intellectual frameworks proposed in canonical texts by philosophers and international lawyers.[87] In this sense, our approach cannot avoid 'a clear separation between the object of historical research and the researcher's own context', and therefore, is 'unavoidably – and fruitfully – conditioned by the historian's prejudices and pre-understandings, conceptual frames and interest of knowledge'.[88] The six periods are not decisive criteria but merely symbolic for the authors of each chapter to assess the academic life of relevant scholars. Thus, the periodisation does not aim to overstate the particularity of the Japanese context in terms of solipsism by relativising the boundaries of theories in the West and Non-West, but prepares the ground for conversations.

## Structure of the book

### *Initial stage: passive acceptance*

With the arrival of Western powers in the latter half of the nineteenth century, Japan changed its isolation policy (*Sakoku*) and actively embraced civilisation in various sectors.[89] The standard of civilisation was also engraved in modern international law, and Japan had an encounter with it in the form of the conclusion of unequal treaties. To overcome this asymmetrical relationship, the practical and theoretical levels of international law in Japan

87 Ignacio de la Rasilla, 'The Problem of Periodization in the History of International Law' (2019) *Law and History Review (FirstView)* 1–34.

88 Martti Koskenniemi, 'Histories of International Law: Significance and Problems for a Critical View' (2013) 27 *Temple International and Comparative Law Journal* 215.

89 AKASHI Kinji, 'Japan–Europe' in Bardo Fassbender and Anne Peters (eds), *The Oxford Handbook of the History of International Law* (Oxford University Press 2012) 724–743.

had to meet those of civilised nations. In response to this demand, Japanese international lawyers actively accepted a large volume of literature and knowledge and strove to gain civilised membership of international society. During this period, particular focus on research was placed on international law related to war (the Sino-Japanese War and the Russo-Japanese War) and sovereignty issues such as unequal treaties and the annexation of Korea.

During this period, the general tendency of international lawyers has been to passively accept modern international law as applicable to civilised nations. It is pointed out that 'their positivistic method was the result of their passive attitude towards international law in that they unilaterally accepted the way of writing and reasoning of the Western internationalists'.[90] NISHI Amane might be called 'father of international law in Japan', but his main achievement was to import and translate the then-influential Western teaching. Similarly, ARIGA Nagao and TAKAHASHI Sakuei made considerable contributions to both the practice and academia of international law in Japan at that time; their approach is quite descriptive, drawing on their own experiences.

One of the most unique among them was TACHI Sakutaro, a scholar of international law who also served as a legal adviser to the Ministry of Foreign Affairs. While scholars up to the Meiji era focused on detailing and accurately describing facts based on what they had actually experienced, Tachi elaborated on the interpretation and even theory of international law.[91] A symbolic example of this is the controversy between Tachi and MINOBE Tatsukichi, a constitutional scholar serving at the imperial institution, over sovereignty and the annexation of Korea. While Minobe supported the supremacy of international law over domestic law, Tachi differentiated the common will of nations from state consent and maintained that domestic law is valid at the domestic level but incompatible with international law, which entails state responsibility at the international level.[92]

Another exceptional figure was SENGA Tsurutaro (千賀鶴太郎 1857–1929), who published his academic work in European languages, which was rare for a Japanese international jurist of the time, raising harsh criticisms

90 AKASHI Kinji, Japanese Predecessors of Judge Oda in the World Courts: Works and Method' in Nisuke Ando, Edward McWhinney and Rüdiger Wolfrum (eds), *Judge Shigeru Oda: Liber Amicorum* (Brill 2002) 20–22.

91 TSUTSUI Wakamizu and HIROBE Kazuya, 'International Law (100 Years of Doctrinal History) (Kokusaiho (Gakusetsu 100 Nenshi))' (1968) 400 *Jurist* 216–227 (in Japanese).

92 EBARA Yoshiyasu, 'Debate Between MINOBE and TACHI on the Relationship Between International Law and Domestic Law: The Annexation of Korea and the Territorial Rights and Sovereignty Dispute' (2002) 181 *Historia* 1–25 (in Japanese).

against the Western powers that imposed the standards of civilisation. As documented by TOYODA Tetsuya in Chapter 1, Senga condemned the imposition of civilising standards by Western countries that denied Japan and Qing China full capacity in the community of international law for accepting consular jurisdiction. By choosing a positivist perspective on legal bindingness, he developed a rationale that guaranteed Japan's autonomy under international law in opposition to the European powers. As shown in the chapter, however, Senga could not escape from double standards, thinking like many Japanese intellectuals of the Meiji period, and he did not feel much compassion for Korea colonised under Japanese imperialism.

### *Inter-war period and wartime*

In comparison with the preceding era, where Japanese international lawyers passively accepted civilised norms, they began to proactively engage in civilising international law. After rectifying the unequal relationship with Western countries, Japan contributed to the peaceful settlement and codification of international law within the League of Nations. One internationally acclaimed figure is ADATCI Mineichiro, who worked as a member of the Advisory Committee of Jurists that drafted the Statute of the Permanent Court of International Justice (PCIJ) and later served as the Court's Judge.[93] When the League of Nations was working on the codification of international law, JSIL submitted its own draft code to the League, and in 1928, the League's General Assembly resolution expressed its gratitude to JSIL, demonstrating the presence of the academic society.[94]

In comparison with the preceding approach that focused on accepting international law with descriptive methods, a few researchers in the inter-war period elaborated their own normative approach. Their distinctive theories provided prescriptive suggestions by consciously analysing values in international law, which are of particular significance in the transition from peace to war. During the inter-war period, the positivist *Reine Rechtslehre* (pure theory) of Hans Kelsen had been influential in Japanese academia. YOKOTA Kisaburo (横田喜三郎 1896–1993), as explained by TAKATA Hinako in Chapter 2, was known as 'Kelsen of the Orient', who espoused the positivist programme of value-neutral legal science and persistently

93 ADACHI Mineitciro (Masaharu Yanagihara (ed.)), *Peace among All Nations: A Collection of Mineitciro Adachi's Writings* (University of Tokyo Press 2019) (in Japanese). In addition to Adachi's seat (1931–1933), ODA Yorozu (1922–1930) and NAGAOKA Harukazu (1935–1942) were also elected as judges of the Court.

94 TAKAHASHI Rikiya, *Weaving International Law: The Codification Enterprise of International Law in the League of Nations and Japan* (*Kokusaiho wo Amu: Kokusai Renmei no Hotenka Jigyo to Nihon*) (University of Nagoya Press 2023).

asserted the juridical pyramid (*Stufenbau*) crowning international law as *Grundnorm*.[95] While inheriting the Kelsenian legacy, Yokota also elaborated his legal philosophical foundation in light of the value-driven *international democracy*.

TAOKA Ryoichi (田岡良 1898–1985) was another exceptional theorist in this era. As explicated by FUKUSHIMA Ryoshi in Chapter 3, Taoka developed an approach called 'historical positivism', by which politics and authority of international law are revealed in relation to social situations and specific values of the international community.[96] For example, Taoka classified the *Caroline* case, which is generally taken as a precedent of the right to 'self-defence', as rather one of 'self-preservation' and underscored that it should not be overly generalised. By applying the history-based positivist approach, Taoka rigorously interpreted the legitimacy of invoking the right to self-defence under the Non-Belligerency Pact in light of the situation in the international community, and rejected the government position that the Manchurian Incident constituted a 'war', for which Japan's military actions were justified due to the right to self-defence.[97]

As Japan plunged into the Greater East Asia War and its imperialist path, Japanese intellectuals, in support of the liberation of Asia from Western modernity, argued for 'Overcoming Modernity'.[98] The academia in the field of international law also offered theoretical bases for normative ambition, different from the Western model based on the Enlightenment tradition. Japanese international law scholars envision a new framework of the 'Greater East Asia Mutual Prosperity Sphere'.[99] In Chapter 4, YAMASHITA Tomoko introduces YASUI Kaoru (安井郁 1907–1980), who contributed to the idea of *Daitoa Kokusai Ho* (Greater East Asian International Law).

95 YOKOTA Kisaburo, '*Kokusaiho to Kokunaiho tono Ronriteki Kankei* (*The Logical Relations Between International and National Law*)' in KAMIKAWA Hikomatsu (ed.), *Festschrift in Celebration of the Sixtieth Birthday of Professor YAMADA* (Yuhikaku 1930) 511.

96 TABATA Shigejiro, 'The Late Professor TAOKA Ryoichi: His Contributions to the Study of International Law' (1985) 28 *Japanese Annual of International Law* 1.

97 Urs Matthias Zachmann, 'Taoka Ryoichi's Contribution to International Legal Studies in Pre-War Japan: With Special Reference to Questions of the Law of War' (2014) 57 *Japanese Yearbook of International Law* 148.

98 For an analysis of overcoming modernity in terms of international law, Takao Suami, 'Global Constitutionalism for East Asia: Its Potential to Promote Constitutional Principles' in Takao Suami, Anne Peters, Mattias Kumm and Dimitri Vanoverbeke (eds), *Global Constitutionalism from European and East Asian Perspectives* (Cambridge University Press 2018) 533–571.

99 IKEDA Josuke, 'Japanese Vision of International Society: A Historical Exploration' in Kosuke Shimizu, Josuke Ikeda, Tomoya Kamino and Shiro Sato (eds), *Is There A Japanese IR? Seeking an Academic Bridge Through Japan's History of International Relations* (Afrasia Research Series 2008) 5–28.

Yasui advocated that the legal system of the Greater East Asia would be guided by Japan's inherent principles, as the leading state of the broad area.[100] This theory, which justified colonialism and imperialism in Asia, was not commensurable with the liberal international legal order at that time. Meanwhile, Japanese scholars draw inspiration from critics of Western liberal democracy, such as Hans Morgenthau, E. H. Carr and Carl Schmitt.[101] In particular, Schmitt's concept of *Völkerrechtliche Großraumordnung*, espousing the Nazi regime, was a driving force to sophisticate Greater East Asian International Law. In the West, there is a tendency to exclude Nazi-like traditions as *undialoguable*, but in Japan, this Greater East Asia concept has been construed as a theoretical basis for a regional order that differs from the Western model. In this regard, it is necessary to continue to critically examine its negative legacy within a *conversational* framework.

### *The post-war period (from 1945 to the 1970s)*

After being defeated by the USA, the Japanese Government was forced to accept the Potsdam Declaration, which defined the terms for surrender.[102] Japanese scholars offered the 'bureaucratic' doctrine of international law to the practical conundrums arising from the defeat in the Pacific War.[103] Their interests were directed at the transformation of internal sovereignty through constitutional amendment through the intervention by the triumphant states and the restoration of external sovereignty by returning to it.

In contrast to the positivist approach mainstreaming in bureaucratic practices, TANAKA Kotaro (田中耕太郎 1890–1974) developed his own theory as OGURI Hirofumi writes in Chapter 5.[104] Against the experience of the Second World War and the militarist régime in Japan as backgrounds,

100 YASUI Kaoru, *Ohshu Koiki Kokusaiho no Kiso Rinen* (*Basic Ideology of European Broad-Area International law*), Kokusaiho Gakkai (Japanese Society of International Law), Daitoa Kokusai Ho Sousyo (Greater East Asian International Law Series), vol. 1 (Yuhikaku Publishing 1942), Introduction and Chapter 6 (in Japanese).

101 SOGAWA Takeo and MATSUDA Takeo, 'International Legal Scholarship in the Inter-War Period' (1978) 50 *Horitsu Jiho* 51–66 (in Japanese).

102 TAKENAKA Yoshihiko, 'The Postwar Visions of the International Lawyers in Wartime Japan: From the Pursuit of the Greater East Asian International Law to the Idealization of the United Nations: Japan's Wartime Diplomacy and the Postwar Visions' (1995) 109 *International Relations* 70–83 (in Japanese).

103 OBATA Kaoru, 'Historical Function of Monism with Primacy of International Law: A View Based on the Japanese Experience during the Early Period of the Allied Occupation' (2006) 49 *Japanese Annual of International Law* 1–35.

104 Kevin M. Doak, *Tanaka Kōtarō and World Law: Rethinking the Natural Law Outside the West* (Springer 2018).

Tanaka acknowledged 'the defects in relying simply on the positivistic method and positive norms of international law that had been constructed by the Westerners'.[105] When taking the seat on the International Court of Justice (1961–1970), typically in the *South West Africa* case, Tanaka advanced the concept of world law derived from the natural law tradition.[106] By reevaluating the general principles of law as a foundation for international law, Tanaka's theory was expanded to bridge the gap between national and international legal systems within the framework of world law.

With the establishment of the United Nations after the Second World War, the use of force and colonialism, which were permissible under traditional international law, became illegal. To assess such transformations, Japanese scholarship took preliminary steps to elucidate the structure of modern international law.[107] For this structural analysis, the Marxist approach provided a critical perspective on the hegemonic ideology of international law, particularly when synthesised with the historical–social methodology of the Kyoto School.[108] TABATA Shigejiro (田畑茂二郎 1911–2001) is discussed in Chapter 6 written by KANETAKE Machiko. During wartime, Tabata criticised modern international law that had traditionally rested on the principles of sovereign equality and state voluntarism, and instead advocated the basic ideal of 'the common moral consciousness' as the foundation for Greater East Asian International Law. After the War, he reflected on the Prosperity's simple denial of sovereign equality and reappraised its significance as the hallmark principle opposable to the great powers. Tabata also showed his interest in the emergence of the Third World based on the principle of self-determination (cf. issue of 'bearer of sovereignty').

Another eminent critical lawyer in this era was SOGAWA Takeo (祖川武夫 1911–1996), whose theory is elucidated by NISHI Taira in Chapter

105 AKASHI Kinji, 'Japanese Predecessors of Judge Oda in the World Courts: Works and Method' in Nisuke Ando, Edward McWhinney and Rüdiger Wolfrum (eds), *Judge Shigeru Oda: Liber Amicorum* (Brill 2002) 20–22.

106 *South West Africa*, Second Phase, Judgment, I.C.J. Reports 1966, 6, Dissenting Opinion of Judge Tanaka, Reports, 250.

107 FUJITA Hisakazu, 'Steps and Prospects of International Legal Scholarship' (1977) 5 *Science in Law* 73–86.

108 MATSUI Yoshiro, 'The Social Science of International Law: Its Evolution in Japan (Syakai Kagaku to shite no Kokusaiho-gaku: Nihon ni okeru Sono Keisei to Hatten)' in YAMATE Haruyuki and KOZAI Shigeru (eds), *The Structure of the International Society: Its History and Current Situation*, vol. 1 (Toshindo 2003) 5–45 (in Japanese); Yoshiro Matsui, 'The Social Science of International Law: Its Evolution in Japan' (2003) 45 *Japanese Annual of International Law* 1–33.

7.[109] In line with Hans Morgenthau, Sogawa took the anti-positivist position to address the issue of dispute settlement, particularly the question of which procedures would provide adequate settlements to political disputes. In sympathy with Schmidtian criticism of the ideology of international law under Western liberalism, Sogawa also developed his theory of the prohibition of the use of force. Meanwhile, he certainly inherited the universal fortunes of the liberal tradition in favour of weaker nations or colonies opposing the great powers.[110]

## *From the 1970s to the end of the Cold War*

As reflective analyses of Pacific War events gradually settled, the interests of Japanese international legal scholars shifted to specific and practical issues (international institutional law, human rights law, economic law, maritime law and so on) that are contingent on the functionalisation of international society. The functionalist trend entails, consciously or unconsciously, the prevalence of positivism in methodological choice. As international law became increasingly fragmented, the expertise of international lawyers in various fields became an important source of knowledge in diplomacy.[111] The prominent figure in this era is ODA Shigeru (1976–2003), who bridged academia and practice, including his decisive arguments that led the Federal Republic of Germany to victory in the North Sea Continental Shelf case and his service as a judge at the International Court of Justice.[112]

The most influential in this era was YAMAMOTO Soji (山本草二 1928–2013), who embodied this positivist and functionalist approach in theory and served as a judge of the International Tribunal for the Law of the Sea (ITLOS) (1996–2005). Yamamoto's vast body of work across all areas of international law, and the textbooks he compiled from it, have enriched the coming generations of scholars and practitioners. As MORITA Akio reflects in Chapter 8, Yamamoto deepened positivism and functionalism by emphasising the historical contexts of international law and diplomacy. Yamamoto's works on international administrative law, while uniquely

109 NISHI Taira, 'The German Antipositivist Tradition in International Law: Schmitt, Morgenthau and Sogawa' (2005) 55 *The Law Review of Kansai University* 60–85 (in Japanese).

110 MATSUI, 'The Social Science of International Law' 24 (n).

111 KITA Yasuo, 'The Legal Advice System of the Ministry of Foreign Affairs of Japan: Between Legal Advisers and Foreign Policy Makers' in Andraž Zidar and Jean-Pierre Gauci (eds), *The Role of Legal Advisers in International Law* (Brill 2016) 128–147.

112 ANDO Nisuke, Edward McWhinney and Rüdiger Wolfrum (eds), *Liber Amicorum Judge Shigeru Oda* (Kluwer Law International 2002) vol. 1, 570.

developed in Japanese based on European findings, have the potential to be compared to contemporary global administrative law and his jurisprudence on international administrative law is cited in the main text as prior research in the works of Kingsbury and others.

In parallel with the passivist trend, some fundamental theorists, building on earlier analyses of the structure of modern international law, sought to reveal the dynamic transformation of the structure towards contemporary international law. The concept of 'structural transformation of international law' in Japanese academia is based largely on the arguments developed by ISHIMOTO Yasuo (石本泰雄 1924–2015).[113] In Chapter 9, WANI Kentaro expounds the dual transformation: the outlawry of war and the incorporation of private law principles. On the one hand, Ishimoto traced the historical evolution from classical international law that built the dualistic structure of peace and war to modern international law that limits and prohibits war. On the other hand, Ishimoto discerns three changes in incorporating private law principles into international law in the contemporary era: international legal personality is expanded beyond sovereign states, the right of states to govern national territory is limited to protect individuals, and treaties may be invalidated in violation of peremptory norms.

MATSUI Yoshiro (松井芳郎 1941–), introduced by KODERA Satoshi in Chapter 10, builds on his predecessors' studies on the structural transformation of international law, mainly based on the Marxist approach. Against the backdrop of the Vietnam War and the *Anpo* (Japan–United States Security) Struggle, Matsui brought international legal theory to the forefront as a social science to deal with realities. Inspired by Tabata's question of 'bearer of sovereignty', Matsui rejects the conception of the state as a black box and resituates the people and non-state actors as constituting the inner reality of the state. In this direction, as Kodera rightly notes, Matsui's textbook adopted a 'conversational' style to invite citizens to utilise international law for changing the state and international society.

### *From the end of the Cold War to the present*

After the collapse of communism and the establishment of the liberal international legal order, Japanese scholars have increasingly engaged in the legal-technical discourse in the sectoral sub-fields of international law. The horizontal fragmentation of international law has led to a tightening of

113 KIRIYAMA Takanobu, 'ISHIMOTO Yasuo and His Legacy of International Legal Theory' (2016) 62 *Journal of Law and Politics of Osaka City University* 347–365 (in Japanese).

international law and domestic law in each sub-field.[114] Against the fragmented and deformalised trend, MURASE Shinya (1943–) revisited the sources theory of international law, which touches upon the meaning of positivism in the contemporary era.[115] He applied his outstanding scholarship to the practice at the International Law Commission (2009–2022) and contributed as Special Rapporteur on the protection of the atmosphere, where many legal regimes are intertwined. As regards the approximation between the international and domestic legal spheres, IWASAWA Yuji published a monograph which influenced both theorists and practitioners, especially domestic lawyers and judges applying international law.[116] His academic expertise has been applied as a member of the Human Rights Committee (2007–2018) and currently as a judge at the International Court of Justice (2018–).

While belonging to this mainstream positivism, KOTERA Akira (小寺彰 1952–2014) continued to take a unique position. Chapter 11 by MEGURO Maiko illustrates how Kotera sought to develop an interactive relationship between international law and Japanese domestic law. While recognising that the disciplinary and practical framework of international law itself is Eurocentric, Kotera firmly insisted that international law should essentially be understood as a code of judicial norms, and that maintaining the rule of international law is necessary, even if imperfectly, to control the rule of power. For this reason, he did not align himself with the critical jurisprudence of his time. On the other hand, he recognised the changing assumptions about the international order brought about by globalisation and the deepening of international trade, and pointed out the blurring boundary between international law and domestic law in the newly emerging realm of international economic law. He attempted to build a foundation for a new international law that reflects the circumstances of each country through its interpretation and application, and for this purpose, he educated international law experts, who had previously been passive in international law,

114 YOKOTA Yozo, 'Theory and Practice of the Application of International Law in Japan' in Budislav Vukas and Trpimir Sosic (eds), *International Law: New Actors, New Concepts – Continuing Dilemmas: Liber Amicorum Božidar Bakotić* (Brill 2010) 75–94.

115 MURASE Shinya, 'The Changing Views on the Sources of International Law (Gendai Kokusai Ho ni okeru Hogen Ron no Doyo: Kokusai Rippo Ron no Zenteiteki Kosatsu to shite)' (1985) 25 *St Paul's Review of Law and Politics* 81–111 (in Japanese). See also, *Murase Shinya, International Law-Making: Sources Theory of International Law* (*Kokusai Rippo: Kokusai Ho no Hogen Ron*) (Toshindo 2002).

116 IWASAWA Yuji, *Domestic Applicability of Treaties: What are 'Self-Executing' Treaties?* (*Joyaku no Kokunai Tekiyo Kanousei: Iwayuru 'Self-Executing' na Joyaku ni Kansuru Ichi Kosatsu*) (Yuhikaku 1985).

in seeking to develop the said interactive relationship between international law and Japanese law and policies. However, Kotera published very few works in English, so in that sense, it could be said that he entrusted the 'conversation' and 'dialogue' he idealised to the practitioners he educated and advised in his time.

In parallel with the positivist, practice-oriented approach, fundamental theories are sophisticated to overcome the rigid binary between universalism and relativism. As KAKU Shun evaluates in Chapter 12, ONUMA Yasuaki (1946–2018) is one of those rare theorists who has actively sought 'conversations' with international lawyers around the world. His early writings included a war crimes theory involving the two World Wars, the rectification of Japan's past wrongs of colonial rule over Korea and a study of Hugo Grotius' on *De jure belli ac pacis*. His critique of colonialism led to a civic movement that left its mark on the Repatriation of the Koreans Left Behind in Sakhalin and the Asian Women's Fund. Gradually, Onuma disseminated his own idea of *A Transcivilizational Perspective on International Law*, from which international law exists 'as globally shared perception' or 'as an inter-subjective historical product of humankind'.[117] His original perspective aims to correct unreflective bias towards non-Western societies in international law, and therefore, is beneficial to continue 'conversations' with the incommensurable.

While sympathetic to Onuma's approach, rooted in civic activism, MOGAMI Toshiki (最上敏樹 1950–) established an original theory by immersing himself in the world of discourse. As NEGISHI Yota depicts in Chapter 13, his intellectual mind has been shaped by the political science of the World Order Models Project (WOMP) led by Richard Falk, and by the Christianity of Hammarskjöld and Bonhoeffer, who have dedicated themselves to anonymous sacrifice. The concept of 'normative multilateralism', refined through research on international organisations, became specialised in law governing inter-state violence (*jus contra anarchiam*), particularly law against institutionalised hegemonic powers (*jus contra oligarchiam*). His critical perspective is comparable to that of Martti Koskenniemi, a leader in critical international legal studies, but also includes a future vision of *After International Law* beyond agnosticism.

117 ONUMA Yasuaki, *International Law in a Transcivilizational World* (Cambridge University Press 2017) Chapter 1-II.

## Conclusion

Through this Introduction, we have discussed the framework and practice of the mode of communication in conversation, which is also the theme that runs through this compilation. The primary objective of 'conversation' is to continue the conversation, which is a form of communication that does not divide into one-sided listeners and speakers. It does not seek to transcend boundaries; rather, it respects the fact that different traditions create their own boundaries as systems and define what is related to them and what is not according to their own rationality.

It is our claim that a legal tradition must be responsive to embody its own history of legal thought in order to start a conversation on equal footing. From this perspective, as defended in this edited volume, the editors aim to provide an intellectual overview of international legal thought in Japan, embodied by the lens of Japanese tradition, using the vocabulary and concepts of international law as well as of Western legal thought, such as positivism, naturalism and Marxism. (Otherwise, Western counterparts cannot understand the Japanese legal thought within the framework of international law and its history.) While the project cannot fully escape from Western centrism to the extent that we must rely on the vocabulary and concepts of Western origin, chapters will be written by authors who have the right expertise to address these concepts, such as positivism in Europe and 'positivism' in Japan.

Simultaneously, the compilation does not deny that the term 'international law' implies that we accept that each international law tradition loosely constitutes a common system. However, from the perspective advocated in this book, we should first continue the conversation, rather than hastily trying to find commensurable dimensions, based on the premise of the plurality of laws that make up 'international law' and the proposition of achieving the coexistence of different traditions. From the perspective defended here, it is emphasised that there are possible downsides for the scholars from a particular cultural sphere to clearly depict a comprehensive framework, basis or commonality that includes the habitat of others, and that this could be an act that moves away from the ultimate formation of an inclusive foundation for international law, at least currently.

Furthermore, this Introduction notes that the perspective of conversation is useful not only in spatial terms but also in terms of communication between different points in time. The legal order assigns a legal or illegal label to actions and behaviours within the boundaries of the order. The main boundaries indicated in this Introduction are spatial, and on this, it is argued that international law can only define a very shallow part of the legal order, and that much of the legal substance relies on regional and cultural orders defined by different rationales that overlap with the international legal order. However, the boundaries drawn by the legal order are not limited to regions and cultures. The same is true of time and contemporaneity. The closure of the legal order is an unavoidable premise, as legal norms regulate and shape the actions of the subjects confined within its boundaries.

The necessity of the communicative mode of conversation is based on the premise that there is a possibility of a realm outside of the *limits of* the specific order in which we find ourselves. From this premise, rather than making a unilateral judgment on the legality or illegality of an action from the perspective of a particular era, we can recognise the limitations of the closed world (temporality) that defines legality and illegality, and shelve that judgment, or take it as a different legal order ('a-legality'/'a-illegality') that coexists. This perspective can be useful for addressing intergenerational topics such as climate change, post-war peace-building and so on. Through conversation as a communication mode, it may be possible to continue to critically examine the negative legacy of the past by treating even those subjects that had to be treated as unforgivable, hence *undialoguable beings* in the previous discussions, but possibly as conversational beings.

# 1

# SENGA Tsurutaro: positivism against civilisational Eurocentrism in international law

*TOYODA Tetsuya*

## Introduction: Eurocentrism and resentment

After receiving his doctorate from the University of Berlin in 1897, SENGA Tsurutaro (1857–1929) was appointed professor of Roman law in 1899 and of international law in 1900 at Kyoto University, where he taught until 1923. Senga is worthy of a chapter in the historiography of international law in Japan for at least three reasons. He was the first professor specialising in international law at Kyoto University, one of the country's two major centres for the study of international law before the Second World War. Furthermore, he represents the patriotic strand of Japanese international law scholars who were critical of the Eurocentrism that was, to some extent, visible in international law theories at the turn of the twentieth century. Finally, he was the first Japanese professor of international law to express anti-Eurocentric sentiments in a European language.

Civilised or uncivilised, that was a crucial question for many non-European political entities in the nineteenth century. If labelled as uncivilised, they would be subject to the European powers' civilising mission. James Lorimer's civilisational theory of international law was widely shared, with some variations, by many intellectuals in European countries and European colonies, and even in non-European independent countries, as represented by FUKUZAWA Yukichi in Japan. Fukuzawa claimed that 'the nations of Europe and the United States of America are the most highly civilized, while the Asian countries, such as Turkey, China, and Japan, may be called semi-developed countries, and Africa and Australia are to be counted as still primitive lands'.[1]

Only the civilised states were apt and entitled to full sovereignty under international law. According to this view, the Ottoman Empire was accepted

1 FUKUZAWA Yukichi, *An Outline of a Theory of Civilisation* (*Bunmeiron no gairyaku*), translated by D. A. Dilworth and G. C. Hurst III (2008 [1875]) 17.

into the community of the law of nations only after the 1856 Paris Treaty at the end of the Crimean War, and the Qing dynasty of China remained outside the protection of international law until its fall.[2] For their primitive legal systems with the torture of criminal suspects by the public authorities or other brutal practices, the half-civilised governments were considered incapable of governing themselves in a modern and civilised fashion, while they were capable of concluding unequal treaties with the civilised governments of the West. Such a vision was often subjective or even absurd in reality, but it justified, at least in British eyes, the invasion of China for the sake of freedom of trade in opium.

Such a worldview was not to be maintained forever. By the time the First Peace Conference was convened in 1899, several non-European powers had gained European recognition, among them were China, Japan, Persia, Siam and Turkey, which sent their delegations to The Hague. However, the conference was dominated by nineteen European powers[3] and two powers of European descent in North America (the United States and Mexico). The international society was still mostly European. In the preamble to the Second Hague Convention on the Laws and Customs of War on Land of 1899, the contracting parties declared that:

> the principles of international law, as they result from the usages established between civilized nations, from the laws of humanity and the requirements of the public conscience.

The concept of civilised nations then was virtually synonymous with that of Europeanised nations.[4]

This concept was incorporated twenty years later in the Statute of the Permanent Court of Justice (PCIJ) in its Article 38(1):

> The Court, whose function is to decide in accordance with international law such disputes as are submitted to it, shall apply: … c. the general principles of law recognized by civilized nations.

This wording had a lasting impact on international law. The text of Article 38 of the PCIJ Statute was inherited word for word by the Statute of the

2 Cf. A. de La Pradelle, 'La question chinoise' (1901) 8 *Revue générale du droit internaitonal*.

3 Germany, Austria-Hungary, Belgium, Denmark, Spain, France, the UK, Greece, Italy, Luxembourg, Montenegro, the Netherlands, Portugal, Romania, Russia, Serbia, Sweden and Norway, Switzerland and Bulgaria.

4 ONUMA Yasuaki, *Transcivilizational Perspective on International Law* (2010) 85.

International Court of Justice. Since then, throughout the twentieth century or even in the twenty-first century, few international lawyers bothered to look at non-European practices of law in identifying the general principles of law as defined by Art. 38(1)(c) of the ICJ Statute. It is only in the last decade of the twentieth century that the voice against Eurocentrism in international law started to attract serious attention.

The prevalence of civilisational Eurocentrism in international law evoked anti-Eurocentric resentment, of which the Japanese government became its major proponent in the early twentieth century. Two instances require mention: one is the proposal for a racial equality clause in the Covenant of the League of Nations, and the other is the proposal for a pluricivilisational clause in the PCIJ Statute. The racial equality clause proposal was rejected by Woodrow Wilson at the peace conference at Versailles,[5] but the pluricivilisational clause proposal was accepted at The Hague in a modified form in the text of Article 9 of the PCIJ Statute, which was inherited word for word by the ICJ Statute:

> the whole body [of the Court] … should represent the main forms of civilization and the principal legal systems of the world.

The pluricivilisational clause proposal was made at the personal initiative of a Japanese diplomat-scholar, ADACHI Mineichiro, who was the *de facto* representative of Japan in the drafting committee for the PCIJ Statute in 1919, not an official proposal of the Japanese government.[6] The government in Tokyo was influenced more by purely nationalistic discourses than Adachi's anti-Eurocentric universalism.

Since nationalistic discourses were translated less often into foreign languages than universalist ones, they were not well known overseas. Exceptional was that of Senga (1857–1929), the first professor of international law at Kyoto University, who championed the nationalist strand of thought in the Japanese scholarship of international law with his book on the *Gestaltung und Kritik der heutigen Konsulargerichtsbarkeit in Japan* (*Form of and critical considerations on the consular jurisdiction in Japan today*), published in Berlin in 1897. In this chapter, we will consider his positivism strategy in the fight against civilisational Eurocentrism in international law.

5 Kristofer Allerfeldt, 'Wilsonian Pragmatism? Woodrow Wilson, Japanese Immigration, and the Paris Peace Conference' (2004) 15(3) *Diplomacy and Statecraft* 545–572.

6 TOYODA Tetsuya, 'Japan's Early Challenge to Eurocentrism and the World Court' in Felix Rösch and Atsuko Watanabe (eds), *Modern Japanese Political Thought and International Relations* (2018) 43.

### Civilisational Eurocentrism and consular jurisdictions

Before being replaced by the Meiji imperial government in 1868, the government of the Tokugawa shogunate concluded a series of treaties with five Western powers: the US, the UK, France, Russia and the Netherlands in 1858. They all had a clause for consular jurisdiction. For example, article 6 of the 1858 Treaty between Japan and the United States provided that 'Americans committing offenses against Japanese shall be tried in American Consular courts, and, when guilty, shall be punished according to American law'. Treaties with Portugal (1860), Prussia (1861) and Italy (1866) included similar provisions. After the fall of the shogunate in 1868, the Meiji imperial government signed another treaty with a consular jurisdiction clause with Austria-Hungary in 1869, as well as with a few others.

With increasing activities of foreigners in Japan, the Meiji imperial government started to understand how much consular jurisdiction could damage public order and provoke dissatisfaction among citizens.[7] There were countless incidents involving consular jurisdiction, of which it would be enough to mention three: the Hesperia incident in 1879, the Normanton incident in 1886 and the Ravenna incident in 1892.

The first notable case was the Hesperia incident. In a desperate attempt to curb the spread of cholera, the Meiji imperial government issued quarantine regulations in 1878 and port control regulations for international vessels in July 1879. The US, Chinese and Italian legations accepted the new regulations, but the German, French and British legations refused, arguing that Japanese courts should not have jurisdiction over the violation of quarantine regulations by their respective nationals. In the same month, escorted by a German gunboat, a merchant ship, Hesperia, from China, where cholera was ravaging, entered the port of Yokohama despite the quarantine injunction from the Japanese authorities. The chief staff-surgeon of the German legation inspected the ship and cleared Hesperia, without following Japanese regulations. Since cholera was already spreading in the western part of Japan, it is not fair to attribute all the blame to Hesperia alone, but the death toll in Japan exceeded 100,000 in 1879, and the German attitude angered the Japanese public.[8] Former US President Ulysses Grant was passing by Tokyo on his world tour and was reported by American and German

7 Harald Fuess, 'Unequal Treaties, Consular Jurisdiction, and Treaty Port Society' in Sven Saaler and Christopher W. A. Szpilman (eds), *Routledge Handbook of Modern Japanese History* (2017) 47–61.

8 Harald Fuess, 'Informal Imperialism and the 1879 "Hesperia" Incident: Containing Cholera and Challenging Extraterritoriality in Japan' (2014) *Japan Review* 103–140.

newspapers to have recommended that the Japanese government sink the German ship.[9]

Seven years later, a very much criticised case of consular jurisdiction occurred: the Normanton incident in 1886. A British merchant ship, the Normanton, sank off the coast of Wakayama. The British captain took only European passengers in lifeboats and let all the Japanese passengers drown. The declaration of the captain's innocence by the British consul at Kobe sparked an uproar in Japanese newspapers. The consul-general at Yokohama overruled the decision and sentenced the captain to three months' imprisonment, but refused any compensation to bereaved families.

Six years after the Normanton incident, the most politicised case of consular jurisdiction happened: the Ravenna incident (or the Chishima incident). The British merchant ship Ravenna collided with the Japanese light cruiser Chishima of the Japanese navy off the coast of Matsuyama in 1892. While the Ravenna suffered only physical damage and could continue its navigation, the Chishima sank immediately and the lives of seventy-four sailors were lost. The judgment by the consular court at Yokohama, in favour of the Japanese government, was overturned by the court of appeal at Shanghai, which denied any reparation or compensation. In the House of Commons of the Imperial Diet, opposition leaders blamed the government for its inability to rectify the allegedly unfair practice of consular jurisdiction. The Japanese government appealed the case to the Privy Council in London, which quashed the judgment of the court of appeal at Shanghai and remanded the case to the consular court at Yokohama in July 1895. The case was settled two months later with a compromissory agreement under which the shipping company, P&O Steam Navigation Company, agreed to bear the costs of litigation incurred by the Japanese government and pay a rather small settlement sum of 1 million pounds, while the Japanese government gave up all claims.[10]

The judicial complications of the Ravenna case coincided with the final stage of negotiations to abolish British consular jurisdiction. The revised Treaty of Commerce and Navigation was signed in July 1894 by the Japanese minister in the UK and the British government and entered into force five years later. Similar treaty revisions were made with the US and Italy in 1894, Russia in 1895, Germany and France in 1896 and Belgium,

9 *New York Times* (28 August 1879) and *Frankfurter Zeitung* (11 September 1879) cited by ibid 108, footnote 33.

10 Christopher Keepfer Roberts, *The British Courts and Extra-Territoriality in Japan, 1859–1899* (2014).

Peru, Brazil, Sweden, the Netherlands, Switzerland, Spain, Portugal and Austria-Hungary in 1897.

In revising the unequal treaties, the Japanese government needed to convince the European powers that it was as civilised as they were. To support the Japanese government in its negotiations with the Europeans, Italian professor of international law, Alessandro Paternostro, who served as a counsel for the Japanese Ministry of Justice from 1889 to 1892, published an article[11] in the *Revue générale du droit international et de législation comparée*, one of the most influential journals of international law at the time, to claim that the legislative and administrative developments in Japan

> have made Japan a country that has the culture, the political life, the political structure, social conditions, in brief, of Western countries (ont fait du Japon un pays qui a la culture, la vie politique, l'organisation d'État, l'état social en un mot, des pays d'Occident).

Paternostro argued that Japan was then almost a European country because the Japanese government sought to present itself as a quasi-European government worthy of equality with European powers. It had modernised its education, judiciary and legislation, and even constructed a gorgeous dance hall, the *Rokumeikan*, which was used from 1883 to 1887 to advertise the Europeanisation of Japanese society. The much-ridiculed construction of the *Rokumeikan* was a desperate attempt by Inoue Kowashi, the earnest proponent of the treaty revision. The Rokumeikan strategy did not bear fruit immediately and was often ridiculed by Japanese newspapers, but, in the end, it was the Europeanisation of Japanese institutions that convinced the British and other Western powers to abolish consular jurisdiction in Japan. Inoue was right.

It should be noted that the Japanese government did not reject consular jurisdiction as a matter of principle. Consular jurisdiction was loathsome to them as long as it was introduced to give foreigners immunity in Japan. While striving for the abolition of consular jurisdiction, the Japanese government imposed on Korea in 1876 a treaty of commerce with a consular jurisdiction clause for the immunity of Japanese citizens in Korea. For the Joseon dynasty of Korea, the treaty with Japan was the first with a foreign power, followed by treaties with the Western powers and with Qing China,

11 Alessandro Paternostro, 'La révision des traités avec le Japon au point de vue du droit international' (1891) 18 *Revue générale du droit international et de législation comparée* 5–29.

all of which included consular jurisdiction clauses. Japan was not simply an innocent victim of consular jurisdiction.

## Life and writings of Senga Tsurutaro

Senga, born in 1857 in a samurai family, studied in Germany from 1884 to 1899 and received the degree *Doctor Utriusque Juris* from the University of Berlin for his thesis on consular jurisdiction in Japan. Upon the establishment of the School of Law at Kyoto University, he was appointed professor of Roman Law and also taught international law until 1927 (even after his retirement in 1923). Senga died in 1929 at the age of seventy-two.

His only published work in a foreign language, *Gestaltung und Kritik der heutigen Konsulargerichtsbarkeit in Japan*, was 160 pages long and had two parts: the first part on consular jurisdiction in Japan and the second part on its critical considerations. While the first part is only a flat description of the consular jurisdiction in Japan, the second part contains its critical and theoretical considerations.

It was still a predominant perception in Germany that consular jurisdiction was indispensable to protect Westerners in Asian countries that were not colonised by European powers. Senga criticised such views for the arbitrariness of the concept of civilisation and argued that:

> The theory that the fundamental rights of a state must be limited because of its lack of culture is just as untenable as another possible theory that the fundamental rights of citizens must be limited because of the deficiencies in their intellectual education, for example, of the working-class people or peasants. (*Die Theorie, dass die Grundrechte eines Staates wegen seiner Unkultur beschränkt werden müssen, ist eben so wenig haltbar, wie eine andere mögliche es sein würde, dass die Grundrechte der Staatsbürger, wegen der Mängel ihrer geistigen Bildung, etwa des Arbeiter- oder Bauernstandes, beschränkt werden müssen.*)[12]

and that:

> A so-called uncivilised state is just as much a state, a sovereign state, as a civilised one, and as such has the same claim to the full enjoyment of its fundamental rights as the latter. (*Ein sg. uncivilisirter Staat ist ebenso ein Staat, ein*

12 Tsurutaro SENGA, *Gestaltung und Kritik der heutigen Konsulargerichtsbarkeit in Japan* (1897) 138.

> *souveräner Staat, wie ein civilisirter, und hat, als solcher, denselben Anspruch auf vollen Genuss seiner Grundrechte, wie der letztere.*)[13]

As rightly pointed out by Arnulf Becker Lorca, non-European international lawyers could make use of positivism as a strategically optimal choice which should 'give preponderance to the sources of law that unequivocally expressed the will of their sovereign'.[14] This was particularly true for Senga for his resentment of cultural Eurocentrism in international law and, as pointed out again by Lorca:

> Positivism was indeed the theoretical approach more amicable [than natural law doctrines] to Senga's efforts to reduce the latitude to interpret unequal treaties beyond Japan's sovereign will and as such opposed the use of natural law doctrines to limit the sovereign autonomy of non-Western states.[15]

As to the arbitrariness of the concept of civilisation, Senga added a long footnote running for four pages to harshly criticise the writings of Martens and Holtzendorff, among others.[16] He appears to be somewhat emotional when he wrote:

> The definition of 'civilisation' is of course outside jurisprudence. But which discipline has ever defined this expression? Never! (*Die Definition von 'Civilisation' steht selbstverständlich ausserhalb der Jurisprudenz. Aber welche Wissenschaft hat je diesen Ausdruck definirt? Keine!*)

Senga was particularly angry with the identification of civilised nations with Christian nations or European nations. Senga advanced the idea of Buddhist-Confucian civilisation as an alternative to European civilisation:

> The East Asians really cannot give him [Martens] a better answer than to just call 'Buddhist-Confucian' states 'civilised' states, which Chinese writers often do. (*Die Ostasiaten könnten ihm wahrlich keine bessere Antwort geben als*

13 Ibid.

14 Arnulf Becker Lorca, *Mestizo International Law: A Global Intellectual History 1842–1933* (2014) 57.

15 Ibid.

16 F. Martens, *Das Consularwesen und die Consularjurisdiction im Orient* (1874) and Frantz von Holtzendorff, *Handbuch des Völkerrechts auf Grundlage europäischer Staatspraxis* (1885–1890). See also Andreas T. Müller, 'Friedrich F. Martens on "The Office of Consul and Consular Jurisdiction in the East"' (2014) 25(3) *European Journal of International Law* 871–891.

*ihrerseits 'buddhistisch-confutseanische' Staaten einfach 'civilisirte' Staaten zu nennen; was chinesische Schriftsteller vielfach auch thun.*)[17]

Senga did not develop his civilisational approach any further, but we can see there a prototype of pluricivilisationalism, later developed by Adachi: if the Europeans claim their culture to be the only civilisation, the East Asians can also claim their culture to be the only civilisation. There is no superiority or inferiority between European and East Asian civilisations, but if there is, East Asian civilisation is superior at least in terms of its antiquity.

Senga's anti-Eurocentrism was expressed again in his 'Qing China's Being in the International Society' (1906).[18] In this article, Senga blamed the Western scholars who denied Qing China's full capacity in the community of international law for its acceptance of consular jurisdiction. We can see that Senga's anger against Eurocentrism extended to the consular jurisdiction in China.

However, while sympathetic to the difficulties Qing China had been going through, Senga did not feel much compassion for Korea. This makes his academic integrity dubious. If he were to be consistent with his respect for sovereignty in international legal relations, he should have opposed the consular jurisdiction in Korea, introduced there first by the Japanese government. Quite the contrary, the only writing of Senga on the topic of Korea was a short opinion paper in a newspaper against autonomy in Korea in 1919, which had a long title: 'A Serious Worry, The Monroe Doctrine's Double Standards, and Impossible Autonomy in Korea: Are Our 70 million Compatriots Ready?'[19]

For Senga, Korean autonomy, let alone independence, was out of the question, and Japanese citizens should prepare themselves to fight against US interference in the Japanese sphere of influence in East Asia. The Monroe Doctrine was an arbitrary doctrine used by the US government; it may be true, but it was used for political convenience. However, Senga's criticism was no less arbitrary. Senga, who criticised the European arbitrariness of the concept of civilisation, was very much arbitrary in determining which government was qualified for sovereignty.

17 SENGA 136–137 (n 12), footnote 39.

18 SENGA Tsurutaro, 'Qing China's Being in the International Society (Shin-koku-ha Kokusai-Shakai-no Naka-ni Ari)' (1906) 10(11) *Nihon Hosei Shinshi* 1–14.

19 SENGA Tsurutaro, 'A Serious Worry, The Monroe Doctrine's Double Standards, and Impossible Autonomy in Korea: Are Our 70 Million Compatriots Ready? (*Shin-ni Yuryo-ni Taezu. Monroe-Shugi-ha Go-Tsugo-Shugi-nari, Chosen-ni Jichi-wo Yurusu-ha Fuka-nari: Waga Nana-Sen-Man-Doho-no Kakugo-ha Ikan?*)' *Osaka Jiji Shimpo* (18 June 1919).

## Peripheral universalists as Senga's enemies: Martens and Takahashi

It is no accident that Friedrich Martens, the most prominent proponent of international law as the public law of civilised nations, served the Russian government (even though he was ethnically Estonian). The Russian government needed a theorist to bring the Russian Empire into the European community, and the Russian imperial family had been eager to take the initiative to promote European unity.[20] Emperor Alexander I's initiative for the Holy Alliance in 1815 is a good example. Martens served Nicholas II, who reigned over the empire from 1894 to 1917 and pursued the policy of European peace. Nicholas II was the principal promoter of the First Peace Conference at The Hague in 1899, and Martens led the Russian delegation.[21]

Geographically far from Europe, Japan also sought to be included in the European community in its struggle to eliminate consular jurisdiction. Even after the abolition of consular jurisdiction, it seemed beneficial for the Japanese Empire to be included in the society of civilised nations. TAKAHASHI Sakuye (1865–1920) represented this strand of thought in the Japanese scholarship of international law.

Senga was known for virulent attacks against Takahashi. One contemporary recorded his anti-Takahashi zeal:

> Dr. Senga on the podium attacked false scholars often with blazing fire. His attacks against Friedrich Martens of Russia and Takahashi of Japan were particularly fierce as if to perish them with dreadful vituperation. Dr. Senga exercised extreme strength in his words against Martens, who wrongly criticized the Japanese attack without declaration of war on Port Arthur at the beginning of the Russo-Japanese War. Dr. Senga indicated wrong translations in Dr. Takahashi's *International Law* and ridiculed the latter's arguments on the protectorate and the vassal states, even to declare that 'they have no knowledge in international law'.[22]

20 In a broader ideological context, there was a deep divide between the Westernising school and the pan-Slavist school, Russian international law scholars such as Martens and Taube against Nikolay Yakovlevich Danilevsky (1822–1885), who emphasised the distinction between Russian civilisation and European, i.e., Germano-Roman civilisation (Lauri Mälksoo, *Russian Approaches to International Law* (2015) 40).

21 Arthur Eyffinger, 'Feodor Martens, Architect of the Hague Tradition of International Law' (2009) 3 *East-West Studies* (http://publications.tlu.ee/index.php/eastwest/article/viewFile/806/593; accessed 7 July 2024).

22 Sendagi Senshi (ed.), *Gakkai-Bundan Jidai-no-Shinjin* (*New People in Academia*) (1908) 274–277 (http://kindai.ndl.go.jp/; accessed 7 July 2024).

Senga published thirteen articles that specifically criticised Takahashi's writings, of which the first was on the definition of international law, the second on the sources of international law and the eighth on the binding nature of treaties.

As to the concept of public international law, Takahashi defined international law as 'the rules recognised by the civilised nations to regulate the relations between the nations that belong to the community of civilised nations as well as the relations between the civilised nations and private persons (or entities) that belong to those nations'. With his anti-Eurocentric sentiment, it was quite natural for Senga to reject the relevance of civilisedness to the status of sovereignty under international law.[23]

As to the sources of international law, Senga, as a positivist, was wary of law-making treaties. Takahashi advanced the possibility that 'provision of bilateral or multilateral treaties may become sources of international law when they are likely to be recognised by nations'. Senga criticised Takahashi for the confusion between the direct sources of international law, treaties and international custom that create international legal obligations and the indirect sources of international law that motivate sovereign states to conclude treaties or practise international custom. According to Senga, Takahashi confused the two kinds of sources and wrongly expected multilateral and even bilateral treaties to create legal rules for the international community in general, including the governments which never signed such treaties.[24]

As to the binding nature of treaties, Takahashi quoted in his textbook of international law the argument by Martens as the most appropriate argument:

> The most appropriate argument is that the binding nature of international treaties flows from the concept of the international community (*die Verbindlichkeit der internationalen Verträge fliesst aus dem Begriff der internationalen Gemeinschaft*) by Martens, *Völkerrecht: das internationale Recht der civilisirten Nationen*, 1er Band, 1883, S. 391. Wherever there is society, there is law (*ubi societas ibi jus est*). A state, as a member of the international community, has the obligation to comply with international legal rules, which prescribe the compliance with treaties. Therefore, the binding nature

23 SENGA Tsurutaro, 'Takahahi-Hakase-Cho-no Kokusai-Koho-naka Yo-no Shoken-to Kotonaru-ten-ni-tsukite (What is different from my view in Dr Takahashi's writings on public international law) (1)' (May 1909) 4(5) *Kyoto Hogakkai Zasshi* 19–31.

24 SENGA Tsurutaro, 'Takahahi-Hakase-Cho-no Kokusai-Koho-naka Yo-no Shoken-to Kotonaru-ten-ni-tsukite (What is different from my view in Dr Takahashi's writings on public international law) (2)' (November 1909) 4(11) *Kyoto Hogakkai Zasshi* 1–11.

of treaties is based on international legal regulations. (However, the binding nature of international legal regulations goes back to the maxim of *ubi societas ibi jus est*, and we see a circularity in reasoning. This is the reason why the binding nature of treaties remains an important question in the theories of international law.)[25]

To point out that Takahashi misread Martens' textbook, Senga quoted the passage more at length:

> the binding nature of international treaties flows from the concept of the international community. Wherever there is society, there is law. By entering into international transactions, the states subject themselves to the effectiveness, through non-arbitrarily changeable life needs and relationships, which alone enable them to achieve their rational purposes. These conditions take the form of legal norms, and since the living relationships existing between states appear formulated in international treaties, these norms must also influence the treaties concluded by the states: as long as the real relationships bind them, the treaties themselves remain binding. (*die Verbindlichkeit der internationalen Verträge fliesst aus dem Begriff der internationalen Gemeinschaft. Ubi societas, ibi jus est. Indem sie in den internationalen Verkehr eintreten, unterwerfen sich die Staaten der Wirksamkeit durch nicht willkürlich abänderbare Lebens-Bedürfnisse und -Beziehungen fest bestimmter Bedingungen, bei deren Einhaltung allein sie ihre vernünftigen Zwecke zu erreichen vermögen. Diese Bedingungen nehmen die Gestalt von Rechtsnormen an, und da in den internationalen Verträgen die zwischen den Staaten bestehenden Lebensverhältnisse formulirt erscheinen, so müssen jene Normen auch auf die von den Staaten abgeschlossenen Verträge influiren: soweit die relaen Verhältnisse verbinden, soweit sind auch die Verträge selbst verbindlich.*)

Senga quoted Martens only to point out how wrong Takahashi was and did not mean to agree with Martens. After the long quote above, Senga criticised Martens for making the bindingness of treaties dependent on life relationships (*Lebensverhältnisse*), which would, in reality, make it dependent on politicians' subjective judgments. For Senga, the question of the basis of the binding nature of treaties is an extra-legal question, and there is no practical value in discussing it. Here, we see again Senga's enmity against the subjectivity of international law as advanced by European and Eurocentric scholars.

25 Quoted by SENGA Tsurutaro, 'Criticism against Dr Takahashi's Theory on the Nature of Treaties (Takahahi-Hakase-no Kokusai-Joyaku-no Seishitsu-ni Kansuru Setsu-wo Hibaku-su)' (August 1914) 9(8) *Kyoto Hogakkai Zasshi* 56–68.

## Senga's legacy from pretended universalism to hegemonic Japan-centrism

Except for his thesis paper, which was published in German, Senga did not publish anything in European languages. Senga's virulent attack against Martens was received only by the Japanese audience, and Takahashi was the only one who was in any way affected by Senga's criticisms.

During the first two decades of the twentieth century, Japanese international lawyers played an important role in promoting aggressive nationalism in public opinion. When seven professors of Tokyo Imperial University published in June 1903 an open opinion letter in newspapers to push the government for more assertive negotiations with Russia over Japanese rights to Korea and Manchuria (known as the 'Seven-Doctors' Claim'), three of the seven were professors of international law. In response to the professors' authoritative contention, newspapers condemned the government. Pushed by increasingly irritated public opinion, the Japanese government severed diplomatic relations in February 1904 and hostilities started immediately.

The war ended with a Japanese victory, only by a close margin. After the Peace Treaty of Portsmouth was concluded in September 1905, Senga published a nationalist opinion article in the Osaka-Mainichi newspaper to accuse the government of compromising too much with Russia and of being naive about the maleficent intermediation of peace negotiations by the US government.

Meanwhile, the Permanent Court of Arbitration rendered the award in the House Tax case in 1905 to Japan's disadvantage. Japanese international lawyers were unanimous in blaming the unfairness of international adjudication.[26] In 1906, Senga published an article on 'Arbitration on the House Tax case' to clarify how wrong the arbitral award was.[27] It is noteworthy that none of these criticisms were expressed in European languages. In the 1900s, anti-Eurocentric discourses were still only for domestic consumption.

As mentioned earlier, the Japanese government started to openly question the Eurocentric biases in international law after the First World War. The civilisational anti-Eurocentrism, of which an early version was developed

26 It should be noted not only that Japanese lawyers but also many lawyers in the West disagreed with the arbitral award, including Hersch Lauterpacht (Douglas Howland, 'The Japan House Tax Case, 1899–1905: Leases in Perpetuity and the Myth of International Equality' (2015) 75(2) *Zeitschrift für ausländisches öffentliches Recht und Völkerrecht* 413–434).

27 SENGA Tsurutaro, 'Arbitration on the House Tax Case (Kaoku-Zei-Mondai-no Chusai-Saiban) (1)-(2)' (February and March 1906) 1(2) and 1(3) *Kyoto Hogakkai Zasshi* 15–27 and 20–34.

by Senga in his 1897 book, was then developed into a most formal text of international adjudication, the PCIJ Statute, by Adachi. In a meeting of the drafting committee, Adachi declared that:

> all different kinds of civilisation must be taken into account, among them the civilisation of the Far East, of which Japan was perhaps the principal representative. (Advisory Committee of Jurists, Procès-Verbaux of the Proceedings of the Committee, 16 June-24 July 1920, with Annexes (Van Langenhuysen Brothers 1920) 136.)

Adachi's claim for the plurality of civilisations and Japan's status as the representative of the Far Eastern civilisation was taken seriously. The final version of the Statute did not recognise the plurality of civilisations per se, but did recognise that the plurality of forms of civilisation was ascertained as a compromise between universality and plurality.

Adachi later became a judge of the PCIJ and advocated for Japan's acceptance of compulsory jurisdiction. There was virtually no support from academia, and the Japanese government never considered such a possibility seriously. Adachi could cater for support only as long as he was fighting against universalism.[28]

The idea of Japan being a civilisational representative of East Asia outlived Adachi. In November 1943, the Greater East Asia Conference was convened in Tokyo with the participation of leaders of Japan, Manchukuo, China (the reorganised National Government of China), Burma, the Second Philippine Republic and the Kingdom of Thailand. It was to build an 'East Asian Co-Prosperity Sphere' with Japan as the leading nation. The conference declared that 'the countries of Greater East Asia by respecting one another's traditions and developing the creative faculties of each race will enhance the culture and civilization of Greater East Asia'.[29]

Senga's intuitive anti-Eurocentrism and pluri-civilisationalism developed into Adachi's sophisticated arguments, which left footprints in the text of the PCIJ Statute. Those ideas then developed into the ideology of the East Asian Co-Prosperity Sphere, which formed the official policy of the

28 TOYODA Tetsuya, 'A Civilizational Pluralist and Inegalitarian: Mineichiro Adachi (1869–1934)' in P. Sean Morris (ed.), *The League of Nations and the Development of International Law* (2021) 74–90.

29 Ministry of Foreign Affairs, 'Final Record of Proceedings of Greater East Asia Conference, Joint Declaration of Greater East Asia' (1943) *Digital Archives of Japan Center for Asian Historical Records*. Reference code B02032957800 (https://www.jacar.go.jp/english/; accessed 7 July 2024).

Japanese government during the final years of the Empire before its collapse in August 1945.

## Conclusion: a lasting dilemma between universalism and pluralism

The first major agenda for Japanese international law scholarship was the abolition of consular jurisdiction. The so-called unequal treaties concluded by the Tokugawa shogunate and the early Meiji imperial government had two defects: the installation of consular jurisdiction and the loss of tariff autonomy. In economic terms, the redemption of tariff autonomy was much desired, but in domestic politics, the abolition of consular jurisdiction was far more important.

The early Meiji imperial government was too weak, both internationally and domestically, to effectively counter the Western powers and reluctantly continued to conclude new treaties with them that included consular jurisdiction clauses. For the revision of these treaties, the acceptance of European values and institutions was indispensable or, to be precise, the appearance of accepting them to European eyes was indispensable.

Senga's thesis paper on consular jurisdiction came out when British–Japanese negotiations had already been completed two years earlier. Senga's work, published in Berlin, thus did not contribute in any way to Japanese diplomacy.[30] Senga's book should be seen as a confession of anti-Eurocentric *rancœur* of a Japanese student who had suffered racism in Europe for more than ten years. His case exemplifies a nationalist interpretation of international law, reflecting anti-European sentiment in Japan. As such, it surely represents one strand of thought in Japanese scholarship on international law, rather than a single instance of a nationalist perception of international law presented in a European language.

The Japanese government continued its policy of Europeanisation even after the abolition of consular jurisdiction in 1899, which allowed its ascendancy in the international hierarchy. The 1902 Japan–UK alliance to end the Glorious Isolation of the British Empire surprised diplomats and politicians around the world. The victory over the Russian Empire was celebrated as

30 In this regard, Gustavo Gozzi is wrong in claiming SENGA's contribution to the abolition of consular jurisdiction in Japan (G. Gozzi, 'The Particularistic Universalism of International Law in the 19th Century' (2010) 51 *Harvard International Law Journal Online* 83). Gozzi wrongly refers to Kinji Akashi, 'Japanese "Aacceptance" of the European Law of Nations' in M. Stolleis (ed.), *East Asian and European Perspectives on International Law* (2004) 1–21, which mentions SENGA's intention of contributing to the abolition of consular jurisdiction, but not the actual contribution (14).

that of an originally non-European nation over a European nation. After the First World War, it became one of the five permanent members of the Council of the League of Nations, the other four all from Europe (with the problematic absence of the United States).

It was part of the Japanese campaign for apparent Europeanisation to publish Ariga Nagao's *La guerre sino-japonaise au point de vue du droit international* in 1896, *La guerre russo-japonaise au point du vue du droit international* in 1906, Takahashi's *Le droit international dans l'histoire du Japon* in 1901 and *International Law Applied to the Russo-Japanese War with Decisions of the Japanese Prize Courts* in 1908. These works created the impression that the Japanese government was becoming increasingly Europeanised and passionate about the universal project of international law.

To the eyes of European observers, the emergence of the ideology of East Asia Co-Prosperity was a bad surprise. It is sometimes interpreted as a doctrine of political convenience catering for rising militarism or as a Japanese version of Schmittian *Grossraum* theory. Such an interpretation overlooks the nationalist strand of thought as *basso continuo* in Japanese international law scholarship. International law scholarship is usually associated with universalism. YKOTA Kisaburo, later the chief justice of the Supreme Court, is remembered for his support for the Kelsenian pure theory of law (*reine Rechtslehre*) and Tanaka Kotaro, later the chief justice of the Supreme Court and also an ICJ judge, for his theory of world law, but there was also a nationalistic and anti-Eurocentric strand of thought in the Japanese scholarship of international law.

Lorca may be wrong in considering that Senga was exceptional among the semi-peripheral (i.e. non-European) scholars, most of whom internalised the Eurocentric vision of the international legal order. Senga was exceptional among Japanese scholars only in that he expressed his rejection of Eurocentrism in a European language, be it only in one footnote, but not in his rejection of Eurocentrism.

# 2

# YOKOTA Kisaburo: between value-neutrality, and internationalist, pacifist and democratic ideals

*TAKATA Hinako*

## Introduction

YOKOTA[1] Kisaburo was born in 1896 in Aichi Prefecture and embarked on his scholarly career at the Faculty of Law, Tokyo Imperial University (now the University of Tokyo) in 1922 as an assistant. He became a professor in 1930, served as dean from 1948 to 1951 and retired in 1957. He was a member of the United Nations International Law Commission from 1957 to 1961, the Chief Justice of the Supreme Court of Japan from 1960 to 1966 and a member of the International Labour Organization (ILO) Committee of Experts on the Application of Conventions and Recommendations from 1967 to 1975. He died in 1993 at the age of ninety-six.

Yokota has made major contributions to the theory and practice of international law throughout, and in every important moment of Japan's turbulent times: its militarisation and invasion of Manchuria (Manchurian Incident) in the 1930s;[2] its launch of and defeat in the

1 His original family name was IWATA. He got married to Shizuko YOKOTA and was adopted into the YOKOTA family in March 1924.

2 See, for example, YOKOTA Kisaburo, 'War as an International Crime' in YOKOTA Kisaburo, *Collections on International Law II* (Yūhikaku 1978) (hereinafter '*YOKOTA's Collections on International Law II*') (first published in 1931); YOKOTA Kisaburo, 'Prevention of War' in *YOKOTA's Collections on International Law II* (first published in 1934); YOKOTA Kisaburo, 'Manchurian Incident and International Law' (1932) 31(4) *Kokusai-hō gaikō zasshi* 357; YOKOTA Kisaburo, 'Manchurian Incident and Hoover Doctrine' (1933) 32(1) *Kokusai-hō gaikō zasshi* 46; YOKOTA Kisaburo, 'Security Issues' (1934) 33(1) *Kokusai-hō gaikō zasshi* 6; YOKOTA Kisaburo, 'Stimson Doctrine as an International Law Doctrine' (1934) 33(8) *Kokusai-hō gaikō zasshi* 711. Although YOKOTA wrote several articles in newspapers and non-academic journals to elaborate on issues of public concern to non-experts, this chapter cites only academic works. Note that all works cited in this chapter, except for the following, are written in Japanese: YAMAMOTO and NEGISHI, *infra* note 22; OBATA, *infra* note 86; ZACHMANN, *infra* note 103; IKEDA, *infra* note 111; and MURASE, *infra* note 129. Due to space constraints, it cites only the English translations of the works' titles.

Asia–Pacific War;[3] the occupation of Japan by the Allied Powers;[4] the creation of the new Japanese Constitution and its denunciation of wars;[5] prosecution of Japanese leaders in the International Military Tribunal for the Far East;[6] the conclusion of the Treaty of Peace with Japan (San Francisco Peace Treaty);[7] creation of the United Nations and Japan's participation in it;[8] and Japan's national security policies in the face of the increasing tensions of the Cold War.[9] Yokota provided important works on a wide range of topics, most importantly international adjudication,[10] and published the most up-to-date and detailed commentaries in many

3 Due to severe restrictions on freedom of expression against governmental policies, YOKOTA was unable to publish papers that directly criticised Japan's commencement of the Greater East Asian War during the war. Thus, he indirectly dealt with the issue in the following articles. YOKOTA Kisaburo, 'Grotius' Just War Theory' in *YOKOTA's Collections on International Law II* (n 2) (first published in 1941); YOKOTA Kisaburo, 'Doctrine of Non-Belligerency (1)' (1942) 60(4) *Hōgakukyōkaizasshi* 545; YOKOTA, 'Doctrine of Non-Belligerency (2)' (1942) 60(5) *Hōgakukyōkaizasshi* 759.

4 See, for example, YOKOTA Kisaburo, 'Unconditional Surrender and Japan' (1946) 45(1–2) *Kokusai-hō gaikō zasshi* 1; YOKOTA Kisaburo, 'The Legal Status of Japan' (1946) 1(1) *Nihon kanri hōrei kenkyū* 11; YOKOTA Kisaburo, 'Basic Forms of Control over Japan' (1946) 1(1) *Nihon kanri hōrei kenkyū* 27.

5 See, for example, YOKOTA Kisaburo, *Renunciation of War* (Kunitachi shoin 1947).

6 See, for example, YOKOTA Kisaburo, *Studies on War Crimes* (Yūhikaku 1947).

7 See, for example, YOKOTA Kisaburo, 'Methods for Concluding a Peace' (1948) 17 *Nihon kanri hōrei kenkyū* 79; YOKOTA Kisaburo, 'Basic Characteristics of the New Peace Treaty' (1948) 1 *Kokusai jiji kenkyū* 9.

8 See, for example, YOKOTA Kisaburo, 'Post-War Project by the Anti-Axis States on an International Organization' (1944) 44(11) *Kokusai-hō gaikō zasshi* 39; YOKOTA Kisaburo, *United Nations: Studies and Commentary* (Seiji fukyū-kai 1946); YOKOTA Kisaburo, *Studies on the United Nations* (Ginza shuppansha 1947); YOKOTA Kisaburo, 'Japan after Joining the United Nations: Its Interests and Responsibilities' (1957) 36(1) *Kokuren hyōron* 4.

9 See, for example, YOKOTA Kisaburo, *Korean War and Japan's Future* (Keisōshobō 1950); YOKOTA Kisaburo, 'The Concept of Security and Japan–U.S. Security Treaty' (1959) 961 *Gaikōjihō* 2; YOKOTA Kisaburo, 'Limits to the Renunciation of War: In light of Sunagawa Judgment' (1960) 59(1–2) *Kokusai-hō gaikō zasshi* 182.

10 IWATA Kisbauro, 'Historical Studies on International Adjudication (1)' (1923) 37(2) *Kokka Gakkai Zasshi* 219; IWATA, 'Historical Studies on International Adjudication (2)' (1923) 37(3) *Kokka Gakkai Zasshi* 427; IWATA, 'Historical Studies on International Adjudication (3)' (1923) 37(4) *Kokka Gakkai Zasshi* 558; IWATA, 'Historical Studies on International Adjudication (4)' (1923) 37(5) *Kokka Gakkai Zasshi* 685; IWATA, 'Historical Studies on International Adjudication (5)' (1923) 37(6) *Kokka Gakkai Zasshi* 897; IWATA, 'Historical Studies on International Adjudication (6)' (1923) 37(7) *Kokka Gakkai Zasshi* 1068; IWATA, 'Historical Studies on International Adjudication (7)' (1923) 37(8) *Kokka Gakkai Zasshi* 1272; YOKOTA Kisaburo, *The Essence of International Adjudication* (Iwanami shoten 1941).

fields based on his experience as a practitioner. He immediately released a commentary on the law of the sea[11] after serving as a legal adviser to the Japanese delegation at the United Nations Conference on the Law of the Sea in 1958. He published commentaries on diplomatic[12] and consular law[13] based on his experience with the United Nations International Law Commission in drafting the Vienna Conventions on Diplomatic and Consular Relations. He also left work on international labour law, given his experience in the ILO Committee of Experts.[14]

Despite the existence of the above-mentioned rich and important works, in light of the overarching theme of this book, this chapter focuses on Yokota's three major and interrelated contributions to the field of theory and approach to international law: his introduction of Hans Kelsen's pure theory of law (*Reine Rechtslehre*) in Japan; his argument on the supremacy of international law over domestic law in the face of monist/dualist debates; and his development of the theory of international democracy. Finally, this chapter discusses whether these three theories presented by Yokota are consistent and finds that Yokota's approach to international law fluctuated between value-neutrality and internationalist, pacifist and democratic ideals in response to the changing realities of Japan and international society.

Although the detailed autobiographies written by Yokota himself in the later years of his life[15] are useful for understanding his subjective motivations, they should not be given undue weight when evaluating his work. To provide an overall picture of Yokota's theories, this chapter draws on evaluations of his work by his Japanese colleagues[16] and the historical context in which Yokota's works are situated.

11 YOKOTA Kisaburo, *Law of the Sea I* (Yuhikaku 1959).
12 YOKOTA Kisaburo, *International Law on Diplomatic Relations* (Yuhikaku 1963).
13 YOKOTA Kisaburo, *International Law on Consular Relations* (Yuhikaku 1974).
14 See, for example, YOKOTA Kisaburo, *Freedom of Association: International Standards and Japan* (Yuhikaku 1979).
15 YOKOTA Kisaburo, *My Life* (Tōkyō shinbun shuppan-kyoku 1976); YOKOTA Kisaburo, *The Remaining Years of the Remaining Years of My Life* (Shinzansha 1987).
16 See, generally, TSUNETO Takeji, 'Discussing YOKOTA Kisaburo: His Legal Ideology' (1961) 33(1) *Hōritsu jihō* 4; TERASAWA Hajime, 'Discussing YOKOTA Kisaburo: His International Law Theories I: YOKOTA's Pre-War Academic Activities' (1961) 33(1) *Hōritsu jihō* 10; TAKANO Yuichi, 'Discussing YOKOTA Kisaburo: His International Law Theories II: YOKOTA's Post-War Academic Activities' (1961) 33(1) *Hōritsu jihō* 14; OWADA Hisashi, HATANO Ribo, MIYAZAKI Shigeki and YAMAMOTO Soji, 'Roundtable Discussion: In Memory of YOKOTA Kisaburo' (1994) 1041 *Jurist* 66; YAMAMOTO Hajime, 'An "International Democrat" Who Descended to the Supreme Court: The Formation and Development of YOKOTA Kisaburo's Legal Thinking" in HIGUCHI Yoichi et al. (eds), *Dignity of the Constitution* (Nihonhyōronsha 2017) 463.

## Yokota and pure theory of law

### *Disseminating the pure theory of law in Japan*

In the early stages of his academic career, Yokota was attracted to Hans Kelsen's pure theory of law. According to Yokota's summary:

> The pure theory of law aims at the pure recognition of law. … Law here means positive law. Its pure recognition requires the capture of law as law, to the exclusion of any extra-legal factors. Thus, influence by ethical, political, psychological, social, historical, economic, and any other factors are eliminated, and they never transform or alter positive law. Especially, analysis based on natural science and sociology, and ethical and political considerations are eliminated, as they are most detrimental to the pure recognition of law.[17]

Since first publishing a book review on Kelsen's monograph, *Das Problem der Souveränität und die Theorie des Völkerrechts* (1920), in 1923,[18] he devoted his academic passion to research on the pure theory of law, especially in the 1930s. He published a Japanese translation of Kelsen's monograph, *Reine Rechtslehre* (1934),[19] and wrote a number of articles on this theory, of which many were later compiled into two-volume collections.[20] Such articles include, in addition to the ones cited below, 'Junsuihōgaku no ippan riron (General Theories of the Pure Theory of Law)' (1932), 'Junsuihōgaku no tetsugaku-teki kiso (Philosophical Foundations of the Pure Theory of Law)' (1936) and 'Hō to kyōsei (Law and Enforcement)' (1938).[21] Yokota contributed greatly to the diffusion and acceptance of the pure theory of law among international law scholars and legal scholars in Japan. Thus, Yokota is sometimes referred to as 'Kelsen of the Orient'.[22]

17 YOKOTA Kisaburo, 'Pure Theory of Law' in *YOKOTA's Collections on Pure Theory of Law I*, *infra* note 20 (first published in 1934) 1, 3.

18 IWATA Kisaburo, 'Introduction and Critique: H. Kelsen, Das Problem der Souveränität u. die Theorie des Völkerrechts, 1920' (1923) 37(12) *Kokka Gakkai Zasshi* 145.

19 KELSEN Hans (translated by YOKOTA Kisaburo), *Pure Theory of Law* (Iwanami Shoten 1935).

20 YOKOTA Kisaburo, *Collections on Pure Theory of Law I* (Yūhikaku 1976) (hereinafter, '*YOKOTA's Collections on Pure Theory of Law I*'); YOKOTA Kisaburo, *Collections on Pure Theory of Law II* (Yūhikaku 1977) (hereinafter, '*YOKOTA's Collections on Pure Theory of Law II*').

21 They are all contained in *YOKOTA's Collections on Pure Theory of Law I* (n 20).

22 YAMAMOTO Hajime and NEGISHI Yota, 'Japan' in PALOMBINO Fulvio Maria (ed.), *Duelling for Supremacy: International Law vs. National Fundamental Principles* (Cambridge University Press 2019) 210, 215.

### *Supplementing the pure theory of law with his original insights*

Yokota not only effectively described Kelsen's argument and disseminated it among his Japanese colleagues, but also supplemented and strengthened it with his own interpretations and insights. Unfortunately, owing to Yokota's writing style containing few citations and quotations, and no clear section dedicated to a literature review – a style not uncommon in Japan's legal scholarship at the time – it is difficult, unless the reader possesses thorough and comprehensive knowledge of Kelsen's theory, to clearly distinguish his original contributions from Kelsen's pre-existing arguments; often forming an integrated whole. However, Yokota's original contributions are evident in certain fields and topics. The clearest example is his promotion of the monist theory of the supremacy of international law over national law, which is discussed in the next section.

Another major example is his elaborate examination of the relationship between the pure theory of law, legal interpretation and judicial adjudication. Kelsen and other scholars belonging to the Vienna School of Law did not closely examine how the law should be interpreted or how judges should adjudicate under the pure theory of law. Thus, Yokota decided to explore this 'maiden soil'[23] in his two interrelated and largely overlapping articles, 'Saiban to hōritsu (Judicial Adjudication and Law)'[24] and 'Hōritsu no kaishaku (Interpretation of Law)'.[25] Yokota argued in accordance with the pure theory of law that legal scholarship as a science and judicial adjudication as a practice should be strictly separated.[26] Under the pure theory of law, when law leaves a lacuna, it should be presented as it is. Legal lacunae cannot be filled by legal techniques, such as analogy, *a contrario* interpretation or resorting to the spirit of the law.[27] Thus, under the pure theory of law, judges who are tasked with filling such lacunae need not adjudicate based on positive law and should fill lacunae based on extra-legal considerations concerning what is just, whose standards are not derived from law or the pure theory of law.[28] One should never pretend that such extra-legal considerations are part of law, as that would confuse the concept of law

23 YOKOTA Kisaburo, 'Judicial Adjudication and Law' in *YOKOTA's Collections on Pure Theory of Law II* (n 20) (first published in 1933) 88, 89 (fn 1).
24 Ibid.
25 YOKOTA Kisaburo, 'Interpretation of Law (1)' (1934) 48(12) *Kokka Gakkai Zasshi* 1; YOKOTA, 'Interpretation of Law (2)' (1935) 49(1) *Kokka Gakkai Zasshi* 75; YOKOTA, 'Interpretation of Law (3)' (1935) 49(2) *Kokka Gakkai Zasshi* 77.
26 YOKOTA, 'Interpretation of Law (3)' 110 (n 25).
27 YOKOTA, 'Interpretation of Law (1)' 23–26 (n 25).
28 YOKOTA, 'Judicial Adjudication and Law' 98–100 (n 23).

and destroy its integrity as a science.[29] Although Yokota is fully aware that this conclusion may run contrary to the traditional view that judicial adjudication should always be based on law, which is derived from the principles of separation of powers and independence of the judiciary, he rejected this view by arguing that these principles are mere political demands and dependent on the specific historical context.[30] Thus, Yokota clarified the scope of the functions of the pure theory of law by excluding the function of providing standards for judicial interpretation and adjudication.

### *Defending the pure theory of law from its opponents in Japan*

Yokota's active engagement in academic debate with his Japanese colleagues on the pure theory of law has greatly deepened the understanding of this theory within the community of Japanese legal scholars.

In response to the criticisms by KIMURA Kameji (1897–1972), a legal philosopher and criminal law scholar,[31] and YASUI Kaoru (1907–1980), an international law scholar,[32] that the pure theory of law plays a function to endorse and justify the existing legal order and state authority, Yokota published an article 'Junsuihōgaku no jissaiteki kinō (Practical Functions of the Pure Theory of Law)' in 1933. Yokota established a distinction between the concept of law and that of legal theory: legal theories are used to recognise law, capture the existing law as it is, ascertain its content and order and systematise it. They cannot create or modify law.[33] Thus, he argued that

> The pure theory of law, a legal theory that aims to capture positive law as it is, is not conservative or liberal, and does not play either capitalistic or socialistic functions. It is completely neutral. Indeed, the law recognized and described in accordance with Pure Theory of Law may be conservative and capitalistic. Nevertheless, that is only because the law itself is originally conservative and

29 Ibid 113.
30 Ibid 103–107.
31 KIMURA Kameji, 'Denial of Natural Law Theory by Kelsen: Introduction and Critique: H. Kelsen, Die philosophischen Grundlagen der Naturrechtslehre und des Rechtspositivismus, 1928' (1931) 45(5) *Kokka Gakkai Zasshi* 122, 137; KIMURA Kameji, 'Reading Kelsen's Pure Theory of Law' (1932) 4(10) *Hōritsu jihō* 43, 46–47.
32 YASUI Kaoru, 'Introduction to Marxist International Law Scholarship' (1933) 32(2) *Kokusai-hō gaikō zasshi* 106; YASUI Kaoru, 'Studying the Theory of Temporary International Law' (1933) 51(4) *Hōgakukyōkaizasshi* 149, 150.
33 YOKOTA Kisaburo, 'Practical Functions of Pure Theory of Law' in *YOKOTA's Collections on Pure Theory of Law I* (n 20) (first published in 1933) 72, 77–78.

capitalistic. ... In this case, it is law itself that is conservative and capitalistic, and not the pure theory of law as a legal theory.[34]

Yokota's intense debate with Professor MINOBE Tatsukichi (1873–1948), a constitutional law scholar, is well known. In his article 'Keruzen kyōju no kokuhō oyobi Kokusai-hō riron no hihyō (Critique of Professor Kelsen's Theories on State Law and International Law)' in 1930, Minobe criticised Kelsen's distinction of *Sein* (is) and *Sollen* (ought) and his characterisation of law as falling solely in the domain of *Sollen*, as well as his exclusion of social and psychological considerations from the scope of legal scholarship. Minobe argued that the essential nature of law lies in *Sein*; legal research should not rely solely on simple logic but should instead encompass the observation of social facts.[35] Whereas Kelsen argued that the question of why a law is valid as law, or the essential nature of law, is outside the scope of legal research, Minobe suggested that such a question should form the foundation of legal research.[36] According to Minobe, 'the essence that makes law a law is the recognition by the people who are members of the society, in their general state of mind, of the norm as law, namely, regulation that cannot be violated'.[37] If this element is overlooked, one cannot explain why a robber's order to hand over money under the threat of a gun is not a law, while a similar order by the monarch in a state of absolute monarchy is a law.[38] Therefore, Minobe concluded that 'social and psychological elements are never extra-legal elements, as argued by Kelsen, but are the essential elements of law'.[39] Additionally, Minobe asserted that 'situating law into the domain of *Sollen* is the consequence of the confusion between the content of law and its essential nature'.[40] He classified law into two categories: the first grants humans the legal power and authority that they do not originally enjoy, and the second restricts the freedom they originally possess.[41] According to Minobe, the characterisation of law as *Sollen* only applies to the second category, and the first category regulates *Können*, not *Sollen;* when a man is over twenty-five years old, he has the power to vote as

34 Ibid 82.
35 MINOBE Tatsukichi, 'Critique of Professor Kelsen's Theories of State Law and International Law (1)' (1930) 44(8) *Kokka Gakkai Zasshi* 1177, 1181.
36 Ibid 1191–1192.
37 Ibid 1197.
38 Ibid 1192.
39 Ibid 1201.
40 Ibid 1183.
41 Ibid 1185.

a natural consequence of the relevant legislation, and it is no different from the phenomenon that materials expand when heated.[42]

Given these criticisms, Yokota wrote an article titled 'Hōritsu ni okeru tōi to sonzai: Minobe kyōju no keruzen no hihan ni taishite (*Sollen* and *Sein* in Law: A Response to Professor Minobe's Critique of Kelsen)' in 1931.[43] In answering the question of whether law is *Sollen* or *Sein*, Yokota first attempted to clarify the meanings of these two concepts. After categorising *Sein* into physical and psychological beings, he argued that a third category exists: conceptual being.[44] When *Sein* is interpreted broadly, law is part of *Sein* within the meaning of conceptual *Sein*.[45] He then categorised propositions on existence into those representing natural causal relations – such as 'materials expand when heated' – and those representing relations based on values – such as 'when one commits a theft, he/she shall be punished'.[46] Only the latter relations qualify as *Sollen*. Law differs from natural causal relations. Causal relations mean that a cause necessarily (*muss*) leads to a certain outcome, but law does not necessarily lead to certain outcomes as a matter of natural causal relations; it only normatively dictates that certain outcomes should (*soll*) occur.[47] In rebutting Minobe's example of the voting power of men over the age of twenty-five, Yokota explained that there is no natural causal link between the fact that he is a man over the age of twenty-five and the result that he has the power to vote in elections. In fact, not only men over twenty-five years old, but also women and younger men can go to the polling station, write a candidate's name and put it into the ballot box. Law does not enable such factual acts, but gives a legal effect to such factual acts.[48] Moreover, when there is a fact that a material is heated, it naturally and inevitably expands as a result, at any time and place. In contrast, even when there is a fact that a man is over twenty-five years old,

42 Ibid 1186.

43 For a commentary on this article, please see TAMURA Tokuji, 'What Kind of Existence is Law? Examination of Professor YOKOTA's Paper "Sollen and Sein in Law" (1)' (1931) 25(5) *Hōgakuronsō* 731; TAMURA, 'What Kind of Existence is Law? (2)' (1931) 25(6) *Hōgakuronsō* 895; TAMURA, 'What Kind of Existence is Law? (3)' (1931) 26(1) *Hōgakuronsō* 82; TAMURA, 'What Kind of Existence is Law? (4)' (1931) 26(3) *Hōgakuronsō* 395; TAMURA, 'What Kind of Existence is Law? (5)' (1931) 26(4) *Hōgakuronsō* 563.

44 YOKOTA Kisaburo, 'Sollen and Sein in Law: In Response to Professor Minobe's Critique of Kelsen' in *YOKOTA's Collections on Pure Theory of Law I* (first published in 1931) 115, 126–132 (n 20).

45 Ibid 159.

46 Ibid 136–138.

47 Ibid 165.

48 Ibid 178.

voting rights do not follow as a necessary consequence; they arise only in today's Japan.[49] Yokota analysed that Professor Minobe had defined *Sollen* narrowly by including only those legal norms that provide for obligations, perhaps due to his focus on the term '*soll*'.[50] However, as Kelsen interpreted the concept of *Sollen* in a wider manner as relations based on values that are distinct from natural causal relations, Professor Minobe's criticism was not in the right ballpark.[51]

Professor Minobe quickly wrote a follow-up article titled 'Hōritsu wa tōi nari ya sonzai nari ya (Is Law *Sollen* or *Sein*?)' in 1931,[52] and argued that even if the content of law (*Rechtsinhalt*) may be classified as *Sollen* and is different from natural causal relations, the characterisation of the essence of law (*Rechtswesen*), the very basis that makes law a binding law, is a distinct question. Other norms, such as morals, religions and customs, normatively dictate certain conduct, and they cannot be distinguished from law in terms of content. Thus, it is necessary to debate what essence or basis of law distinguishes it from other norms.[53]

In response, Yokota published an article titled 'Hōritsu no datōsei (Validity of Law: A Response to Professor Minobe)' in 1931.[54] Yokota reframed Minobe's critique as, 'What is the validity of law? What does it mean? In what cases is law considered to be valid?'[55] Yokota classified theories on the validity of law into three types.[56] The first type of theory, value validity, considers that law is valid because and when it is right and consistent with justice. The second type, causal validity, posits that law is valid because and when it is complied with. The third type, positive validity, suggests that law is valid because and when the law should be complied with as law. Only the third category falls within the scope of legal studies. Yokota found that although Minobe originally relied on the second type, the pure and direct application of the theory would lead to an absurd result: a law is valid only among those who know and comply with the law.[57] Thus, Minobe himself modified the theory to the extent that even when the general public

49 Ibid 178–179.
50 Ibid 180.
51 Ibid 180.
52 MINOBE Tatsukichi, 'Is Law Sollen or Sein? (1)' (1931) 45(4) *Kokka Gakkai Zasshi* 1; MINOBE, 'Is Law Sollen or Sein? (2)' (1931) 45(5) *Kokka Gakkai Zasshi* 26; MINOBE, 'Is Law Sollen or Sein? (3)' (1931) 45(7) *Kokka Gakkai Zasshi* 62.
53 MINOBE, 'Is Law Sollen or Sein? (1)' 8–9 (n 52).
54 YOKOTA Kisaburo, 'Validity of Law' in *YOKOTA's Collections on Pure Theory of Law I* (first published in 1931) 182 (n 20).
55 Ibid 184.
56 Ibid 184–201.
57 Ibid 227.

is unaware of the detailed content of laws, it suffices that they generally believe that they should comply with what the legislature provides.[58] With this modification, Yokota argued that Minobe had substantially changed his position concerning the basis of validity from causal to positive validity by admitting that the most decisive element for validity is the fact that the legislature enacted the law.[59]

Lastly, the debate of Yokota with Professor MAKINO Eiichi (1878–1970), a criminal law scholar and supporter of the Free Law school (*Freirechtslehre*), should be briefly introduced. In his extensive article titled 'Hōritsu-teki shōkyokushugi (Legal Passivism)',[60] Professor Makino criticised the pure theory of law as put forward by Yokota for its passiveness. The pure theory of law requires understanding positive law as it is, without adding value judgment of the interpreter; thus, the theory cannot give guidance on the interpretation of abstract terms and concepts in positive law, runs the risk of leading to legal lacunae, and cannot explain the possibility of 'désuétude'.[61] Yokota published an article, 'Hōritsu-teki sekkyokushugi: Makino kyōju no hihyō ni kotaete (Legal Activism: In Response to Professor Makino)' in 1932[62] and addressed these problems. Yokota argued that the pure theory of law helps clarify the meaning of abstract terms and concepts in positive law by situating the law in question within the overall unity of the legal system, including customary law.[63] Thus, although the pure theory of law admits legal lacunae, such cases are more limited than Makino assumed.[64] The pure theory of law endorses désuétude when such an interpretation is consistent with the overall unity of the legal system.[65] In addition, Yokota made a critical comment on legal activism: adding extraneous and extra-legal elements to law in the name of legal activism is detrimental to the unity of the legal system. Legal activism seems to assume that 'just-

58 Ibid 227–231.
59 Ibid 231–232.
60 MAKINO Eiichi, 'Legal Passivism (1)' (1932) 34 *Hōgaku-shi-rin* 1; MAKINO, 'Legal Passivism (2-1)' (1932) 34 *Hōgaku-shi-rin* 129; MAKINO, 'Legal Passivism (2-2)' (1932) (34) *Hōgaku-shi-rin* 561; MAKINO, 'Legal Passivism (3-1)' (1932) 34 *Hōgaku-shi-rin* 769; MAKINO, 'Legal Passivism (3-2)' (1932) 34 *Hōgaku-shi-rin* 897; MAKINO, 'Legal Passivism (3-3)' (1932) 34 *Hōgaku-shi-rin* 1025; MAKINO, 'Legal Passivism (3-4)' (1932) 34 *Hōgaku-shi-rin* 1301; MAKINO, 'Legal Passivism (3-5)' (1932) 34 *Hōgaku-shi-rin* 1429.
61 MAKINO, 'Legal Passivism (1)' 6–47 (n 60).
62 YOKOTA Kisaburo, 'Legal Activism: In Response to Professor Makino' in *YOKOTA's Collections on Pure Theory of Law I* (first published in 1932) 245 (n 20).
63 Ibid 250–252.
64 Ibid 276.
65 Ibid 264–271.

ness' is another basis of the validity of law, in addition to the positive validity, thereby advocating two different *Grundnorms*.[66] However, it is logically impossible for a single legal system to have two *Grundnorms*. Legal activism's attempt to add a new *Grundnorm* would even destroy the unity and integrity that the legal system had previously earned.[67]

## International law and national law

### *Supremacy of international law over national law*

The issue of the relationship between international and domestic laws emerged in Japan in the early twentieth century, soon after Western international law was introduced.[68] Yokota joined the debate in the 1930s and advocated for a monist approach with the supremacy of international law over domestic law. In his article 'Kokusai-hō to kokunai-hō to no ronri-teki kankei (The Logical Relationship between International Law and National Laws)' in 1930,[69] Yokota first noted that although the issue of the relationship between international and national laws had been thoroughly addressed by the Vienna School, especially Kelsen, these studies have focused exclusively on the logical aspect of the issue.[70] Yokota then proposed that both the logical and legal aspects of the issue should be investigated.[71]

According to Yokota, there are three logically possible options for the relationship between international and national laws: separative (bunritsu-teki), equal-rank (dōi-teki) and hierarchical (jōge-teki) relationships.[72] In the separative relationship – substantially equivalent to what we call 'dualism' today – the two legal orders are totally independent and do not recognise each other as valid legal orders, as if law is separate and independent from

66 Ibid 294–299.

67 Ibid 298–299. Note that Professor MAKINO published a follow-up article: MAKINO Eiichi, 'Active Meaning of the Pure Theory of Law' (1933) 35(2) *Hōgaku-shi-rin* 98.

68 For a summary of the history of the debate on the relationship between international and national laws in Japan, see KOBAYASHI Tomohiko, 'The Significance of Discussing the "Relationship between International Law and Domestic Law": In Light of the Development Process of Academic Theories in Japan' (2003) 54(5) *Tōkyōdaigaku shakai kagakukenkyūjo kiyō* 81.

69 YOKOTA Kisaburo, 'Logical Relationship between International Law and National Law' in KAMIKAWA Hikomatsu (ed.), *Collection of Papers Celebrating Professor YAMADA's 60th birthday* (Yūhikaku 1930) 551.

70 Ibid 512.

71 Ibid 512.

72 Ibid 514–531.

morals.[73] In an equal-rank relationship, the two legal orders are parallel. However, this relationship is possible only when there is an overarching, hierarchically higher third normative order that regulates the relationship between the two legal orders. Thus, an equal-rank relationship is a branch of a hierarchical relationship.[74] The hierarchical relationship – equivalent to 'monism' – posits that one normative legal order derives its validity from the other normative legal order. The former order is hierarchically lower, and the latter is higher. When legal orders are understood in this manner, they form a single legal order. Hierarchical relationships can be divided into those with supremacy of national law and those with supremacy of international law.[75]

Yokota then argued that the separative relationship is inconsistent with the reality that both international and national laws are considered valid law and that there is a relationship of delegation between them, such as a reference by treaties to national laws on technical rules and rules for implementation.[76] Although national laws that conflict with international law may remain valid, such conflicts incur the state's international responsibility, meaning that the two legal orders are not independent.[77] The equal-rank relationship is not feasible either, as a third legal order that overarches both international and national laws has not been developed.[78] The hierarchical relationship with the supremacy of national laws cannot be adopted because it would deny the widely shared understanding that all national legal orders are equal, and thus, would undermine the basis of international law – agreement among equal states.[79] Yokota proposed adopting a hierarchical relationship with the supremacy of international law. Only this relationship can explain the reality that each national law is valid within a certain geographical and personal scope demarcated by international law, and lay the foundation for equality among different national laws.[80]

Yokota's argument largely supports that of Kelsen in adopting the monist – what Yokota called 'hierarchical' – vision of international and national laws. However, his original contributions lie in the combination of a logical approach with an empirical approach – what Yokota calls the 'legal' approach. Although Kelsen concluded that it is not possible to choose

73 Ibid 514–517.
74 Ibid 516–517.
75 Ibid 517–519.
76 Ibid 532–534.
77 Ibid 535–536.
78 Ibid 538–539.
79 Ibid 539–542.
80 Ibid 543–545.

between the monist vision of the supremacy of national law and that of international law, Yokota observed that the latter is more consistent with empirical reality.

### *The status of international law in Japan's 1946 Constitution*

Although Yokota supported the hierarchical (monist) vision with the supremacy of international law, he refused to adopt the radical view that national laws that conflict with international law are immediately invalid. In his monograph 'Kokusai-hō no kiso riron (Basic Theories of International Law)' in 1949, Yokota stated that

> Generally, states are presumed to have no intention to violate international law, and national law should be interpreted to avoid conflicts with international law as much as possible. This can be explained reasonably only by grasping two legal orders as constituting a single and uniform legal order with international law occupying a higher, and national law a lower status. Nevertheless, international law does not have immediate effects in national law. ... For international law to have effects in national law, express or implied recognition by national law to that effect is necessary.[81]

Thus, Yokota studied the provisions of national constitutions, including Japan's, on the national effects of international law. The Constitution of the Empire of Japan (Meiji Constitution), adopted in 1889, had no provisions on this matter. In contrast, Article 98(2) of the Japanese Constitution, newly adopted in 1946, stipulates 'The treaties concluded by Japan and established laws of nations shall be faithfully observed'. Yokota interpreted this provision as binding on the Japanese state, state organs and nationals.[82] Thus, the Japanese courts must apply treaties and international law.[83] When international law and the Constitution are in unavoidable conflict, with which do the state and individuals comply? In answering this question, Yokota paid attention to Article 98(1) of the Constitution, which reads 'This Constitution shall be the supreme law of the nation and no law, ordinance, imperial rescript or other act of government, or part thereof, contrary to the provisions hereof, shall have legal force or validity'. He argued that the overall structure of Article 98 indicates, and the developed and closely related international society necessitates, that the Constitution be the supreme law

81 YOKOTA Kisaburo, *Basic Theories of International Law* (Yuhikaku 1949) 125–126.
82 Ibid 143–144.
83 Ibid 145.

only within Japan, and in its external relationship, Japan should faithfully comply with treaties and international law.[84] He thus concludes 'in case of conflict between treaties and international law, and the Constitution, treaties and international law prevails, and [Japan] must respect them'.[85]

### *Yokota's monist theory on the supremacy of international law in the historical context*

OBATA Kaoru found that Yokota's theory of the supremacy of international law over national law played a vital role during Japan's occupation and transition after its defeat in the Second World War.[86] Japan's acceptance of the Potsdam Declaration on 14 August 1945 caused fundamental changes to its constitutional system. As the 1889 Constitution of the Empire of Japan provided that the emperor had sovereignty in Japan, it was argued that the new Japanese Constitution of 1946, which accords sovereignty to the people of Japan, was justified only as a 'revolution', not a product of normal amendment processes.[87] It has been suggested that this theory – the theory of the so-called 'August revolution' – was inspired by Yokota's monist vision with the supremacy of international law, as the theory needs to build on the supremacy of international commitments embedded in the Potsdam Declaration.[88] Moreover, Obata highlighted that after Japan lost the authority to conduct external and diplomatic affairs under the Allies' occupation, monist theory contributed to justifying the authority of the Emperor and the Ministry of Foreign Affairs to continue conducting external and diplomatic affairs by deriving such authority directly from international law, as well as constraining the power of the Allied occupying force in accordance with international law.[89]

84 Ibid 146–149.
85 Ibid 146.
86 OBATA Kaoru, 'Historical Function of Monism with Primacy of International Law: A View Based on the Japanese Experience during the Early Period of the Allied Occupation' (2006) 49 *Japanese Annual of International Law* 1.
87 MIYAZAWA Toshiyoshi, 'August Revolution and Popular Sovereignty' (1946) 1(4) *Sekaibunka* 64.
88 YAMAMOTO and NEGISHI 216 (n 22).
89 OBATA (n 86).

## International democracy

### *The concept of democracy*

Although Yokota's theoretical arguments examined in the previous sections are largely based on Kelsen's theories, the theory of 'international democracy' is indeed Yokota's original contribution. This theory was presented in his monograph, *Kokusai minshushugi* (*International Democracy*) in 1947, in the most comprehensive manner.

First, when examining the concept of 'democracy' as a preliminary observation, he asserted that 'the fundamental notion in democracy is equality. Democracy recognizes all persons as equal persons, and aims to achieve this equality in reality'.[90] Every person should be able to participate in politics equally.[91] Thus, sovereignty should not be attributed to a single person or a small group of people but to all people collectively.[92] Moreover, equality in a democracy requires that politics be conducted for all people.[93]

Second, he argued that in democratic governance, both individuals and the community are valuable, and that their purposes should be achieved harmoniously.[94] When individuals are given excessive weight, such absolute individualism is equivalent to anarchy.[95] In contrast, when the community is given excessive weight, it is extreme nationalism and totalitarianism and not democracy.[96] Democracy 'unites individuals to the community...by enabling individuals to participate in the will-making of the community, and at the same time unites the community to individuals ... by forming the will of the community based on the will of individuals'.[97] Thus, Yokota observes that in a democracy, the will of the community must be formed through the integration of the will of all individuals.[98] Yokota emphasised the important role of the majority vote as a practical means of achieving such a relationship between individuals and the community. Although admitting that the will of the majority is not necessarily objectively right, Yokota argued that 'presumably, what the majority considers right and thus wishes for is more

90 YOKOTA Kisaburo, *International Democracy* (Kakushinsha 1947) 19.
91 Ibid 20.
92 Ibid 21.
93 Ibid 21.
94 Ibid 27.
95 Ibid 28.
96 Ibid 28.
97 Ibid 28.
98 Ibid 28–29.

likely to be objectively right than what the minority thinks and hopes for'.[99] Moreover:

> when the will of the majority is respected and followed, many people feel satisfied subjectively and become happy. By contrast, when the will of the minority is realized, ... the majority of the people are dissatisfied and unhappy. Thus, from the perspectives of subjective satisfaction and happiness, respecting and following the majority's will ... has a sufficient reason and a stronger basis.[100]

Third, Yokota emphasised that the fundamental rights of individuals should be protected, including the rights to life and security of the person, freedoms of religion, expression, assembly, press, conduct and movement.[101] Democracy aims to ensure these fundamental rights are protected.[102]

### *The theory of international democracy*

Yokota is generally known for his tendency to draw structural parallels between domestic and international regimes[103] – an approach potentially leading to what we call 'international constitutionalism' today.[104] In this topic too, Yokota applied the above observations on democracy, developed in national law contexts, to the international plane by analogising individuals to states and national society to the international society. He proposed international democracy as a form of governance where 'international sovereignty belongs to all states collectively, all states participate in the international politics, and the politics are conducted for all states'.[105] Regarding the concept of 'international sovereignty', he explained:

> When the international society is established, the authority should exist that regulates various relations within the society and determines the code of

99 Ibid 30–31.
100 Ibid 31.
101 Ibid 36.
102 Ibid 37.
103 ZACHMANN Urs Matthias, 'YOKOTA Kisaburō: Defending International Criminal Justice in Interwar and Early Post-War Japan' in MÉGRET Frédéric and TALLGREN Immi (eds), *The Dawn of a Discipline: International Criminal Justice and Its Early Exponents* (Cambridge University Press 2020) 335, 343–344.
104 For the constitutionalist approach to international law and the centrality of domestic law analogy in the approach, see BIANCHI Andrea, *International Law Theories: An Inquiry into Different Ways of Thinking* (Oxford University Press 2016), Chapter 3 'Constitutionalism'.
105 YOKOTA, *International Democracy* 52 (n 90).

> conduct for its members. Sovereignty signifies such supreme authority – international sovereignty. Until now, there was no person or organization to which such sovereignty concretely belongs, or which represents such sovereignty. ... [Such authority] was dispersed among states. States ... shared the ownership over international sovereignty. ... Regulation of the relations of the international society was made possible by agreement of states, that is, collecting pieces of sovereignty owned by different states. Indeed, this approach was very primitive and is not the appropriate one to exercise international sovereignty. Practically, it has significant flaws and has caused various harms.[106]

Yokota advocated for the principle of majority voting as a means of integrating the will of states into the will of international society. Yokota highly praised the principle as 'genius' and even 'mystic', as it would

> allow all states to make speeches based on free will and give them equal opportunities, and at the same time, to create a common will, establish common purposes, and set up necessary control and authorities. Thus, all states and the international society are united in an integrated manner and achieved harmoniously and coordinatedly.[107]

In international democracy, all states should be treated equally and have equal values, and all states should be recognised for their dignity, honour, opportunities and participatory rights in international politics and economic activities.[108] Deriving from such equality is the freedom of all states in speech, policy and conduct, but it is subject to the limitations necessary to ensure equal freedom for all states.[109]

### *'World state' and the unit of democracy*

As a closely related concept to international democracy, Yokota presented the concept of the 'world state' most comprehensively in his monograph titled *Sekai kokka no mondai* (*Questions of the World State*) published in 1948.[110] He argued that the intensification of international interactions in various fields, and most importantly, the invention of nuclear weapons, had necessitated the creation of the 'world state', as the only means to prevent

106 Ibid 53–54.
107 Ibid 62.
108 Ibid 44.
109 Ibid 44–45.
110 YOKOTA Kisaburo, *Questions of the World State* (Dōyūsha 1948).

the next world war.[111] Theoretically, there are two ways to establish a world state: one is where a world state is directly composed of individuals as world citizens without the mediation of nation-states, and the other is where a world state comprises existing states, not individuals.[112] Yokota observed that only the second option was feasible and desirable, with the first option being too utopian and inattentive to the cultures of different races and ethnicities.[113] Thus, in Yokota's theory of international democracy, the national state is considered a necessary unit, and the so-called 'cosmopolitan' democracy is denied. Although Yokota briefly stated that internationalism could harmonise nationalism/statism and cosmopolitanism, this point was not elaborated on further.[114]

### *Evaluating existing organisations and making normative proposals*

Yokota evaluated two international organisations, the League of Nations and the United Nations, under these frameworks. First, Yokota observed that the principle of equality among states was upheld in both the League of Nations and the United Nations, which aimed to treat all states equally, contribute to their interests and development equally, give them equal opportunities for speech and seek equal contributions from all states.[115] Although exceptions exist, such as the system of permanent members in the Council of the League of Nations and the United Nations Security Council, these are justifiable from a practical point of view because the actual implementation of policies requires the cooperation of powerful states.[116] Regarding the protection of the fundamental rights of states and individuals, both the League of Nations and the United Nations aim to protect the territorial integrity and political independence of member states from external interference and the right to decide on their internal affairs, including the political system.[117] Although the Covenant of the League of Nations is silent on the fundamental rights of individuals, such protection is substantially implied

111 Ibid 5–8. For a discussion on YOKOTA's idea of 'world state', see IKEDA Josuke, 'Japanese Vision of International Society: A Historical Exploration', in SHIMIZU Kosuke et al., *Is There a Japanese IR? Seeking an Academic Bridge through Japan's History of International Relations* (Afrasian Centre for Peace and Development Studies, Ryukoku University, Research Series 5, 2008) 5, 14–15.

112 YOKOTA, *Questions of the World State* 9 (n 110).

113 Ibid 9–10.

114 YOKOTA, *International Democracy* 70–71 (n 90).

115 Ibid 101, 122–123.

116 Ibid 102–103, 123.

117 Ibid 112, 130–131.

in provisions concerning international cooperation on economic, social and humanitarian issues.[118] The United Nations Charter is more explicit and willing to protect fundamental rights, given the seriousness of human rights violations committed in Nazi Germany and Japan during the Second World War/Asia–Pacific War.[119]

The critical difference between the two organisations lies in their decision-making procedures. Yokota severely criticised the League of Nations for adhering to the principle of unanimity in both the Assembly and the Council. Although unanimous decisions are theoretically the most consistent with democracy, as they reflect all states' will, practically speaking, such decisions are impossible on important matters.[120] If unanimity is required, even one state may block decision-making and prevent cooperation for common interests and development. This is almost equivalent to anarchy.[121] As a result, the League of Nations was unable to take necessary and effective action when the Manchurian Incident or the Ethiopian War broke out.[122] By contrast, the United Nations adopts the principle of majority voting in all principal organs, which endorses democratic governance in international society.[123] As an exception, decisions on non-procedural matters in the Security Council require concurring votes of all permanent members. While this is the United Nations' largest flaw, it is inevitable from a practical perspective, as the cooperation of powerful states is necessary to maintain the order and security of international society.[124]

Yokota then analysed the positive future prospects of the United Nations, given the strong leadership of the United States and the real threat and danger to peace and human lives caused by the development of nuclear weapons.[125] The United Nations embodies international democracy; thus, the development of the United Nations certainly contributes to the proper functioning of international democracy.[126] The veto power of permanent members of the Security Council should be abolished in due course to ensure true international democracy.[127] Yokota characterised the United Nations

118 Ibid 113.
119 Ibid 132–133.
120 Ibid 105.
121 Ibid 106.
122 Ibid 108.
123 Ibid 124–126.
124 Ibid 128–129.
125 Ibid 137–153.
126 Ibid 152.
127 Ibid 152.

Charter as 'the constitution of the international community, international society, and the world'.[128]

### Yokota's theory of international democracy in the historical context

Yokota's theory of international democracy should be understood in its historical context: it was presented in the immediate aftermath of Japan's defeat in the Asia–Pacific War and the inauguration of the United Nations. Presumably, Yokota's deep regret and criticism of Japan's pre-war foreign policy motivated him to introduce the theory, with a heavy focus on the principle of majority voting. Yokota is one of the few international law scholars who consistently criticised Japan's imperialism and militarism from the Manchurian Incident in the 1930s to the attack on Pearl Harbor.[129] In the last chapter of the above-mentioned book *International Democracy*, titled 'Kokusai minshushugi to nihon (International Democracy and Japan)', Yokota noted that throughout the process of the Manchurian Incident, both the Council and the Assembly of the League of Nations repeatedly adopted resolutions critical of Japan with the concurring votes of all member states but Japan (Siam abstained in one case).[130] Japan never abandoned its self-interest and acted against international democracy. Eventually, Japan was completely defeated in the Asia–Pacific War and was forced to accept unconditional surrender, which was a necessary consequence of acting against the will of the majority of states, that is, international democracy.[131]

Yokota asserted that for Japan to settle its wrongful past and rehabilitate as a healthy state, it must not only establish a democratic regime at the national level but also behave in accordance with the democratic principles on the international plane by recognising the principle of majority voting and respecting the will of the majority. He concluded that

> the creation of the United Nations has given clear form to international democracy and has contributed to the achievement of meaningful international democracy. Japan should keep pace with such progress. It should

128 YOKOTA, *Studies on the United Nations* 60 (n 8).
129 MURASE Shinya, 'One Hundred Years of the ILA Japan Branch' in KASSEDJIAN Catherine, DESCAMPS Olivier and FABRIZI Teodolinda (eds), *Au Service du Droit International: Les 150 ans de l'Association de droit international* (Panthéon-Assas 2023) 393, 397. See YOKOTA Kisaburo, 'The Manchurian Incident and the League of Nations' *Teitodaigaku Shinbun* (5 October 1931). For a more comprehensive list of relevant papers, see YOKOTA, *My Life* 133–137 (n 15).
130 YOKOTA, *International Democracy* 156–162 (n 90).
131 Ibid 166–167.

> understand the meaning, theories, and development of international democracy sufficiently, and make efforts towards respecting, practicing, and realizing international democracy. This is the only direction that Japan should move toward.[132]

In Japan's post-war period, Yokota's theory of international democracy provided strong support for the Japanese government's policy of pursuing national security through the Japan–US Security Treaty under the umbrella of the United Nations collective security system.[133] One may even speculate that his theory of international democracy was devised for this practical purpose. In fact, this speculation may explain some of the flaws in Yokota's theory of international democracy, such as its inattention to the potentially harmful effects of majority voting[134] – its tendency to benefit those in power, like the United States and its allies –[135] and its placing of priority on democracy within the framework of the United Nations without sufficient analysis of cosmopolitan democracy.[136] Moreover, although Yokota insisted on the necessity of democracy at both the national and international levels, he avoided discussing the possibly contradictory relationship between international and national democracies – how should the concept of democracy address situations where a state, as a result of national democracy, wishes to deviate from the outcome of international democracy – and seems to have prioritised international democracy without elaborate reasons. This may reflect his distrust of national democracy, given his experiences of the failure of democracy in pre-war Japan and Nazi Germany, and his hope and faith in the newly established United Nations.[137]

132 Ibid 170–171.
133 YOKOTA, *Renunciation of War* 169–171 (n 5). For the analysis on the role of YOKOTA's theory of international democracy in post-war Japan's foreign policy, see HAYASHI Naoyuki, 'The Sovereign State and World Federalism: UN Centrism in Post-War Japan' (2014) 637 *Ritsumeikan bungaku* 1427, 1418–1417 (33–34).
134 TSUNETO 9 (n 16).
135 KOBAYASHI Keiji, 'Post-War "World Citizenship" Ideology and Japanese Constitutional Theory: The Triad of Human Rights, Democracy, and Peace' (2019) 12 *Ōsakaichiritsudaigaku-shi kiyō* 3, 20.
136 Cf. TAKANO Yuichi, 'Book Review: The United Nations and World Peace: Through Various Literatures' (1950) 6 *Hōtetsugaku shikibō* 99, 107; KOBAYASHI 18 (n 135).
137 It has been highlighted that many international law scholars, including those who advocated the theory of Greater East Asian International Law during the Asia–Pacific War and/or provided a justificatory basis for Japan's militarisation, have become supporters of the United Nations. See, TAKENAKA Yoshihiko, 'The Post-War Visions of the International Lawyers in Wartime Japan: From the Pursuit of the Greater East Asian International Law to the Idealization of the United Nations: Japan's Wartime Diplomacy and the Post-War Visions' (1995) 109 *Kokusai seiji* 70, 81.

## Evaluation: consistency in Yokota's theories

Yokota's three main theoretical contributions presented in the previous sections are important and valuable. Nevertheless, it is doubtful whether there is consistency and coherence among them. When introducing the pure theory of law, Yokota repeatedly emphasised its value-neutral character, in that the theory strictly excludes any extra-legal considerations and requires describing the state of law as it is. However, in arguing that Article 98(2) of the Japanese Constitution should be interpreted to give priority to treaties and international law over the constitution in case of conflict, Yokota relied on normative considerations based on the internationalist ideology by stating that 'the understanding that the constitution prevails over international law and treaties would reflect the legacy of the old statism, and are not legitimate in today's developed and closely interconnected international society'.[138] This deviates from the pure theory of law.[139] It is further obvious that in proposing the theory of international democracy, Yokota relied on internationalist, democratic and pacifist values, and criticised positive law based on such normative values. MARUYAMA Masao described this contradiction as follows: 'an advocate of the pure theory of law, who is supposed to distance himself from any political confrontations, [Yokota] is a strong supporter of the League of Nations, and then a powerful pacifist and democrat'.[140] He thus suggested that Yokota 'should be aware of his own political position' to be able to contribute to solving real-world problems.[141] YAMAMOTO Hajime also noted that Yokota, as an 'international democrat', actually provided normative judgments based on internationalist and democratic values, thus looking like a natural lawyer.[142] Although Urs Matthias Zachmann seems to grasp this as the development of Yokota's 'own variant of a pure theory of law' instead of inconsistency within his theories,[143] it is questionable how the commitment to value-neutrality of the pure theory of law and reliance on normative substantive values may be bridged and integrated into a single theory.

138 YOKOTA, *Basic Theories of International Law* 149 (n 81).

139 TSUNETO 9 (n 16).

140 MARUYAMA Masao, 'Critique of the Three Professors at the Faculty of Law', in MARUYAMA Masao, *Collections of Maruyama's Works* (Iwanami shoten, 1996) (first published in 1937) 35, 40.

141 Ibid 40.

142 YAMAMOTO, 'An "International Democrat" Who Descended to the Supreme Court' 472–473 (n 16).

143 ZACHMANN 343 (n 103).

Moreover, the relationship between Yokota's pure theory of law and his practice as a judge on the Japanese Supreme Court (1960–1966) remains unclear. As noted earlier, in the 1930s, Yokota repeatedly argued that under the pure theory of law, when interpreting and applying abstract provisions, a single answer cannot be discovered based on law and legal techniques. Judges decide such cases based on extra-legal considerations concerning what is 'just'. Yokota asserted that the pure theory of law is a science of law and does not intend to provide techniques for judicial adjudication.[144] Yokota's colleagues wondered how he could uphold this argument after becoming a judge expected to write judgments in legal terms.[145] Yokota appears to have distorted his earlier observations when he served as Chief Justice in the Japanese Supreme Court. In his autobiography, published later in his life, Yokota stated that while serving as a judge, he interpreted and applied the law in accordance with the pure theory of law. 'I have tried to understand and apply the meaning of the law purely, and in accordance with the wording of the law, without being affected by my own subjective morals and political visions'.[146] As an example, he referred to his dissenting opinion in the case concerning the Interest Rate Restriction Act of 1962, where he argued that the amount that a debtor has voluntarily paid beyond the interest rate provided in the Act should be allocated to the principal.[147] In this dissenting opinion, in the absence of an express provision on the matter, Yokota relied on the legislative intent of the Act that, according to his understanding, was to protect debtors who were in an economically weak position. He considered that this should prevail over conflicting considerations such as the smooth operation of the financial sector. Considering his earlier argument, Yokota's reasoning in this case can be precisely described as filling a legal lacuna with an extra-legal value judgment that prioritises protecting the economically weak over ensuring the smooth operation of the financial sector. Pretending that such a value judgment derives from law through legal techniques is precisely what Yokota had emphatically rejected. In this regard, Yamamoto critically analysed that 'presumably, Yokota invalidated his own theoretical premises presented in the pre-war period under the temptation to justify his judicial activities during his office as a judge'.[148]

144 YOKOTA, 'Judicial Adjudication and Law' 118 (n 23).
145 TERASAWA 13 (n 16).
146 YOKOTA, *My Life* 141 (n 15).
147 Supreme Court of Japan (Plenary), Judgment on 13 June 1962, Minshū 16(7), 1340.
148 YAMAMOTO, 'An "International Democrat" Who Descended to the Supreme Court' 469 (n 16).

Although it is difficult to justify these inconsistencies from a theoretical perspective, they may be explained by Yokota's motivation to support the pure theory of law from a subjective perspective. A crucial factor that attracted him to Kelsen's theory of the pure theory of law was the substantive and practical advantage that Kelsen's theory of the supremacy of international law would offer. Yokota said that

> It was the immediate aftermath of the WW1 that this monograph [Kelsen's *Das Problem der Souveränität und die Theorie des Völkerrechts*] was published and I read it. It was the period where the League of Nations, a new worldwide international organization, was created, and where world peace and order were strongly aspired, and seemed feasible. For these purposes, the concept of state sovereignty, which is the philosophical fortress of the statism, should be fundamentally criticized and new international law theories should be developed.[149]

He believed that the theory of international law's supremacy, derived from the pure theory of law, was instrumental in such endeavours. The fact that Yokota's motivation to support the pure theory of law was not pure is probably the fundamental cause of the ambivalence in his theories.

In the pre-war period of Japan, as UKAI Nobunari analysed, 'given its formality, the pure theory of law in [Japan] has played sufficient roles as a scholarship resisting the Nazi political legal theories'.[150] In the midst of increasing nationalistic militarism, the pure theory of law helped Yokota as a shield to protect his internationalist, pacifist and democratic ideals from temptation and pressure to use international law to support and justify Japan's imperialism.[151] In contrast, in post-war Japan, where internationalist, pacifist and democratic ideals could be openly promoted, Yokota no longer needed a shield and used theories such as the supremacy of international law and international democracy as a sword to advance such ideals.

149 YOKOTA Kisaburo, 'Kelsen and Me' in *YOKOTA's Collections on Pure Theory of Law II* (first published in 1967) 282, 283 (n 20).

150 UKAI Nobunari, 'Vienna School' in UKAI Nobunari et al. (eds), *Lecture on the History of the Development of Modern Japanese Law* vol. 7 (Keisōshobō 1959) 142.

151 Cf. KATAGIRI Nobuo, *YOKOTA Kisaburo 1896–1993: The Trajectory of His Realist-Pacifist Arguments* (Fujiwara shoten 2018) 31–32.

# 3

# TAOKA Ryoichi: doctor eximius as a steadfast origin point in Japanese tradition

*FUKUSHIMA Ryoshi*

## Introduction

During the most difficult period, which spanned the years before and after the Second World War, TAOKA Ryoichi engaged in conversation with a number of prominent figures, including the Foreign Minister, the Supreme Commander of the Allied Powers and distinguished scholars of his generation. Taoka can be considered a model of academic conversation. This is made possible by his unwavering position and keen intelligence. Taoka stuck to a prudent approach as a scholar, which occasionally led him to exhibit conservative tendencies. His meticulously crafted arguments, however, garnered widespread admiration.

Taoka graduated from Kyoto University in 1922. He held the position of Professor of International Law at Tohoku University until 1940, after which he became a professor at Kyoto University until his retirement in 1960. He served as President of the Japanese Association of International Law and was appointed a judge of the Permanent Court of Arbitration by the Japanese Government. Throughout his academic career, Taoka consistently demonstrated leadership in the field of international law. He has been identified as a pioneer in establishing an international jurisprudence based on a rigorous methodology. This methodology, which has come to be known as 'historical positivism', represents a departure from the previous period.[1]

> At this stage, however, emphasis was on learning the theories of Western international law and simply applying them to the actual events occurring in international society. It was after the beginning of the Showa period in 1926 that Japanese international law studies became established as a systematic juridical science with a firm methodological foundation. There were two great leaders in this endeavour, Professors Kisaburo Yokota and Ryoichi Taoka. Though different in content, the academic contributions of both of these scholars,

1 TABATA Shigejiro, 'The Late Professor TAOKA Ryoichi: His Contributions to the Study of International Law (1985) 28 *Japanese Annual of International Law* 1.

based on solid methodologies, exerted significant influence on the succeeding generations in the field.

Most Japanese researchers tried to advocate a progressive or idealistic aspect of law. Japan had to catch up with the rest of the international community after 'Kaikoku' – open foreign policy – at the end of the Edo era. In the aftermath of two world wars, Japan was to 'occupy an honoured place in an international society striving for the preservation of peace', as its constitution states. In order for Japan to achieve these policy goals, international lawyers believed that progressive perspectives and interpretations of international law were desirable. Taoka, on the other hand, was of the conviction that the principles of international law should be based on a precise comprehension of the real-world dynamics of international relations. He was always worried that an optimistic vision of the foundation and development of international law would lead to an overabundance of international law when a serious situation arose in the international sphere. His perspective aligns closely with that of Charles de Visscher, who also emphasised the need to reconcile the theoretical and practical dimensions of international law. This awareness stemmed from his commitment to preserving the legacy of international law. In the context of contemporary global instability, it is becoming increasingly apparent that Taoka's pioneering contributions to the field of international law, which were aimed at preserving the authority of international law, are of growing importance.[2]

## Between Tokyo and Vienna

It is a historical fact that the legacy and authority of international law were once threatened by Japan itself. The Manchurian Incident is a case in point. As noted in Chapter 2, YOKOTA Kisaburo was one of the few international law scholars who had criticised Japan's imperialism and militarism from the Manchurian Incident in the 1930s. Taoka was also among the few. His position and argument based on his definition of war and self-defence have already been introduced in an English article.[3] It confirms as follows: 'He rejected the view that Japan's actions were justified, because they did

2 YANAGIHARA Masaharu, '"A Hundred Volumes of International Law Are No Match for a Few Cannon" Still Apply Today?' (2022) 710 *Kokusaimondai* (*International Affairs*) 4.

3 Urs Matthias Zachmann, 'TAOKA Ryoichi's Contribution to International Legal Studies in Pre-War Japan: With Special Reference to Questions of the Law of War' (2014) 57 *Japanese Yearbook of International Law* 148.

not constitute a war and only an "incident". Moreover he contradicted the opinion that Japan had acted in 'justified self-defence' against Chinese troops, as this did not fit the narrow definition of self-defence'.

The month after the outbreak of the Pacific War, which was triggered by the attack on Pearl Harbor, Taoka contributed an article, 'Kokusaihouhiteiron to shoraino kokusaihougaku (Denial of International Law and the Future of International Law)', which is still regarded as the manifesto of international law scholars.[4] While researchers in Tokyo tended to support government policy, Taoka, who taught in Kyoto, 550 km from the capital, was kept at a distance from the political mainstream. Even within the academic community of Kyoto University, TABATA Shigejiro, his younger colleague, espoused a divergent perspective. In the period following the Second World War, Tabata was supportive of the UN system. Tabata was relatively flexible in his approach to methodology. He could, for instance, research the historical context of a particular issue at one time and then apply this to the interpretation of a specific treaty article.

As a significant opponent of the UN system and numerous Japanese foreign policies, Taoka consistently proposed alternative strategies for achieving Japan's security and international society in general. He could do so on the basis of this solid theoretical framework in international relations. In the field of theoretical studies, Taoka received little assistance from Japanese scholars. It can reasonably be assumed that researchers in the field of domestic law could rely on German legal studies, such as that of Georg Jellinek. Indeed, many of them studied in Germany. Japan accepted legal arguments and frameworks from the German-speaking sphere. The tradition of legal positivism, which originated in the Pandekten, was well known. The ongoing debates over methodology and the form of government in Europe were re-enacted in Japan among followers of the opposing schools. In international law, it can be observed that there has been a notable delay in the acceptance of the European legal paradigm, let alone that of positivism. At the time Taoka began his academic career, positivism was facing a significant challenge from the younger generation, namely Hans Kelsen, Carl Schmitt, Hermann Heller and Rudolf Smend. In this context, Taoka was not primarily concerned with the positivist argument; rather, he focused on the relationship between social reality and law. Jellinek was no longer to be regarded as an authority figure.

4 TAOKA Ryoichi, 'Kokusaihouhiteiron to Shoraino Kokusaihougaku (Denial of International Law and the Future of International Law)' (1941) 101 *Gaikojiho* (*Revue diplomatique*) 1–14.

In 1927, Taoka travelled to Milan, where he discovered a book by Dionisio Anzilotti. He subsequently obtained a French translation of this text and dedicated himself to a detailed study of it, examining it page by page.[5] It is well known that Anzilotti accepted Hans Kelsen's theory of the Grundnorm in 1923.[6] Therefore, Taoka must also be aware of Kelsen's theory, given that he read Anzilotti's work. Yokota, a significant adversary of Taoka, self-describes as the Kelsen of the Orient. In the Japanese academic context, the Vienna School's influence on Taoka has been overlooked. The confrontation with Yokota is not conducive to the investigation of either the method or the theory of both sides. Yokota's doctrine is not merely a consequence of theoretical considerations. Each doctrine and legal practice of Yokota is distinct from Kelsen's theoretical framework. This implies that Taoka was solely opposed to Yokota's own opinions and assertions, rather than to the theoretical framework Yokota advocated in general. Indeed, Taoka was in favour of the theories put forth by the Vienna School and even of the monism of international law. He compared theories of Anzilotti and Verdross concerning dualism/monism controversies and demonstrated a well-elaborated explanation that the two theories are not as contradictory as they appear. If one understands the meaning of the 'void' as both authors use it, it becomes evident that facial differences do not affect the actual interpretations.[7] He openly admires the strict conceptualisation and theorisation of Kelsen and Verdross and adds cynically that it would be desirable to 'import' those skills and methods to Japan.[8]

Taoka expressed a critical view of Tokyo, and the rationale behind his convictions was derived from a theoretical framework which he self-disciplined through close analysis of Anzilotti and the Vienna School.

### *The three commandments of Taoka*

Under the influence of Anzilotti and the Vienna School, Taoka was a strong advocate of rigorous demonstration and argument in the field of international law. His lessons have been handed down to the present day. Although there are minor variations between the versions, they can be summarised as

5 TAOKA Ryoichi, 'Shippitsu wo Oete (After Writing)', *Houritsugaku Zennshu*, Leaflet, 27 (1957) 213–214.

6 Giorgio Gaja, 'Positivism and Dualism in Dionisio Anzilotti' (1992) 3(1) *European Journal of International Law* 127–128.

7 TAOKA Ryoichi, *Kokusaihougaku Taikou* (Ganshodo 1943) 57–59.

8 TAOKA Ryoichi, Kokusaihoujyono Jieikenn (*The Right of Self-Defence in International Law*) (Keisoshobo 1981) 20.

follows: 'You shall not employ deductive reasoning'; 'You shall not employ domestic analogy'; 'You shall not employ lex ferenda'.

### *You shall not employ deductive reasoning*

The similarity of the legal systems in question was not the only reason why Japanese academics were so eager to research German studies. As a nascent player on the global stage, Japan, like Germany, gravitated towards theoretical arguments. In the absence of substantial legal documentation, such as treaties and court decisions, they may be inclined to treat international law only at an abstract level. Given Germany's rich history of philosophical thought, its academics were highly adept at theoretical demonstration, particularly deductive reasoning. For Japanese researchers, the meanings of complex terminology are often more readily discernible than the intricacies of European historical case law and documentation, which span a vast and convoluted historical timeline.

In this context, Hans Kelsen was the most desirable author; thus, we have the Kelsen of the Orient, Yokota, who introduced and translated Kelsen's works. Kelsen's writings encompass a wide range of studies, whereas Yokota's interest was primarily focused on highly theoretical topics such as the validity and legality of international law. One of the topics that could be considered to be of a highly theoretical nature was the debate surrounding the Potsdam Declaration and Japan's subsequent acceptance of it. Yokota asserted that the acceptance of the declaration and additional memorandum demands the sovereignty of the people. Given that Japan was a monarchy with an Emperor based on a hereditary system, it can be argued that the transition was a legal and peaceful revolution. An insightful analysis of Yokota's doctrine reveals that this legally and politically radical claim was supported by Yokota's theory, namely, the supremacy of international law over domestic law.[9] In comparing the doctrines of Yokota and Taoka, the same author expressed high regard for Taoka.

Certainly, it could be submitted that there is essentially no difference between Taoka's argument and Yokota's observations on the status of Japan. But, compared with Yokota's characterisation of Japan as 'a quasi-sovereign state', it is remarkable that Taoka starts with the presupposition

9 OBATA Kaoru, 'Senryoshoki Nihonn niokeru Kennpouchitsujyono Tennkann nitsuiteno Kokusaihouteki Saikentou: "Hachigatsukakumei" no Housyakaishinotameni (Sociology of the Constitutional Transformation in Japan under the Allied Occupation: Review of "August Revolution" in the Light of International Law)' (2009) 230 *Nagoya Housei Ronnshu* 80–81.

of Japan's sovereignty. From such a position, he casts strong doubt on the Allied Powers' measure for suspension of Japanese diplomatic intercourse. Indeed, if the Instrument of Surrender is a kind of armistice, or a contractual agreement that affects only *in personam*, it would never prejudice Japan's right to communicate with neutral Powers, such as Switzerland or Sweden. Yokota fails to explain how the Instrument of Surrender and so on provide Japan's objective status *in rem* as a quasi-sovereign. In this regard, Taoka's reasoning is based on a more solid legal foundation[10].

The assertion by Taoka that the Allied Powers bear the burden of proving that an order issued by the Allied Powers falls within the range of obligations imposed by the Potsdam Declaration on Japan is examined in particular.[11] Yokota tends to employ abstract theories in order to advance concrete and controversial interpretations. In contrast, Taoka was meticulous in his approach to legal matters, conducting thorough in-depth investigations and analyses. In examining the texts of the treaties in question, Taoka did not neglect the confusion that frequently arises among terminology and concepts. Furthermore, he did not fail to identify logical leaps that other researchers had made. He also made it clear how risky it can be to apply deductive reasoning from abstract theories.

Naturally, Taoka selected a concrete research topic of his own choice. In 1944, he published a book entitled *Sennsouhouno Konnponnmondai* (*Fundamental Questions of the Law of War*). In this book, the author critiques the view that the protection of private persons and property can be on the basis of the assertion that 'war is a relation between state and state', as put forth by Rousseau.[12] That view fails to acknowledge the continuity between this view and the classical doctrine of bellum justum. Taoka provides a detailed account of the comprehensive doctrine of the Spanish theologian Francisco de Vitoria on the protection of civilians.[13] The critical issue is that if one relies on Rousseau's theorem, the obligation of civil protection would coincide with this theorem. Indeed, some writers contended that in the era of total war, war became a relationship between people and people. This is why Taoka felt the need to clarify the true basis of the norm protecting private persons and property.

10 OBATA Kaoru, 'Historical Functions of Monism with Primacy of International Law: A View Based on the Japanese Experience during the Early Period of the Allied Occupation' (2006) 49 *Japanese Annual of International Law* 29.

11 Ibid.

12 TAOKA Ryoichi, Sennsouhouno Konnponnmondai (*Fundamental Questions of the Law of War*) (Iwanamishotenn 1944) 24–25.

13 Ibid 10.

Similarly, he elucidates the assertion that 'the people of hostile countries are enemies of each other', which is a position commonly advanced by Anglo-American international lawyers. He demonstrates that this does not negate the protection of private persons and property.[14] He compared the meaning of the term 'enemy' in the context of the English-speaking sphere and that of continental countries such as France and Germany. In the English context, the assertion only means that trade transactions between individuals are prohibited. Commercial restrictions of this nature are also common among continental countries, even though they do not have a specific term for that situation. Once more, he draws our attention to the fact that we can be easily misled by abstract sentences and that we may draw erroneous conclusions.

### *You shall not employ domestic analogy*

One of the reasons Taoka was attracted to Anzilotti was his clear distinction between the domestic and international legal systems. The constitution of Japan is a civil law system. In Japan, the legal system is divided into two distinct categories: domestic and international law. The legal and social contexts suggest that Taoka considered the analogy between the legal systems proposed by common law scholars to be both inconsistent and useless. In his book, *The Right of Self-Defence in International Law*, Taoka provides a detailed examination of the Caroline case, offering a comprehensive analysis of the circumstances surrounding the incident and its implications for self-defence. He classified the case as one of self-preservation, given that no previous illegal acts were found. In the view of Taoka, however, the case did not serve as a leading case for the right of self-preservation in international law. It should therefore not be generalised.

His contributions facilitated a deeper understanding of the specific provisions on self-defence as outlined in Article 51 of the United Nations Charter. This article stipulates that the use of armed force is permissible only in response to an armed attack. Taoka reminds us that the practice and existence of the right of self-preservation in the domestic legal system of each country do not prove that it exists in the international sphere in a similarly valid manner. The existence of the right of self-preservation must be proven by specific evidence, such as state practice and the opinion of jurists.[15] He makes it clear that there must be sufficient solidarity among

14 Ibid 77.

15 TAOKA Ryoichi, *Kokusaihoujyono Jieikenn* 139.

nations if they are to accept the possibility of legal interests being damaged by other members.[16]

> The institution of legitimate defence, which permits members of the community to injure the legally protected interest of an illegal offender, is a necessary institution within the community where its organ cannot always safeguard members of the community against illegal injury, and, in this sense, the right of legitimate defence can be called a sort of primitive right, to be found in every legal community worth its name. On the other hand, the institution of necessity [self-preservation] described above presupposes that it has developed in the community to a certain degree. This institution can be founded on the moral basis that a member of the community is willing to share the hardships of others as his own. Does this moral basis exist among the members of the community of nations in their dealings with each other, to the same extent as we find it within a national community composed of individuals? This is the question. And it must be answered by a fact-based observation of the practices of nations.

Taoka believed that Yokota's doctrine contains a loophole which allows for the justification of an act in the absence of self-defence, provided it is covered by a self-help justification. This arises from the crude borrowing of the right of self-defence concept from domestic law.[17] It is of greater consequence that Taoka posited that in instances where reprisals are acknowledged within the legal framework, the right of self-defence cannot be upheld. He held the conviction that the right of self-defence could be established in international law only once all reprisals had been vanquished from the international sphere collectively under an efficacious legal mechanism.

As previously stated, George Jellinek was not a primary source for Taoka, yet he did conduct a critical analysis of Jellinek's work. His focus was on how Jellinek established the legal foundation of international law. Jellinek regarded the state as the primary law-making organ, from which the entire legal system is derived. International law is constructed through mutual recognition and treaties as a product of state action. Thus, international law is dependent on each state. In this context, the state is regarded as the primary source of authority for its legitimacy. For Taoka, this is the most problematic form of domestic analogy: the attempt to deduce basic legal consequences from the domestic sphere. Despite its elaboration, Jellinek's reasoning ultimately leads to the denial of the legality of international law.[18]

16 Ibid 130.
17 Ibid 253–254.
18 TAOKA Ryoichi, *Kokusaihougakutaikou* 63–67.

### *You shall not employ lex ferenda*

Taoka did not adhere to the discipline of the German legal positivist tradition, yet he was a positivist in the broader sense of the term. It does not mean he was against the natural law doctrine. In contrast, he openly opposed the tendency towards the lex ferenda argument. Taoka posited that written and signed treaties should be considered just a lex ferenda, an ideological scheme, under certain conditions. The Kellogg–Briand Pact is an example of such treaties. He refused the Kellogg–Briand Pact because of the lack of a judicial mechanism.[19]

Following the ratification of the Convention, armed conflicts within the international community became increasingly overt and large-scale. The Manchurian Incident, the Czech War and the Italian–Ethiopian War, all fought after 1928, led to the Second World War in 1939. It would be a mistake to regard this fact as due to desuetude, the disobedience to conventional obligations. From its inception, the Treaty was inherently impracticable.

It is observed that Taoka was more forthright in his refutation of the Pact's efficacy than Tachi.[20] While explicitly declaring the Pact to be void, Taoka never provided a rationale for the Japanese actions in Manchuria. He was a loyal follower of the traditional international law that had been accumulated and evolved over the course of the Age of Francisco de Vitoria. It is not possible for international law to enter a new stage instantaneously through the implementation of a single treaty. The regulations regarding war or the use of force were to be achieved through a static or conventional interpretation of valid treaties and related legal history. According to Taoka, those qualified treaties had to include an institutional mechanism, especially for dispute settlement. The application of teleological or dynamic interpretations to mere ambitious treaties is tantamount to employing the lex ferenda.

The academic inclination towards the lex ferenda argument was not limited to the treaty itself, but also extended to the international organisation. Tabata suggests that state equality may be modified in order to facilitate the organisation of international society more firmly or to develop existing institutions.[21] In stark contrast to Tabata's perspective, Taoka asserted that the inequality between states in the United Nations system was implemented by the victorious states for the purpose of perpetuating their dominance.[22]

19 TAOKA Ryoichi, *Kokusaihou III* (*International Law III*) (Yuhikaku 1973) 144.
20 Urs Matthias Zachmann, 'TAOKA Ryoichi's Contribution to International Legal Studies in Pre-War Japan' 148.
21 TABATA Shigejiro, *Kokkabyoudoukannnenn no Tenkann* (Akitaya 1946) 308.
22 TAOKA Ryoichi, *Kokusaihou* (*International Law*) (Keiso Shobou 1973) 68.

The League of Nations also exhibited some inequalities. However, in the UN system, the disparity was worsened, and the P5 held exclusive power.[23]

Takano, another Japanese researcher specialising in international organisations, had a somewhat ambivalent stance towards the regional agreement within the UN system. As a long-time commentator on the United Nations, he argued that the use of force should be centralised within the Security Council. Nevertheless, when the Japanese government became involved in the Japan–US alliance through the Japan–US Security Treaty, it was necessary for him to demonstrate some degree of support for the regime, which was essentially a regional agreement with considerable autonomy. He stated that the treaty, a regional agreement, would harmonise with the UN system. His sole lead was that the 'advance consultation' between the US and Japanese governments, which is supposed to precede any forceful action, should be held.[24] As was to be expected, Taoka expressed a decidedly pessimistic view of the regional agreement in the UN system. At the San Francisco Peace Conference, the right to self-defence was modified because of the difficulty of implementing a worldwide security arrangement. Taoka described them as neo-regional arrangements that have acquired autonomy as representing a 'decomposition trend' in the collective security of the United Nations.[25]

The Japanese constitution comprises three fundamental principles. One of these is pacifism, which is enshrined in Article 9, which prohibits the declaration of war and the maintenance of military forces. In the post-Second World War political context in Japan, with its new constitution and international security system, the expectation was that a war in the traditional sense would no longer occur. This was a topic on everyone's minds. It was widely believed that the establishment and maintenance of peace could be facilitated by the law, whether at the domestic or international level. It was clear that the Security Council was incapable of maintaining peace. Indeed, the discussion pertained to the concept of lex ferenda. Taoka evidently hoped that large-scale or cruel wars would be abandoned; however, he stated that the international community could permit coercive measures if the development of peaceful conflict is impeded. It is argued that the 'use of coercion for the benefit of society' should be preserved. However, it is difficult to distinguish in reality between means of 'coercion for the benefit of individual states' and 'coercion for the social benefit of the international

23 Ibid 70.

24 TAKANO Yuichi, *Shudanannzennhosho to Jieiken* (*The Collective Security and the Right of Self Defence*) (Toshindo 1999) 250.

25 TAOKA Ryoichi, *Kokusaihou* 92–93.

community'. Nevertheless, it is essential that the distinction be adhered to in both theory and practice.[26]

Zachmann points out that Taoka's method has been partly criticised on the grounds that, although it possessed the potential for ideological critique, Taoka applied it to interpret the existing international order, ultimately resulting in the normative legitimisation of that order.[27] The author also indicates that Taoka's stance on positivism is by no means simplistic.[28] As mentioned at the beginning of this chapter, Taoka's rigorous approach sometimes led him to affirm the status quo. From a Japanese domestic perspective, Taoka also adhered to a strict interpretation of the Constitution's pacifist principles. This forced him to bridge the gap between Japan's idealistic dependence on collective security and the reality of the UN system.

It is notable that, while openly criticising the lex ferenda argument in theoretical terms, he did not hesitate to elaborate on quite naive or idealistic concepts such as 'coercion for the social benefit of the international community'. From a different perspective, it could be argued that his theory enabled Taoka to propose a plan for an institutional or legal policy without resorting to the use of lex ferenda.

### *Institutional development*

Taoka rejected the irrevocable joining of lex lata to lex ferenda and instead proposed a blueprint for international institutions that would be directly involved in policy-making, rather than the interpretation of law. Taoka was particularly interested in the legal framework for the settlement of disputes, with the aim of preventing a war. Taoka elaborated on the axiomatic and systematic enumeration and composition of the requisite elements, as proposed by Saint-Pierre in his theory of perpetual peace (the five fundamental clauses for perpetual peace):[29]

> (1) The society is obliged by its norms to settle disputes by this means, rather than leaving it to the discretion of its members, who may initially settle the dispute by any means of their choice, but if they are unable to do so, they must eventually submit to this means, which is prescribed by the norms of

26 TAOKA Ryoichi, *Kokusaihou III* 268–269.
27 Urs Matthias Zachmann, *Voelkerrechtsdenken und Aussenpolitik in Japan, 1919–1960* (Nomos 2013) S.155.
28 Ibid 153.
29 TAOKA Ryoichi, *Kokusaihou III* 132.

> the society. If they are unable to resolve the dispute in this way, they should always resort to the means provided for by the norms of society.
>
> (2) When the dispute is referred to, this means it is not optional but obligatory for the parties to accept a black/white ruling on the claims of the parties to the dispute by the social organisation in charge of the settlement, and to accept the terms of settlement offered by the social organisation.
>
> (3) That the society's measure is applied to the members who do not comply with the obligations of the right.
>
> Components who do not comply with their obligations are: (a) those who do not rely on the peaceful means of settlement provided by society, and attempt to settle disputes by appealing to their own strength; and (b) those who do not comply with the results of the means of settlement provided by society, i.e. those who break their obligations as mentioned in (2) above.

Taoka has asserted that the establishment of an effective dispute resolution mechanism is a fundamental prerequisite for collective security.[30] He has also expressed his opposition to the proposed enhancement or 'evolution' of enforcement measures within the UN system.[31] For Taoka, the dispute settlement was regarded as a cornerstone for the future of international peace.

Taoka rejected the categorisation of non-judicial disputes as fixed or existing a priori. 'A dispute not fit to be referred to court means that it is unfit for final settlement by peaceful means. We are unable to understand that there are disputes of any kind that should not be settled by peaceful means'.[32] This does not imply that Taoka assumed that existing positive international law could adequately cope with all potential disruptions. Taoka observed that Hersch Lauterpacht advocated the so-called completeness of the law system. Lauterpacht held that there are no gaps in positive law and that all disputes can be settled on the basis of positive law. This theory incorporates the theorem of the 'completeness of law' (Geschlossenheit der Rechtsordnung), which applies not only to international law but also to all law. According to this theory, international law always contains norms that provide solutions to all disputes in the society it governs, i.e. the international community, and there should be no disputes that cannot be resolved by applying international law. Taoka conducted an in-depth analysis of Lauterpacht's legal tools. It was argued that it is possible to resolve the dispute by dismissing a legal action on the grounds that the plaintiff's action is groundless under the

30 Ibid 134.
31 Ibid 147–148.
32 Ibid 197.

legislation. They advocate this method of resolving disputes by ex contrario interpretation of the legislation.[33]

> The idea that, if the law is silent on a matter, the dispute can be settled by ex contrario interpretation is premised on the view that where international law makes no provision for a matter, it leaves the disposal of that matter to the discretion of the States, and therefore, if a State takes a certain step in this matter, the Court must recognise that State's right to take this step. The Court must therefore recognise that if a State takes a certain measure in this matter, [the] State's right to take this measure. However, this view does not explain all cases of legal silence but is true for only part of them. The absence of a law on a matter can mean either (1) that the law leaves the treatment of the matter at the disposal of the members of society, or (2) that the matter is of such a nature that it requires the intervention of the law to maintain order in social life, but due to the negligence of the legislator, for example because of severe conflicts of interest among the members of society, it is difficult to make uniform rules ... It is therefore incorrect to say that the dispute can be resolved by ex contrario interpretation in all cases of silence of the law.

Taoka opposed non-liquet-avoiding window-dressing rulings that ignored the will of the parties. Taoka posited that it was the legal scholar's responsibility to determine the limits of positive law. This position calls to mind the ideas expressed by Carl Schmitt regarding the dictatorship of the Reich President. 'Despite all the terminology such as "unchecked power" and "naked power" with regard to the Reich President's various powers under Article 48(2), it would still be impossible to exercise sovereign dictatorship under this constitutional provision, even with the Reich Government's deputy signature'.[34] The concepts of court decision and dictatorship appear to be distinct, yet both were cases in which a nebulous understanding of law or an image of legal order led to a mistaken conclusion. Those who espouse legal positivism tend to rely on the term 'legal order', which implies that all legal issues and matters are covered under the system. Taoka and Schmitt concur that the legal order in question is distinct from a legal universe that is without limit or vacancy. For both Taoka and Schmitt, the positivist illusion of the completeness of law is to be overcome by the determined judgment of legal scholars.

33 Ibid 190–192.

34 Carl Schmitt, 'Die Diktatur des Reichspräsidenten nach Artikel 48 der Weimarer Verfassung', *Die Dictatur von den Anfängen des modernen Souveränitätsgedankens bis zum proletarischen Klassenkampf*, 3 Aufl. (Duncker & Humblot 1964) 238.

A question arises as to how we can say that all disputes are solvable when international law is not sufficiently comprehensive to address all cases. In such instances, Taoka advocated for the arbitration of disputes. The lack of a positive legal basis means that ex aequo et bono is a potential resort for those engaged in such practices. Taoka anticipated that the establishment of the Permanent Court of International Justice (PCIJ) would result in the functional differentiation of arbitration tribunals. The arbitration tribunals were designed to settle cases, particularly by ex aequo et bono. Relying on arbitration tribunals is not always a negative consequence of a legal deficiency.[35]

> A significant proportion of the post-World War I Intermediate Court treaties provide for the resolution of both legal and non-legal disputes by assigning legal disputes to the Permanent International Court of Justice and non-legal disputes to ad hoc arbitral tribunals. The former applies Article 38(1) of the Permanent International Court of Justice. The latter can proceed with 'judgment not bound by law', which is expressed by 'ex aequo et bono' (equity and good), 'les pouvoirs d'amiable (the powers of amiable)' and 'principes l'equite (principles of equity)'.
>
> It is fitting that post-WWI treaties should differentiate between a court of law and a court of equity, with the former being represented by the Permanent International Court of Justice and the latter by ad hoc arbitral tribunals.

A similar analysis was conducted regarding mediation. However, the object or scope of mediation was considered more comprehensive. Mediation can be applied to a range of disputes, both non-legal and legal in nature.[36]

> A considerable number of treaties on the peaceful settlement of disputes have stipulated that legal disputes shall be referred to court and other disputes (non-legal disputes) shall be referred to mediation.
>
> However, it cannot be concluded from this fact that there is a general belief that non-legal disputes are suitable for mediation.

In each analysis, the author explained that treaties delineate the legal and non-legal nature of disputes, assigning them to distinct procedural pathways, including the Permanent Court of International Justice (PCIJ), arbitration or mediation. A further question arises as to the criteria by which

35 Ibid 234–235.
36 Ibid 245.

certain disputes are classified as legal or non-legal. The most recent research on Hans Morgenthau provides a definitive answer to the question of what constitutes a legal or illegal dispute.[37] The criteria in question are referred to as subjective criteria. It is the state party's decision on what is legal and what is not. The parties to a dispute base their respective claims on international law; therefore, the dispute can be settled by the interpretation and application of international law. If the parties base their claims on a basis other than international law, it is a non-legal dispute. Taoka is regarded as a proponent of such subjective criteria.

> If a party in a dispute does not base its claim on existing international law, it is natural to assume that it will base its claim on some value or principle of justice different from existing law. If this is the case, then the party should be claiming the validity (at least for the case in question) of some value or principle of justice that changes existing law. Therefore, a 'non-legal dispute' in the sense of the subjective criteria theory can be understood as a dispute arising over a demand for a change in existing international law, i.e. a 'dynamic dispute'.

It is possible to evaluate Taoka's argument regarding the disruption of settlement in the context of international academic discourse. The discourse sought to encompass even the most radical challenges to the status quo of international law. Taoka's vision for the development of the institution or procedure was not merely a single chapter in the history of its evolution. Should one wish to pursue the discourse that originated during the era of the League of Nations, one must confront Taoka. He is one of the authors with whom you are going to have a conversation.

## *Reversing method*

Taoka's methodology was evaluated by his colleague Tabata as 'historical positivism'. The positivism Tabata refers to is not the legal positivism commonly understood in German legal theory. He was merely stating that Taoka held a strict demonstration based on facts in high regard. It is of significant importance to acknowledge that the fact in question was not, in and of itself, a historical fact. It is evident that Taoka was consistently inclined to substantiate his assertions with tangible evidence. However, the evidence he presented was not limited to a specific domain. Taoka was a scholar of

37 NISHI Taira, 'Labor Law Model for International Law in the Era of the League of Nations' (2017) 36 *Yearbook of World Law* 45–46.

multiple disciplines. He chaired an academic study group on international relations, which brought together researchers from various fields, including political studies. He was well versed in the history of international relations, state practices and international organisations, although he was not a trained historian in the strict sense. The evidence and facts presented in his work were compiled by other legal researchers for a specific purpose. It can be asserted that these documents are not neutral primary sources. In a positive light, he employed a wide range of resources, regardless of their academic discipline, to substantiate his argument. Taoka's precise use of concepts, strict logic and persuasive demonstration all contribute to his reputation as a respected scholar. However, when it comes to methodology, he does not adhere to any particular methodology. In other words, he lacked a methodology.

A different evaluation may be reached if the term 'methodology' is paraphrased as 'approach'. Taoka was more of a theoretician than a historian. He invoked several approaches to support his theory. As previously stated, the material in question could be constituted by the text of treaties, the travaux préparatoires, state practices and legal doctrine. For the most part, he utilised all the material to classify or categorise different legal concepts. In legal history, such an abstraction of the object should be avoided. Conversely, Taoka's primary objective was to provide support for his legal arguments by clarifying various concepts. For example, Taoka authored a book on the subject of permanent neutrality. The work appears to be purely historical research, yet Taoka's primary focus is the derivation of the category of unilateral collective security/defence alliance.[38]

> The principle of collective security posits that a war in one corner of the world is a matter of vital concern to all other nations, and therefore all nations must act in concert to rescue the aggrieved state and sanction the aggressor. Consequently, only the United Nations, a global security organisation, can be considered a collective guarantee. This does not apply to narrowly scoped international organisations such as the Locarno Guarantee Treaty. However, as Yokota itself cites the Locarno Treaty as an example of collective security, it must be acknowledged that this definition is not consistent with the concept of collective security. Even if the argument is directed to the International League, it does not identify the collectiveness of the League's guarantees as a critical element, but rather the 'global' nature of the League's guarantees mechanism.

38 TAOKA Ryoichi, *Eiseichuritsu to Nihonn no Anzennhosyo* (*Perpetual Peace and Security of Japan*) (Yuhikaku 1950) 169–170.

> Furthermore, if the definition of collective guarantees is that 'all the countries of the Treaty are mutually obliged to guarantee each other, and that for none of them can the guarantee be unilateral', then, as in the Locarno Treaty of Guarantee, this is not an example of collective security. The fact that the United Kingdom and Italy provide guarantees to France, Germany and Belgium, while the latter are not obliged to provide guarantees to the United Kingdom and Italy.

By referencing the Locarno Treaty and other historical cases, Taoka identified several categories: (1) mutual obligation/unilateral obligation; (2) regional/worldwide regime. Taoka's objective was to highlight Yokota's inconsistency when he argued about collective security, which was the most politically sensitive issue in Japan. Clarifying those categories was the necessary means of refuting Yokota. Taoka's historical research has consistently been driven by a specific motivation and objective. For Taoka, historical facts and resources were merely secondary tools. His area of expertise was theoretical, and his primary instrument was his acuity in using concepts.

In his celebrated work on self-defence, he also elucidated the distinction between self-preservation and self-defence against armed attack. With regard to the question of requirements or conditions of self-defence in the UN system, it is noteworthy that the prerequisite of a preceding armed attack is critical. Nevertheless, the question remains whether an act undertaken in self-preservation, such as Canada's in the Caroline Incident, is permitted under the UN Charter. This is because it may not constitute the use of force against territorial integrity or political independence. Moreover, with regard to the underlying rationale for each action, self-preservation was a factor that could be considered. It is still possible to argue that self-preservation is the fundamental basis for all actions, with the exception of the trigger requirement, which is limited to instances of being attacked. Taoka did not pursue this line of inquiry. For Taoka, the right of self-defence as outlined in the UN Charter represented a revolutionary concept in a negative sense. It was not a solid legal concept rooted in traditional international law. As previously stated, Taoka maintained that the use of force against another country in self-defence was not permitted under traditional international law. This implies that, according to Taoka's doctrine, some degree of vacancy remained. The question remained unanswered: on what basis could a state take forceful action towards another state?

The lacunae in Taoka's historical account can be attributed to his understanding that international law in the classical period was primarily concerned with dispute resolution.[39]

39 TAOKA Ryoichi, *Kokusaihou III* 272–273.

> It was previously stated that the ideal of international law is the abolition of coercive measures. However, it is theoretically impossible to call war illegal under the present organisation of the international community. Therefore, in order to achieve the ideal of international law, the present system of international society must be further developed in order to complete the system of dispute settlement within society.
>
> The just-war doctrine was based on the idea that only sovereigns can settle disputes. The just-war doctrine serves as a means of sanctioning illegal actors in a society without a sovereign and redressing the rights violated by illegal acts. This theory is not incorrect in this context.

There should have been instances of states engaging in forceful attacks against one another from the medieval to the nineteenth century. The victim state must have exercised its right of self-defence. Taoka did not address or discuss such instances directly. It is highly probable that Taoka was dealing in all instances within his understanding of the framework of his understanding of the just-war theory – dispute settlement. In theory, even an armed attack could be considered an 'illegal act' in general. A further insight may be gained by examining Taoka's writings once more in the context of Yokota's 'contradiction'.[40]

> We have no choice but to consider that the use of force and other coercive measures taken in a manner that does not meet the definition of the right to self-defence, as such, are not prevented from being illegal.
>
> However, the same scholar [Yokota] has elsewhere in their international law writings explained under the heading 'reprisals' that the right of self-help is recognised under general international law, which is broader than the right of self-defence in domestic law, or, in other words, is limited by fewer conditions. The two theories are contradictory, but no effort has been made to resolve this contradiction and rationally unify the causes of inhibition of illegality in the international legal order. It appears that the contradiction is probably one that he does not notice.

In essence, Taoka thought that self-defence and reprisals could not co-exist simultaneously. At the time, the use of force was not limited to armed attacks. Each form of use of force was therefore justified as a reprisal. In the event of an armed attack, the response is still a reprisal. It is evident that reprisals are legally equivalent to the coercive measures identified by Taoka in the just-war doctrine. This leads to the conclusion that every legally

40 TAOKA Ryoichi, *Kokusaihoujyono Jieikenn* 353–354.

permitted act in that era was conducted within the framework of dispute settlement. This conclusion appears to deviate significantly from the historical and factual realities. A state engaged in a conflict should not perceive itself as engaged in a process of dispute resolution. That supposition is too theoretical to be evaluated as historical positivism.

In contrast, Verdross espoused an alternative perspective regarding the relationship between self-defence and reprisals or self-help. The concept of self-help can be understood as a method of dispute resolution, as Taoka posits. However, self-defence can be seen as a more urgent and reactive use of force. In his textbook, Verdross presented a systematisation of the forceful act, as follows:[41]

> *Die Sanktionen des Volkerrechts* [The sanction of international law]
> *A. Selbsthilfe, Beistandsrecht und Beistandspflicht* [Self-help]
> *B. Arten der Selbsthilfe* [Types of self-help]
> *I. Die Retorsion* [The retorsion]
> *II. Die Repressalie* [Reprisals]
> *III. Die Notwehr* [Self-defence]
> *IV. Der Selbstschutz* [Self-preservation]
> *V. Der Krieg* [War]
> *a) Der Kriegsbegriff* [The concept of war]
> *b) Angriffs-und Verteidigungskrieg*
> [War of aggression and defence]
> *c) Erlaubte und verbotene Kriege (jus ad bellum)*
> [Authorised and prohibited wars (jus ad bellum)]

Nothing is clearer and more well-organised than this table of contents. Reprisals, self-defence, self-preservation and war are all listed in parallel. Taoka separated the concepts of reprisals, self-defence and self-preservation according to the criteria of an illegal act, an armed attack or the absence of both. Verdross, on the other hand, has not made a decisive segmentation, as every concept is covered by the notion of sanctions. Taoka himself carried out the segmentation analysis[42].

> The Vienna School posits that in the context of the international legal order, the right of self-defence is superseded by a broader concept of self-help. Despite Verdross' efforts to maintain the term self-defence within the confines of international law, he differentiates between self-defence and self-help primarily on

41 Alfred Verdross, *Völkerrecht*, 3 Aufl. (Springer-Verlag 1955) xi.
42 TAOKA Ryoichi, *Kokusaihoujyono Jieikenn* 19–20.

the basis of the initiating procedure, rather than on the question of whether the act in question is a justifiable cause for noncompliance with the law.

Taoka's assessment of Verdross' clarification is incorrect, as it is not merely a matter of procedure or formality. According to Verdross, the justification for self-defence is derived from the concept of war for defensive purposes as espoused in the just-war theory tradition.[43]

> This can be either the defence against an unlawful attack (defensive war) or the enforcement of a legally justified claim (restitution of injustice, surrender of unlawfully occupied territory) against a state that does not want to voluntarily fulfil the claim (execution war). Therefore, from the very beginning, just-war was understood as a reaction against an injustice. Some writers, such as Vitoria and Suárez, demand, in addition to the fact that reparation for the injustice cannot be obtained by peaceful means, that it is a serious injustice on the part of the enemy, since the consequence of the injustice must be proportionate to the offence taken.

Legality and illegality are to be determined by the proportionality of the action taken, which, of course, is not known at the initial stage. This is what they argue as a topic on the continuous and simultaneous application of ad bellum and in bello proportionality.[44] Taoka's differentiation of the concepts was based on the preceding conduct of the state in question, whether that conduct was illegal, an armed attack or otherwise. In this context, Taoka makes the distinction between self-defence and self-help primarily on the basis of the initiation process, which led his approach to be non-historical.

As he concentrated on disproving the domestic law analogy, he occasionally failed to consider the broader vision of the field of war and the use of force. In general, Taoka demonstrated considerable skill in critiquing his opponents and elucidating related concepts. However, he exhibited less proficiency in the area of systematic construction. His colleague, Tabata, was good at such systematic construction, although he lacked any methodology whatsoever. ONUMA Yasuaki's comparison of Taoka, Tabata and Takano seems to reflect the general underestimation of Japanese academics.[45]

43 Alfred Verdross, *Völkerrecht* 355.

44 Eliav Lieblich, 'On the Continuous and Concurrent Application of Ad Bellum and In Bello Proportionality' in Claus Kreß and Robert Lawless (eds), *Necessity and Proportionality in International Peace and Security Law* (Oxford University Press 2020) 41–76.

45 ONUMA Yasuaki, 'Takana Yuichi: Personification of a Liberal Mind and Solid Scholarship' (2010) 53 *Japanese Yearbook of International Law* 394.

> Taoka was an outstanding professor of international law whose shrewd analyses of international law, based on realistic and meticulous historical and political research, and rigid, logical reasoning, were stunning. Taoka's textbooks on international law reflected these characteristic features of high quality and could be assessed as competitive with [those of] his contemporary Western international lawyers. Yet, although his textbooks remain an important contribution, in my view, Taoka was more impressive as a monograph writer than as a textbook author.

> Tabata is the most appropriate contemporary to compare with Takano, in terms of evaluating the academic and professional accomplishments of Takano, as well as to appreciate the era of these great international lawyers in Japan. Like Takano, Tabata was outstanding in writing both monographic studies and textbooks.

It is possible that Tabata respected Taoka's academic rigour and believed that it originated from Taoka's involvement with historical resources. It can be reasonably assumed that cause and effect are inversely related. Due to his rigorous theoretical tool, Taoka was able to engage with a diverse range of resources, including texts, charters and historical documents. If the identification of complex concepts in precise detail is merely a tool, rather than a method, then it can be argued that Taoka also lacked a method. One possible reason for the absence of a successor in the academic sense is the lack of a method to follow or emulate, given the unique nature of Taoka's intellect. His sharp intellectual skill is not something that can be easily learned.

### *Conversation with Taoka*

Given the number of rivals he faced, Taoka regularly engaged in debate with them, often using sarcasm even in his old age. Those who attempt to engage Taoka in contemporary conversation face a considerable challenge because of his unwavering logic. Even a researcher from a similar generation to Taoka's finds it challenging to evaluate his doctrine in the context of contemporary debate.[46]

A typical example of Taoka's historical surveys of international law is his 'I'nintochi no Honshitsu (The Essence of the Mandate)'. Here, he sought out a unitary yardstick to criticise the theories of sovereignty over mandated territories by examining the history of the formation of this institution. His conclusion, that the sovereignty of mandated territories rested on

46 MATSUI Yoshiro, 'The Social Science of International Law: Its Evolution in Japan' (2002) 45 *Japanese Annual of International Law* 9.

mandataries, was, in effect, in Japan's favour after her withdrawal from the League of Nations. However, Taoka's analysis here may unintentionally reveal that the mandate system was a means of colonial redistribution among the victorious powers.

Despite the book's title, 'The Essence of the Mandate', the main purpose of this book was to demonstrate that there was no mandate system in international law.[47]

> From a jurisprudential perspective, the term 'mandate' as used in Article 22 of the Covenant of the League of Nations is not an accurate reflection of the substance expressed in the term. The term 'mandate' was only connected to the substance of the instrument in the original drafts of Smuts and Wilson. Following the fundamental amendment to the substance of the instrument by the Supreme Council in the Peace Conference in Paris, the term 'mandate' became disconnected from the substance of the instrument.

It was explicitly stated by Taoka that the terminology employed did not reflect the legal status of the Mandates or Mandate Clauses.[48] This interpretation was overturned by the ICJ in a series of decisions and ultimately advisory opinions in 1971.[49]

> As the Court indicated in 1962, 'this Mandate, like practically all other similar Mandates' was 'a special type of instrument composite in nature and instituting a novel international régime. It incorporates a definite agreement ...'. The Court stated conclusively in that Judgment that Mandate '... in fact and in law, is an international agreement having the character of a treaty or convention'.

Taoka's work continues to appear in the bibliography of commentary on the case, but his argument is not pertinent to the subject matter.[50] Had Taoka provided some reflection or feedback on this conclusion, it would have been a more sustainable argument. Instead, he shifted his focus and topic intermittently. His most recent academic work pertained to the Japanese domestic court decision concerning the injury to a Russian prince, the Otsu Incident. Should we wish to continue the conversation through Taoka and

47 TAOKA Ryoichi, *Ininntouchi no Honnshitsu* (*The Essence of the Mandate*) (Yuhikaku 1941) 212–213

48 Ibid 97–98.

49 Legal Consequences for States of the Continued Presence of South Africa in Namibia (South West Africa) notwithstanding Security Council Resolution 276 (1970), Advisory Opinion, ICJ Reports (1971) 16.

50 MORITA Akio, 'Jyudaina Ihannniyoru Jyoyakuno Shuryo: Namibia Case', *Leading Cases in International Law* (Yuhikaku 2021) 126–127.

his work as a moderator, we must extend him an invitation to join our own circle. The conclusions and positions Taoka adopted were often unwavering in nature. In contrast, his line of reasoning can be traced and understood.

If we incorporate questions and newly acquired information or knowledge into the logical steps he has outlined, we may be able to orient his theory within our circle of conversation. In other words, we can propose an alternative interpretation of Taoka's argument, which would shift the focus towards a more contemporary perspective.

In a positive light, Taoka's consistent position enabled him to serve as a point of origin in Japanese tradition. From this origin of the coordinate axes, we are able to estimate and measure our own positions with a broader perspective. This origin point of Japan serves the same function in comparative studies in international law. Taoka would identify the most suitable researchers to initiate a conversation with.

Speaking of the issue of international comparison, Yokota described himself as the Kelsen of the Orient. A question might also be raised as to Taoka. It is perhaps fair to propose that he was the Francisco Suárez of the Orient. Suárez demonstrated remarkable skill in classifying questions and defining concepts typical of scholastic theologians of the period. From a political standpoint, Suárez was similarly unwavering in his convictions, particularly regarding the state-church situation in England. In contrast to Francisco de Vitoria, Suárez is a legal professional rather than a well-inspired thinker with a global vision. Among the numerous shared characteristics, both Suárez and Taoka can be referred to as a 'doctores eximius', an eminent doctor.

# 4

# YASUI Kaoru: from academic to activist

*YAMASHITA Tomoko*

## Introduction: 'the road lies before and behind me'

YASUI Kaoru (1907–1980) stands as a complex and contentious figure within the history of Japanese international law. Dedicating his life to pursuing radical social change in pre-war, wartime and post-war Japan, he emerged as a significant activist and scholar. Despite his extensive engagement with the dialectical method in international law, Yasui's influence within Japanese legal scholarship remains remarkably limited.

This marginalisation can be attributed, at least in part, to political considerations. Yasui actively contributed to the development of 'Greater East Asian International Law', a legal framework designed to legitimise Japan's expansionist aims during the Second World War. This association with wartime propaganda undoubtedly alienated him from the post-war legal scholarship, which embraced a more liberal orientation.

However, Yasui's post-war activism for peace, particularly his resolute opposition to the atomic and hydrogen bombs (A- and H-bombs), garnered widespread support. This grassroots movement culminated in the publication of *Michi: Yasui Kaoru Sei no Kiseki* (The Road: Yasui Kaoru's Path of Life) in 1983, a memorial collection of essays honouring his life and legacy.[1] Notably, with the exception of HOSOYA Chihiro (Professor Emeritus of Diplomacy and Foreign Relations, Hitotsubashi University), the publication committee lacked prominent academics. Instead, it comprised Yasui's alumni from both the University of Tokyo (*Dojyu Kai*) and Hosei University

1 Michi Publishing Committee (*Michi Kanko Iinkai*), *The Road: YASUI Kaoru's the Path of Life* (*Michi: YASUI Kaoru Sei no Kiseki*) (Hosei University Press 1983) i. This book was a posthumous publication put together by YASUI's disciples. It is a collection of his literary remains, including unsorted manuscripts, essays, tanka (Japanese poems) and eulogies.

(*Yuho Kai*), as well as members of a reading group in his residential area (*Suginoko Kai*).

Significantly, *Michi* offers a multifaceted portrait of Yasui. The collection encompasses his diverse essays, delving into his personal history, philosophical and religious beliefs, political ideologies, dedication to public education, anti-nuclear activism and his broader view of humanity. It also includes tributes from his former students, providing a more personal perspective on his life and influence. The reason why he was so curious about divergent fields of thinking appears in the following sentences, which were cited in Hosoya's preface to the book as follows:

> The road lies before and behind me. [...] There is a road before me. [...] I inherit that road and continue to walk it. Praying that a new path will be created behind me as a sign that I lived in a new era, I continue to walk. (Translated by the author.)[2]

The examination of Yasui's life reveals a figure deeply engaged with the critical issues of his time. This suggests a high degree of sensitivity to the prevailing social and political climate. One could argue that he actively sought to fulfil the roles expected of him by the era. This chapter delves into Yasui's intellectual and activist responses to the tumultuous period spanning the pre-war and post-war eras. Against this background, the first section focuses on Yasui's early intellectual trajectory. It explores the theoretical contributions he made during the first half of his life, which unfortunately culminated in justifications for Japan's wartime militarism and expansionism. The second section examines the latter half of Yasui's life, marked by a shift from academic pursuits to activism. It delves into his regret over his wartime contributions and his subsequent commitment to peace advocacy. Finally, the chapter concludes by critically evaluating Yasui's overall contribution to Japanese international law, considering both his wartime justifications and his later activism.

This chapter's analysis is primarily informed by two key sources: Yasui's seminal work, *Kokusai Ho to Bensho Ho* (*International Law and the Dialectic*), published in 1970, and *Michi*, a 1983 memorial essay collection edited by his former students after his death. These volumes encompass Yasui's scholarship across various periods – pre-war, wartime and post-war – providing a comprehensive view of his four-decade-long intellectual trajectory in the field. Notably, Yasui's 1970 work is particularly valuable for understanding his evolving perspective on the study of international law.

2 Ibid i.

Here, he emphasises the need to strike a balance between realism and scientism, a theme that recurs throughout his writings. When citing these edited volumes, the author employs the original publication dates of the included works within the text, allowing readers to trace the development of Yasui's thought over time.

## As an academic: Yasui's legal contribution justifying Japan's militarism and expansionism during the Second World War

Born in 1907 at Ohwada Village (present-day Kadoma City), Osaka Prefecture, Yasui initially enjoyed a distinguished academic career. A student of TACHI Sakutaro, Yasui graduated from the Division of Political Studies at Tokyo Imperial University (later renamed the University of Tokyo in 1947) in 1930. He was appointed Research Associate at the young age of twenty-three and subsequently secured a position as Associate Professor of International Law at the prestigious university.

However, Yasui's trajectory shifted in 1943. His nomination for promotion to full Professor encountered fierce opposition from YOKOTA Kisaburo (*see* Chapter 2), a senior colleague at Tokyo Imperial University. This incident, known as the 'Professor Y Problem' after Yasui's surname initial, exposed a rift within the faculty. Notably, Yasui's wartime cooperation with the Japanese military contributed to the controversy. In protesting the approval of Yasui's promotion, Yokota and TANAKA Kotaro (*see* Chapter 5) submitted their resignations to the university.

Prior to the disagreement, Yasui had been actively involved in Japan's militaristic national policies. In 1938, the workload of the Second Division of the Treaty Bureau of the Ministry of Foreign Affairs expanded. In response to the newly added task of 'research and investigation of international law and extraterritorial legislation', a Legal Affairs Office was established. This was because, since the outbreak of the 1931 Mukden Incident (also known as the Manchurian Incident), international law-related issues had increased, and it was urgent to improve the international law research system, given Japan's leading position in East Asia. With the opening of the Legal Affairs Office, the Ministry of Foreign Affairs hired young international law researchers at the time as commissioned investigators. One of them was Yasui.[3] Yasui had also been appointed in 1941 to the Current

3 TAKAHASHI Rikiya, *Weaving International Law: The Codification Project of the League of Nations and Japan* (*Kokusaiho wo Amu: Kokusai Renmei no Houtenkajigyo to Nippon*) (Nagoya University Press 2023) 338–339.

Affairs Committee, the Wartime International Law Committee, and most significantly, the East Asian International Law Committee (EAILC) of the Japanese Society of International Law. The EAILC aimed to legitimise the Pacific War as a 'holy war' aimed at achieving equal footing for 'East Asian peoples' with the British and Americans under international law. This objective necessitated the 'abolition of the British and American systems of extraterritoriality and evacuation' and the development of 'legal principles governing the relationships within the Greater East Asian Co-Prosperity Sphere, thereby establishing the foundation of East Asian international law'.[4]

As part of the EAILC's activities, Yasui published a book titled *Ohshu Koiki Kokusaiho no Kiso Riron* (*Basic Theories of European Broad-Area International Law*) in 1942, which triggered the fury of Yokota as well as the reason to be purged in 1948 by order of the Allied Forces' General Headquarters after Japan's defeat. This publication, along with his cooperation with the military, likely contributed to Yokota's strong disapproval and ultimately led to Yasui's purge from the university in 1948, ordered by the Allied Forces' General Headquarters after Japan's defeat. Yokota was very critical of Yasui's inconsistent academic attitude and later wrote in his essay as follows:

> Initially, he [Yasui] was a 'liberal', but with the introduction of Soviet international law theories, he became 'leftist'. When the Sino-Japanese War began, he associated with the military and sought to develop a theory to defend the claims of the Greater East Asian Co-Prosperity Sphere advocated by the military and the right wing, and he published a series of books for this purpose. (Translated by the author.)[5]

According to Yokota, Yasui's studies at Tokyo Imperial University demonstrated a broad interest in diverse legal theories. Yasui himself stated that the first half of his life was dedicated to identifying the fundamental principles and methodologies of international law.[6] This section focuses on

4 TAKENAKA Yoshihiko, 'The Postwar Visions of the International Lawyers in Wartime Japan: From the Pursuit of the Greater East Asian International Law to the Idealisation of the United Nations Japan's Wartime Diplomacy and the Postwar Visions (*Kokusaiho Gakusha no 'Sengo Kohso': 'Daitoa Kokusaiho' kara 'Kokuren Shinko' he*)' (1995) 109 *Kokusai Seiji* 70–83.

5 YOKOTA Kisaburo, *My Whole Life* (*Watashi no Issho*) (Tokyo Shimbun Publishing 1976) 349.

6 YASUI Kaoru, *International Law and the Dialectics* (*Kokusai Hohgaku to Bensyoho*) (Hosei University Press 1970) i.

his contributions concerning the inherent nature of international law and broad-area ideologies among his various scholarly pursuits.

### *The debate between legal pluralism and monism supporting the supremacy of international law*

Yasui's initial and most notable scholarly endeavour centred on the character of international law, with a particular emphasis on the interplay between international and national legal systems. This topic first captured his attention during his research assistantship at Tokyo Imperial University and remained a core focus of his research for nearly four decades. His doctoral dissertation, titled 'Kokusai Ho to Kokunai Ho no Kankei (The Relationship Between International Law and National Law)', submitted in 1960, ultimately led to his award of a Doctor of Law (LLD) from Hosei University.

In this context, his fluency in German allowed him to engage with the dominant tradition of German legal scholarship within Japanese legal studies at the time. During his tenure at Tokyo Imperial University, Yasui published a series of articles introducing German doctrines advocating the supremacy of international law over national law. Interestingly, Yasui later acknowledged that he had originally intended to study the work of Heinrich Triepel, a prominent dualist scholar on this topic, particularly his influential book *Völkerrecht und Landesrecht* (*Law of Nations and Municipal Law*). However, limited access to resources, as evidenced by the unavailability of this key text even at the library of Japan's most prestigious university, forced him to focus on the writings of other German scholars.[7]

The initial corpus of his scholarly output consists primarily of translations of German scholarship, serving as foundational introductions to Japanese society on the relationship between international and domestic law.

His first published article, originally published in *Kokusai Ho Gaiko Zasshi* (the *Journal of International Law and Diplomacy* published by the Japanese Society of International Law) in 1931, examined the theory of the supremacy of international law. Drawing on the work of Alfred von Verdross and other scholars, Yasui analysed the historical context and contemporary status of this theory, which was once dismissed as merely an academic question. Yasui's conclusion suggested that the realities of the time hinted at a trend towards the supremacy of international law within a monist framework. However, he recognised that this emerging monist understanding still contained elements resembling a modified dualistic approach.

7 Ibid 556.

This suggested that a fully developed monist system, characterised by a supranational legal order, was not yet established. In other words, the political reality of the time had not yet reached a point where international law functioned as a truly superior legal system independent of individual nation-states.[8]

This emphasis on translation is especially pronounced in his following articles. The second article, published in 1934, was indeed a condensed translation of Gustav Adolf Walz's work, 'Völkerrecht und staatliches Recht (International Law and State Law)', which appeared in *Kokka Gakkai Zasshi* (Tokyo Imperial University, *Journal of the Association of Political and Social Science*). Drawing on Triepel's scholarship, Walz reframed the traditional monist-dualist debate on the relationship between international and domestic law by proposing a framework of pluralism and monism. Although Yasui maintained a monist understanding of the supremacy of international law, he appreciated Walz's dualistic approach as a form of criticism of his approach.[9] Then, his third article in *Hogaku Kyokai Zassi* (*Journal of the Jurisprudence Association*) in 1938 considered Hans Kelsen's pure theory of law, which placed importance on the principle of *pacta sunt servanda* as a kind of 'Grundnorm (Basic norm)' in international law. Yasui argued that Kelsen's adoption of a monist perspective on the supremacy of international law stemmed not from purely theoretical considerations but rather from his underlying philosophical outlook.[10]

Another article, included in *Tokyo Teikoku Daigaku Gakujutsu Taikan* (*Tokyo Imperial University Academic Overview*) of 1942, focused on the monist–dualist debate in Japanese scholarship. Yasui identified YAMADA Saburo's 1906 article as the first to address this topic, followed by the MINOBE Tatsukichi–TACHI Sakutaro debate. YOKOTA Kisaburo's work in 1930 defended Kelsen's pure theory, while Minobe challenged it. On the other hand, TAOKA argued that the prevailing view favoured a dualistic approach, as international law lacked the automatic power to nullify domestic law. He further contended that a monist understanding of international law's supremacy could not, in theory, preclude the possibility of war.

Drawing on analytical insights from German and Japanese scholarship, Yasui, in his 1960 doctoral thesis, reached an original conclusion about the primacy of international law. His analysis focused on doctrines that position international law as the apex of the global legal order. He identified a common thread among these doctrines: the notion that domestic legal validity is

8 Ibid 184–188.
9 Ibid 262–263.
10 Ibid 277.

ultimately derived from international law. These doctrines posit that domestic law receives its legitimacy through a process of delegation from international law, thus attributing 'primacy of delegation (Delegationsprimat)' to international law.[11]

However, he considered that this theory of primacy of delegation could not explain the reality of law and misunderstood the essence of international law. While acknowledging that international and domestic law have distinct bases of validity, he argued that the distinction between the two is relative. In this sense, he rejected a compartmentalised structure and adopted a unified framework. However, he maintained that the unified relationship between international law and domestic law, each with its own validity, was established only through the intermediation of state will. Within this complex unified relationship between international and domestic law, intermediated by state will, various arguments, such as the relative distinction between international law and domestic law, the partial primacy of international law and the partial primacy of domestic law, were all incorporated to a correct extent.[12]

## *Broad-area ideologies: pan-Asianism and greater East Asian international law*

In the early 1940s, the theory of greater East Asian international law (GEAIL) gained significant traction within the Japanese Society of International Law. To fully grasp the theoretical underpinnings of GEAIL, it is essential to first delineate its intended geographical scope. In Article 2 of the Tripartite Pact signed in Berlin on 27 September 1940, Germany and Italy recognised and respected the leadership of Japan in the establishment of a new order in 'Greater East Asia (GEA)', which included French Indochina (Cambodia, Laos, Chinese territory of Guangzhouwan and Vietnam), Bilma, Dutch East Indies (Indonesia), Straits Settlements (Penang, Singapore, Malacca and Dinding), New Guinea and New Caledonia. On the other hand, Japan considered in its negotiations for the Pact that GEA extended not only to these regions but also to Thailand, Australia, New Zealand and India.[13] In 1942,

11 Ibid 307.
12 Ibid 312–314.
13 MATSUI Yoshiro, '*"The Universality" and "the Regionality" in the Globalizing World: A Critical Study on Criticism of Universalism by the Idea of Greater East Asian Co-Prosperity Sphere* (*Gurobaru ka suru Sekai ni okeru "Fuhen" to "Chiiki": "Daitoa Kyoeiken" Ron ni okeru Fuhensyugi Hihan no Hihan teki Kento*)' (2004) 102(4) *Kokusaiho Gaiko Zasshi* 567–588.

the Imperial Headquarters-Government Liaison Conference (*Daihonei Seifu Renraku Kaigi*), a Japanese government body that coordinated military and civilian operations during the Second Sino-Japanese War and the Second World War, decided GEA meant the area of Southeast Asia and Oceania that is located between 90° east longitude and 180° east longitude, and north of 10° south latitude, but the precise area would have been decided based on the situation.[14]

As previously noted, Yasui, a member of EAILC, actively contributed to the theoretical development of GEAIL during this period, despite not having conceptualised GEAIL itself. Within the context of the EAILC's activities, Yasui's 1942 publication delved into the concept of European broad-area international law. As he noted, this theory emerged as a challenge to British universalism, the dominant paradigm within the European-centric world order. In this order, East Asia occupied a peripheral position, evidenced by the unequal treaties imposed on Japan in the late nineteenth century, which included provisions for consular jurisdiction. These treaties reflected the prevailing perspective that shaped East Asian international law under the old order. Significantly, Yasui identified European broad-area international law as possessing world-historical importance. He saw it as a force working from within to dismantle the global dominance of old European international law. Having ostensibly liberated itself from the constraints of the old-world East Asian international law, Japan, according to Yasui, was now spearheading the liberation of all peoples within GEA. This vision entailed a new order free from European domination, with a GEA Co-Prosperity Sphere centred on Japan. GEAIL, a newly formulated legal system, would govern both external and internal relations within the GEA Co-Prosperity Sphere. Notably, Yasui emphasised that this legal system would be guided by the inherent principles of Japan, the leading state of the GEA.[15]

It is evident that the theoretical framework of Yasui's European broad-area international law drew heavily on Carl Schmitt's concept of 'Völkerrechtliche Großraumordnung', which was prominently invoked during the Nazi era in Germany. According to Yasui's essay published in 1938, the 1931 Mukden Incident served a historical purpose: the creation of a GEA Co-Prosperity Sphere. This vision, though seemingly disruptive to existing static peace mechanisms and international law, might ironically

14 Ibid 569.

15 YASUI Kaoru, *Basic Ideology of European Broad-Area International Law* (*Ohshu Koiki Kokusaiho no Kiso Rinen*) in Japanese Society of International Law (*Kokusaiho Gakkai*), *Greater East Asian International Law Series* (*Daitoa Kokusai Ho Sousyo*) vol. 1 (Yuhikaku Publishing 1942) Introduction and Chapter 6.

suggest a shift. This shift would be from a rigid, flawed peace system to a more adaptable one that reflected dynamic, changing historical realities.[16]

Notably, prior to his 1942 book, Yasui engaged with Marxist international law. During this earlier phase, he had not yet settled on a specific theoretical framework to underpin his arguments, likely viewing these critiques as tools to challenge the dominant liberal theory of international law.[17] Despite this initial lack of a settled theoretical framework, it appears Yasui maintained a consistent focus on the liberation of Asian peoples from the constraints of Western-centric international law.[18]

GEAIL, alongside the concept of the GEA Co-Prosperity Sphere, can be understood as a form of regionalism and a critique of Western-centric universalism and imperialism. However, it is crucial to acknowledge that these ideas, despite the intentions of scholars like Yasui, were ultimately manipulated for political purposes to legitimise Japan's aggression towards Asian nations. In the wake of his purge by the Allied Forces' General Headquarters in 1948, an article authored by Yasui appeared in the University of Tokyo newspaper. This article endeavoured to elucidate the rationale behind his wartime contributions to GEAIL in stating that:

> I attempted to establish the concept of East Asian liberation academically, driven by an irresistible inner demand, but I was swept away by the tides of the times and failed to achieve the desired results. To equate my actions with cooperation in aggressive wars and label them as militarism or extreme nationalism is to trample on the freedom of conscience. (Translated by the author.)[19]

Following Japan's defeat in the Second World War, GEAIL fell out of favour and remained largely undiscussed until the late 1970s in the Japanese Society of International Law. This period of renewed interest coincided with the work of several scholars, including SOGAWA Takeo (*see* Chapter 7), MATSUDA Takeo, ONUMA Yasuaki (*see* Chapter 12) and MATSUI Yoshiro (*see* Chapter 10), who began a historical analysis of the theory.[20] Particularly noteworthy is Matsui's deep insight into GEAIL and critique of Yasui. Matsui argues that an 'irresistible inner demand' does not absolve

16 Michi 16–17 (n 1).
17 YASUI 7 (n 15).
18 TAKENAKA 76 (n 4).
19 Michi 46 (n 1).
20 AKASHI Kinji, 'The Modern Law of Nations and the "Greater East Asia Coprosperity Sphere" ("*Daitoa Kokusaiho" Riron: Nihon ni okeru Kindai Kokusaiho Jyuyo no Kiketsu*)' (2009) 82(1) *Hogaku Kenkyu* 261–292.

scientists, particularly those actively involved in Japan's wartime militarisation, of their social responsibility.[21] As Matsui argues, while the dreams of the scholars of that time for the liberation of Asian peoples from Western domination through the realisation of the Greater East Asia Co-Prosperity Sphere were sincere, the biggest problem with GEAIL was its failure to make an effort to discern the true policy objectives and the realities of the Co-Prosperity Sphere hidden behind it.[22]

## As an activist: Marxist 'Japanese peace worker' after the purge in 1948

Following his dismissal from academia in 1948, Yasui briefly registered as a barrister. However, he soon transitioned back to a scholarly role, albeit at private institutions. He held positions at Kanagawa University (1951) and Hosei University (1952–1978).

The latter half of Yasui's life witnessed a shift in his focus. He leveraged his expertise in international law to contribute significantly to the anti-nuclear movement. This period (until his passing in 1980 at the age of seventy-two) was marked by a dedication to grassroots activism rather than purely academic pursuits. Beyond his individual efforts, Yasui's wife, Tazuko, actively supported the cause. She held leadership roles in the Suginami Ward women's book club '*Suginoko kai*' and the '*Kusa-no-ne Heiwa no Tsudoi* (Grassroots Peace Gathering)' (1985–1991). The latter group included figures like OHISHI Buichi, a former Minister of Agriculture and Forestry, and SIMMURA Takeshi, a linguist and scholar of French literature. Yasui's contributions extended to local governance as well. In 1953, he became the first and emeritus director of both the Suginami City Library and the Suginami Public Hall, which served as a focal point for the local anti-nuclear movement. These local initiatives eventually laid the groundwork for his broader activism on the world stage, as will be discussed in a subsequent section.

A cursory examination of Yasui's later activities might suggest a prioritisation of activism over conventional academic methods. This is evident in his critiques of Western dominance, colonialism and capitalism. However, Yasui himself viewed this period as an application of the analytical methodology he developed in the first half of his life.[23] Notably, he explicitly mentions his exploration of Marxist frameworks, culminating in his embrace of *Juche*, the official ideology of the Democratic People's Republic of Korea

21 MATSUI 588 (n 13).
22 Ibid 586–587.
23 YASUI i (n 6).

(DPRK). This section will delve deeper into Yasui's transformation into an activist, analysing his anti-nuclear movement work and his demonstrably strong ties to communist countries during the Cold War era.

## *Karl Marx, Max Weber and* Juche

Yasui's most notable contribution to Japanese international law scholarship was his introduction of Marxist international law.[24] Early in his academic career, Yasui focused on Marxist international law and the relationship between international and national law. Building on his conclusions regarding the latter, which he established in his 1960 doctoral thesis, he developed a Marxist theoretical framework in the latter half of his life.

In 1933, Yasui published two book reviews: one in *Kokusai Ho Gaiko Zasshi* (vol. 32, no. 2) and another in *Hogaku Kyokai Zassi* (vol. 51, no. 4). Both reviews examined Evgeny Aleksandrovich Korovin's *International Law in the Transition Period* (the original Russian version was published in 1924 and translated into Japanese by YONEMURA Shoichi in 1933). Four years later, in 1937, in *Hogaku Kyokai Zassi* (vol. 55, no. 9), Yasui published a review of Evgeny Bronislavovich Pashukanis' Course on Soviet Economic Law (the original Russian version was published in 1935 and translated into Japanese by YAMANOUCHI Ichiro in 1937). It is worth noting that Yasui's reliance on German or Japanese translations for these reviews suggests a potential limitation – a possible inability to understand the source material in Russian. This raises questions about the depth of his engagement with the original arguments and nuances presented by the authors. It should also be noted that the Japanese version of the text contained numerous censored passages due to wartime restrictions. To fully understand the content, the translator engaged in direct negotiations with the author.

Despite these limitations, Yasui's contribution merits recognition. As a scholar of international law, he transcended mere translation by introducing an analytical perspective on Soviet international law theory to prominent Japanese international law journals. He pointed out that the evolution of Soviet international law can be divided into three phases. During the initial phase, Soviet international law vehemently repudiated all norms of modern international law, branding them as vestiges of the bourgeoisie. This stance aligned with the Soviet Union's struggle against all forms of oppression,

24 For example, YASUI Kaoru, 'The Soviet Union's Peace Institution (*Rohno Rosia no Heiwa Kiko*)' in YOKOTA Kisaburo (ed.), *International Law Essays: Commemorative Collection for Professor Tate's Sixtieth Birthday* (*Tate Kyoju Kanreki Shukuga Kokusaiho Ronsyu*) (Yuhikaku Publishing 1934).

including military intervention by capitalist states. In the second phase, Soviet international law sought to establish a distinct theoretical framework governing relations between socialist and capitalist states during the transitional period leading to world revolution. This approach corresponded to the era when the Soviet Union, implementing the New Economic Policy, sought recognition from capitalist states and established international relations with them. Korovin's discussions reflect this period. The third phase witnessed Soviet international law endeavouring to interpret modern international law in light of Soviet practice. This shift coincided with the period when the Soviet Union maintained peaceful relations with capitalist states while pursuing the construction of a socialist state through successive five-year plans. Pashukanis' arguments epitomise this era.[25]

Yasui appears particularly drawn to Pashukanis' arguments that position Soviet international law as an antithesis to the emerging imperialist forces seeking another world war. Pashukanis grounded Soviet international law in the Marxist concept of the proletarian base structure influencing the exploitative superstructure. According to Pashukanis, this framework aligned with the Soviet Union's consistent pursuit of peace since its inception and its genuine rejection of national subjugation, annexation and oppression. Pashukanis further argued that Soviet international law represented the interests and will of the vast majority of working people. Yasui acknowledged the tragic dismissal and disgrace Pashukanis faced in 1937, coinciding with the Trotskyist purge in the Soviet Union. While expressing sympathy for Pashukanis' fate, which Yasui viewed as inevitable for an international legal scholar who completely subordinated objective analysis to political ideology, he maintained that Pashukanis' arguments still embodied the theoretical framework of Soviet international law at the time.[26].

The original publication date of these comments in the 1937 book review is noteworthy. It raises a question of Yasui's possible foresight regarding his own future involvement with Japanese militarism and the GEAIL during the Second World War. However, without further evidence, it is difficult to definitively determine whether Yasui's embrace of Pashukanis' arguments foreshadowed his later shift towards supporting Japanese expansionism.

In the aftermath of the 1948 purge, Yasui's theoretical orientation pivoted decisively towards Marxist international law. He likely viewed it as a theoretical framework that not only championed world peace but also provided a critical lens for resisting Western dominance, colonialism and imperialism. In addition, despite publishing only a brief book review of Karl

25 YASUI 89–90 (n 6).
26 YASUI 99, 103 (n 6).

Jaspers' work (translated into Japanese by MORI Akira) in 1942,[27] Yasui considered his study of Max Weber to be methodologically significant. This is further underscored by his explicit statement in his 1970 book that his methodology was built on the combined insights of 'Marx and Weber', not 'Marx or Weber'.[28] This suggests a more nuanced approach, in his words, a 'dialectic approach', potentially seeking to integrate both Marxist critiques of capitalism and Weberian analyses of power and bureaucracy into his understanding of international law.

In his later years, Yasui's intellectual focus shifted towards *Juche*, the North Korean state ideology. This shift can be interpreted as a continuation of his prior engagement with Marxist international law and his pursuit of a more realistic framework for international law. In 1972, he established and chaired the Japan–DPRK Social Scientists Solidarity Committee. This period also saw his appointment as a representative for both the Japan–DPRK Normalisation National Council and the Japan–DPRK Cultural Exchange Association. Building on his growing engagement with the DPRK, Yasui played a key role in the founding of the International Institute of *Juche* Idea in 1978. The institute's establishment stemmed from a resolution adopted at an international conference held in Pyongyang. Yasui became the institute's first Director-in-Chief.

There, his earlier experience at the Ministry of Foreign Affairs likely played a significant role in shaping this ambition. He may have been particularly motivated by the potential to translate legal arguments into concrete political strategies capable of achieving these desired social changes.

### *The movement against A- and H-bombs*

Yasui emerged as a prominent figure in the anti-nuclear movement during the 1950s and 1960s. A pivotal moment arrived in 1954 with the contamination of the Japanese fishing vessel F/V Lucky Dragon 5 by fallout from the US thermonuclear test at Bikini Atoll. This incident galvanised Yasui to organise anti-nuclear movements in Japan. In 1954, he assumed leadership roles as Chair of the Suginami Council for the Petition Movement Against A- and H-Bombs and Secretary General of the Japan Council for the Petition Movement Against A- and H-Bombs. He subsequently became the first Chair of the Japan Council Against A- and H-Bombs in 1955. Yasui's influence extended beyond Japan. He served as a powerful representative in various international conferences aligned with the Third World movement,

27 YASUI Kaoru, 'Max Weber as a Seeker after Truth (*Kyu Do Shya to shite no Max Weber*)' (1942) 56(12) *Kokka Gakkai Zasshi* 1527–1535.

28 YASUI ii (n 6).

including the Conference of Lawyers in Asia (Calcutta, 1955), the Asian–African Conference (Cairo, 1957) and the World Congress for General Disarmament and Peace (Moscow, 1962).

Complementing his political activism, Yasui provided expert testimony on international law from 1955 to 1963 at the Tokyo District Court. He supported the plaintiffs in the *Shimoda case*, who were atomic bomb victims from Hiroshima and Nagasaki. The case argued that the US atomic bombings constituted illegal acts under international law. Interestingly, Yasui's wartime colleague at the EAILC, TABATA Shigejiro (see Chapter 6), also served as an expert witness for the plaintiffs. Notably, the lawsuit did not seek compensation directly from the United States, but rather from the Japanese government. The plaintiffs contended that the Treaty of Peace with Japan (1952) arbitrarily relinquished their individual rights to claim compensation from the US.

While the court ultimately dismissed the case in 1963, citing the lack of individual rights under international law without specific treaty recognition, the judgment held significant weight. The court remarkably declared the bombings of Hiroshima and Nagasaki unlawful based on the Draft Rules of Air Warfare (1923) and analogous rules governing land and naval bombardments. The court's reasoning hinged on the illegality of indiscriminate attacks on undefended civilian populations, a principle considered customary law, and the fact that the supposed adoption of 'total war' by belligerents did not nullify this principle.

Yasui actively participated in the intellectual life of post-war Japan through his involvement with the Legal Affairs Committee of the Democratic Scientists' Association (*Minshu Shugi Kagakusha Kyokai*, often abbreviated as *Minka*). Founded in 1946, Minka was a prominent Japanese scholarly organisation that significantly influenced the intellectual landscape, particularly in the fields of science and social sciences. Yasui's contributions extended beyond membership. He delivered several academic presentations titled 'Current Issues in International Law' in 1954 and 1965. These presentations addressed a broad range of contemporary international legal issues concerning Japan, with a particular focus on anti-nuclear movements.[29]

Throughout his anti-nuclear activities, Yasui self-identified as a 'Japanese peace worker'. This commitment was exemplified by his act of laying a wreath at the USS Arizona Memorial in Pearl Harbor, Hawaii, during a 1963 visit.[30] As Chair of the Japan Council Against A- and H-Bombs that year, he embarked on a nationwide 'peace lecture' tour across the United States, with Hawaii as his first stop. This peace movement, rooted in humanist

29 Ibid 551–552.
30 Michi 205 (n 1).

principles, consistently advocated for global solidarity and cooperation for peace, transcending East–West divides.[31] His dedication to this cause was recognised with the Lenin Peace Prize in 1958, followed by his appointment to the Prize's selection committee in 1961. According to Matsui's analysis, Yasui's later involvement in the anti-nuclear movement can be interpreted as a form of apology for his past contributions to GEAIL, which provided justification for Japan's wartime militarism and invasions of neighbouring countries.[32]

## Conclusion: legacy of the era

Yasui's intellectual journey began with a comparative approach to international law theories. This initial focus on diverse legal perspectives likely laid the groundwork for his later engagement with social activism.

This chapter examined Yasui's evolving intellectual stance in the context of a rapidly changing Japan. The author suggests that Yasui exhibited a high degree of adaptability, readily aligning himself with the dominant intellectual currents of his time. This adaptability is particularly evident during the tumultuous period spanning the pre-war and post-war eras. Here, Japanese society grappled with the profound impact of war, the challenges of reconstruction, and the adoption of democratic principles. It also highlights a potential inconsistency in Yasui's approach, as mentioned in Yokota's objection to Yasui's promotion at Tokyo Imperial University in 1943. In the aftermath of the Second World War, Japanese academia witnessed a significant shift in the dominant intellectual currents. Marxist thought, with its emphasis on social critique and class struggle, emerged as the preeminent social science framework. Yasui, demonstrably adaptable to the prevailing intellectual trends, aligned his scholarly pursuits with this Marxist resurgence.

These societal shifts undeniably shaped the nation's identity and trajectory in the modern world. As he noted for Pashukanis' fate, Yasui might have considered it an inevitable fate for an international legal scholar to be completely subordinated to political ideology. Through his social activities, he arguably developed a transformative understanding of international law. He emphasised the need to strike a balance between realism and scientism, a theme that recurs throughout his writings. While this emphasis on realism and scientism offers valuable insights, it is important to acknowledge another consistent theme in Yasui's work: his view of international law as a tool for dynamic social change. He envisioned international law as a means

31 Ibid 207.
32 MATSUI 588 (n 13).

to liberate people oppressed by Western-centric universalism and imperialism, and to contribute to the construction of a new legal order built upon this liberation. This ambition was likely fostered by his earlier experience at the Ministry of Foreign Affairs, where he may have been motivated by the prospect of translating legal arguments into real-world political strategies that could achieve these goals.

Despite his evolving intellectual positions, Yasui appears to have garnered considerable respect from his colleagues and students. This positive regard is evidenced by several factors. Notably, his successful promotion during the 'Professor Y Problem' suggests strong support within the Faculty of Law. Additionally, his colleagues actively protested the 1948 purge, a move that implies a strong belief in his character. Finally, the efforts of his former students, manifested in the formation of several alumni associations, grassroots movements and a posthumously published edited volume, further reinforce the positive impact he left on those he mentored.

The positive regard for Yasui may have stemmed, in part, from a philosophical perspective he developed early in his academic career. This perspective, potentially emphasising the limitations of human knowledge, could have fostered a sense of intellectual humility and a willingness to engage with diverse viewpoints. Such qualities, if present, would likely contribute to his positive relationships with colleagues and students. He sought a universal principle capable of achieving the complete liberation of humanity. This liberation encompassed freedom from the contradictions between humans and nature/society, as well as internal human contradictions. Yasui dedicated his life to pursuing and enacting this ideal across various domains, including academia, faith, art and politics.[33] Further insight into his philosophical outlook can be gleaned from his 1977 collection of Japanese poems, *Eigou no Dampen* (*Fragments of Eternity*).[34] This collection, containing 468 poems, affirms the essence of life. While not subscribing to a specific religion, the works reflect the profound understanding Yasui gained through over five decades of research into Buddhism and Christianity.

In conclusion, the author portrays Yasui as a noteworthy and unconventional figure within Japanese international law scholarship. While he may not have established a dominant school of thought in the field, his enduring engagement with social movements in pre-war and post-war Japan undeniably signifies his significant contribution to the broader intellectual landscape of the time.

33 Faculty of Law, Hosei University, 'Bibliography and Works of Professor YASUI Kaoru (*Yasui Kaoru Kyojyu Ryakureki Gyoseki*)' (1978) 76(1) *Hogaku-shirin* 101–105.

34 YASUI Kaoru, *Fragments of Eternity* (*Eigou no Dampen*) (Tanka Shimbun Publishing 1977).

# 5

# TANAKA Kotaro: an unparalleled jurist with natural law tradition

*OGURI Hirofumi*

## Introduction: a well-known but overlooked public figure in scholarship

TANAKA Kotaro (1890–1974),[1] the first Japanese judge to serve on the International Court of Justice (ICJ), is an underexamined figure in Japanese international legal scholarship despite his distinguished career. After graduating from Tokyo Imperial University, Tanaka briefly worked at the Ministry of Internal Affairs for eighteen months before joining the Faculty of Law at Tokyo Imperial University in 1917 as an assistant professor. Following a three-year sabbatical in Europe, he returned to Japan and was promoted to full professor, specialising in commercial law, in 1923. Notably, Tanaka did not specialise in public international law in the strictest sense, nor did he leave behind a significant body of work on the discipline. His most widely known contribution to international legal scholarship is his three-volume *Theory of World Law*, published between 1932 and 1935, based on his dissertation submitted to the university in 1929.

Tanaka's career subsequently took him into high-level governmental and judicial roles. In 1946, he became Minister of Education in the first Yoshida Cabinet, was a member of the House of Peers in June of the same year and later served as a member of the House of Councillors for three years starting

The author has previously analysed TANAKA Kotaro's theory of world law with reference to sources of international law. This chapter elucidates the comprehensive formation and evolution of Tanaka's world law theory, which underpins the discussion in the published article, and further explores its standing within Japanese international legal scholarship. See OGURI Hirofumi, 'Conceptions of International Law in Tanaka Kotaro's Theory of World Law: Their Natural Law Basis and the Roles of General Principles of Law' (2008) 39 Yearbook of World Law 64–92.

1 For his biography, see TANAKA Kotaro, *My Autobiography* (Shunju-Sha 1961); SUZUKI Takeo (ed.), *TANAKA Kotaro: His Character and Works* (Yuhikaku 1977); MAKIHARA Izuru, *TANAKA Kotaro: The Fighting Founder of the Judiciary and An Explorer of World Law* (Chuokoron-Shinsha 2022).

in 1947. In 1950, he was appointed Chief Justice of the Supreme Court, a position he held until 1960. In the following month, he was elected as a judge of the ICJ, where he served for nine years, participating in eight cases (seven contentious and one advisory opinion), contributing individual and dissenting opinions.

The main focus of Tanaka's *Theory of World Law* was on uniform law and private international law – what he termed 'world law in a narrow sense'. He acknowledged that his arguments on public international law through the lens of his conception of world law were merely a 'sketch',[2] and not fully developed. After publishing this volume, his engagement with world law theory was limited, apart from a 1936 lecture at the University of Paris and other writings on uniform law within the context of commercial law, his core specialisation. Later in his career, particularly from a world peace perspective, he produced several scholarly works while serving as a Supreme Court judge. However, Tanaka's views on the relationship between international and world law only became clearer after his appointment to the ICJ in 1960.

An examination of Tanaka's legacy, particularly regarding his world law theory, reveals that this area of his scholarship has been largely neglected.[3] From the establishment of the World Law Association in 1965 to the present,[4] there has been scant analysis of his theory, likely due in part to the fact that Tanaka himself did not fully develop it. Nonetheless, his later writings and his opinions as an ICJ judge suggest that he sought to expand his theory on world law, particularly in relation to public international law, although these efforts have yet to be thoroughly explored in scholarship.

Against this backdrop, this chapter aims to map out his theory of world law in relation to the international legal scholarship of the time. The analysis

2 TANAKA Kotaro, *Theory of World Law*, vol. 3 (Iwanami Shoten 1934) 5.

3 This aligns with the observation that Tanaka has not been adequately represented in the historiography of international law in Japan. See, ITO Fujio, 'One Hundred Years of International Law Studies in Japan' (1969) 13 *Japanese Annual of International Law* 19–34. Cf. AKASHI Kinji, 'One Hundred Years of Japanese International Law Scholarship and International Outreach' in ONUMA Yasuaki (ed.), *One Hundred Years of Japan and International Law*, vol. 1 (Sanseido 2001) 221. For his position within Japanese scholarship on private international law, see TAKESHITA Keisuke, 'Sadajiro Atobe and Kotaro Tanaka: The Universal Private International Law School of Thought in Japan' (2013) 56 *Japanese Yearbook of International Law* 217–242.

4 For the background to its establishment and the initial state of the study group, see, for example, TAKANO Yuichi, 'On the Launch of Proceedings of the World Law Research Association/World Law Association' (1987) 7 *Yearbook of World Law* 38–39; TABATA Shigejiro and FUKATSU Eiichi, 'Interview with TABATA Shigejiro Sensei: On the Philosophy of World Law' (1998) 8 *Yearbook of World Law* 33–43.

will be divided into two phases: the formative phase and the expansion phase. First, the formative phase will examine his early writings, including his magnum opus, *Theory of World Law*, with attention to the role of international law in his theoretical framework. The second phase will focus on his post-war career, particularly his tenure as Chief Justice of the Supreme Court and as an ICJ judge, examining how his views on international law evolved and how his world law theory expanded during this period. Through a detailed analysis of Tanaka's works, including primary documents such as personal notes and essays, this chapter will illuminate the (in)significance of his world law theory within Japanese international legal scholarship.

## The birth of world law theory

### *Two rudiments of world law theory*

#### *Development of research questions and conversion*

According to Tanaka's recollections, his serious engagement with commercial law began when he was preparing to lecture on the law of bills at the Tokyo Imperial University. This preparation sparked his academic interest in the subject. As a result of his work on the lecture, Tanaka published an article titled 'The Essence of Bills and Notes' in 1925, two years after his promotion to professor of commercial law. The article posited that, despite differences in the bill laws of various countries, there might be something universal about the very nature of bill regulations. The central question raised was: Is the unification of bill laws possible, and if so, what is its theoretical foundation?[5] From this inquiry into the law of bills, Tanaka expanded his study to encompass the foundational concepts of commercial law more broadly. He identified the global nature of commercial law, noting the existence of uniform provisions across municipal laws and the rational, technical nature of commercial law as governing principles of human commercial activity.[6]

Although Tanaka began his career as a researcher in commercial law, his intellectual interests were always more aligned with legal philosophy than

5 TANAKA Kotaro, 'The Essence of the Bills Relationship' (1925) 43 *Journal of the Jurisprudence Association* 11.

6 TANAKA Kotaro and YANAGISAWA Ken (eds), *The Path I Have Walked* (Sekai-no-Nippon-Sha 1955) 138.

positive law.[7] A significant turning point for him occurred in September 1923, about six months after his appointment as a professor of commercial law and shortly after the Great Kanto Earthquake. His colleague, TAKAYANAGI Kenzo, asked him to teach a general course on jurisprudence at the First Higher School. Tanaka agreed and taught the course for six years. During this period, he gained a foundational understanding of legal philosophy and an overview of common law. Tanaka later recalled that his lectures on jurisprudence at the school significantly broadened his intellectual horizons and contributed to the depth of his opinions delivered at the Hague Court.[8]

In 1927, as a result of his preparation for the lecture, he published serialised essays on jurisprudence. In relation to his later work, *Theory of World Law*, it is important to note that in this article, Tanaka recognised two foundational methodologies in legal study: the objective analysis of legal phenomena and systems, and the sociological method for analysing the various elements of legal reality. He described these two approaches as 'two different halves of a single whole',[9] underscoring their interdependence in legal studies.

Beyond his discovery of the phenomenon of 'unification' within commercial law, another pivotal event in shaping Tanaka's world law theory was his conversion to Catholicism. Initially, Tanaka followed the Non-church Movement after being influenced by UCHIMURA Kanzo's *How I Became a Christian* (1895), which he read during a serious illness in high school. However, after a falling-out with Uchimura over the marital issues of some of Uchimura's followers, Tanaka began to question the Protestant doctrine of *sola fide*. He grew convinced that an external authority was necessary to guarantee the objectivity of faith. On 3 April 1926, he was baptised as a Catholic.

This baptism played a crucial role in the development of Tanaka's world law theory. In his view, the conception of legal values, which seeks to determine the ultimate purpose of law and the state, is closely tied to an individual's worldview. His conversion to Catholicism led him to believe that legal values are neither rooted in individualism nor institutionally derived, but rather in natural law as an objective ethical standard.[10] His shift to Catholicism, in short, liberated the concept of law from the constraints of

7 TANAKA Kotaro, 'My Legal Philosophy' (1950) 22(1) *Horitsu-Jiho* 30.
8 TANAKA Kotaro, 'Jurisprudence: My Own Way (3)' *Asahi Shimbun* (23 April 1970) 7.
9 TANAKA Kotaro, 'Jurisprudence (fin.)' in Nippon Hyoron Sha (ed.), *Socio-Economic System*, vol. 8 (Nippon Hyoron Sha 1927) 92.
10 TANAKA Kotaro, 'Jurisprudence: My Own Way (2)' *Asahi Shimbun* (21 April 1970) 6.

the state, allowing him to argue that true law must align with natural law – a departure from conventional legal theory, which placed excessive emphasis on the authority of the state.

*The prototype of world law theory*

Tanaka's early reflections on legal philosophy can be found in *Law, Religion, and Social Life*, published in 1927. Tanaka described the work as 'an argument on legal values in a nutshell' and viewed it as both an expression of his conversion to Catholicism and his confirmation of the significance of legal studies.[11] The book was written during the conceptualisation and drafting of *Theory of World Law*, which Tanaka submitted as a dissertation to Tokyo Imperial University in 1929. A close examination of its content reveals certain ideas that would later be expanded in *Theory of World Law*. Notably, Chapter IX, titled 'Issues on World Law', indicates that these issues 'would be studied in detail at another time'.[12] As will be discussed below, Tanaka's theory of world law can be understood as having its prototype in this early work.

The first key idea in Tanaka's work is the assertion that the concept of law should be free from ethnic or national bias. He argued that the laws governing social life should be universal for all humanity. Although he acknowledged that municipal laws need not be identical in every detail, he claimed that many legal differences arose not out of necessity but from arbitrary traditions and that these differences often created unnecessary problems. Therefore, he emphasised the need for as much unification of laws as possible.[13]

Second, Tanaka distinguished between two types of law: ethical and technical. He argued that only technical norms, which are concerned with the most rational means of achieving certain objectives, could serve as the foundation for the unification of laws. Technical norms, in his view, are a form of social technology designed to meet specific goals.[14] However, Tanaka also acknowledged that the multiplicity of goals in human society often leads to conflicts. In response, ethical norms, he suggested, offer a framework for resolving such conflicts.[15] He explained that 'the essence of technical norms lies in their purposiveness (*Zweckmässigkeit*) for a given set of objectives, whereas ethical norms are about making value-based judgments

11 TANAKA, *My Autobiography* 59 (n 1).
12 TANAKA Kotaro, *Law, Religion and Social Life* (Kaizo-Sha 1927) 208.
13 Ibid 21–22.
14 Ibid 214–215.
15 Ibid 17–19.

to harmonise different goals, which is to say, justice in the broadest sense (*Gerechtigkeit*)'.[16] This distinction between technical and ethical norms reflects the same two methodologies Tanaka outlined in his earlier work 'Jurisprudence', where he described the objective and sociological methods as 'two different halves of a whole'.[17]

Third, Tanaka argued that the ideal of law must be sought in a higher order beyond human-made law, specifically in natural law, which he described as the rational world order established by God. While he recognised the factual and relative nature of law, he simultaneously emphasised its ideal nature. He anticipated objections to this view but sought to elevate natural law to an absolute, giving it the same validity as positive law, akin to the natural law doctrines of the Enlightenment.[18] However, Tanaka made it clear that his conception of natural law differed from that of Enlightenment philosophes and other contemporary theories of natural law. He hinted at a deeper exploration of 'the relationship between natural law, St. Thomas Aquinas' *lex aeterna*, and world law',[19] although he did not delve into this subject in detail at the time.

Fourth, Tanaka outlined a broad vision for world law, asserting that it encompasses not only uniform law but also private international law and public international law. As will be discussed below, Tanaka's world law theory began with the concept of uniform law, which was referred to at the time as 'world law in the narrow sense', a term originally coined by Ernst Zitelmann.[20] However, Tanaka argued that once law is freed from the constraints of state sovereignty and is viewed through a sociological and ideological lens, all legal systems are fundamentally altered.[21] In this transformed framework, 'international law is recognised as the public law of global humanity. Its scope is not limited to states alone, but also includes other entities and private individuals, allowing individuals to engage in international legal relations with states in their own capacity'.[22]

16 Ibid 220.
17 Ibid 235–236.
18 Ibid 237–238.
19 Ibid 239–240. On Tanaka's theory of natural law, see HANZAWA Takamaro, *Modern Japanese Catholicism: A Study of History of Ideas* (Misuzu Shobo, 1993) 113–225; José Llompart, 'TANAKA Kotaro's Natural Law Theory' in *Japan Association of Legal Philosophy* (ed.), *Annual Review of Legal Philosophy 1979: Japanese Legal Philosophy* (Yuhikaku 1980) 1–23.
20 Ernst Zitelmann, 'Die Möglichkeit eines Weltrechts' (1988) 39 *Allgemeine österreichische Gerichts-Zeitung* 193–195, 201–203, 209–212.
21 TANAKA, *Law, Religion and Social Life* 240–241 (n 12).
22 Ibid 245.

It is evident from the above that the arguments presented in *Law, Religion, and Social Life* – specifically in its ninth chapter on world law – were not yet fully developed or persuasive. Rather, the ideas are presented as preliminary sketches of arguments that would be refined later. In particular, the relationship between world law and international law, which Tanaka referred to as a 'Copernican turn in legal thought',[23] would take years to be articulated in a coherent and comprehensive form, as will be explored in the following section.

## The birth of *Theory of World Law*: dissertation (1929) and book volume (1932–1934)

### *'Seeking refuge in natural law' and developing his natural law theory (1929–1930)*

Tanaka's three-volume *Theory of World Law* was based on his doctoral dissertation of the same title, submitted to Tokyo Imperial University. He received his doctorate in law from the university in April 1929. Initially, Tanaka intended to focus solely on the uniformity of laws, a concept of 'world law in the narrow sense', as advocated by Zitelmann. However, while writing, he expanded the scope to encompass not only the regulation of the world economy and global society but also private international law and public international law. This marked a broadening of his theoretical framework, moving beyond the initial premise of private international law to include public international law as well.[24]

A notable divergence exists between his doctoral dissertation and the published three volumes. According to a newspaper interview on 25 January 1935,[25] the argument on public international law was only added in the third volume of the book. In fact, Chapter 9 of the dissertation, titled 'International Law and World Law', which would later appear in the third volume, is absent from the original dissertation.[26] This suggests that

23 Ibid 245–246.
24 TANAKA, 'My Legal Philosophy' 30 (n 7).
25 'A *Magnum Opus* from Ten Years of Study: Dr Tanaka's *Theory of World Law*' *Asahi Shimbun* (25 January 1935) 5.
26 Upon reviewing Tanaka's doctoral thesis, it becomes apparent that despite the outline presented in the first chapter ('Introduction'), which lists 'Chapter 8: World Law and International Law', neither the table of contents nor the main text actually contains Chapter 8. The final paragraph of the 'Introduction' is recorded as follows, but it appears to have been crossed out, possibly indicating removal: 'Finally, this paper primarily focuses on private law, but in order to roughly complete the system of world

Tanaka's theory of public international law as part of his broader world law theory took shape between 1929, when his dissertation was submitted, and 1934, when the third volume was published. Indeed, the evolution of his ideas on international law is seen in several essays on natural law written between 1930 and 1931, which are examined below.

Furthermore, although *Theory of World Law* is grounded in natural law, the preface to the second volume of 1933 reveals that Tanaka 'sought refuge in natural law' after three or four years of grappling with the subject, modifying the work to reflect this shift in perspective.[27] The corresponding section on 'Natural Law and World Law', found in Chapter 6 of the second volume, was absent from his doctoral thesis, implying that this part was conceived and written after the thesis was submitted.

The foundation of Tanaka's ideas on the relationship among natural law, world law and international law can be traced to his 1930 article on natural law. Regarding world law, Tanaka references his earlier work, *Law, Religion, and Social Life*, where he argues that 'the fact that commercial law is rooted in universal human reason demonstrates how a unified world law can be established in commercial law'.[28] He further asserts that world law – a legal system that transcends national boundaries and ethnic differences – began to take shape and was referred to as 'world law'. This development, he contends, cannot be fully grasped through the lens of Friedrich Carl von Savigny's historical school of jurisprudence, and then he posits that world law derives directly from natural law.[29]

Moreover, Tanaka highlights that when a legal system is deficient, it is supplemented by natural law.[30] He argues that the function of natural law is most apparent in international law, which lacks many positive rules. To create a new international order following the First World War, Tanaka calls for a departure from the traditional view that the will of states is the sole source of international law, advocating instead for a 'return to natural law,

law, it is necessary to make a brief comment on international law, which should be a world public law opposing world private law. This is an observation of international law from the perspective of world law, and it is what Chapter 8, "World Law and International Law", seeks to address'. TANAKA Kotaro, *Theory of World Law* (Dissertation submitted to the Imperial University of Tokyo 1929) 34.

27 TANAKA Kotaro, *Theory of World Law*, vol. 2 (Iwanami Shoten 1933) 2.

28 TANAKA Kotaro, 'The Past of Natural Law and Its Contemporary Significance' in Tokyo Imperial University Catholic Study Group (ed.), *Catholic Study*, vol. 1 (Iwanami Shoten 1930) 52.

29 Ibid 53–54.

30 Ibid 56.

the ancient foundation of international law'.[31] This argument is also found in his articles in 'Introduction to Jurisprudence', serialised from 1930 to 1931, where he asserts that natural law provides the philosophical basis for international law.[32] He emphasises that natural law's supranational nature challenges the absoluteness of states, critiques their actions and promotes the development of international organisations.[33]

From this, one can conclude that Tanaka's conception of world law was driven both by his interest in the phenomenon of unification in commercial law and by his adoption of natural law theory following his conversion to Catholicism. While this conversion compelled him to embrace natural law, it took him some time to fully integrate it into his legal thought. As Tanaka deepened his understanding of natural law, he simultaneously developed his vision of international law within his theory of world law. The recognition that emerged before the publication of *Theory of World Law* reflected a need for a new foundation for international legal thought in the wake of the Great War, as Tanaka sought to supplement the weak and underdeveloped international legal system by rooting it in natural law.

## *An overview of* Theory of World Law *and international law as 'world public law'*

Tanaka's theory of international law, developed in Chapter 9 of the third volume of *Theory of World Law* (1934), was, like his earlier work *Law, Religion, and Social Life* (1927), described by Tanaka as merely a 'sketch'.

31 Ibid 61. In a footnote to the text, reference is made to the following work by Joseph Mausbach on the role of natural law in addressing deficiencies within positive international law: Joseph Mausbach, *Naturrecht und Völkerrecht* (Herdersche Verlagshandlung 1918). This was part of a series of publications produced by the Commission for Christian International Law in Germany, established in November 1917, with Mausbach serving as chairman. Although further analysis is needed, it appears that, in addition to Mausbach's work, Tanaka drew considerable insight from two other studies in his essays written in 1930/1931 and in *Theory of World Law*: Viktor Cathrein, *Die Grundlage des Völkerrechts* (Herdersche Verlagshandlung 1918), and Otto Schilling, *Das Völkerrecht nach Thomas von Aquin* (Herdersche Verlagshandlung 1919).

32 TANAKA Kotaro, 'Introduction to Jurisprudence (1)' in SUEHIRO Izutaro (ed.), *Collected Works on Modern Legal Theory*, vol. 31 (Nippon HyoronSha 1930) 36–37.

33 TANAKA Kotaro, 'Introduction to Jurisprudence (7, fin.)', in SUEHIRO Izutaro (ed.), *Collected Works on Modern Legal Theory*, vol. 38 (Nippon Hyoron Sha 1931) 144, 153. This essay was the first to articulate Tanaka's conception of international law in a coherent form, with most of its assertions later revisited in detail in the third volume of *Theory of World Law*.

Tanaka noted in the preface that, having originally focused on private law, a more detailed exploration of public international law as public law on a global scale would have to wait for a later occasion.[34]

In Chapter 1 of its first volume, Tanaka states that his aim was to bridge gaps between law, morality, custom and religion within jurisprudence, as well as between legal studies and positive law.[35] Acknowledging the dominant views of the time that linked law to the state and ethnicity, he presents the existence of law in societies beyond the state, including supranational entities. While recognising the influence of ethnic identity on law, Tanaka argues that such identity stems primarily from 'consciousness (*Bewusstsein*)', which itself arises from religion.[36] He challenges the prevailing theories and thereby lays the groundwork for his concept of world law.

On this basis, Tanaka posits that since human societal relations transcend national borders and ethnic groups, global societal relations also exist. Where there is society, there must also be law; hence, a body of world law exists, which Tanaka defines as both the sociological foundation and the metaphysical foundation of law appropriate to global society. According to him, world law must be regulated by legal principles common to all nations and peoples, and these principles are rooted in natural law.[37] From this premise, Tanaka identifies three types of world law that enable the unification of legal systems: (1) international law, which governs relations between sovereign states; (2) private international law, which reconciles conflicts between different national legal systems; and (3) uniform law, a form of 'world law in the narrow sense' that applies equally across multiple states. Tanaka defines world law as law that transcends national boundaries, distinct from law governing individual nations, emphasising its 'transboundary' nature.[38]

Following this introduction, Tanaka reviews the development of international legal scholarship up to the nineteenth century and introduces what he

34 TANAKA, *Theory of World Law*, vol. 3 665 (n 2).

35 TANAKA, *Theory of World Law*, vol. 1 (Iwanami Shoten 1932) 16. For a summary of *Theory of World Law*, see ORIMO Yutaka, 'World Law' in SUZUKI (ed.), *TANAKA Kotaro* 76–90 (n 1); YAZAWA Makoto et al., 'In Memory of TANAKA Kotaro Sensei (Round Table I): His Scholarship and Thought' in ibid 530–537.

36 TANAKA, *Theory of World Law*, vol. 1 25 (n 35).

37 Ibid 38. Anticipating criticism for combining these two methodologies, Tanaka nonetheless contends that in a social science like jurisprudence, such a synthesis is essential. He argues that relying solely on the elaboration of empirical facts 'succumbs to the flaw of positivism', while exclusive metaphysical speculation 'degenerates into mere subjectivism, devoid of any grounding in real life', Ibid 30.

38 Ibid 278.

calls 'international legal thought after the Great War'.[39] This new thought critiques nineteenth-century international legal positivism, which was centred on state sovereignty. He identifies three emerging trends: (1) psychological and sociological approaches (e.g. Hugo Krabbe and Léon Duguit); (2) logic-based tendencies (e.g. Hans Kelsen and Alfred Verdross); and (3) scholastic natural law approaches (e.g. Joseph Mausbach). According to Tanaka, these trends differ from traditional international law in seeking foundations beyond the state, and all share an underlying aspect of natural law. However, he clarifies that while the first two trends focus on relations between individuals, his own approach, aligned with Scholastic natural law, emphasises relations between states and employs both empirical and speculative methods. He incorporates these perspectives into his own theory.[40]

Tanaka's discussion on the nature of international law relies on the dualistic methodology that he argued in the first chapter of the first volume. He asserts that, from an empirical standpoint, the international community exhibits a weak form of supranational authority greater than the state, providing the sociological foundation for international law as world public law. Simultaneously, Tanaka contends that the essence of international law is the same as that of law within any state: law binds individuals regardless of their personal will, and international law similarly possesses an objective existence independent of the will of states. This objective existence, he argues, is grounded in natural law, which provides the metaphysical foundation for international law as world public law.[41]

Tanaka then addresses four key issues arising from this metaphysical ground of international law: (1) the sources of law; (2) fundamental rights and duties of states; (3) the scope of the international legal community; and (4) the problem of war. His discussion of sources is particularly significant. Tanaka argues that the supranational foundation of international law, derived from natural law, offers a 'guiding principle for correct solutions' to major issues in international law. He contends that where positive rules of international law are deficient, they must be supplemented by natural law principles, regardless of the de facto recognition by individual states. He dismisses the positivist explanation that customary law fills such gaps as merely an 'explanation of a quandary'. Tanaka also addresses general principles of law, asserting that 'commutative justice (*iustitia commutativa*)' governs relations between states and is equally valid within the international community, even in the absence of positive rules. In many instances, he

39 Ibid 665–676.
40 Ibid 685–690.
41 Ibid 696–677.

argues, the source of positive international law is the embodiment of natural law; put differently, positive law is generally the manifestation and concretisation of already existing natural law principles.[42]

To fully understand Tanaka's view of the relationship between natural law and international law, one must recognise that, for him, the supranational character of international law depends fundamentally on natural law. While empirical considerations, such as solidarity among states and the global economy, can confirm this supranational character, they alone cannot justify international law as applicable to all humanity. For Tanaka, international law attains its universality – its status as world law – only through natural law, the universal legal principle derived from human nature. However, he distinguishes between natural law and international law: while many rules of international law reflect natural law, the validity of positive international law is subject to the same temporal and spatial constraints as municipal law. As a result, international law evolves in response to changes in the international community and the global economy, highlighting the importance of sociological and economic studies in international law scholarship.[43]

As noted earlier, Tanaka conceived of world law as the legal framework governing the global economy. Reflecting on this issue, he returns at the conclusion of the third volume to discuss the sociological foundations of international law as world public law. Acknowledging that international law has historically regulated not only economic but also non-economic matters, Tanaka accepts the importance of comity in inter-state relations.[44] He focuses on international cooperation for administrative, technical and humanitarian purposes, arguing that this transforms international law into world public law, distinct from private international law and uniform law. This, in turn, allows states to regulate international economic relations directly through treaties and indirectly influence the global economy. In concluding his work, Tanaka asserts that 'the metaphysical foundation of international law, which is world law, is natural law, just as in the case of

42 Ibid 698–699. The remaining three topics are as follows: (i) the rights and duties traditionally regarded as fundamental rights of states, despite lacking a clear basis in treaty or customary law, can only be justified through natural law; (ii) the distinction between 'civilised' and 'non-civilised' states is based on the recognition by state will, but from the perspective of natural law, such a distinction is untenable, and the scope of international legal community must encompass the entire world; and (iii) natural law acknowledges war as a self-defence remedy, similar to the concept of *justa causa* in traditional just war theory, thereby enabling a legal distinction between legal and illegal wars, which allows for the legal regulation of warfare. Ibid 699–708.

43 Ibid 709–710.

44 Ibid 718–720.

municipal law', and then emphasises that 'only through natural law can the unity of national and world law be achieved'.[45]

## The expansion of world law theory and its application to practice

### *Plan for the fourth volume of* Theory of World Law

Shortly after the end of the Second World War, university-affiliated scholars were invited to reform the education system, and Tanaka was appointed Director of the School Education Bureau of the Ministry of Education in October 1945. By May 1946, he became Minister of Education and played a crucial role in shaping the post-war educational system, as demonstrated by his involvement in drafting the Fundamental Law of Education.[46] Despite being occupied with his official duties, Tanaka continued writing. In his draft titled 'Ideological Foundations of the United Nations', completed on 18 February 1946, he highlighted key differences between the League of Nations and the United Nations, particularly the latter's reliance on majority rule and an international police force. Tanaka asserted that the UN must aim at 'the realisation of international justice', governed by 'supranational principles of natural law – the democratic ideals of international life'.[47] In essence, Tanaka viewed the new post-war international organisation, the UN, as being founded on natural law, much like the League.

In January 1947, Tanaka resigned as Minister of Education and ran for election to the newly established House of Councillors, winning a seat on 3 May of the same year. He continued writing during his time as a legislator, publishing numerous essays in both specialised and non-academic journals. Many of these reiterated the arguments already made in the third volume of *Theory of World Law*. However, Tanaka did address new phenomena in international law, as seen in his 1948 essay, where he discussed crimes against peace as 'one expression of the revival of natural law philosophy in international law'.[48]

Tanaka was appointed Chief Justice of the Supreme Court in March 1950, and the ten years before his retirement were marked by his efforts

45 Ibid 723–724.

46 For a detailed account of Tanaka's major activities during this period, see, MAKIHARA, *TANAKA Kotaro* 127–175 (n 1).

47 TANAKA Kotaro, 'The Ideological Basis of the United Nations' (1946) 1(2) *Asahi Hyoron* 16. The English translation can be found in the *Nippon Times* (29 May 1946) 4.

48 TANAKA Kotaro, 'The Logic and Ethics of Pacifism' (1948) 28(1) *United Nations* 8.

to supplement and expand his world law theory, which he later called 'the jurisprudence of peace'. In January 1950, just before assuming the position, he declared, 'if I have the rest of my life to live, my task hereafter will be to complete this labour by publishing, as a continuation of *Theory of World Law*, world organisational law based on the Universal Declaration of Human Rights and grounded in the principles of natural law'.[49] Here, Tanaka renewed his commitment to completing his unfinished theory of world law.

In fact, in a legal philosophy essay submitted on 23 January 1950, Tanaka refused to accept that peace could not be fully addressed only in terms of legal studies. He briefly discussed how peace is first linked to achieving legal stability within the global human society, and second, that the content of peace is the realisation of both *Gerechtigkeit* and *Zweckmässigkeit*.[50] He also touched on the theory of just war, noting that war with *justa causa* remains legitimate in the current international system, particularly in cases of self-defence.[51]

Alongside his focus on peace, Tanaka's efforts to complete his world law theory were also centred on what he named 'world organisational law'. In several articles published during this period, he presented his views on the international community. One noteworthy piece, 'Law and the World', was completed in 1951 and later included in the fourth volume of his *Philosophical Treatise on Law*, subtitled *The Jurisprudence of Peace*, published in 1954. In this article, Tanaka argued that 'international law will dissolve into the municipal law of a world state once it is established, but even in its current state, it can be called public law within the world community'.[52] He emphasised that this law governs not individuals or private groups but the relations between states and international organisations, particularly entities like the League and the UN.

Tanaka's evolving theory of the international organisation became even more concrete in his 1958 article, which he described as a draft for the fourth volume of *Theory of World Law*. In this essay, he connected his ideas to broader questions of war and peace, asserting that the primary aim of the

49 TANAKA, 'My Legal Philosophy' 30 (n 7).

50 TANAKA Kotaro, 'Some Legal Philosophical Reflections on Peace' (1950) 6 *Legal Philosophy Quarterly* 1–28. Tanaka's views on war were clearly articulated not only in his academic papers but also in his address as Chief Justice of the Supreme Court. See TANAKA Kotaro, 'New Year's Address of 1951' (1951) 73 *Court Times* (*Saibansho-Jiho*) 1.

51 TANAKA, 'Some Legal Philosophical Reflections on Peace' 11–14 (n 53).

52 TANAKA Kotaro, 'Law and the World' in TANAKA Kotaro (ed.), *Collected Works on Legal Philosophy*, vol. 4: *The Philosophy of Peace* (Yuhikaku 1954) 25.

international community is to maintain peace and security. He emphasised that this aim is founded on a natural and global moral order that supports interdependence and solidarity among peoples. According to Tanaka, the UN collective security system plays a key role in realising these objectives.[53]

In his interpretation of the pacifism in Article 9 of the Constitution of Japan, Tanaka argued against the notion that Japan's renunciation of war also means renouncing the right to self-defence. He maintained that such an interpretation is unjust because it allows for the unlawful use of force by aggressors. He further argued that exercising the natural law-based right of resistance – whether individually or collectively – should be prioritised over legal stability if it means upholding justice. Tanaka believed that defending another state against aggression is a moral obligation of the international community and that exercising the right of self-defence in response to wars of aggression contributes to the realisation of the rule of law in the international arena.[54] In this sense, Tanaka affirmed that just war theory remains relevant within the UN collective security system. This argument influenced his judicial opinions during his tenure as Chief Justice.[55]

However, Tanaka also believed that peace was unattainable in a world divided between liberal democracies and communist states. He argued that true peace could only be achieved with the victory of the liberal democracies.[56] This position highlighted Tanaka's strong liberalism and his sharp critique of communism. As Chief Justice,[57] Tanaka continued to expand his vision of world law by working to establish the post-war Japanese judicial system while advocating for a world of liberal democracies, which he saw as the only path to lasting peace.

53 TANAKA Kotaro, 'Basic Conditions for World Peace' in TAKANO Yuichi (ed.), *Challenges of Modern International Law: A Festschrift in Honor of Professor Yokota's Sixtieth Birthday* (Yuhikaku 1958) 10–14.

54 Ibid 15–26.

55 In the *Sunagawa* case, which raised the issue of whether the stationing of US troops violated the Constitution as the time for revising the US–Japan Security Treaty approached, Tanaka reiterated the views he had expressed in his 1958 article. Supreme Court of Justice, '1959 (A) 710 (16 December 1959)' (1959) 13(13) *Supreme Court Reports (Criminal Cases)* 3239–3247.

56 TANAKA, 'Basic Conditions for World Peace' 51–57 (n 53).

57 For an analysis of the relationship between Tanaka's activities as Chief Justice and his scholarly works, see, OGATA Takeshi, 'The Indefatigable Natural Law Theorist: TANAKA Kotaro' in WATANABE Yasuyuki et al. (eds), *Supreme Court Justices from a Constitutional Law Perspective: Seventy Years of Supreme Court Justices* (Nippon Hyoron Sha 2017) 49–63.

## The application of world law to practice in the ICJ

### *Judge of the world court*

Tanaka, who was set to retire as Chief Justice of the Supreme Court in October 1960, initially planned to spend his post-retirement years reading and pursuing scholarly interests. However, he soon found himself 'living like an exile in a hotel in The Hague, the Netherlands'.[58] The reason for this, of course, was his election as a judge of the ICJ. His candidacy had been proposed by YAMADA Saburo, who, in an August 1959 letter, described Tanaka as 'a scholar of natural law jurisprudence, well-known in Europe and the United States, and a distinguished judge' and, therefore, 'the best candidate that our country can offer'.[59] On 1 March 1960, after consultations with experts, in accordance with the recommendation stipulated in Article 6 of the ICJ Statute – among whom was Yamada, the President of the Japan Academy at the time – the National Group of the Permanent Court of Arbitration, including KURIYAMA Shigeru, TAKAYANAGI Kenzo, NISHIMURA Kumao and YOKOTA Kisaburo, formally nominated Tanaka for the ICJ position.[60]

Tanaka received the Order of Culture on 7 October 1960, just before his retirement as Chief Justice. That evening, in his office, he reflected on his future, stating:

> After retiring, I wish to rebuild the theory of world law, the subject of my award. I want to fulfil your expectations as part of my life's work by reading the classics that I was unable to explore during my tenure. I also hope to strengthen the ICJ and contribute to the transition from arms reduction to total disarmament, as the idea of an international community will dominate the world in the future.[61]

58 TANAKA, *My Autobiography* 88 (n 1).

59 YAMADA Saburo, 'Tributes to the Election of Dr. K. Tanaka as a Judge of the International Court of Justice' (1961) 59 *Journal of International Law and Diplomacy* 851–855; 'Letter from YAMADA Saburo to TANAKA Kotaro (18 August 1959)', TANAKA Kotaro Private Papers (Manuscript Division of the Center for Modern Japanese Legal and Political Documents, Graduate Schools for Law and Politics, University of Tokyo), Part II, 2(21), 36.

60 'Memorandum of Deliberations of the Advisory Committee on the Nomination of Candidates for Judges of the International Court of Justice (2 March 1950)', B'.2.5.0.1-2, Diplomatic Archives of the Ministry of Foreign Affairs Japan.

61 MATSUO Keiichi, *Dr. TANAKA Kotaro* (Saga Shimbun 1975) 334.

Upon his election to the ICJ on 16 November 1960, Tanaka made world law a key focus of his academic life. According to him, the coexistence of numerous nations and peoples must be guaranteed by common judicial ties, which exist as world law – a moral law common to all of humanity and grounded in natural law.[62] Though he was somewhat pessimistic about his life in The Hague, referring to it as living 'like an exile', he expressed his excitement at applying his theory of world law to practice: 'A noiseless academic life in this city awaits me'.[63]

During his nine-year tenure, Tanaka contributed individual and dissenting opinions in about half of the eight cases he participated in.[64] His focus was often on the general principles of law, which he viewed as one of the most crucial sources of international law.[65] Below, this chapter outlines his development of arguments on international law from the perspective of his theory of world law, particularly in terms of (1) the concept of world law, (2) the natural law approach underlying his theory and (3) the general principles of law, which he considered key to understanding international law.

First, Tanaka invoked the concept of world law several times in his individual opinions.[66] The most notable example is his dissenting opinion in the 1969 *North Sea Continental Shelf* case. While the majority rejected the equidistance principle as customary international law, Tanaka believed otherwise. He argued that the 1958 Continental Shelf Convention had initially been *lex ex contractu* but had evolved into part of the law of the

62 'Speech Upon Election as Judge of the International Court of Justice', TANAKA Kotaro Private Papers, Part II, 3(2), 3 (n 59). 'I personally put the general term of "the world law" to all such existing laws, which are based on the natural law, – the moral law common to all mankind transcending antagonisms between nations and races'. In addition to English, this speech was also prepared in French, German and Spanish.

63 TANAKA, *My Autobiography* 88 (n 1).

64 For a comprehensive examination of Tanaka's opinions, see Ijaz Hussain, *Dissenting and Separate Opinions at the World Court* (M. Nijhoff 1984) 156–204; TAKANO Yuichi, 'The International Court of Justice and Dr. TANAKA Kotaro' (1977) 633 *Jurist* 119–128.

65 Tanaka consistently showed interest during his tenure and actively developed his own views in individual opinions, particularly regarding issues arising from the dissolution of the League of Nations and the Permanent Court of International Justice. In this context, Tanaka identified the conflict between formalist and functionalist tendencies in legal thought, adopting the latter approach to derive the legal continuity between the old and new organisations.

66 See Kevin M. Doak, *Tanaka Kotaro and World Law: Rethinking the Natural Law Outside the West* (Palgrave 2019) 101–105; Otto Spijkers, 'Application of World Law by International Courts and Tribunals to Protect the Environment', in Edgardo Sobenes et al. (eds), *The Environment Through the Lens of the International Courts and Tribunals* (TMC Asser Press 2022) 691–695.

international community – or world law – through its implementation.[67] Tanaka suggested that the equidistance principle had universal character and technical applicability, elements he long argued were essential for world law in its narrower sense as uniform law. In his view, the ICJ could have further contributed to the development of international law by granting the equidistance principle the status of world law.[68]

Second, Tanaka's world law theory was grounded in natural law, a concept that appeared frequently in his opinions. He often contrasted natural law with the legal positivism dominant in state-centric approaches. In his dissenting opinion in the *North Sea Continental Shelf* case, Tanaka argued that legal positivists, who see international law's binding force as dependent on the will of sovereign states, are rigid in recognising customary law. By contrast, he advocated a more flexible approach that recognises the objective existence of law independent of state will. He argued for prioritising the substance and content of customary law over its formation process, highlighting natural law's role in creating an objective legal order.[69] The reasoning grounded in natural law also appeared in his dissenting opinion in the second stage of the *South West Africa* case (1966), where Tanaka justified the inclusion of the principle of equality in the mandate agreement despite its absence in explicit text. He argued that equality was implicit in the agreement by virtue of natural law.[70] Here, he relies on his idea that positive international law is generally the embodiment of natural law.

Finally, Tanaka placed significant emphasis on the general principles of law, which he regarded as central to world and public international law. He viewed these principles not merely as a means of filling gaps in positive international law but as a way to bridge municipal and international law, thereby advancing the formation of world law. In his dissenting opinion in the *South West Africa* case, he examined whether norms protecting human rights could be considered general principles of law. Tanaka argued that with the recognition of these principles, 'international law could have the foundation of its validity extended beyond the will of States, that is to say, into the sphere of natural law and assume an aspect of its *supra*-national

67 'Dissenting Opinion of Judge Tanaka', Judgment of 20 February 1969, *North Sea Continental Shelf Cases (Federal Republic of Germany v. Denmark; Federal Republic of Germany v. Netherlands), ICJ Reports 1969*, 176.

68 Ibid 194–196.

69 Ibid 178.

70 'Dissenting Opinion of Judge Tanaka', Judgment of 18 July 1966 (Second Phase), *South West Africa Cases (Ethiopia v. South Africa; Liberia v. South Africa), ICJ Reports 1966*, 301.

and *supra*-positive character'.[71] He traced this development to the Advisory Committee of Jurists' drafting process in 1920.

Moreover, Tanaka asserted that general principles of law, custom and treaties operate on a hierarchical basis. In his view, general principles come first, as treaties and customary law are often expressions of these pre-existing principles, 'if we accept the fact that convention and custom are generally the manifestation and concretization of already existing general principles'.[72] By advocating for the primacy of general principles of law over other sources of international law, Tanaka underscored their paramount importance in shaping world law.

### *An extension of the naive argument? On the relationship between natural law and general principles of law*

As previously mentioned, Tanaka's tenure at the ICJ involved not only applying his theory of world law, grounded in natural law, but also a sustained focus on general principles of law listed in Article 38(1)(c) of the ICJ Statute. These themes, prominent in his individual opinions at the Court, were also reflected in academic works published contemporaneously.

One of the most important examples is his article 'From International Law to World Law', originally written in French in 1964 and translated into Japanese three years later. Here, as in his earlier work from 1958, Tanaka argued that the recognition of general principles of law as the third source of international law introduced a 'non-positivistic element' into the legal framework. This, he claimed, represented 'a remarkable concession made by the positivist school in favour of natural law'. Tanaka further argued that, insofar as general principles of law are applied to international relations, they incorporate principles governing various fields of municipal law, thereby granting international law a world law character. He proposed that general principles of law enable a merging of national and international law, dismantling the traditional separation between the two.[73]

In his 1965 publication 'Law and Sovereignty', Tanaka revisited the idea that general principles of law could bridge the gap between national and international legal systems.[74] He specifically highlighted the Japanese

71 Ibid 298–299.

72 Ibid 300.

73 TANAKA Kotaro, 'Du droit international au droit mondial', in *Études juridiques offertes à Léon Julliot de la Morandière* (Dalloz 1964) 564–567.

74 TANAKA Kotaro, 'Japanese Law', in Arthur Larson et al. (eds), *Sovereignty within the Law* (Stevens & Sons 1965) 240–241.

legal system's inheritance of Western legal tradition, which he believed contributed to the formation of general principles and provided material for the development of world law. This line of argument marked a significant departure from his earlier view, which held that general principles of law merely filled substantive gaps in international law. In light of the development of his theory, Tanaka's new idea was revolutionary: it suggested that general principles could facilitate the combination of national and international law, as he also articulated in his 1966 dissenting opinion in the *South West Africa* case.

During his final years, Tanaka continued to develop these ideas, publishing three articles in English before collecting his previous work into two volumes of *Sequel to the Theory of World Law* in 1972.[75] One notable piece from this period was his 1971 article, 'The World Law Character of the International Court of Justice'. In it, Tanaka reiterated that general principles of law serve as the metaphysical foundation of positive rules of international law. He argued that treaties and customary law are merely 'detailed embodiments of the general principles of law in special circumstances' and that logically, general principles of law precede these other sources. Tanaka described general principles as 'universal principles inherent in the law as a whole or in each legal system – a sense that distinguishes between right and wrong – what we may call judicial truth or natural law'.[76]

This statement highlights a critical point in Tanaka's philosophy: while he seemed to equate general principles of law with natural law, he also acknowledged a distinction between the two. Shortly thereafter, however, it is acknowledged that 'while general principles of law can, of course, be distinguished from natural law, the latter constitutes a significant component of them'.[77] If one interprets this segment of the argument intrinsically, it seems that Tanaka suggested general principles of law equate to natural law because they encompass non-positivistic elements, grounded in the dichotomy between state-will-centric positivism and natural law. Regardless of whether this interpretation is accurate, this nuanced view illustrates a tension in Tanaka's thinking about the relationship between natural law and general principles of law.

The complexity of Tanaka's ideas on this topic may reflect a naive understanding of the relationship between natural law and general principles of

75 TANAKA Kotaro, *Sequel to the Theory of World Law*, 2 vols (Yuhikaku 1972). This collection of papers includes translations into Japanese of articles that Tanaka authored in foreign languages during this period.

76 TANAKA Kotaro, 'The Character of World Law in the International Court of Justice' (1971) 15 *Japanese Annual of International Law* 21.

77 Ibid.

law. He seemed to simplify the connection between the two, particularly when referencing Pope John XXIII's encyclical *Pacem in Terris* (1963). According to Tanaka, taking a natural law approach to general principles of law provided a strong theoretical foundation. He argued that 'if one accepts that imperfect positive international law must be supplemented by natural law, or that natural law underlies positive law, or even that positive law is a manifestation or embodiment of natural law, then giving confidence to legal arguments'.[78]

For Tanaka, general principles of law were essential to grounding international law in natural law, forming the basis of his world law theory. He confirmed his commitment to this position in his later years. In his congratulatory address at the Japanese Society of International Law's seventy-fifth-anniversary conference in 1972, he introduced general principles as 'the prerequisite for the realisation of world peace'.[79] In his post-war contributions, Tanaka thus emphasised the role of general principles not only as gap-fillers in international law but as a means of bridging international and national legal systems within the framework of world law.

However, while Tanaka's ideas were groundbreaking in many respects, they also faced certain limitations. His relatively simplistic understanding of the relationship between natural law and general principles prevented him from fully exploring the depth of this connection, and the debate was not taken further. Tanaka passed away on 1 March 1974 at the age of eighty-three, leaving behind a complex yet not fully developed theory regarding the intersection of natural law and general principles of law.

## Echoes of silence: intellectual isolation and the absence of engaged dialogues

In summing up the lines of argument explored earlier, one key conclusion emerges: Tanaka's conception of international law, particularly as articulated in his world law theory, was ultimately unfinished. While his theory was initially developed to address the unification of legal systems, it never fully matured in the interwar period, particularly with respect to international law. Even after the Second World War, when Tanaka sought

78 TANAKA Kotaro, 'International Society and Natural Law (Dialogue)' (1964) 169 *Century: Journal of Catholic Thought* 31.

79 TANAKA Kotaro, 'Congratulatory Address on the Seventy-Fifth Anniversary of the Founding of the Japanese Association of International Law' (1972) 71 *Journal of International Law and Diplomacy* 696.

to expand the scope of his theory and apply it practically at the ICJ, the conception of international law within his world law framework remained underdeveloped.

Tanaka's emphasis on natural law as a foundation for international law – something he believed was necessary after the Great War – was linked to his idea that general principles of law could fill gaps in positive law. However, he was unable to sufficiently conceive the role of general principles in relation to natural law. Ultimately, the post-war expansion of his theory was more about broadening the range of issues considered in world law than about deepening the theory itself. In other words, Tanaka's post-war work often sought to refine what he had previously sketched, but it did not transform his theory into a coherent, systematic framework.

This lack of depth can largely be attributed to Tanaka's focus on the essential, philosophical foundations of international law, rather than its specific institutions and structures. Despite his assertion that legal studies require both analytical and integrative approaches,[80] Tanaka himself rarely engaged in the kind of detailed, analytical research that might have strengthened his theoretical contributions to international law. He did not systematically examine international legal structures or principles as part of legal studies.

Finally, an important question is the extent to which Tanaka's world law theory and his concept of international law were received, both domestically and internationally. One striking point is the apparent lack of recognition Tanaka received from Japanese international lawyers. While some colleagues acknowledged learning from his work, particularly from his *Theory of World Law*,[81] there were no detailed reviews of the book by international lawyers, nor was it widely referenced in the discipline.[82] Even scholars who engaged with the concept of world law often failed to mention Tanaka's contributions to or its significance in the scholarship.[83]

There are several potential explanations for this neglect. One reason is that Tanaka's primary field of expertise was commercial law. Despite his

80 TANAKA, 'Jurisprudence (fin.)' 73–75 (n 9).

81 See, for example, TAKANO, 'On the Launch of Proceedings of the World Law Research Association/World Law Association' 38 (n 4).

82 Cf. Kevin M. Doak, 'Beyond International Law: The Theories of World Law in Tanaka Kotaro and Tsuneto Kyo' (2011) 13 *Journal of the History of International Law* 209–234.

83 See, for example, OHFUCHI Niuemon, 'The Road from International Law to World Law', in *Collected Papers Celebrating Thirty-Fifth Anniversary of Ritsumeikan*, vol. 2: Law and Economics (Ritsumeikan-Shuppan 1935) 81–98; OHIRA Zengo, 'From International Law to World Law' (1946) 45 *Journal of International Law and Diplomacy* 265–290; YASUI Kaoru, *World, International and Domestic Law: Recognition of the Present Stage of the Development of International Law* (s.n. 1937).

later role as a judge at the ICJ, he was not regarded as an international lawyer. For instance, Yokota, one of Tanaka's long-time associates, noted that while he deeply respected Tanaka, he did not consider him an international lawyer, emphasising Tanaka's background in commercial law and jurisprudence.[84]

Another reason for Tanaka's lack of interlocutors in Japan could be the state of Japanese international legal scholarship at the time. While Tanaka's approach to international law was grounded in natural law, scholarship in Japan had matured under the influence of legal positivism, particularly through the work of scholars like TACHI Sakutaro. This positivist tradition, carried forward by figures such as Yokota, TAOKA Ryoichi and TABATA Shigejiro, dominated the discipline during Tanaka's lifetime. Even debates about general principles of law, which Tanaka discussed extensively, were framed within the positivist tradition, as evidenced by the so-called 'Yokota–Taoka debate'.[85] Given the positivist focus of Japanese international legal scholarship, Tanaka's natural law-based arguments – which sometimes presupposed the existence of God – found little resonance.[86] Throughout his life, Tanaka focused on discussions such as the 1920 Advisory Committee of Jurists debate on whether general principles of law were part of international law or natural law. However, in a scholarship where positivism had firmly taken root, there was little room for Tanaka's theory of natural international law.[87]

84 YOKOTA Kisaburo, 'In Memory of Dr Tanaka' (1974) 27(5) *Kokoro: A Literary Magazine* 106–108. In an article on the history of international legal scholarship in Japan, Yokota highlights theoretical research on the nature of international law as one of the characteristics of international legal studies during the interwar period. However, only the works of OHSAWA Akira of Kyushu Imperial University and Yokota's own work are mentioned in that context, with no reference to Tanaka's writings. YOKOTA Kisaburo, 'International Legal Scholarship in Our Country', *Tokyo Imperial University Academic Overview: Faculty of Law and Faculty of Economics* (Tokyo Imperial University 1942) 244–245. See also, SOGAWA Takeo and MATSUDA Takeo, 'International Law Studies in the Interwar Period' (1978) 50(13) *Horitsu-Jiho* 51–66.

85 MURASE Shinya, 'Studies on the Sources of International Law in Japan' (1997) 96 *Journal of International Law and Diplomacy* 736.

86 Although not an international lawyer, it is noteworthy that a criminal lawyer has critiqued Tanaka's natural law theory for its medieval elements, specifically the invocation of God's existence in the argument. In his review of *Theory of World Law*, he argued that from the perspective of empirical and scientific analysis, one should be cautious about unnecessarily invoking God. MAKINO Eiichi, *Evolutionary and Universal Aspects in Law* (Yuhikaku 1937) 172.

87 However, considering that contemporary scholars, including Yokota, highly valued the theoretical aspects of OHSAWA Akira's work – who was Tanaka's high school

Despite this absence of engaged dialogue in Japan, Tanaka was relatively active on the international stage. He wrote more articles in foreign languages and delivered more lectures abroad than many of his contemporaries. His international communications were often linked to his career as Chief Justice of the Supreme Court and his later role at the ICJ. Even during his interwar years as a professor of commercial law, he spent time in Italy from December 1935 to October 1936 as an exchange professor and delivered a lecture in Paris titled 'L'idée du droit mondial'.[88] Despite only three years having passed since the publication of his book on the subject, Tanaka was pleased with the reception of his lecture, firmly believing 'it had stimulated the European academic circle'.[89]

However, this self-assessment is questionable. While his dissenting opinion in the *South West Africa* case attracted significant international attention and was examined in detail,[90] his subsequent works did not receive the same level of engagement.[91] His post-ICJ contributions were largely based on his judicial experience, touching on a range of topics, from judicial independence and peace to human rights and the invalidity of treaties that conflict with *jus cogens*. Ultimately, these late-career essays merely expanded

---

classmate and developed a natural law theory rooted in Catholic theology – it may be premature to conclude that natural international law itself was undervalued. This issue will be examined in a separate paper through a comparative analysis of the arguments between the two naturalists. See OHSAWA Akira, *Theory of International Legal Order: The Legal Status of International Law within a Unified Legal Order* (Iwanami Shoten 1931).

88 TANAKA Kotaro, 'Une esquisse d'une théorie de droit mondial', (1938) 3 *Annales de l'Institut de Droit Comparé de l'Université de Paris* 303–315. He also delivered approximately ten lectures in Italy addressing fundamental issues in legal philosophy and commercial law. The content of these lectures was 'published across all relevant specialised journals', including *Rivista internazionale di filosofia del diritto* and *Rivista del diritto commerciale e del diritto generale delle obbligazioni*, facilitated by the efforts of figures such as Del Vecchio, the Dean of the Faculty of Law at the University of Rome. On lectures and articles, see, TANAKA Kotaro Private Papers, Part II, 1(2), 10 (n 59).

89 Ibid.

90 See, for example, Richard Falk, 'The South West Africa Cases: An Appraisal' (1967) 21 *International Organization* 1–23; Rosalyn Higgins, 'The Identity of International Law', in Bin Cheng (ed.), *International Law Teaching and Practice* (Stevens & Sons 1982) 28–31; Patrick Thornberry, *International Law and the Rights of Minorities* (Oxford University Press 1991) 314–318.

91 TANAKA Kotaro, 'Some Observations on Peace, Law, and Human Rights' in Wolfgang Friedmann et al. (eds), *Transnational Law in a Changing Society: Essays in Honour of Philip C Jessup* (Columbia University Press 1972) 242–256; TANAKA Kotaro, 'Independence of International Judges' in Roberto Ago et al. (eds), *Il processo internazionale Zusatz: Studi in onore di Gaetano Morelli* (Giuffrè 1975) 855–872.

the scope of his earlier discussions and did not lead to a more systematic engagement with world law as a unified theory.

In the end, Tanaka's arguments on international law were hindered by his simplistic dichotomy between subjectivist positivism and natural law. This framework complicated his efforts to establish a natural law foundation for international law through general principles of law. However, this cannot be attributed solely to the limitations of his conceptual imagination; it must also be recognised that it stems from the inherent nature of natural law theory, which is grounded in epistemological assumptions about the 'community', or, in Tanaka's terms, 'worldview'.[92] Consequently, Tanaka's conception of international law as world public law has not gained traction within Japanese post-war international legal scholarship, which has remained reluctant to actively engage with such a 'worldview', despite its own alignment with a particular worldview.

92 See Geoff Gordon, 'Natural Law in International Legal Theory: Linear and Dialectical Presentations', in Anne Orford and Florian Hoffmann (eds), *The Oxford Handbook of the Theory of International Law* (Oxford University Press 2016) 279–305.

# 6

# TABATA Shigejiro: Japan's leading authority in the twentieth century on international law and its history

*KANETAKE Machiko*

## Introduction

As an undergraduate student of international law, I read Shigejiro Tabata's work with much admiration. Such admiration must have multiple sources. It must be not only due to the large volume and density of his work *per se*, but also owing to the prevailing epistemic assumption of the time that Tabata was one of the 'leading authorities' of international legal scholarship in Japan and that you were expected to study his work, should you wish to do some research in this field. In a society with so many levels of formal and informal hierarchy, I duly consulted Tabata's work, assuming it was important to read. I indeed found some of his books, including *The Idea of World Government** (1950)[1] and *Human Rights Issues in the Age of Internationalisation* (1988),[2] fascinating. At the same time, I wish I had kept some distance from the sociologically embedded idea of who was supposed to be the field's leading intellectual authority, in order to allow more critical space for myself and others to learn from his scholarship. Now, after many years of studying and working in international law, I am still not sure whether I have succeeded in maintaining a critical eye towards his scholarship, although I will try in this chapter.

Shigejiro Tabata (1911–2001) has, for much of the twentieth century, been regarded as one of the most influential legal scholars in international law in Japan. After graduating in 1934 from the Faculty of Law at Kyoto Imperial University, Tabata quickly climbed the academic ladder, being appointed as a lecturer in 1936, associate professor in 1938 and full professor in 1945

* The Japanese titles of books and articles are translated by the author.

1 TABATA Shigejiro, *Sekai seifu no shiso* (*The Idea of World Government*) (Iwanami Shoten 1950).

2 TABATA Shigejiro, *Kokusaika jidai no jinken mondai* (*Human Rights Issues in the Age of Internationalization*) (Iwanami Shoten 1988).

at his alma mater.[3] Apart from his professorship at Kyoto University, he assumed various representative or advisory roles at diplomatic conferences and legal proceedings.[4] Among many leadership roles in academia, Tabata served as president of the Japan Branch of the International Law Association. Tabata was also the first president of the Japanese Association of World Law. Tabata has established himself as a prolific writer on international law, having published more than twenty books as well as a large number of articles and commentaries. Through these writings, he came to be seen as a scholar eager to express his own philosophical views on international law and legal scholarship. His interests centred on understanding the historical and political considerations that shaped international law and its theories.

This chapter aims to introduce a fraction of Tabata's writings on international law. Given that Tabata's scholarship is vast in volume, the chapter is by no means designed to provide any overview of his contribution. The chapter will begin with an analysis of Tabata's writings published during the Second Sino-Japanese War and the Pacific War, in which Japan invaded many Asian-Pacific countries. I believe that it is important to start with a consideration of his 'wartime' literature – which I was not exposed to during my university studies – because such literature undoubtedly forms part of the 'histories of international legal theories in Japan' used as the theme of the present edited volume. As explained below, some of Tabata's wartime works did not escape the influence of Japan's nationalistic militarism. This leads me to address Tabata's studies on the equality of states and the doctrines of recognition in international law. The chapter then outlines his literature on the status of individuals in international law and his dedication to advancing scholarship on international human rights. The chapter further investigates Tabata's contribution to diplomatic conferences and litigation practices, including his expert opinion in the 1963 *Shimoda* case before the Tokyo District Court. Finally, the chapter refers to his iconic piece entitled *The Idea of World Government*. By introducing some of Tabata's scholarship, this chapter concludes with some characteristics common to his scholarship.

## Earlier and wartime literature

Tabata's first analytical piece was published in 1935 by the *Kyoto Law Review*, concerning the exclusion of so-called 'political disputes' from

3 ISHIMOTO Yasuo, 'Dr. Shigejiro TABATA (1911–2001)' (2001) 44 *Japanese Annual of International Law* 1–4.

4 Ibid 3.

international adjudication.[5] Tabata considered the extent to which the 'political' nature of international disputes might prevent international courts and tribunals from exercising their adjudicative functions, which was one of the classic issues concerning the scope of international dispute settlement. In this article, Tabata argued that we cannot make sense of the distinction between 'legal' and 'political' disputes (and academic debates concerning such a distinction) without considering the political tensions surrounding a particular international dispute.[6] This earliest publication already demonstrates Tabata's iconic analytical steps. Namely, he was interested in examining the structural considerations behind ostensibly legalistic arguments and primarily engaged with theories written in German, French and English by scholars based in Europe and the US. After this publication, in 1936–1938, Tabata produced a series of journal articles concerning the status of individuals under international law, which I will touch upon later.

While Tabata was busy writing a series of academic articles, the political climate in Japan was shifting further towards nationalistic militarism. It is not the purpose of this chapter to analyse the Second Sino-Japanese War and the Asia-Pacific front of the Second World War, but the Japanese military's invasions, occupation, forced labour, sexual slavery and mass killings altered and devastated many parts of Asia and the Pacific. What matters for the sake of this chapter is that Tabata's academic work during the war was affected by, and in fact ended up advocating, a facet of the Japanese war propaganda. Perhaps it was not surprising that Tabata, then an associate professor of Kyoto Imperial University, was influenced by, or deferential to, the imperial war policies, although he was certainly not the only one.[7] Illustrative in this regard is Tabata's article published in 1943 regarding the 'international legal scholarship of Nazi Germany'.[8] In this article, Tabata gave a nuanced appreciation of the scholarship, on the basis that it formed part of 'pluralism' in the international legal order in revising 'monotonous

5 TABATA Shigejiro, 'Exclusion of Political Disputes in International Adjudication: A Study of Its Actual Significance (Kokusai Saiban ni okeru Seijiteki Hunso no Jogai ni tsuite: Sono Genjitsu-eki Imi no Kosatsu)' (1935) 33 *Hogaku Ronso* 803–829. Before this publication, TABATA published a review of the work of Georges Scelle in (1934) 31 *Hogaku Ronso*.

6 Ibid.

7 For analysis, AKASHI Kinji, '"Daitōa kokusaihō" riron: Nihon ni okeru kindai kokusaihō juyō no kiketsu (The Modern Law of Nations and the "Greater East Asia Co-prosperity Sphere")' (2009) 82(1) *Journal of Law, Politics, and Sociology* 261–292.

8 TABATA Shigejiro, 'Natis kokusaihō gaku no tenkai to sono mondai teki igi (International Legal Scholarship of Nazi Germany and Its Problems and Their Significance)' (1943) 107(1) *Gaiho Jiho* 5–17.

universalism'.[9] Needless to say, it is hard to imagine this 'scholarly' observation without the political context of the time and the alliance between Nazi Germany and Imperial Japan.

In the summer of 1944, Tabata published his first monograph, *The Transformation of the Concept of the Equality of States*.[10] At one level, this book is an eloquently written piece on the historical development of the context of the equality of states and the notions of equality developed by a range of European and US scholars. Based on historical and conceptual investigation, Tabata problematised the principle of the equality of states under modern international law. In his view, the principle contained 'fundamental difficulties' as a 'regulatory principle of international society'.[11] He argued that such a principle effectively facilitated unequal relations among states and allowed states to engage in arbitrary activities.[12] At another level, however, this book made a claim which was intertwined with one of Japan's wartime ideologies. Such an ideology was the concept of the 'Greater East Asia Co-Prosperity Sphere' (*dai tōa kyōeiken* in Japanese), with which Imperial Japan asserted its military advancements into East and Southeast Asia. Such a wartime claim was partly influenced by claims such as the Monroe doctrine, and by the theory of a 'large space' (*kōiki*; 'Großraum' in German) developed by Carl Schmitt.[13]

For the sake of this chapter, it suffices to say that the story of the Greater East Asia Co-Prosperity Sphere remains contested, partly depending on who gets to speak about its concept and consequences. According to Jeremy A. Yellen, a historian who has written a book about this subject, the Co-Prosperity Sphere had two broad dimensions. On the one hand, it was the story of 'Japan's revolt against the older order and attempt to build Asia anew'[14] by advocating the 'end of imperialism and colonialism'.[15] In the emerging total war, the Co-Prosperity Sphere 'became the focus of a process by which military and civilian elites imagined a new order in international politics, one that asserted Japanese leadership over the expanse of Greater East Asia under the guise of "Asian liberation"'.[16] On the other hand, how-

9 TABATA Shigejiro, 'International Legal Scholarship of Nazi Germany' 16–17 (n 8).

10 TABATA Shigejiro, *Kokka byōdō kannen no tenkan* (*The Transformation of the Concept of the Equality of States*) (Nihon Gaisei Kyōkai 1944; Akitaya 1946).

11 Ibid 56.

12 Ibid.

13 AKASHI 266 (n 7).

14 Jeremy A Yellen, *The Greater East Asia Co-Prosperity Sphere: When Total Empire Met Total War* (Cornell University Press 2019) 5.

15 Ibid 206.

16 Ibid 207–208.

ever, as the war progressed, the Co-Prosperity Sphere 'took on a distinctly *imperial* cast', and, by 1942, 'political intellectuals and politicians alike reimagined it as a political-economic hierarchy of nations and territories under Japanese leadership'.[17] 'Despite the promise of a new and inclusive Pan-Asian order' as part of Japan's imperial dreams, 'Japan delivered little more than war, oppression, control, cruelty, and hardship'.[18] Interestingly, the idea of the Sphere continued after the end of the Pacific War. According to Yellen, this was partly because of the Greater East Asia Conference of November 1943, in which Japan – apparently contrary to its actions in the Asia-Pacific – put forward 'a new commitment to liberal internationalist ideals of independence, equality, and cooperative regionalism'.[19]

Returning to the analysis of Tabata's book of 1944, I would argue that Tabata was one of many 'intellectuals' who paradoxically imagined the Co-Prosperity Sphere as both the sphere of 'cooperative internationalism'[20] and as a 'political-economic hierarchy of nations and territories under Japanese leadership'.[21] According to Tabata, the equality of states within the 'co-prosperity sphere' should not be based on the absolute equality of states. Instead, the relationships should be built on 'relative equality'.[22] In the view of Tabata, the 'values (*rinen*) of the co-prosperity sphere' serve as a yardstick for determining the relative legal status of states within the sphere.[23] In the co-prosperity sphere, however, there is still a 'leading state'.[24] While Tabata argued that the 'leading state' was also subject to the 'values of the co-prosperity sphere',[25] Tabata's 1944 book took it for granted that 'our country should be the leading state of the East Asia co-prosperity sphere'.[26]

As Tetsuya Sakai rightly observed, there is a clear contradiction in the reasoning of Tabata and other scholars who academically supported the rationale of the co-prosperity sphere. Namely, the idea of such a sphere

17 Ibid 206.
18 Ibid 206.
19 Ibid 208.
20 Borrowing the words of Yellen (ibid 208). Yellen's book does not analyse TABATA's work, however.
21 Borrowing the words of Yellen (ibid 206).
22 TABATA, 'The Transformation of the Concept of the Equality of States' 60 (n 10).
23 TABATA (1944) 60 (n 10).
24 This idea of a 'leading state' in the co-prosperity sphere was commonly discussed by legal scholars during the war: AKASHI 269–271 (n 7).
25 SAKAI Tetsuya, 'Kokusai kankeiron no seiritsu to kokusai hōgaku–Nihon kindai-shi kenkyū kara no ichikōsatsu (The Establishment of International Relations Theories and International Legal Scholarship: A Study from Modern Japanese History Studies)' (2003) 22 *Sekaiho Nenpo* 95–106.
26 TABATA, 'International Legal Scholarship of Nazi Germany' 3 (n 10).

denies mechanical sovereign equality in order to ensure a better 'freedom' of the region, while, at the same time, using the concept to defend the role of the 'leading state' in the region.[27] While Tabata's work was a product of wartime indoctrination, a large part of his 1944 book could easily be read as a 'usual' scholarly piece on the equality of states. In this sense, his 1944 book illustrates that wartime nationalism was deeply embedded in academic writings of the time.

Interestingly, Tabata's post-war writings continued to engage with the general idea of a legal order based on a 'large space' (*kōiki*). He no longer made any explicit reference to the Greater East Asia, however. His writings instead imagined the 'large space' as a sphere for 'cooperative internationalism', in the words of Yellen.[28] We can see this continued yet revised version of his idea in Tabata's articles entitled 'The Pluralistic Structure of the International Legal Order' published in 1947–1948. According to Tabata, the evaluation of the 'large-space orders' (*kōikiken*) depends on one's conceptualisation of international law. For some, such a 'space-based' order is not permissible, precisely because they characterise the international legal order as 'universally unified'. For others, however, large-space orders are possible because the international legal order is understood as pluralistic.[29] Perhaps not surprisingly, Tabata supported the latter position that international law was pluralistic and accommodated a set of special rules applicable to a given area. According to Tabata, the fact that some of the abstract and formalistic rules are commonly applicable does not mean that modern international law is a 'truly unified order'. The international legal order is rather based on a 'pluralistic structure' that accommodates the existence of special legal orders that are premised on a variety of legal values.[30]

Having reviewed some of Tabata's 'wartime' writings, I should probably add that, after the end of the Second World War, Tabata quickly endorsed the mechanism of the Tokyo Trial that prosecuted individuals on the basis of international crimes, including the crime against peace. In his short article on the Tokyo Trial, Tabata advocated that the war crimes tribunal

27 SAKAI, 'The Establishment of International Relations Theories and International Legal Scholarship' 99 (n 25).

28 Borrowing the words of Yellen (ibid 208). Yellen's book does not analyse TABATA's work, however.

29 TABATA Shigejiro, 'Kokusaihō chitsujono tayūtekikōsei (ichi) (The Pluralistic Structure of the International Legal Order (Part One))' (1947) 47(3) *Kyoto Law Review* 382–402.

30 TABATA Shigejiro, 'Kokusaihō chitsujono tayūtekikōsei (san, kan) (The Pluralistic Structure of the International Legal Order (Part Three))' (1948) 48(6) *Kyoto Law Review* 908–934.

prosecute individuals, despite apparent legal difficulties. In the words of Tabata, 'under absolutist political institutions such as those in Japan, it is not surprising that all responsibility is placed on those who planned, prepared, and launched the war of aggression'.[31] Tabata observed that denying individual criminal responsibility would prevent the locus of responsibility from being identified.[32]

## Recognition of states

As epitomised by Tabata's aforementioned book published in 1944, Tabata had a broad interest in the theory and practice of the equality of states under international law. For example, Tabata has analysed the writings of Hugo Grotius through the lens of the equality of states. According to Tabata, while Grotius made significant contributions to the foundations of international law in terms of suggesting a set of restrictions on the freedom of states on the basis of natural law, Grotius should not be understood as having conceptualised the equality of states in international law.[33]

In connection with his work on the equality of states, Tabata was also interested in the role of recognising a new state. In his separate writing on the recognition of states, published in 1943, Tabata analysed not only the legal status of the recognition of states in itself, but also the 'implications of the [very] fact that the recognition of [a] state was accepted as a mechanism under general international law'.[34] On the basis of the analysis of different scholarly views, Tabata criticised the constitutive theory of recognition. He did so essentially based on the logical consequence of the theory to reduce international law to relations between individual states. According to Tabata, the constitutive theory was not consistent with general international law, given that 'it should have been a logically natural demand to recognise the existence of some form of international law *prior* to the recognition of a state'.[35] In the view of Tabata, 'general international law is fundamentally

31 TABATA Shigejiro, 'Tokyo saiban no hōri (The Jurisprudence of the Tokyo Trial)' (1949) 42 *Sekai* 12–20.

32 Ibid.

33 TABATA Shigejiro, 'Gurochūsu to kokka byōdō (Grotius and the Equality of States)' (1950) 50(5–6) *Kyoto Law Review* 416–440.

34 TABATA Shigejiro, 'Kokka shōnin to sono mondai (san, kan) (State Recognition and Its Issues (Part Three))' (1943) 43(1) *Kyoto Law Review* 86–111.

35 Ibid 90 (emphasis added by the author).

applicable beyond the effect of state recognition', and unrecognised states were the 'subjects [*juhansha*] of general international law'.[36]

What would then be the legal effect of an act of recognition? According to Tabata, recognition should be characterised as a means by which states establish rights and obligations applicable among them, as if they had concluded a treaty.[37] In that sense, Tabata did not see the recognition of states as a unilateral act. Instead, to Tabata, the recognition of states should be logically understood as a mutual act, which, in theory, entitles newly emerged states to explicitly deny the act of recognition by another state.[38] Although I must acknowledge that it is difficult to imagine any circumstances in which state recognition is denied by the recipient of the recognition, Tabata's overall claim was that the recognition of states should not be discussed solely as a matter of the *legal personality* of states.[39] Tabata emphasised the need to pay much more attention to the specific rights and obligations that new states enjoy under international law.

## Status of individuals in international law

Beyond the personality and equality of states, Tabata's longstanding interests lie in the status of individuals in international law. In 1936–1938, he published a series of journal articles regarding the legal personality of individuals under international law,[40] the relevance of individuals in international adjudication,[41] state responsibility in connection to private conduct[42] and the meaning of individuals as subjects of international law.[43] Tabata

36 Ibid 91. Similarly, ibid 94.
37 Ibid 108–109.
38 Ibid 110.
39 Ibid 111.
40 TABATA Shigejiro, 'Kojin no kokusai hō shutai-sei ni kansuru ronsō ni tsuite (ichi) (On Controversy regarding the Status of Individuals as Subjects of International Law (Part One))' (1936) 35(4) *Kyoto Law Review*; TABATA Shigejiro, 'Kojin no kokusai hō shutai-sei ni kansuru ronsō ni tsuite (ni-kan) (On Controversy regarding the Status of Individuals as Subjects of International Law (Part Two))' (1937) 36(2) *Kyoto Law Review*.
41 TABATA Shigejiro, 'Individual Litigation and International Litigation (Kojin sōshō to kokusai sōshō) Part One' (1937) 37(3) *Kyoto Law Review*; Part Two (1937) 37(4) *Kyoto Law Review*.
42 TABATA Shigejiro, 'State Responsibility in International Law for the Conduct of Private Actors (Shijin kōi ni yoru kokka no kokusai sekinin) Part One' (1939) 39(5) *Kyoto Law Review*; Part Two (1939) 39(6) *Kyoto Law Review*.
43 TABATA Shigejiro, 'Kokusaihō juhansha toshite no kokka to kojin (ichi) (States and Individuals as Subjects of International Law (Part One))' (1938) 38(4) *Kokusaihō*

was interested in examining the historical significance of the increased relevance of individuals in the principles, rules and practices of international law. As an extension to these articles, Tabata has written separate pieces on the legal personality of minorities in international law.[44]

These earlier writings already manifest Tabata's iconic analytical style that made him a leading figure in the Japanese scholarly circle. He seems to have enjoyed unveiling some of the contextual factors that inform legal practices and related scholarly debates. For example, in his articles on the status of individuals as international legal subjects,[45] Tabata examined not only the typology of connections individuals have with international law, but also why some traditional theories had taken for granted the tenet that states were the only subjects of international law. According to Tabata, such an assumption had historical and ideological roots in the idea of absolute monarchy, which subjugated individuals to its control. Given that the idea and system of absolute monarchy played an important role in the formation of modern states, the traditional theories of international law had upheld the assumption that states and individuals should be fundamentally different in their status under international law. On this basis, Tabata appreciated the then-new theories of international law that began to recognise the legal status of individuals, precisely because such theories represented, according

*Gaikō Zassi* (*Journal of International Law and Diplomacy*); S. TABATA, 'Kokusaihō juhansha toshite no kokka to kōjin (ni) (States and Individuals as Subjects of International Law (Part Two))' (1938) 38(5) *Kokusaihō Gaikō Zassi* (*Journal of International Law and Diplomacy*); S. TABATA, 'Kokusaihō juhansha toshite no kokka to kōjin (san) (States and Individuals as Subjects of International Law (Part Three))' (1938) 38(6) *Kokusaihō Gaikō Zassi* (*Journal of International Law and Diplomacy*); S. TABATA, 'Kokusaihō juhansha toshite no kokka to kōjin (shi – kan) (States and Individuals as Subjects of International Law (Part Four – Conclusion))' (1938) 38(7) *Kokusaihō Gaikō Zassi* (*Journal of International Law and Diplomacy*).

44 TABATA, 'Shoyū shōsū minzoku no kokusaihō shutaisei ni tsuite (ichi) (On the Legal Personality of So-Called National Minorities in International Law (Part One))' (1938) 38(3) *Kyoto Law Review*; TABATA, 'Shoyū shōsū minzoku no kokusaihō shutaisei ni tsuite (ni) (On the Legal Personality of So-Called National Minorities in International Law (Part Two))' (1938) 38(3) *Kyoto Law Review*; TABATA, 'Shoyū shōsū minzoku no kokusaihō shutaisei ni tsuite (san) (On the Legal Personality of So-Called National Minorities in International Law (Part Three))' (1938) 38(3) *Kyoto Law Review*.

45 TABATA, 'Kojin no kokusai hō shutai-sei ni kansuru ronsō ni tsuite (ichi) (On Controversy regarding the Status of Individuals as Subjects of International Law (Part One))' (1936) 35(4) *Kyoto Law Review* 886–927; TABATA, 'Kojin no kokusai hō shutai-sei ni kansuru ronsō ni tsuite (ni-kan) (On Controversy regarding the Status of Individuals as Subjects of International Law (Part Two))' (1937) 36(2) *Kyoto Law Review* 288–333.

to Tabata, a sign of 'value transformation' regarding states and their connection to individuals.[46]

Tabata's fascination with the role of individuals in international law is also evident in writings on diplomatic protection, among others. Having examined the historical development of diplomatic protection, Tabata acknowledged that under existing international law, diplomatic protection was state-centric and that it was up to the state of nationality to decide whether and how diplomatic protection would be exercised.[47] Tabata's claim – characteristic of his analytical approach to put the status quo in a historical context – was that the state-centric characteristic was the historical product of mercantilism in the seventeenth and eighteenth centuries and, as such, was subject to further changes.[48] As the structure of states has undergone changes in such a manner that states' positions are no longer equated with those of individuals therein, the state-based conceptualisation of diplomatic protection was 'designed to be denied', according to Tabata's paradigm.[49]

In connection with these lines of scholarship, Tabata has also written extensively on human rights under international law. For example, he published a book on *Human Rights and International Law* in 1952.[50] Tabata also introduced, in his 1956 article, the role of the UN, including the Commission on Human Rights, in promoting international human rights and analysed the tensions among states within the UN.[51] That being said, one of the most widely read texts of Tabata in the domain of human rights is his book on *Human Rights Issues in the Age of Internationalization* published in 1988.[52] In this book, Tabata analysed the development of international human rights law according to the three generations of human rights, and explained the importance of, and challenges associated with, the third generation of human rights.

46 TABATA, 'Part Two' (1937) (n 45) 332.S. TABATA, 'Part Two' (1937) 332 (n 45).

47 TABATA, 'Gaikō-teki hogo no kinō henka (ni, kan) (The Changes in the Functions of Diplomatic Protection (Part Two – Conclusion))' (1953) 53(1–2) *Kyoto Law Review* 393–414; S. TABATA, 'Gaikō-teki hogo no kinō henka (ni, kan) (The Changes in the Functions of Diplomatic Protection (Part Two – Conclusion))' (1953) 53(1–2) *Kyoto Law Review* 393–414.

48 TABATA, 'Diplomatic Protection (2)' (1953) 404 (n 47), 411–412.

49 TABATA, 'Diplomatic Protection (2)' (1953) 412 (n 47).

50 TABATA, *Jinken to kokusaihō* (*Human Rights and International Law*) (Nippon Hyoron Shinsha 1952).

51 TABATA Shigejiro, 'The United Nations and Human Rights Issues' (1956) 55(2–4) *Kokusaihō Gaikō Zassi* (*Journal of International Law and Diplomacy*) 364–385. TABATA, *Human Rights Issues* (1988) (n 2).

52 TABATA, *Human Rights Issues* (1988) (n 2).

## Opinions concerning the *Shimoda* case

As noted at the beginning of this chapter, Tabata was also involved in diplomatic conferences and legal proceedings during his career. One of the noteworthy instances in this regard was his testimony in the *Shimoda* case (1963) before the Tokyo District Court.[53] In this case, the Japanese victims of the atomic bombs brought action against the state (Japan), claiming damages for the dropping of atomic bombs, which the plaintiffs argued were contrary to international law. The plaintiffs further argued that the state had an obligation to pay damages to the plaintiffs, whose claims for damages against the US (as part of the Allied Powers) were waived by Article 19(a) of the Treaty of Peace with Japan.[54] The Tokyo District Court dismissed the plaintiffs' claims, on the basis that, on the one hand, individuals in this case did not have specific rights under international law to bring claims for damages, and, on the other hand, individuals cannot resort to domestic court proceedings against the US for its actions due to state immunity.[55] Despite the result of this case, the *Shimoda* case still drew attention, in part because the Tokyo District Court observed that the dropping of the atomic bombs 'may be regarded as contrary to the fundamental principle of the law of war which prohibits the causing of unnecessary suffering'.[56]

The Court's observation with regard to the aforementioned points was largely the view expressed by Tabata, who, at the request of the state, provided his testimony during the proceedings as an expert.[57] Tabata was requested to answer a series of questions, including whether the dropping of atomic bombs in Nagasaki and Hiroshima constituted a violation of international law, whether such an action was contrary to the domestic law of Japan and the US, whether the victims who were not combatants possessed the right to claim for damages under international law and whether such a claim can be sought at the domestic level.

In his testimony, Tabata argued that, in the light of the rules of international law regulating aerial bombardment:

> considering that both Hiroshima and Nagasaki were so-called undefended cities at that time, it is necessary to conclude that the use of atomic bombs, which

53 *Ryuichi Shimoda v. The State*, 14(12) Kaminshu 2435, 32 ILR 626 (District Court of Tokyo, 7 December 1963).

54 *Ryuichi Shimoda v. The State*, ibid 626–627 (ILR Report).

55 Ibid 638.

56 Ibid 634.

57 TABATA, 'Testimony' (5 April 1962), available at https://www.hankaku-j.org/shimoda/tokyo02.html (in Japanese) (accessed 29 July 2024).

> have the effect of destroying everything indiscriminately, without distinguishing between military and non-military targets, was illegal.[58]

Furthermore, Tabata observed that the dropping of the atomic bombs was contrary to the principle of unnecessary suffering under the laws of war. According to Tabata's testimony, 'the dropping of the atomic bombs in Hiroshima and Nagasaki has led not only to the loss of many lives. Those who managed to escape death are still today living under a tragic fate and in danger of losing their lives, due to the effects of radiation'.[59] On this basis, Tabata concluded that the use of those weapons was contrary to the principle of unnecessary suffering. Importantly, Tabata confirmed that these principles under the laws of war also had a domestic legal effect in both the US and Japan and, therefore, that the dropping of the atomic bombs constituted a breach of domestic law as well.[60] At the same time, Tabata denied the procedural routes open to individuals. According to his testimony, the non-combatant victims of the unlawful conduct of hostilities are not entitled to seek compensation for damages, both internationally and domestically, unless there is a specific treaty or a piece of legislation to enable such proceedings.[61] As noted earlier, this is largely the reasoning that the Tokyo District Court in the *Shimoda* case provided in its judgment with regard to the violations of the laws of war and the right of individuals to seek compensation for damages. Neither the plaintiff nor the state appealed the judgment.

## The idea of world government

Returning once again to the sphere of Tabata's scholarly work, among the vast amount of literature Tabata has produced during his career, the book on *The Ideas of World Government*, published in 1950,[62] continues to occupy a special place among the circles of scholars who are familiar with Tabata's work. The book partly describes various ideas and initiatives that supported the establishment of a form of 'world government'. The book begins with an overview of the development of the ideas about world government before the Second World War and moves on to an in-depth analysis of several publications and initiatives developed during and shortly after

58 Ibid, 'Testimony' (1962) 4.
59 Ibid, 'Testimony' (1962) 22.
60 Ibid, 'Testimony' (1962) 23–30.
61 Ibid, 'Testimony' (1962) 30–42.
62 TABATA, *World Government* (1950) (n 1).

the Second World War. Tabata analysed, for instance, the ideas put forward by Emery Reves in *The Anatomy of Peace* (1945)[63] and Cord Meyer in *Peace or Anarchy* (1948).[64] Tabata also examined the 'Preliminary Draft of A World Constitution' released in 1948 by the Committee to Frame a World Constitution, based at the University of Chicago.[65] Tabata described a series of movements in the US, UK, France, Italy and Germany and explained some of the international initiatives that supported the idea and creation of world government.[66] Tabata compared a series of ideas and initiatives, particularly in terms of their rationale, content and plans to materialise an idea of world government.[67]

Having introduced a series of proposals and criticisms levelled against them, Tabata moved on to explain his own perspectives about the ideas of world government. In principle, Tabata was rather approval of the *motivations* for world government. In view of Tabata, while it is 'of course dangerous' to uncritically praise the ideas of world government, it is not appropriate either to dismiss the ideas entirely.[68] What matters for him was to clearly identify the pros and cons of the proposals, Tabata added.[69] In the eyes of Tabata, the ideas of world government featured an element of 'protest' against the 'flaws in the existing international legal order', which merit close examination.[70] There are many flaws in the existing legal order, owing to the existence of power asymmetries. While the UN has a collective security system, it relies upon states' provision of forces and is ineffective against powerful states, as Tabata pointed out.[71] In terms of aspirations, Tabata therefore expressed his 'endorsement' for the movement of world government:

> There is absolutely no room for opposition to the aims and objectives of the world government movement, and I think that, as world government advocates say, it is indeed necessary to create a world government based on the wills of the people of the world and to make efforts in the direction to

63 Emery Reves, *The Anatomy of Peace* (Penguin Books 1947).
64 Cord Meyer, *Peace or Anarchy* (Little, Brown 1948).
65 Committee to Frame a World Constitution, *Preliminary Draft of a World Constitution* (University of Chicago Press 1948).
66 TABATA, *World Government* (1950) 1–23 (n 1).
67 Ibid 25–158.
68 Ibid 187.
69 Ibid 187.
70 Ibid 186.
71 Ibid 188–190.

> completely eliminate war from the earth by the authority and military power of the world government.[72]

In particular, Tabata expressed his sympathy for the movement driven by the need to prevent a possible nuclear war.[73]

Despite such endorsement, Tabata was, overall, highly critical of the *existing proposals* for world government. What Tabata problematised most was that a series of proposals for world government were based on some 'abstract' understanding of the causes of war and the mechanisms of state sovereignty.[74] There is a question of the feasibility of establishing a world government,[75] but even leaving that aside, there is a conceptual problem, according to Tabata. He observed the following:

> If a world government were to be created under the current circumstances, it would probably be a world government that would leave behind, and namely solidify, various international and domestic contradictions, as well as a variety of contradictions that are overlooked owing to the abstract nature of the thinking of world government proponents, would, in a sense, freeze them in place.[76]

Tabata criticised here the world government proponents' tendency to place blame on the abstract notion of state sovereignty as a systematic problem. Each state's domestic structure and economic and political conditions are some of the significant factors in the state's decision to go to war, and Tabata highlighted the need for analysing the domestic governance structure of each state and its connection to wars, before casting an optimistic eye on a world government as a solution for world peace.[77] The Pacific War waged by Japan no doubt serves as a painstaking example here, although Tabata did not use this book as a site for reflecting on Japan's decisions to go to war in any detail.[78]

As part of the critiques of the existing proposals of world government, Tabata also referred to their implications for national independence movements in colonial territories:

72 Ibid 192.
73 Ibid 201.
74 Ibid 193.
75 Ibid 202.
76 Ibid 193.
77 Ibid 194–197.
78 See ibid 195 (a brief reference to the Pacific War).

> National independence movements in the colonies will be suppressed, and the current ruling relationship in the colonies will be reflected, as it is, in the world government. The problem of liberating the colonies from the ruling relationship is not a problem that can be easily solved in a short time and by only deliberations and discussions in a council, as the world government proponents argue.[79]

Tabata indicated that any world government which suppresses national liberation movements would not be able to achieve a durable peace. In short, Tabata argued that a world government, without addressing the existing 'power relations' at the domestic and international levels, would end up representing the interests of dominant classes and states.[80]

Many decades after its publication, Tabata's book *Ideas of World Government* is still a fascinating read, I must say. Tabata's book continues to be discussed in academic circles of international law in Japan. In fact, the annual conference of the Japanese Association of World Law in 2010 adopted the reflection of '60 years of "The Idea of World Government"' as a common conference theme, based on which a series of scholars discussed the implications of the idea of world government in the theories and practices of international law.[81]

In many respects, the book embodies Tabata's analytical styles and approaches, which I will also revisit in the concluding section. The book represents Tabata's skill in surveying existing writings on this topic, unpacking their logic and offering a typology to help readers make sense of the debates, before providing his own critical insights. In terms of perspectives with which critiques are raised, this book is also representative of Tabata's approach. One of the final sentences of the book embodies his perspective. He argued that 'the problem of realising a world government should not be limited to the narrow domain of simply realising a world government *organisation*'.[82] Instead, he argues, the realisation of world government 'bears a wide range of challenges across political and economic spheres'.[83] As illuminated by this sentence, it was Tabata's willingness to situate institutional and legal mechanisms in historical, political and economic contexts

79 Ibid 203.
80 Ibid 203, 207.
81 The Japanese Association of World Law, 2010 Annual Conference, 'Common Theme', https://www.jawl.jp/annualconf/2010summary.pdf (in Japanese) (accessed 29 July 2024); Yoshiro Matsui, '"Idea of World Government" and Its Relevance in the Age of Globalization' (2011) 30 *Yearbook of World Law* 109–147 (written in Japanese).
82 Ibid 217 (emphasis original).
83 Ibid 217.

that made his scholarship unique and highly influential in Japan's academic communities of international law.

## Conclusion

As mentioned at the beginning of this chapter, Tabata's scholarship is vast in volume and themes. This chapter touched upon merely a small segment of his scholarship to highlight some of his interests. In addition to the writings I mentioned in this chapter, Tabata has published, for instance, a series of general textbooks on public international law. In 1951, he released *International Law*,[84] followed by the series of *International Law* textbooks published in 1955–1957.[85] In 1968–1970, Tabata further wrote *Lectures on International Law*.[86] These textbooks must have been read by many students of international law in Japan, and the textbooks are usually the most effective medium through which scholars disseminate their knowledge and perspectives. While it is difficult to assess the impact of these textbooks, I assume they further affirmed the epistemic assumption that Tabata is a leading authority in international law.

Having revisited and discovered new writings of Tabata, I would like to share my observations regarding several prominent characteristics of his scholarship. I narrowed them down to the following five interrelated aspects. To begin with, I must admit that Tabata was extremely skilled in 'unpacking' underlying assumptions about legal principles, rules and practices. As far as I can see from his writings, Tabata was not particularly interested in simply describing what applicable rules were, but rather curious about how the rules emerged, why they were interpreted in a certain manner and what alternative interpretations could have meant for the development of international law and scholarship. In unpacking the contexts about law, Tabata did not hesitate to criticise what he perceived as a 'mainstream' reading of international law.

Second, and in relation to the first point, Tabata put a strong emphasis on the history of international law as a basis for his scholarship. It is hard to find texts by Tabata that do not include his explanations of the field's

84 TABATA, *Kokusaihō Ichi* (*International Law I*) (Yushindō 1951).

85 TABATA, *Kokusaihō joukan* (*International Law, Volume I*) (Yushindō 1955); S. TABATA, *Kokusaihō gekan* (*International Law, Volume II*) (Yushindō 1955); S. TABATA, *Kokusaihō* (*International Law*) (Iwanami Shoten 1956).

86 TABATA, *Kokusaihō kougi jou* (*Lectures on International Law, Volume I*) (Yushindō 1968); S. TABATA, *Kokusaihō kougi ge* (*Lectures on International Law, Volume II*) (Yushindō 1970).

historical context or specific topics. In terms of what he considered as relevant 'historical' contexts, Tabata's writings reminded us of how Eurocentric the construction of international law was (and is still largely) in terms of its historical roots. What Tabata's scholarship did was to help students and scholars in Japan learn more about the history of international law developed in Europe between the sixteenth and nineteenth centuries. In this vein, I must note that subsequent generations of scholars in Japan engaged with the critique of the Eurocentric understanding of the history of international law, and thus effectively the critique of Tabata's conceptualisation of international law, as illustrated by other chapters of this volume.[87]

Third, while Tabata's analytical approach was to contextualise law from historical perspectives, such an analytical yardstick was inapplicable, or at best ineffective, with regard to Tabata's own engagement with the co-prosperity sphere during wartime. As illustrated earlier, some of Tabata's writings did not keep a distance from the country's wartime propaganda and nationalistic mobilisation of intellectual resources. As an associate professor at Imperial Kyoto University, one could imagine there was little choice in his involvement in the imperial project of the time. To contemporary eyes, it is still striking to see the way Tabata combined his 'regular' scholarly analysis with his deference to the wartime nationalistic slogan. In his postwar writings on pluralism, he did not reflect on how such an idea politically supported Japanese military expansion. Continuing to remedy this omission should be a task for subsequent generations of international legal scholars in Japan.

Fourth, as it was clear from his earlier publications, Tabata had a linguistic command of analysing the texts of international law and international relations in German, French, Latin and English, which were presumably essential, not only for his study of the history of international law, but for the analysis of what he perceived as the 'mainstream' views about the different sub-topics of international law. In addition to own analytical pieces, Tabata published, especially in the 1930s, a series of review articles on books written in French and German. His linguistic capacity was undoubtedly essential for engaging with the literature on the equality of states, the function of diplomatic protection and the status of individuals, among other topics.

Finally, Tabata's eloquent writing style was an added gift to his scholarly competencies. He has a particular writing style that guides the reader step by step. Tabata writes almost by asking questions to the reader in order to keep them engaged with the story that Tabata tried to convey. In that

87 See Chapter 12 on ONUMA in this volume, for instance.

sense, it is understandable that Tabata's literature kept the audience in the academic community of international law in Japan, even in the twenty-first century. While his work continues to be consulted by students and scholars, a difference may be that subsequent generations of legal scholars can engage with Tabata's work without the strong epistemic assumption about his scholarly authority once predominant in Japan during his career and lifetime. This should encourage, I believe, more critical eyes on Tabata's scholarly work and its lasting legacy within the country's scholarly circles.

# 7

# SOGAWA Takeo: anti-positivist and realist scholar

*NISHI Taira*

## Introduction

Sogawa Takeo (1911–1996) was an international lawyer who occupied a legendary position in Japanese critical approaches to international law. Although he himself published only a very few articles, he was supported by many younger international law scholars with leftist leanings and was very influential in the post-war Japanese international law studies.

Sogawa was regarded as one of the best and brightest elite scholars of his era. He began his academic career as a research fellow at the Faculty of Law at the University of Tokyo immediately after graduating from the faculty. In 1936, he became an associate professor at Keijo (Seoul) University, which was located on the Korean Peninsula under Japanese colonial rule. In the colony, where there was more room for academic freedom than on the mainland, he undertook a detailed study of critical social theories, including Marxism. Following the defeat of his country and Korea's independence, Sogawa assumed a position at Tohoku University. Sogawa was profoundly troubled by Japan's incorporation into the United States' global military strategy during the Cold War. In response, he articulated a series of critiques directed at the Japan–US security treaty regime. In the context of post-war Japan, where the advantages and disadvantages of the Japan–US military alliance were a significant point of contention in political discourse, his arguments had a notable impact beyond the boundaries of international law academia. This chapter aims to elucidate the position of his arguments within the doctrinal history of international law, focusing on the relationship between his theory and German anti-positivism during the Weimar era.

## Background

The study of international law in Japan during the interwar period was more influenced by European legal scholars than it is today. With regard to legal theory, there was a notable inclination towards German jurisprudence, from which a considerable number of arguments were imported. The methodological argument (*Methodenstreit*) between positivist and anti-positivist theories was one of them.

Nineteenth-century German legal positivism criticised subjective value judgments and non-juristic elements present in natural law theories. From the point of view of legal positivism, any speculation about the nature of the human being and the world is merely a subjective judgment of the individual scholar. Furthermore, the eclectic mix of non-juristic elements, including morality, history and politics, is also deemed unacceptable. Positivists held that a complete and comprehensive system of law could be constituted only from juristic elements, namely, objectively verifiable positive legal materials. They further held the view that an interpretative operation on this self-contained, gapless system would offer an appropriate solution to every dispute they faced.[1]

The most prominent theorists of positivism in the field of public law are Carl F. von Gerber (1823–1891) and Paul Laband (1838–1918). Their objective was to exclude political, philosophical and historical considerations from the doctrine of public law and to construct a complete system of positive laws. It is evident that constitutional law and other public law issues are inextricably linked to political questions, in which differences in political ideals and judgments exert significant influence. However, the legal positivists sought to address public law issues in a logical and objective manner, eschewing the consideration of political questions. This doctrine posits that law is founded on the will of a state as a legal person, and that all legal norms should not contradict one another and can be understood consistently because they are derived from the will of a single person. Consequently, the various rules of positive law can be constituted as a coherent system under the umbrella of general legal principles and concepts. Furthermore, through the application of logical operations within this system, objective responses can be provided to all questions, irrespective of any political judgments.[2]

Hans Kelsen's *Reine Rechtslehre* represented the pinnacle of the juristic method as espoused by the legal positivists. It is characterised by the comprehensive exclusion of non-juristic elements from the domain of jurisprudence. In the context of classical legal positivism, the authoritative will of the

1 Franz Wieacker, *Privatrechtsgeschichte der Neuzeit*, 2. Auflage (Vandenhoeck & Ruprecht 1996) 430–437.

2 Carl Friedrich von Gerber, *Grundzüge eines Systems des Deutschen Staatsrechts* (Bernhard Tauschitz 1865) 1–18; Paul Lanand, *Das Staatsrecht des Deutschen Reiches*, Erster Band (H. Laupp'schen Buchhandlung 1876) v–viii; Michael Stolleis, *Geschichte des öffentlichen Rechts in Deutschland*, Zweiter Band (C. H. Beck 1992) 330–348.

state, which creates law, plays a role in linking facts and norms. However, in Kelsen's theory, even the state will is regarded as a concept that is constructed by jurisprudence. Kelsen posits that the psychological will does not generate legal norms; rather, legal norms ascribe specific consequences to an act of a person, with the concept of 'will' in the legal sense serving as an integral element in this attribution. In other words, the will does not beget the law; rather, the law constitutes the will.[3] This understanding of the concept of will in general is directly applicable to the concept of state will. It is not possible for a state to possess a psychological will. Furthermore, the state itself is unable to act, given that it lacks a physical body. Acts of a state are carried out by human beings acting as state organs. Certain behaviours of certain human beings are ascribed to the state by virtue of legal norms, and these behaviours are constituted as acts of the state in accordance with the state's will.[4] 'Der Begriff des Staatswillens hat mit keiner psychologischen Willenstatsache etwas zu tun. Er ist ausschließlich als Produkt der juristischen Konstruktion zu betrachten, und zwar einer zum Zwecke der Zurechnung vollgezogenen Konstruktion'.[5] Since the world of fact (*Sein*) and that of norm (*Sollen*) are so completely distinguished that all positive laws are consistently constructed into a hierarchy of norms, with the fundamental norm at the top.[6] This means that legal science becomes a system that is wholly contained within the domain of norms.

The anti-positivists challenged the exclusion of political ideas and historical considerations from the study of public law, which is essentially a political field. Among law scholars with an anti-positivist orientation, Carl Schmitt is arguably the most prominent in Japan. Schmitt defined the sovereign as a person who makes decisions about exceptional situations that cannot be regulated by normative rules in advance. Schmitt considered it unacceptable to construct the entire field of public law, which is based on political decisions, as a system of objective and logical norms.[7] Other prominent German anti-positivist public law scholars, including Erich Kaufmann (1880–1972), Rudolf Smend (1882–1975) and Hermann Heller (1891–1933), also made significant contributions to the development of Japanese legal scholarship. Despite their considerable divergences in political positions and academic approaches, they collectively endeavoured to reintroduce political ideas

3 Hans Kelsen, *Hauptprobleme der Staatsrechtslehre: Entwickelt aus der Lehre vom Rechtssatze* (J. C. B. Mohr 1911) 97–162.
4 Ibid 162–188.
5 Ibid 184.
6 Hans Kelsen, *Reine Rechtslehre* (Franz Deuticke 1934) 62–89.
7 Carl Schmitt, *Politische Theologie: Vier Kapitel zur Lehre von der Souveränität*, Achte Auflage (Duncker & Humblot 2004).

and values, sociological thinking and historical reflection into the field of jurisprudence.[8]

Hans Morgenthau (1904–1980), a German international law student during the Weimar Republic, demonstrated a profound interest in the methodological argument between positivists and anti-positivists.[9] Consequently, he selected 'the nature and the limits of international justice' as the subject of his doctoral dissertation. The methodological argument was closely related to this subject, which centred on whether systematic interpretation of positive legal norms could provide adequate settlements for all types of disputes. Adopting an anti-positivist stance, he advanced the view that certain disputes were not appropriate for judicial settlement, characterising them as 'political'.[10]

While less overt than in Germany, a parallel methodological argument existed in Japan as well. The method of legal positivism did not emerge in Japanese international law until the early twentieth century. This was largely due to the influence of TACHI Sakutaro (1874–1943), who had studied international law and the history of diplomacy in Europe. Upon returning to Japan, he introduced legal positivism as a sophisticated academic methodology. Tachi criticised the prevailing approach among Japanese international scholars, which he deemed unduly influenced by political and historical considerations, and sought to establish an autonomous juristic discipline of international law, based on a logical and systematic interpretation of positive laws.[11] Tachi's legal work, which employed a logical and well-reasoned approach to justify Japan's position using clearly defined legal concepts, was highly valued by the Ministry of Foreign Affairs. This excellence established him as a de facto advisor on international law to the Japanese government, while he retained his position as a professor of international law at the University of Tokyo. His treatises on the international law of peace and war became the standard textbooks for Japanese students of international law.[12]

8 Michael Stolleis, *Geschichte des öffentlichen Rechts in Deutschland*, Dritter Band (C. H. Beck 1999) 171–186.

9 Christoph Frei, *Hans J. Morgenthau: An Intellectual Biography* (Louisiana State University Press 2001) 115–120.

10 Hans Morgenthau, *Die internationale Rechtspflege: ihr Wesen und ihre Grenzen* (R. Noske 1929).

11 TACHI Sakutaro, 'On typology of protectorate (Hogokoku no Ruibetsu-ron)' (1906) 5 *Kokusaiho Gaiko Zassi* 22–32.

12 TACHI Sakutaro, *International Law of Peace* (*Heiji Kokusaiho-ron*) (Nihon Hyoronsha 1930); *International Law of War* (*Senji Kokusaiho-ron*) (Nihon Hyoronsha 1931).

The next generation of international law scholars sought to challenge Tachi's doctrine and demonstrated a growing interest in critical theories. While YOKOTA Kisaburo, a disciple of Tachi at the University of Tokyo, espoused a Kelsenian version of legal positivism and developed a 'purified' normative system, the still younger generation, including TABATA Shigejiro (1911–2001), YASUI Kaoru (1907–1980) and SOGAWA Takeo (1911–1996), was drawn to the theories of the anti-positivists who incorporated political considerations into jurisprudence. The international legal theories of Carl Schmitt and Hans Morgenthau exerted a considerable influence in Japan during the 1930s and 1940s.

Sogawa's anti-positivist stance was readily apparent. He offered a critical assessment of Dionisio Anzilotti's book on international law, stating:

> Anzilotti analyses legal facts from the standpoint of legal positivism with astonishing acuity and precision and attempts to theoretically formulate each legal issue. ... However, his positivist position also means the limitation of Anzilotti's theory. The approach of sharply separating positive laws from other elements, and of trying to construct a rigorously theoretical system of what are conceived of as the positive law, on the one hand, has led to the dismissal of many different kinds of theories with the stigma of natural law, political and ethical, or legislative arguments, overlooking their historical basis and meaning. On the other hand, it does not question the historically defined nature or political implications of what is conceived as the positive law.[13]

Sogawa acknowledged the theoretical rigour of legal positivism, which has constructed a system of positive laws through logical thinking. However, he challenged this methodology, arguing that such an approach failed to account for the political and historical context that constituted the very foundation of positive law. In the context of Japanese academic discourse, such an argument implies a critique of Tachi's methodology. To express his anti-positivist position, Sogawa, like Morgenthau, addressed dispute settlement, particularly the question of which procedures would provide adequate settlements to political disputes.

## Justiciability question

The question of whether it is possible and appropriate for a given dispute to be settled by a judicial body is known as the justiciability of the dispute. This

13 Review of the Japanese translation of Anzilotti's *Corso di diritto internazionale* (1942) 41(8) *Kokusaiho Gaiko Zassi* 99–100.

question was of great importance during the era of the League of Nations. The Covenant of the League of Nations imposed strict limitations on states' freedom to resort to war to settle international disputes. In accordance with the Covenant, states must first submit any dispute which might lead to a rupture to peaceful settlement procedures. In the case of legal disputes, the matter was to be referred to arbitration or the Permanent Court of International Justice. In contrast, non-legal disputes were to be referred to the Council of the League (Articles 12, 13 and 15). Bilateral or multilateral treaties on dispute settlement also adopted a system for distinguishing between legal and non-legal disputes and assigning each to a judicial tribunal or another form of dispute settlement procedure.[14] Consequently, it seemed to be imperative to determine which disputes were justiciable and which were not, in order to ensure the effective functioning of the peace maintenance system under the League of Nations regime.

The theory of Hersch Lauterpacht is widely acknowledged in contemporary discourse on the subject of justiciability. He posited that all kinds of international disputes could and should be settled through legally binding judgments of judicial tribunals, and that the system of international law constructed under general legal principles would provide an appropriate settlement for each. 'There may be gaps in a statute or in the statutory law as a whole; there may be gaps in the various manifestations of customary law. There are no gaps in the legal system taken as a whole'.[15] Although he positioned this doctrine of the completeness of the international law system as a criticism of positivist doctrines,[16] his argument was, in terms of the doctrinal history of public law, inherited from German legal positivism.[17]

Prior to the war, Lauterpacht's argument on justiciability was not widely accepted in Japan. Rather, it was subjected to rigorous criticism by TAOKA Ryoichi, a distinguished professor at Kyoto University, who introduced Lauterpacht's theory to Japan in an article published in 1938. According to Taoka, there are 'matters which need to be governed by international law,

14 Dietrich Schindler, *Die Schiedsgerichtsbarkeit seit 1914: Entwicklung und heutiger Stand* (W. Kolhammer 1938) 4–28.

15 Hersch Lauterpacht, *The Function of Law in the International Community* (Clarendon Press 1933) 64.

16 Ibid 65–66.

17 NISHI Taira, 'Hersch Lauterpacht as a Positivist: Understood in the Context of the Methodological Argument (*Methodenstreit*)' (2008) 29 *Kansai University Review of Law and Politics* 41–52. Lauterpacht himself noted the methodological differences between positivism in international law and that in other branches of law, and admitted that in the latter, 'it is the essence of positivism that it denies the existence of gaps in the law' (Lauterpacht, *The Function of Law* 67 (n 15)).

but which are not governed by international law in reality due to disagreements in legal opinion between nations with conflicting interests'. Even in such a case, it is of course not impossible to make a legal decision on parties' claims by rejecting the claims that have no basis in international law. However, if there is no international law regulating the issue, rejecting the claims of one party does not mean endorsing those of the other, since neither party's claims have a legal basis. Therefore, the dispute remains unsettled following the decision. In other words, such a dispute cannot be settled by the application of law.[18]

Yokota, another prominent professor of international law at the University of Tokyo, clearly adopted the method of normative science, which focuses on the objective description of positive legal norms. After summarising different theories on the distinction between legal and non-legal disputes, he considered only the provisions of treaties to determine which theory was appropriate. In other words, he attempted to establish the concept of legal disputes through a detailed examination of how each of the dispute settlement treaties formulates legal disputes.

> Needless to say, the consideration [of legal disputes] is a consideration under positive international law. In other words, it is a consideration of what legal disputes are and how the concept of legal disputes should be defined in positive international law. By the way, all positive international laws concerning legal disputes are treaties. There is no provision in customary international law, but only in treaties. Therefore, we should consider how it is defined in treaties.[19]

However, Yokota's methodology did not satisfy Sogawa, his brilliant disciple. Critical of legal positivism, which excludes the consideration of political and historical realities from jurisprudence, Sogawa also criticised Yokota's normativist approach. According to Sogawa, it 'cuts out norms or laws from legal reality and reduces concrete legal existence to abstract norms or laws'. For this reason, Yokota's discussion remains too formalistic and does

18 TAOKA Ryoichi, 'On Distinction between Legal Disputes and Non-Legal Disputes: A Critical Review of Lauterpacht's Doctrine (*Horitsuteki Hunso to Hi-Horitsuteki Hunso no Kubetsu: Lauterpacht Setsu to Sono Hihan*), part 1' (1938) 7 *Hogaku* 18–30.

19 YOKOTA Kisaburo, 'The Concept of Legal Disputes (*Hoteki Hunso no Gainen*), part 1' (1939) 38 *Kokusaiho Gaiko Zassi* 28–29.

not move towards an exploration of the existential and historical foundations of legal institutions.[20]

In studying the distinction between legal and non-legal disputes, Sogawa emphasised the difference between the question of formulation and the question of criterion. The question of how different dispute settlement treaties formulate the concepts of legal and non-legal disputes is different from the question of what the appropriate theoretical criteria are for distinguishing the two types of disputes. Each dispute settlement treaty formulates this distinction in order to assign certain disputes to different procedures. This formulation takes a variety of forms depending on practical considerations. If we were to focus only on the formulation of the treaties, we would lose sight of the principle of this distinction, caught up in the diversity of such expressions. Therefore, from a theoretical perspective, given the realities of the international community, the criteria for distinguishing between legal and non-legal disputes must first be established.[21] This argument, of course, includes the criticism of Yokota.

There were two main competing theories about the criterion for distinguishing disputes. One view is that legal disputes concern issues that can be decided by law.

> According to this view, international law, due to its underdevelopment and its particular character as a consensual law, is an incomplete law with many gaps, and therefore, sometimes it has not established clear and concrete positive laws that should serve as rules for judicial decisions on international disputes. If this is the case, only disputes for which there are positive international laws may be submitted to an international tribunal as legal disputes, and all other disputes must be excluded from the obligatory submission to an international tribunal.[22]

This theory of distinction, based on gaps in positive international law, was unacceptable to those who recognise the completeness, or gaplessness, of international law. Nevertheless, not all who recognise the completeness of international law, like Lauterpacht, recognise the justiciability of all kinds of disputes. Even if it is possible to construct positive international legal norms as a gapless system and to give every dispute a settlement based on positive laws, if the parties to the dispute seek a settlement not based on positive

20 SOGAWA Takeo, 'Review of Yokota's The Nature of International Justice (*Kokusai Saiban no Honshitsu*)' (1941) 55 *Kokka Gakkai Zassi* 91–93.

21 SOGAWA Takeo, 'On the Nature of International Conciliation (*Kokusai Chotei no Seishitsu ni tsuite*), part 1' (1944) 15 *Keijo Teikoku Daigaku Hogakkai Ronshu* 60.

22 Ibid 62.

laws but on an amendment of existing positive laws, then a settlement by application of law is not appropriate. This was the second theory of the distinction. That is, a static dispute in which parties to the dispute seek a settlement based on the application of existing law is a legal dispute, while a dispute in which a party seeks a settlement by changing existing law is a non-legal dispute. In a domestic society, those dissatisfied with the existing law will attempt to change the law through political movements in a public legislative process, such as a congress. Thus, state institutions charged with settling disputes between private parties are not charged with changing the law. However, in the international community, which lacks such a legislative procedure, claims to change the law will be expressed in disputes between states standing on an equal footing. Therefore, unlike domestic courts, international dispute settlement procedures must also address dynamic disputes in which a party seeks to change the law.[23]

Sogawa does not consider the difference between these two theories to be important. This is because both theories are ultimately based on the distinction between static and dynamic settlement of disputes. Non-legal disputes, as formulated by the latter theory, clearly require a dynamic settlement based on a change in the law. If the focus of the dispute concerns a change in existing law, the dispute settlement body must determine whether and how a change in the law should be made to substantively resolve the dispute. According to Sogawa, what the former refers to as non-legal disputes, i.e. disputes in which there is no applicable law, also require a dynamic settlement. This understanding derives from Kelsen's theory of the gap of law.[24] From a formal-logical point of view, it is possible to adjudicate issues that are not regulated by positive laws. In such a case, the party's claims would simply be dismissed by the tribunal because they have no basis in existing law. There is no gap in positive law in this logical sense. However, if such a logical conclusion is considered unjust and does not settle the dispute in a desirable manner, it is claimed that there is a 'lacuna in the law' in the sense that there is no legal norm that should exist. In the absence of a law that

23 Ibid 63–67.

24 'Die sogenannte "Lücke" ist somit nichts anderes als die Differenz zwischen dem positivem Recht und einer für besser, gerechter, richtiger gehaltenen Ordnung. Nur dadurch, daß man eine solche an die positive heranbringt und so an dieser Mängel feststellt, kann so etwas wie eine Lücke behauptet werden. Daß eine solche Lücke nicht durch Interpretation ausgefüllt werden kann, versteht sich von selbst, sobald man das Wesen der Lücke erkannt hat. Die Interpretation hat hier nicht die Funktion, die zu interpretierende Norm zur Anwendung zu bringen, sondern im Gegenteil, sie auszuschalten, um an ihre Stelle die bessere, richtigere, kurz die von dem Rechtsanwender gewünschte Norm zu setzen' (Kelsen, 101–102 (n 6)).

could settle the dispute in a desirable manner, the dispute settlement body may be expected to settle the dispute by supplementing the existing law with appropriate norms. In other words, it settles the dispute by changing the existing law.[25]

In both theories, the criterion for distinguishing between legal and non-legal disputes was whether the dispute should be settled statically by applying the existing law or dynamically by changing the existing law. Sogawa then asked whether the tribunal could settle a dispute dynamically. The answer was yes. For example, according to the General Act for the Pacific Settlement of International Disputes (1928), if conciliation fails to settle a non-legal dispute, the dispute is referred to arbitration. Unless otherwise agreed by the parties, the arbitral tribunal shall apply the rules enumerated in Article 38 of the Statute of the Permanent Court of International Justice (international treaties, customary international law and general principles of law), but 'in so far as there exists no such rule applicable to the dispute, the tribunal shall decide *ex aequo et bono*' (Article 28). In other words, it is possible to provide arbitral tribunals the competence to address non-legal disputes and to provide a dynamic settlement in cases of legal gaps. If the judicial body can also settle non-legal disputes, it follows that non-legal disputes are not necessarily non-justiciable. This means that the theoretical criterion for distinguishing between legal and non-legal disputes is not the same as the criterion for distinguishing between justiciable and non-justiciable disputes.[26]

Then, what are the criteria for the justiciable/non-justiciable disputes? If the judicial tribunal can also provide a dynamic settlement, what kinds of disputes are not suitable for submission to a judicial procedure and should be submitted to other kinds of procedures, such as conciliation or the inquiry by the Council of the League of Nations? To answer this question, Sogawa relied on Morgenthau's theory of political disputes.

According to Morgenthau, a political dispute is one tied to tension. An international dispute is a confrontation between states, involving a claim and a counterclaim. One party clearly and precisely formulates a claim based on generally applicable norms which are considered acceptable to the other party. Because it is constituted by rational arguments based on generally applicable norms, a dispute can be settled by a rational examination of the parties' arguments in a dispute settlement procedure. In Morgenthau's words:

25 SOGAWA, 'On the Nature of International Conciliation (*Kokusai Chotei no Seishitsu ni tsuite*) part 2' (1944) 15 *Keijo Teikoku Daigaku Hogakkai Ronshu* 35–46.
26 Ibid.

> Das sind die zwischenstaatlichen Gegensätze, die in der Form von Forderung und Bestreitung der Forderung einen präzisen, klar formulierten Ausdruck finden, und die ... im Hinblick auf ihre eigene, isoliert von allen Begleitumständen betrachtete Natur ohne Ausnahme Gegenstand eines internationalen Prozesses werden können, da die Begründungen der Parteivorbringen dem Bereich der allgemeiner Anwendung fähigen Normen entnommen sind.[27]

Tension, on the other hand, is a confrontation that arises from desires that have no such rationality. Tensions between states are caused by changes in international power relations. As power relations among states change, newly emerging powerful states seek to revise existing laws in order to gain greater status in the international community commensurate with their growing power. This desire creates tension with the current hegemonic states that seek to maintain the existing law. According to Morgenthau's formulation:

> [Unter dem Terminus 'Spannungen' verstehen wir] diejenigen zwischenstaatlichen Gegensätze ... die eine von einem Staat im Verhältnis zu einem anderen Staat behauptete Diskrepanz zwischen der bestehenden Rechtslage und dem tatsächlichen Kräfteverhältnis zum Inhalt haben.[28]

The tension is based on self-centred desires for power, which cannot be formulated in terms of generally applicable norms and are, in this sense, irrational. This irrational desire itself cannot be expressed in international relations (except in the form of war) and therefore finds its expression in a dispute based on rational claims. This is a political dispute. On the surface, a political dispute is a confrontation of rational claims, but in the background, there is an irrational struggle for power. Political disputes are so strongly tied to the tension arising from the struggle for power that they create very strong antagonism between the parties. For example, a territorial dispute over an uninhabited island of little use can escalate into an international conflict of disproportionate intensity if tensions between the parties are high.[29]

In political disputes, the present and future status of states in the international community is at stake; that is, they concern the entire design of present and future international relations. Only those who are able to make political decisions about the emerging form of international relations can

27 Hans Morgenthau, 10, 73 (n 10).
28 Ibid 78.
29 SOGAWA 50–51 (n 25).

settle such disputes at their own risk and responsibility. Therefore, it is not appropriate to ask professional, neutral judges to settle them.

Mediation by great powers could help settle political disputes. Under the League of Nations regime, it was expected that political disputes would be submitted to the Council's dispute settlement procedures, which can be characterised as organised mediation or political conciliation. Indeed, the Council's dispute settlement procedures were successful in settling international disputes in the 1920s.[30] However, the Council's dispute settlement was strongly criticised for its political nature. Since the Council, composed mainly of representatives of the great powers, was a political body, it was natural that its dispute settlement had a political character. In order to avoid this political character, there was a movement during the League of Nations period to establish a non-political procedure for the settlement of non-justiciable disputes, and many conciliation treaties were concluded for this purpose. In principle, conciliation is not carried out by political representatives of states but by neutral members selected individually. In Sogawa's view, however, this avoidance of politics was the wrong method of settling political disputes. Only those who can take responsibility for political decisions and the risks associated with them are capable of settling political disputes, not a conciliation committee composed of neutral individuals without political power. For this reason, the mediation system has rarely been used.[31]

## After the World Wars

Japan's international political status changed drastically after its defeat in August 1945. Japan's militaristic regime was dismantled, and the country was reestablished as a nation with a pacifist constitution. On the other hand, especially since the Korean War that began in 1950, Japan has also been widely expected to serve as a military ally contributing to the United States' strategy in the Far East. The clearest indication of Japan's contradictory political situation is, of course, Article 9 of the Japanese Constitution and Article 1 of the Security Treaty between the United States and Japan, which was signed on the same day as the San Francisco Peace Treaty (8 September 1951).

Article 9 of the Constitution:

30 Thomas P. Conwell-Evans, *The League Council in Action* (Oxford University Press 1929) 253–259.

31 SOGAWA 53–65 (n 25).

> Aspiring sincerely to an international peace based on justice and order, the Japanese people forever renounce war as a sovereign right of the nation and the threat or use of force as means of settling international disputes.
>
> In order to accomplish the aim of the preceding paragraph, land, sea, and air forces, as well as other war potential, will never be maintained. The right of belligerency of the state will not be recognised.

Article 1 of the Security Treaty between the United States and Japan:

> Japan grants, and the United States of America accepts, the right, upon the coming into force of the Treaty of Peace and of this Treaty, to dispose United States land, air and sea forces in and about Japan. Such forces may be utilised to contribute to the maintenance of international peace and security in the Far East and to the security of Japan against armed attack from without, including assistance given at the express request of the Japanese Government to put down large-scale internal riots and disturbances in Japan, caused through instigation or intervention by an outside power or powers.

Sogawa's stance in the face of post-war political realities is clear. He focused on clarifying the differences between the ideals of the UN Charter and the Japanese Constitution on the one hand, and the Japan–US Security Treaty regime embedded in the Cold War policy of the United States on the other, and harshly criticised the ideology underpinning US hegemony. In particular, he rejected positivist discourses that justified the existing regime by consistently interpreting contradictory positive laws. He repeatedly refuted any argument that the US–Japan Security Treaty was consistent with the UN Charter and the Japanese Constitution.

Sogawa criticised the view that the US–Japan Security Treaty is a regional arrangement for international peace and security recognised by the UN Charter. This view can be summarised as follows. Japan, which has no military force, is unable to defend itself against a powerful aggressor. Under the United Nations system, such a militarily weak country should ideally rely on the collective security measures of the UN Security Council. However, during the Cold War, this system was likely to be paralysed by the veto power of the Council's permanent members. Therefore, Japan must ensure its own security by concluding a regional collective security agreement with the United States, which has sufficient military power. Hence, the Japan–US Security Treaty was concluded.

To refute such a narrative, Sogawa examined the drafting process of Article 51 of the UN Charter to show that the right of collective self-defence underlying the Japan–US Security Treaty is different in nature from the regional arrangements for international peace and is based on the idea of military alliance, which the United Nations system originally sought to overcome. In fact, during the drafting of the UN Charter, the relationship between collective security measures by the Security Council and regional arrangements, especially the regional organisation of American states, was discussed, and this discussion led to the provision of Article 51 of the Charter on the right of collective self-defence. Initially, however, Latin American countries sought legitimate recognition of the functions of regional arrangements in the UN system, proposing, for example, that the peaceful dispute settlement procedures of regional arrangements be given priority or that the veto power of the permanent members of the Council be limited with respect to enforcement measures of regional arrangements. In response, the United States steered the debate towards the right of collective self-defence, which would allow each member state to take military action at its own discretion without Security Council authorisation.[32] This right of collective self-defence of each state was not suited to a regional system that complemented the collective security of the United Nations, but rather developed mechanisms for joint defence against common enemies: mutually hostile military alliances.[33]

Sogawa also rejects an interpretation that attempts to understand the US–Japan Security Treaty and Article 9 of the Constitution consistently. According to this interpretation, Japan, which does not have a military force because of Article 9 of the Constitution, entrusts the defence of Japan to the United States under the 1951 Security Treaty, and in return, Japan provides bases for American troops to use freely. In other words, this interpretation understands the Japan–US Security Treaty as an exchange of Japan's defence for US military bases. Sogawa maintained that such an interpretation was not convincing. First, the Japan-US Security Treaty is not an agreement to provide the US military with specific bases. Article 1 of the treaty provides that Japan grants the United States the right to dispose of its land, air and sea forces in and about Japan, without any restrictions on where they may be stationed. In effect, this is a 'military occupation treaty' that allows US forces stationed in Japan to retain the same extraterritorial status as the occupying forces after the conclusion of the San Francisco Peace Treaty.[34] Second, the Japan–US Security Treaty is not a military alliance between equal nations, but rather 'a new legal form

32 SOGAWA Takeo, 'Collective Self-Defence: The Logical Structure and Practical Functions of So-Called US Formula (Shudanteki Jieiken: Iwayuru US Formula no Rironteki Kozo to Genjitsuteki Kino)', SOGAWA (ed.), *International Political Thought and Sense of International Relations* (*Kokusai Seiji Shiso to Taigai Ishiki*) (Sobunsha 1977) 429–441.

33 Ibid 469–470.

34 SOGAWA Takeo, 'Character of the US–Japan Security Treaty Regime (Nichi-Bei Anzenhosho Joyaku Taisei no Tokushitsu)' (1957) *International Status of Japan* (*Nihon no Kokusaiteki Chii*), special Issue of *Horitsu Jiho* 58–59.

of domination and subordination to be imposed in place of an old one that has been dissolved', just like the subordination treaties concluded at the time of colonial independence, such as the Treaty of Alliance between the United Kingdom and Iraq (1930) and the Treaty of Alliance between the United Kingdom and Egypt (1936). The Japan–US Security Treaty, until its amendment in 1960, granted the United States the right to station its military forces, as stipulated in Article 1 above, but did not impose any obligations. And the purpose of the US military presence in Japan was not only to contribute to 'the security of Japan against armed attack from without' but also 'to contribute to the maintenance of international peace and security in the Far East'. It should be clear that in the 1950s, this meant the use of force in the Korean War and for the defence of Taiwan. On the other hand, Japan was obligated not only to provide bases but also to actively cooperate with US military activities. Article 24 of the Administrative Agreement under Article III of the Security Treaty between the United States and Japan, which set forth the details of the implementation of the Security Treaty, had the following provisions:

> In the event of hostilities, or imminently threatened hostilities, in the Japan area, the Governments of the United States and Japan shall immediately consult together with a view to taking necessary joint measures for the defence of that area and to carrying out the purposes of Article 1 of the Security Treaty.

Such consultations, given the disparity in power between Japan and the US, would force Japan to cooperate fully while allowing the US the freedom to apply the treaty flexibly.[35] Moreover, the Japan–US Security Treaty also had the character of an intervention treaty. Just as at the time of Cuban independence, the United States reserved the right to intervene to preserve Cuban independence, so, at the end of the occupation of Japan, the United States reserved the right to intervene to prevent the spread of the communist revolution to Japan.[36] In summary, Sogawa characterised the Japan–US Security Treaty regime as 'the military subordination of Japan in line with the US strategy towards the Soviet Union', which is alien to the principles of the Charter of the United Nations and the Japanese Constitution.[37]

Sogawa's position was in marked contrast to Yokota's. Yokota understood the Japan–US Security Treaty not as a contradiction of the United Nations Charter and the Japanese Constitution, but rather as a logical consequence of them. Both the Charter and the San Francisco Peace Treaty

35 Ibid 59–61.
36 Ibid 61–62.
37 Ibid 54–55.

recognise the right of self-defence, which is an important element of national security. However, many countries lack sufficient military power to prevent aggression on their own. Japan, in particular, is prohibited by Article 9 of its Constitution from possessing military forces, making it difficult to ensure security through the exercise of the right of self-defence.

> One way to compensate for this is through an international arrangement for security. This arrangement is either general and worldwide, or regional or individual. The former is the maintenance of security by the United Nations, which is believed to apply to Japan. As for the latter, the security treaty between Japan and the United States has been concluded, and Japan's participation in a regional collective security arrangement in the Pacific area will be considered in due course. ... While the security system of the United Nations may not always work effectively today, that of the Japan–US Security Treaty will work reliably, quickly, and effectively.[38]

Yokota also emphasised the compatibility of stationing US forces with the constitutional prohibition on maintaining military forces.

> The provision of the Constitution of Japan that land, sea and air forces, as well as other war potential, will never be maintained means, without a doubt, that Japan shall not maintain such forces. In other words, it means that the state of Japan shall not maintain such forces. ... Therefore, the stationing of foreign military forces in Japan certainly does not violate the provision of the Constitution.[39]

TAKANO Yuichi, Yokota's junior colleague at the University of Tokyo, also took pains to interpret the UN Charter, the Constitution and the Japan–US Security Treaty in a consistent manner, but with more nuance. Regarding the compatibility of a military alliance with the UN regime, he said, 'Alliance treaties are in principle excluded under today's collective security regime. However, within the framework of collective security, they are recognised as regional arrangements for regional security'.[40] The purpose of the regional collective security is to maintain mutual peace and security within the organisation, not to jointly oppose enemies outside the organisation. The regional arrangements, as set forth in Article 52 of the UN Charter, should

38 YOKOTA Kisaburo, 'Security of Japan (*Nihon no Anzen Hosho*)' (1952) 51(1) *Kokusaiho Gaiko Zassi* 26–27.

39 Ibid 17.

40 TAKANO Yuichi, 'The Agreement on Military Bases (*Gunji Kichi Kyotei*)' (1952) 51(1) *Kokusaiho Gaiko Zassi* 45.

be understood as a mechanism for collective security that is distinct from military alliances.

> However, as international politics split into two camps, the collective security and the collective self-defence merged, thereby bringing to the fore the function of jointly opposing external enemies. And several regional arrangements have been set in opposition to each other, resulting in 'a phenomenon not unlike the old alliance rivalries, only on a larger scale.[41]

As for the relationship between the military alliance and the Constitution, Takano tried to remove the contradiction through a subtle interpretation. He defined the right of collective self-defence as 'the right of a state to act in self-defence in the event of an armed attack on another country, when it poses a direct threat to its own legal interests'. Understood in this way, the right of collective self-defence becomes 'an extension of the concept of individual self-defence' and is included in the general concept of self-defence. Such an interpretation may allow Japan to exercise the right of collective self-defence, although it is based on the Japanese government's view that only the exercise of the right of (individual) self-defence is permitted under Article 9 of the Constitution. At the very least, it served to reconcile the Constitution with the commitment to the joint defence of Japan and the United States as stipulated in Article 5 of the 1960 Japan–US Security Treaty.[42] Of course, Sogawa was critical of Takano's interpretation on this point.[43]

The consistent interpretation of positive laws by Yokota and Takano helped to embrace the reality of the Cold War regime in which Japan was forced to engage. In contrast, Sogawa developed an argument that criticised the positive laws by focusing on the political reality underlying them, which led to a critique of the Cold War regime based on the principles of the Constitution and the UN Charter. This was the second round of the methodological argument in Japanese international law scholarship.

41 Ibid 47.

42 The first paragraph of Article 5 of the treaty reads:

> Each Party recognises that an armed attack against either Party in the territories under the administration of Japan would be dangerous to its own peace and safety and declares that it would act to meet the common danger in accordance with its constitutional provisions and processes.

43 SOGAWA Takeo, '1960 Japan–US Security Treaty Regime: A Review of the Revised Security Treaty (60 Nen Anpo Taisei: Shin Anpo Jouyaku no Kento)' (1960) 32 *Horitsujiho* 29–30.

## Sogawa's influence on Japanese scholarship to follow

Sogawa's work on the theory of political disputes under the League of Nations regime has had only a limited impact on post-war Japanese international law studies. The idea, dominant in the League of Nations, of distinguishing disputes by their nature and assigning each to judicial or other dispute settlement procedures, was not carried over into the United Nations era. The International Court of Justice has also repeatedly confirmed that it can provide legal answers to political disputes.[44] Therefore, the significance of the theory of political disputes was lost in post-war international law. Among Japanese international law scholars, the importance of the 'double-track structure' of the dispute settlement system, that is, the allocation of justiciable disputes to tribunals, and of non-justiciable (or political) disputes to other procedures such as conciliation, has been pointed out from time to time, but it has never become a mainstream issue of concern.[45]

Nevertheless, the anti-positivist method that Sogawa used to develop his theory of political disputes, namely, to examine the political and historical foundations of positive international laws and to critically understand the contents of positive laws based on these foundations, had a strong influence even in post-war Japan. This method was also very useful for constructing an academic position critical of the Japan US Security Treaty, which was the biggest political issue in post-war Japan. Sogawa was strongly supported by scholars such as ISHIMOTO Yasuo and MATSUI Yoshiro, who recognised the importance of the critique of ideology. Realist international law scholars with a leftist orientation, who criticised American hegemony and sought Japan's political independence, were attracted to Sogawa's anti-positivism.

44 *United States Diplomatic and Consular Staff in Tehran* (*United States of America v. Iran*), ICJ Reports 1980, para. 37; *Border and Transborder Armed Actions* (*Nicaragua v. Honduras*), ICJ Reports 1988, para. 52. Cf. Gleider I Hernandez, *The International Court of Justice and the Judicial Function* (Oxford University Press 2014) 68–74.

45 TAKANO Yuichi, 'The Convention on Diplomatic Relations and the Clause of Judicial Settlement of Disputes (Gaiko Kankei Joyaku to Shihoteki Hunso Kaiketsu Joko)' in MORIKAWA Toshitaka et al. (eds), *Peaceful Settlement of Disputes and International Law* (*Hunso no Heiwateki Kaiketsu to Kokusaiho*) (Hokuju Syuppan 1981) 339–350; MIYANO Yoichi, 'International Law Doctrines and the Dispute Settlement System (Kokusaiho-gaku to Hunso Shori no Taikei)' in *Japanese Society of International Law* (ed.), *Dispute Settlement* (*Hunso no Kaiketsu*) (Sanseido 2001) 46–49.

# 8

# YAMAMOTO Soji: thorough positivist in Japanese international law society

*MORITA Akio*

## Introduction

YAMAMOTO Soji (山本草二 1928–2013),[1] professor and judge,[2,3] was one of the leading scholars who developed the positivist theory (interpretive approach) of international law[4] in Japan. His approach was based on his realistic understanding of Japan's diplomatic environment, while refuting the ideological confrontation that was often seen, particularly during the Cold War period. His positivist and functionalist research was condensed into a masterpiece textbook[5] that has had a tremendous impact on practitioners

1 Hereinafter as Yamamoto, besides quotations or he is the author in the notes.
2 A member of the initial term of the International Tribunal for the Law of the Sea (ITLOS), from 1 October 1996 to 2005, and as arbiter for the Permanent Court of Arbitration (2000–2013).
3 Yamamoto's English-language biography appears in the *Yearbook of the International Tribunal for the Law of the Sea* (1996) 41 (with pictures). A more precise biography (in Japanese) can be seen in (1998) 42 *Sophia Law Review* (*Jochi Hogaku Ronshu*) 306–329. Yamamoto studied at the University of Tokyo, where he graduated in law in 1953 and earned his doctorate in law in 1969. His professional experience as an academic career is as follows: Research Assistant and Associate Professor of International Law, Faculty of Law and Literature, Kumamoto University, Kumamoto City (1955–1961); Professor of International Law and Organisation, College of Liberal Arts, International Christian University (ICU), Tokyo (1961–1967); Professor of International Law, Faculty of Law, Seikei University, Tokyo (1967–1976); Professor of International Law (1976–1988), Professor Emeritus (since 1988), Faculty of Law, Tohoku University, Sendai City; Professor of International Law, Sophia (Jochi) University, Tokyo (1988–1998). He also served as the President of the Japanese Society of International Law (1988–1991).
4 Readers are cordially requested to read this article with the present author's viewpoint today. Please note that there may be differing opinions, including those of scholars and of Yamamoto himself. Additionally, the author apologises for limiting references due to the subject of this chapter; references in this chapter are mainly limited to works in English or French, resulting in the omission of many Japanese works besides those by Yamamoto.
5 YAMAMOTO Soji, *International Law* (*Kokusaiho*) (Yuhikaku 1985; new ed., 1994).

and scholars in subsequent generations. Furthermore, his theory had a solid basis in the real world through his practical experience, especially enriched by his strong connections with various government agencies, including the Ministry of Foreign Affairs, the Ministry of Posts and Telecommunications (later Ministry of Internal Affairs and Communications), the Japan Coast Guard and more.

## Background of his academic achievements

This section explores it briefly by examining Yamamoto's personal background[6] and semi-practitioner experiences.

### *His personal history*

Although Yamamomo did not spend much time in Europe, he had the 'European spirit'. This could be attributed to his upbringing, as his father was a clergyman of the Non-Church Movement (a group of Protestants advocated by Uchimura Kanzo) and his mother had studied abroad (which was a rare occurrence in Japan at that time).

In his youth, he lived in multiple locations before residing longest in Yokohama, one of Japan's largest international ports. His first foreign language was German, which was not uncommon in pre-war Japan, compared with the thorough English education provided in the post-war period. He received a high school education under the old pre-war Japanese system, renowned for its exceptional quality of European language instruction.

These factors may partially account for his personal background, which later came to be described as having a 'European spirit'.

### *Yamamoto's career as an adviser and a judge*

The role of an adviser to practitioners paved the way for Yamamoto's theories, which are grounded in practical experience and bridge the gap between theory and practice. In this sense, his initial position as an expert in international law was with Japan's Ministry of Foreign Affairs, Treaties Bureau, while he was a graduate student (part-time job, exact dates unknown).

6 This personal history comprises hearsay from Yamamoto himself and his family.

His remarkable contributions as an adviser were many. For example, the Japanese delegation to: UN Legal Subcommittee on Peaceful Uses of Outer Space (Special Adviser, 1967–1982);[7] INTELSAT, Intergovernmental Conference for Definitive Arrangements (Adviser in 1969); Antarctic Treaty Consultative Meeting (Special Adviser, 1976–1979 and 1986); Third UN Conference on the Law of the Sea (Alternate Representative in 1978); and Legal Expert Panel of INTELSAT (1982–1993). His extensive background as a 'Special Adviser to the Japanese Government Delegation' at many governmental conferences and meetings (especially in the field of the law of the sea, outer space, international telecommunications and Antarctic) appears to have developed his practical lawyer's mind. Based on his extensive knowledge, he frequently provided legal advice on international legal issues to Japan's government, such as the Ministry of Foreign Affairs, the Japan Maritime Safety Agency (now Japan Coast Guard), the Ministry of Posts and Telecommunications, the Ministry of International Trade and Industry, the Ministry of Education and so on. Likewise, he submitted his expert opinions to the Japanese courts on numerous occasions.

His most significant career achievement, bridging the two fields, was serving as a judge of the International Tribunal of the Law of the Sea. He endeavoured to contribute to the Tribunal's formation of a majority opinion as often as possible. During this process, he carefully verified whether and to what extent his theory weathered practical trials.

## *Deeply influenced scholars*

Yamamoto seems to be deeply influenced by several scholars. We will pick up only two of them. As an international law scholar, Yamamoto was most influenced by Professor James L. Brierly (Oxford, UK), a well-known figure who requires no introduction. Yamamoto greatly admired his textbook and articles, whose theoretical approach provides deep insight into the relationship between international law and society.[8]

7 This career must have been a turning point for him. His research was enriched not only by the extension to space law, but also by the experience of real diplomatic negotiations.

8 Yamamoto refers to several scholars' books on international law and the law of international organisations in his textbook. Other than Brierly, mentioned are M. Akehurst, D. W. Bowett, I. Brownlie, G. Dahm et al., P.-M. Dupy, L. M. Goodrich et al., K. Ipsen, H. Lauterpacht, I. von Münch, H. Neuhold et al., Nguyen Quoc Dinh et al., L. Oppenheim-H. Lauterpacht, Ch. Rousseau, D. Ruzié, O. Schachter, J. G. Starke, H. Thierry, A. Verdross and B. Simma.

In Japan, despite numerous notable scholars, the author will limit the selection to one international law scholar, who Yamamoto often mentioned was Emeritus Professor TACHI Sakutaro of Imperial University of Tokyo (1874–1943). He is credited with pioneering a genuine positivist approach in international law.[9]

However, it should be noted that the aforementioned scholars predominantly made contributions in the field of traditional international law, also known as the 'international law of coexistence'. Yamamoto's contribution is a pioneering achievement in the field of 'international law of cooperation', which he refers to as 'administrative international law'. Later, we will discuss the two theoretical approaches and the relevant scholars.

## His achievements as a scholar: common features

As a scholar, Yamamoto was quite productive. He wrote numerous books, articles and papers in many fields of public international law. This includes, but is not limited to, the law of international organisations, international environmental law, international telecommunications law, international criminal law, international nuclear law and international economic law.

Representative works, even limited to his most representative monographs, are, for example:

*Uchu Tsushin no Kokusaiho: Kokusaikigyo no Hokeitai toshite* (*International Law of Space Telecommunications: A Type of International Enterprise*) (Yushindo 1967); *INTELSAT Kokyu Kyotei no Kenkyu* (*A Study on the Definitive Agreements Relating to INTELSAT*) (KDD 1973); *Kokusai Gyogyo Funso to Ho* (*International Fishery Disputes and Law*) (Tamagawa University Press 1976); *Hoso Eisei wo meguru Jiyu to Kisei* (*Freedom and Regulation in Direct Broadcast Satellites*) (Tamagawa University Press 1979); Kokusaiho ni okeru Kiken-Sekinin-Shugi (*Function of Liability for*

9 '[H]e established international law study as an interpretative legal science in Japan. He contributed greatly to the elevation of Japanese international law studies to a level truly approaching that of a legal science'. ITO Fujio, 'One Hundred Years of International Law Studies in Japan' (1969) 13 *Japanese Annual of International Law* (later title *Japanese Yearbook of International Law*) 19–34. See also, Yasuo Ishimoto and Kazuya Hirobe, 'Development of Post-War Japanese Studies in Public International Law: Part 1: 1945–1964' (1987) 30 *Japanese Annual of International Law* 89–129; Yasuaki Onuma, 'Japanese International Law in the Prewar Period: Perspectives on the Teaching and Research of International Law in Prewar Japan' (1986) 29 *Japanese Annual of International Law* 23–47. Introduced from a different angle, though, see also Kinji Akashi, 'Sakutaro Tachi: A Blend of Scholarship and Practitionership, and Its Fate in Japan' (2013) 56 *Japanese Yearbook of International Law* 122–143.

*Risk in International Law*) (University of Tokyo Press 1982); *Kokusai Keiji Ho* (*International Criminal Law*) (Sanseido 1991);[10] *Kaiyo Ho* (*Law of the Sea*) (Sanseido 1992);[11] *Kokusai Ho* (*International Law*) (Yuhikaku 1985; new edition 1994).

The following analyses the shared features of his achievements. Initially, it was widely acknowledged that a positivistic approach was adopted,[12] with a significant interest in a historical perspective.[13]

## *Historical approach*

Yamamoto has consistently pondered whether 'history will repeat itself or not',[14] ever since his initial articles reappraised the 'freedom of the seas' between Grotius' argument for 'free seas' and Selden's argument for

10 A book review of this can be found at (1991) 35 *Japanese Annual of International Law* 229–233 (Toshiyuki Tanaka).

11 A book review of this can be found at (1993) 36 *Japanese Annual of International Law* 168–169 (Atsuko Kanehara).

12 'According to editor Tadashi Tanaka in the "Introduction", one of the most remarkable features of Professor Yamamoto's methodology lies in the construction of a general understanding of international law through elaborate analysis in a positivist way of individual international legal phenomena'. (Book Reviews) MATSUI Yoshiro, 'Kazuya Hirobe and Tadashi Tanaka (eds), *Yamamoto Soji Sensei Kanreki Kinen: Kokusaiho to Kokunaiho: Kokusai Koeki no Tenkai* (*International Law and Municipal Law: Development of International Public Interests: In Commemoration of Professor Yamamoto Soji's 60th Anniversary*)' (Keisoshobo 1991) viii, 652, 'List of Professor Yamamoto's Works' (1992) 35 *Japanese Annual of International Law* 235–239. Hereinafter, this Festschrift is referred to as *International Law and Municipal Law: Development of International Public Interests*.

13 It is worth referring to this introduction by Professor Okuwaki. 'Dr Yamamoto's approach to international law belongs to the legal positivist school, with his superb art of treaty interpretation and accurate readings of documents and materials, always offering profound and insightful ideas to academics. However, we must not forget that his legalistic thinking was always based on his profound understanding and real knowledge of the history of international law and diplomacy. In fact, at the start of his research activities, Dr Yamamoto took up Selden's theory of the law of the sea and other thoughts of European jurists in the medieval age as a theme for his doctoral thesis. His theory on the law of international organisations also had its roots in the study of public international unions that were established in the mid-nineteenth century, such as the Universal Postal Union (UPU) and the International Telecommunication Union (ITU)'. OKUWAKI Naoya, 'The Honourable Dr Soji Yamamoto (1928–2013)' (2014) 57 *Japanese Yearbook of International Law* 1–6.

14 You can clearly find this aspect in his thought in YAMAMOTO Soji, 'Postscript' in *International Fishery Disputes and Law* (*Kokusai Gyogyo Funso to Ho*) (Tamagawa University Press 1976).

'closed seas'. These articles were published during the first 1958 Geneva Conference on the Law of the Seas, UNCLOS.[15] He considered the dispute over fishery resources to be a real issue in the argument in the legal system of the sea, rather than a mere confrontation between 'high seas' and 'territorial (coastal) waters', which had appeared as a formal argument. This demonstrates his emphasis on the importance of state practices and historical context. Simultaneously, his functional approach was born due to the recognition of fishery resources being a real issue behind the 'freedom of the seas' argument (which later materialised as the new functional zone, EEZ, in the UNCLOS).

He later moved to contemporary issues. He paid close attention to each issue, analysing its historical development, especially three typical eras in the development of international law: the nineteenth century, the interwar period and the post-war period. In his research, he often consulted German literature and materials, such as volumes of *Nouveau recueil général de traités et autres actes relatifs aux rapports de droit international* (by Georg Friedrich de Martens et al.); *Handbuch des Völkerrechts* (by Franz von Holtzendorff, five volumes, 1885–1889, and succeeded and developed by the famous series of books, beginning in 1912 and successively published in the interwar period); *Wörterbuch des Völkerrechts und der Diplomatie* (by Julius Hatschek and Karl Strupp, three volumes, 1924–1929, *Wörterbuch des Völkerrechts* as the new second edition, three volumes, 1960–1962, succeeded by the *Encyclopedia of Public International Law* (under the direction of Rudolf Bernhardt) and the Max Planck *Encyclopedia of Public International Law* (under the direction of Rüdiger Wolfrum)); and *Internationales Verwaltungsrecht* (by Karl Neumeyer, four volumes,

15 YAMAMOTO Soji, '*Selden Kaiyo Ron no Jissho teki Konkyo* (Positive Basis of Selden's Theory on the Sea)' (1955) 7 *Journal of Law and Literature [Hobun Ronso]* 26–55; YAMAMOTO Soji, '*Chusei Kaiyo Kokusaiho Gainen to sono Henyo: Tordesillas Jyoyaku no Seiritsu wo megutte* (Concept of and its Change in Medieval International Law of the Sea: On the Conclusion of the Treaty of Tordesillas (1494))' (1957) 9 *Journal of Law and Literature* (*Hobun Ronso*) 40–69; YAMAMOTO Soji, '*Haita teki Gyogyoken Gainen no Rekishitekitenkai* (Historical Construction of the Exclusive Right of Fisheries)' (1959) 58 *Journal of International Law and Diplomacy* (*Kokusaiho Gaiko Zassi*) 232–264, 391–418 (this English title is a translation by Yamamoto himself) (1959), all of which are reprinted in YAMAMOTO Soji (KANEHARA Atsuko and MORITA Akio (eds)), *The Positive Basis of International Administrative Law* (*Kokusai Gyoseiho no Sonritsukiban*) (Yuhikaku 2016), which is his posthumous anthology.

1910–1936). Therefore, he had quite a solid basis for his research throughout his scholarly life.[16]

## *Analysis of the relationship between international law and domestic law*

Yamamoto's characteristic preciseness in his positivist analysis was informed by his experiences as a practitioner in preparing for Japan's ratification of multilateral treaties, including space law treaties ('The Rescue Agreement', 'The Liability Convention', 'The Registration Convention'). During this preparatory stage, he was tasked with verifying whether and to what extent implementing acts were required for Japan's ratification of these treaties. Therefore, he possessed a profound understanding of the nuances in language use within treaties, including the distinctions 'right', 'obligation', 'discretion' and so on.

Yamamoto's extensive research examines two interconnected themes. First, the relationship between international law and municipal law. Second, the legal nature of state jurisdiction.[17] These themes are explored from a theoretical point of view below.

16 Not to mention the vast editions of state practices undertaken by Anglo-American endeavours, for example, successive *Digest of International Law* series in the United States or many successive editions of *Oppenheim's International Law* in the United Kingdom.

17 About two characteristic features of Yamamoto's theory, see also Yasuaki Onuma, 'Japanese International Law in the Postwar Period: Perspectives on the Teaching and Research of International Law in Postwar Japan' (1990) 33 *Japanese Annual of International Law* 25–53, 44–45. His view was this (underlines added): YAMAMOTO's theory…has provided ample stimulation for change. One of the two characteristic features of YAMAMOTO's textbook, the emphasis on the significance of the implementative aspect of international law through domestic legal mechanisms, reflects the ongoing transnational penetration of economic, social, informational and cultural activities in the post-war world. The other feature, i.e. the restructuring of the theory of international law from a viewpoint of allocation and adjustment of jurisdiction, is even more challenging. This theory introduces international organisations, international administrative law and international economic law not as separate ingredient subjects, but rather by rearranging the specific legal phenomena associated with these new subjects according to this notion of allocation of jurisdiction. This is slightly different from the views of the present author, as explained below, probably because Yamamoto wrote many other representative works, including a revised new edition of his textbook in the 1990s, after Onuma wrote this article.

## The 'core pillar' in Yamamoto's theory

Not only was his practical knowledge impressive, but he also conducted a thorough analysis of numerous concrete cases using a consistent approach. This approach was based on the analytical method, which differentiates between international administrative law (also known as *internationales Verwaltungsrecht*, *droit administratif international*) and administrative international law (also known as *völkerrechtliches Verwaltungsrecht*, *droit international administratif*). From a domestic law perspective, this analytical method focuses on distinguishing between proper domestic law and internationalised domestic law.

### *Administrative international law theory*

More importantly, the central idea, or 'core pillar' in his theory of administrative international law[18] can be found throughout his achievements as discussed earlier. His numerous works are highly respected for their practical and theoretically consistent aspects. The author would like to highlight his two main articles on this theory[19] in more detail to illustrate the core of his idea.

18 Yamamoto prefers to use 'international administrative law' even in his English Summary, but the author would like to use 'administrative international law' in English, based on the context.

19 Two articles were as follows. YAMAMOTO Soji, '*Kokusai Gyoseiho no Sonritsukiban* (The Positive Basis of International Administrative Law)' (1969) 76 *Kokusaiho Gaiko Zassi* 1–66; YAMAMOTO Soji, '*Kokusai Gyoseiho* (International Administrative Law)' in OGAWA Ichiro et al. (eds), *Systematic Analysis on Modern Administrative Law* (*Gendai Gyoseiho Taikei*), vol. 1: *Gendai Gyoseiho no Kadai* (*Challenges of Modern Administrative Law*) (Yuhikaku 1983) 329–364. Both of them are reprinted in YAMAOTO, *The Positive Basis of International Administrative Law*. There is already a helpful introduction to his theory written by an administrative law scholar. Yukio Okitsu, 'International Administrative Law, a Precursor of Global Administrative Law? The Case of Soji Yamamoto', Jean-Bernard Auby (ed.), *Le futur du droit administratif/The Future of Administrative Law* (LexisNexis 2019) 445–452. Contrasting Yamamoto's two articles above, Okitsu evaluates 'The 1969 article reveals the conceptual framework of [international administrative law] more fully and vividly than the 1983 article, while the 1983 article focuses on the extraterritorial application of domestic administrative law (exemplified by anti-trust law) as well as [international administrative law] as the law of international organisations. This might be because the 1983 article was written to show an outline of [international administrative law], especially to domestic administrative law scholars and practitioners', ibid 446 (n 7). On the other hand, the present author aims to emphasise the positive and developed aspects of the second article.

The first article provides a detailed, positive explanation of the concept of administrative international law. He contrasts two legal schools' viewpoints on international administrative law[20] to establish a clear and objective understanding of the concept. One perspective, advocated by Otto Mayer[21] and Karl Neumeyer,[22] rejects the notion of proper administrative law in the international community and instead views it as a branch of conflict of laws which defines the scope of national administrative laws. The opposing viewpoint, put forth by Alfred Verdross[23] and Georges Scelle,[24] aims to

20 Major references other than those mentioned later are below. Lorenz von Stein, 'Einige Bemerkungen über das internationale Verwaltungsrecht', *Jahrbuch für Gesetzgebung, Verwaltung und Volkswirtschaft im Deutschen Reich?* (1882) Bd. 6, 395; Martens, F. von, *Traité de Droit International* (1886), t. II; Paul Négulesco, 'Principes du Droit International Administratif' (1935–I) t. 51 *Recueil des Cours*, 579; Michel Dendias, 'Les Principaux Services Internationaux Administratifs' (1938–I) t. 63 *Recueil des Cours*, 243; Pierre Kazansky, 'Théorie de l'Administration Internationale' (1902) 9 *Revue Générale de Droit International Public* 353–367; Paul S Reinsch, 'International Administrative Law and National Sovereignty' (1909) 3 *American Journal of International Law* 1–45, reprinted also in YAMAMOTO, *Public International Unions* (1911); V. Ganeff, 'Zu der Theorie der Völkerrechtlichen Verwaltung' (1938) 52 *Niemeyers Zeitschrift für Internationales Recht* S. 36.

21 Yamamoto refers to Otto Mayer, *Deutsches Verwaltungsrecht*, Band II (1896), S. 453–459, which is a part of '§62. Internationales und bundesstaatliches Verwaltungsrecht'.

22 Yamamoto refers to Karl Neumeyer, 'Les Unions Internationales' (1925) 3 *Revue de Droit International, de Sciences Diplomatiques et Politiques* 102–108; Karl Neumeyer, 'Le Droit Administratif International' (1911) 18 *Revue générale de droit international public* 492–497. His most notable works are *Internationales Verwaltungsrecht*, 4 Bände (1910–1936). The present author has heard that Yamamoto studied them in his youth and personally acquired a reprint edition of them.

23 Yamamoto refers to Alfred Verdross, *Die Verfassung der Völkerrechtsgemeinschaft* (1926) 76; Alfred Verdross, *Völkerrecht* (4. Aufl., 1959) 465–478.

24 Yamamoto refers to Georges Scelle, 'Théorie du Gouvernement International' (1935) *Annuaire de l'Institut International de Droit Public* 41–112. He highly evaluates his concept of 'dédoublement fonctionnel' whereby state organs perform dual functions: not only as organs performing administration of the state under its domestic law, but also as organs performing administration of international society under international law. On the other hand, Yamamoto criticises the idealistic aspect of Scelle's understanding of 'dédoublement fonctionnel', particularly regarding Scelle's view of it being of a transitional nature due to his recognition of 'sociétés superétatiques' or federalism as the ultimate, ideal form. Georges Scelle, *Précis de droit des gens: Principes et systématique* (1932) t. 1, 57, 188. Moreover, Okitsu mentions another difference between Yamamoto and Georges Scelle: the subject of international law is the state or the individual. Okitsu, 'International Administrative Law' (n 19) 447–448. In both aspects, Yamamoto would be deemed completely 'positivist'. There are many articles on Scelle's theory, even limited to those in French and English. Worth mentioning are those included in *La technique et les principes du droit public: etudes en l'honneur de Georges Scelle* (1950), 2 tomes; Special Feature: 'The

establish the normative ideal of international administrative law, wherein international legal norms are enforced by the central authority of the international community. Furthermore, critics of the latter theory, such as the 'successors' of Mayer and Neumyer in Germany, criticised this claim as lacking legal proof, but it can only be explained factually. Instead, they suggest that the phenomenon is better understood as an extension of national administrative laws.

Intending to clarify the autonomous and positive basis of international administrative law, he attempted to reconcile these two ideas (similar to the 'aufheben' of thesis and antithesis in German dialectical philosophy, without specifically referencing this term though) through a meticulous analysis of various types of administrative actions by international institutions, and by exploring the proper scope of each legal argument.

In conclusion, he defines international administrative law as a 'legal norm inhering in the existing international communities, which continuously realises 'service public international' established by multilateral administrative treaties and variously influences the national administrations through the administrative actions of international institutions'.[25]

This concept is further expanded upon in the second article, more than ten years after the first. Therefore, he has significantly expanded his idea with considerable modifications. One notable modification is the expansion into new areas, notably international criminal law and international economic law (although the latter is limited to extraterritorial application issues arising from restrictive trade practices, i.e. anti-trust laws in the

European Tradition in International Law: Georges Scelle' (1990) 1 *European Journal of International Law* 193–249. And especially on his *dédoublement fonctionnel* concept, see Antonio Cassese, 'Remarks on Scelle's Theory of 'Role Splitting' (dédoublement fonctionnel) in International Law' (1990) 1 *European Journal of International Law* 210–231, which includes useful information on 'dédoublement fonctionnel' mentioned by Scelle himself and a comprehensive bibliography by other writers at n. 1. On the aspect of his understanding of federalism, see also Ch. Carabiber, 'Le Fédéralisme international dans l'œuvre du Professeur Georges Scelle', in *La technique* (in this note) t. 1, 55–66; Hubert Thierry, 'The Thought of Georges Scelle', in 'The European Tradition in International Law: Georges Scelle' 193–209 (in this note).

25 YAMAMOTO Soji, '*Kokusai Gyoseiho no Sonritsu Kiban* (The Positive Basis of International Administrative Law, English Summary)' (1969) 76 *Kokusaiho Gaiko Zassi* 152. The author would explain it with slight modifications, like this: (the analytical concept of) legal norms inhering in existing international communities established by multilateral administrative treaties, which aim to continuously realise 'service public international' in international communities, and, for that purpose, set up international institutions to influence national administrations through various types of administrative actions.

United States). Of course, the most crucial aspect is the substance of his new idea, and his main theme follows.

He defines international administrative law (in a broad sense), distinguishing between 'international administrative law as conflict of law' and 'international administrative law as international law'. However, it is necessary to elaborate on the nuances of 'international law' to fully comprehend his idea. Also, it should be stressed that this article focuses on the main concept consisting of 'international administrative law as international law', i.e. public international law, which is established and continuously pursued through multilateral treaties.

The key concept, 'service public international',[26] means, according to his first article, services that are performed by multiple states uniformly to

26 There may be remaining complex issues, such as hegemony or ideological criticism, as well as recently popular legitimacy problems. Nonetheless, the present author will only address a specific point below.

The present author interprets Yamamoto's avoidance of certain arguments as intentional for two primary reasons. First, Yamamoto maintains a consistent approach and is wary of diverging into other levels of argumentation. While his approach is an analytical one describing existing law (lex lata), certain aspects of the issues could be more properly treated from a socio-legal approach (cf. J. L. Brierly, *The Outlook for International Law* (Clarendon Press 1944), which is based on a socio-legal approach and contrasts with his other works, although they are closely related) or from law-making analysis because they would primarily function in the process of law-making. Of course, the present author does not deny that there would be counterarguments from a contemporary perspective, given the evolving practices in international organisations or institutions to ensure their legitimacy. Second, presumably, a detailed, thorough analysis of existing law (lex lata) was believed to be an international law approach crucially needed in Japan at that time. Tadashi Tanaka comprehends Yamamoto's thorough positivist approach as expressing criticism of speculative philosophical arguments in methodology, which have been adopted by many previous studies and have formed a prevailing tendency in the academic world of Japanese international law. See YAMAMOTO, 'Introduction', *International Law and Municipal Law: Development of International Public Interests*. On the problem of legitimacy, looking from an administrative law viewpoint, see Okitsu, 'International Administrative Law' 450–452 (n 19). Okitsu pointed out that the legitimacy factor in the theory of Yamamoto was limited to the will of member states, which was a reflection of the 'classical framework of international law' because of the time of writing. He also pointed out that the development of administrative law theory today could contribute to this aspect. See also MATSUI, '*Yamamoto Soji Sensei Kanreki Kinen*' 235–239 (n 12). He reviews this book, commenting as follows: 'On "International Public Interests", Okuwaki, pointing out the socioeconomic foundation of the emergence of this concept, stresses the importance of seeing not only its actuality but also its ideological nature and its limits when the "global problems" occur. The ideological nature of the concept of "International Public Interests" is also referred to by Furukawa and Ueki, and this conception is an important contribution of this volume'

administer and intervene in administrative matters which are rooted in and arise from living conditions in the relevant international community.[27]

This is a product of the establishment of international communities (communauté internationale), composed of corresponding units of administrative matter substantively based on relevant international interests (intérêts internationaux),[28] since interdependent relationships of multiple states have developed as a result of transborder activities by individuals and groups belonging to multiple states and their deepening international communications. These interests[29] differ from those fulfilled and protected within the context of a bilateral, reciprocal relationship, i.e. diplomatic interests as a subject in classical international law. This viewpoint can be termed 'objective international law', meaning that it is independent from the subjective will of each participating state.

Contrasting this, even if there exists 'international law' in the form of treaties or so, they are considered a part of 'international administrative law as conflict of law' when the substantive law is deemed domestic law rather than international law. For instance, a traditional extradition treaty reflects mutual respect for the domestic penal laws of each party and cooperation to the extent of reciprocity, considering 'double criminality' and similar

(note: OKUWAKI Naoya, '"*Kokusai-koeki" Gainen no Rironteki Kento* (Theoretical Examination of the Concept of "International Public Interests")' in *International Law and Municipal Law: Development of International Public Interests* 173–243 (n 12); FURUKAWA Terumi, '*Kokusai-soshiki to Kokusai-koeki* (International Organisations and International Public Interests)' ibid 245–271; UEKI Toshiya, '*Kokusai-soshiki niyoru Kokusai-koeki Jitsugen no Shokeitai* (Forms of Realisation of International Public Interests by International Organisations)' ibid 371–393).

27 See also translations by Okitsu, 'International Administrative Law' 448 (n 19).

28 Yamamoto deems this concept as 'jittaiteki shakaigakuteki kiban (substantive sociological basis)' while he regards 'service public international' as a legal concept. He believes that positive proof of the basis of international administrative law depends on whether and how the former concept can transform into the latter. In essence, this transformation means that traditional sovereign states (politically and territorially separated power units) would transform themselves by consolidating their inherent common interests in each special area into constituent units of an internationally organised community. Yamamoto, *The Positive Basis of International Administrative Law*, 9–10. He refers to Hartwig Bülck, *Der Strukturwandel der internationalen Verwaltung* (Mohr 1962), S. 3–4. Presumably, Yamamoto's ideas were influenced by his works on *internationale Verwaltung* at that time.

29 The sub-title of the *In Commemoration of Professor Yamamoto Soji's 60th Anniversary* is *Kokusai Koeki no Tenkai* (*Development of International Public Interests*), which very well illustrates one main feature of Yamamoto's works, though Yamamoto himself scarcely uses these words. See also MATSUI, 'Yamamoto Soji Sensei Kanreki Kinen' 235 (n 12).

factors.[30] In this context, the relevant extradition treaty serves as a tool for implementing each party's domestic penal law and not as substantive law.

In other words, he aims to divide international legal norms into two categories based on state practice, known as a positive approach. Later, in his textbook, this distinction is developed as a categorisation between 'traditional international law' and 'modern international law', in other words, 'international law of coexistence' and 'international law of (international) cooperation'.[31] The primary legal function of the former is the delimitation of the competence (or jurisdiction) of states. On the other hand, the primary legal function of the latter is twofold: first, the identification of specific rules of public international law to realise the common interest of member states; and second, the establishment of an appropriate international regime through multilateral treaties to realise 'service public international'. Concrete measures for achieving this objective include the allocation of new international objective rights or obligations to member states, and, where necessary, the establishment of international organs or organisations to implement them (e.g. secondary legislation, supervision, enforcement).

Based on this approach, he attempted to analyse all fields of international law to the extent possible. Representative subsequent work was the monograph, *International Criminal Law*, which categorises international crime into two categories: 'crime with foreign element (foreign-related crime)' and 'crime under international law'.[32] The latter is further divided into two types of international crimes. The first category of 'crime against international law (*völkerrechtliches Delikte von Individuen*)' is that individuals can be held directly accountable under international law, without the assistance of domestic criminal law provisions. The second category pertains to 'offences against the law of nations (*delicta juris gentium; crime de droit des gens*)'. These are certain crimes which shall be punished under international cus-

30 In his first article, he picked up and analysed the concept of 'die völkerrechtlich gebundene Verwaltung', which originates with Otto Mayer and Karl Neumeyer, and concluded that it differs from his 'international administrative law' concept.

31 YAMAMOTO, *International Law* Part I, Chapter 1, esp. 30–33 (n 5). 'Traditional international law', as its basic nature, has three characteristics, i.e. (i) 'negative nature' in content of rights and obligations, (ii) respect for 'autonomy' and (iii) 'relative nature' of consent among states. 'Modern international law', as its basic nature, also has three characteristics, i.e. (i) 'active nature' in content of rights and obligations, (ii) 'objective nature' regulating traditional autonomy of will and act of sovereign states by multilateral international institutions and (iii) 'universal nature' of rights and obligations against all members of the international community modifying traditional 'relative nature' in rights and obligations among states.

32 Strictly speaking, there is a third category of 'international crime of a state' in the book, but it will be omitted in this explanation due to its relevance.

tomary law or treaties, as they prejudice certain legal interests of common concern to a large number of states. In response, each state shall enact criminal laws and ensure that the perpetrator is prosecuted and punished. Examples of the latter include multilateral treaties on terrorism or those developed after the Second World War. This technique has recently been developed in other fields, such as the suppression of international organised crime.

The particular feature of the concept of 'crime under international law' is that this includes not only 'crime against international law (*völkerrechtliches Delikte von Individuen*)' that can be prosecuted directly through international criminal tribunals, but also 'offences against the law of nations (*delicta juris gentium; crime de droit des gens*)' that can be prosecuted indirectly through domestic laws of each state. This approach contrasts with widely accepted theories, such as Dietrich Oehler's.[33] His approach is quite consistent with the 'administrative international law' theory mentioned earlier, which involves direct application of international law through domestic law type, i.e. properly limited cases of '*dédoublement fonctionnel*'.

## *Unilateral domestic measures theory*

A new concept and theory of 'unilateral domestic measures'[34] could be called a by-product of the theory of international administrative law. This new

33 In contrast, Oehler's concept of 'International Criminal Law' is limited to Yamamoto's concept of 'crime against international law (völkerrechtliches Delikte von Individuen)'. See Dietrich Oehler, 'Criminal Law, International', Rudolf Bernhardt (ed.), *Encyclopedia of Public International Law*, vol. 1 (North-Holland 1992) 877–882. Even among contemporary Japanese scholars, Oehler's categorisation is influential. See Hiromi Sato, *Multilayered Structures of International Criminal Law* (Springer 2021).

34 Two representative articles are YAMAMOTO Soji, 'The Function of Unilateral Measures by a State in the International Lawmaking Process (*Ippoteki Kokunaisochi no Kokusaiho Keisei Kinou*)' (1991) 33 *Jochi Hogaku Ronshu* 47–86; YAMAMOTO Soji, 'The Changing Function of Opposability as Cause of Action in International Dispute (*Kokusai Funso Yoin toshite no Taikoryoku to sono Henshitsu*)' (1993) 6 *The Yachiyo Journal of International Studies* 63–88 (both are reprinted in *The Positive Basis of International Administrative Law* (n 15)). On the essence of his idea, see YAMAMOTO, *International Law* 64–65 (n 5). This 'unilateral domestic measures' theory was already introduced and developed by several articles by Professor Murase. See, for example, Shinya Murase, 'Perspectives from International Economic Law on Transnational Environmental Issues' (1995) 253 *Collected Courses of the Hague Academy of International Law* 283–431; Shinya Murase, 'Unilateral Measures and the Concept of Opposability in International Law' (1999) 28 *Thesaurus Acroasium*, Thessaloniki Institute of International Public Law 397–454, both are reprinted in

concept and theory presented a new challenge for Yamamoto. It addressed aspects of law-making or legitimacy problems which the theory of international administrative law had not previously dealt with or intentionally avoided.[35] This is a complex and debated concept for some researchers, even in Japan. One possible reason might be that his concept would serve different functions. Therefore, the present author would like to narrow the scope of this concept to the area of 'international law of cooperation' (cited examples in his textbook include trade liberalisation, suppression of the illicit traffic iin narcotic drugs and psychotropic substances, suppression of terrorist acts and humanitarian intervention).

'Unilateral domestic measures' are different from 'unilateral acts'. These are simple applications of pre-existing international laws.[36] On one hand, a unilateral act is a juridical act whose legal requirements and effects are governed by the established rules of international law, whether customary law (e.g. the law concerning recognition of new states or governments) or treaty law (e.g. Article 36, paragraph 2, of the ICJ Statute, i.e. the optional clause). On the other hand, a 'unilateral domestic measure' is, by contrast, an action taken by a state under its domestic law without clearly established international legal (in the strict sense of) 'rules' that either prohibit or permit it. In essence, it can be said to have a 'spillover' effect of a domestic law (usually exercised by hegemonic states or dominant states) into the international arena, which has an object or tendency of general application,[37] where there are no relevant and definite international legal 'rules',[38] i.e. a 'grey zone' area in international law.

A unilateral domestic measure functions in cases of particularly important and serious situations. For instance, when there is a need for an international regime to regulate state jurisdiction to protect or promote certain 'general interests of the international community' (which may be subjective or may not be), there is currently no relevant regime able to respond to such situations. Under those circumstances, as existing laws lack equity and effectiveness, certain unilateral measures would be taken to respond to the

YAMAMOTO, *International Law: An Integrative Perspective on Transboundary Issues* (Sophia University Press 2011).

35 It is dealt with in the chapter 'Sources of international law' in his textbook.

36 See also the work of the ILC, though the result is limited to unilateral declarations, https://legal.un.org/ilc/guide/9_9.shtml

37 In other words, these measures are intended for general application rather than for specific relationships.

38 It would be better to understand this as the absence of relevant legal 'rules', rather than 'principles', as there will always be some relevant 'principles' of international law.

urgent need in serious situations and aim to fill 'gaps or lacunae of law'[39] in order to protect these 'general interests of the international community'. Therefore, objective evaluation of the function or effect of existing law (lex lata) is limited to judgment on 'opposability'[40] as international law does not contain either prohibiting or permitting 'rules'. Therefore, the main focus is on 'lex ferenda', that is, whether it is feasible to agree on and establish a new international regime to address the issues at hand. In this way, unilateral domestic measures may perform law-making functions.

However, when we consider his theory as a whole, this idea appears to be a logical extension of his core idea, that is, 'which is the real substantive law, international law in the true sense (based on 'service public international') or (peculiar) domestic law?' as previously discussed. Furthermore, this idea derives from one aspect of his theory: historical perspective. Since the 'freedom of the seas' argument served as a starting point for his research (as mentioned above), he probably observed various debates or conflicts between states of a general and 'lex ferenda' nature.

The main concern or question (or perhaps criticism) for readers of Yamamoto's articles should be whether or not this opposability effect would be produced ipso facto (i.e. automatically). Presumably, Yamamoto made slight adjustments or improvements to the concept in his second article and in his revised textbook. His conclusion there is as follows: 'third-party states' (affected by the unilateral domestic measure) should argue on the legitimacy of the contents of urgency and equity on which this unilateral domestic measure is based, rather than debating lawfulness or unlawfulness. And they have no choice but to attempt to prevent the accumulation of acts which would result in an opposability agreement (underline added), either by trying to establish an objective determination procedure (on legitimacy) or by use of other feasible means at their disposal, including the representation of effective counter-arguments, for the purpose of bringing such a

39 Although Yamamoto emphasises the role of equity *praeter legem*, it remains a matter of debate as he characterises this situation as 'beyond the framework of positive international law'. It may be prudent to restrict the role of equity *praeter legem* in the context of the 'international law of coexistence' where equity *praeter legem* surely plays a significant role in filling the gap of existing legal rules.

40 Cf. Fisheries Jurisdiction (*United Kingdom v. Iceland*), Merits, Judgment, *I.C.J. Reports 1974*, 3; Fisheries Jurisdiction (*Federal Republic of Germany v. Iceland*), Merits, Judgment, *I.C.J. Reports 1974*, 175. It is also interesting that the ICJ held that the parties were under mutual obligations to undertake negotiations in good faith for an equitable solution on certain matters. It seems that the matter belonged to an area exceeding its judicial ability.

conflict to a normal procedure of international law.[41] Therefore, theoretically (and formally) speaking, the effect of opposability can only be obtained through the consent or acquiescence of the interested states,[42] rather than automatically by fulfilling certain legal requirements.[43]

Furthermore, he must have seen a challenging issue remaining in this argument: how to determine whether certain assertions labelled as 'unilateral measures' would succeed in the long run. His conclusion is general, possibly ambiguous, which could be a persistent problem even for him. Anyway, his remarkable foresight is impressive, as his achievements surpass many recent works on 'unilateral measures' in the law-making function.[44]

## Conclusion

Yamamoto's lifework is a legal analysis of the functional differentiation between international administrative law (*internationales Verwaltungsrecht, droit administratif international*) and administrative international law (*völkerrechtliches Verwaltungsrecht, droit international administratif*), and the gradual development from the former to the latter.

41 When Yamamoto was writing these articles, there were serious cases of unilateral measures taken by the US, including economic conflicts between Japan and the US, especially in the 1980s and 1990s, before the establishment of the WTO. They must have been in his mind and prompted him, at least as important factors, to develop this concept and theory. It would be quite natural for Yamamoto to prefer a multilateral solution rather than a bilateral one, though not negating the latter as a legal 'phenomenon'.

42 In his second article, Yamamoto emphasised the important role of effectiveness. Perhaps Yamamoto was inspired by the Fisheries Case (*United Kingdom v. Norway*), as he once wrote a precedent commentary on it, and this case is referred to in his first article. This could be compared with the theory of consolidation by Charles de Visscher as a root of title. Charles de Visscher, *Théories et réalités en droit international public* (A. Pedone 1953) 244–245. See also D. H. N. Johnson, 'Consolidation as a Root of Title in International Law' (1955) 13 *Cambridge Law Journal* 215–225. Others would explain this phenomenon in terms of acquiescence acquired through long periods of silence, although this should not be lightly presumed.

43 It might be why Murase interprets not only effectiveness but also legitimacy as components of opposability.

44 Picking up just a few works, see Cedric Ryngaert, *Selfless Intervention: Exercising Jurisdiction in the Common Interest* (Oxford University Press 2020); Denys-Sacha Robin, *Les Actes unilateraux des Etats comme elements de formation du droit international* (LGDJ 2022). The latter refers to Murase's article ('Unilateral Measures and the Concept of Opposability in International Law') in the bibliography.

As explained in this chapter, Yamamoto's extended research covers two aspects of this theme. First is the relationship between international law and municipal law, especially regarding which is substantive law. Second is the legal nature of state jurisdiction, with particular focus on the concept of functional differentiation of state jurisdiction (*dédoublement fonctionnel*).

Therefore, as a result of his expertise in these areas, the Festschrift volumes dedicated to him were aptly titled 'International Law and Municipal Law: Development of International Public Interests'[45] and 'State Jurisdiction: International Law and Domestic Law'.[46]

Additionally, he planned to write several scholarly works. He also intended to revise international criminal law and write a monograph on international economic law. Lastly, he proposed to write on administrative international law (in a broad sense) to integrate all subjects. Unfortunately, these monographs were left unfinished. The present author hopes that Yamamoto's legacy will be fully understood, preserved and further developed by future generations, not only in Japan but also around the world.

**Acknowledgements**

The author wishes to express his deep gratitude for the valuable comments of KO Keiko (Professor, Nanzan University) and OKAMATSU Akiko (Professor, Hosei University). Both were supervised by Yamamoto Soji at Sophia (Jochi) University, Faculty of Law and Graduate School.

45 *International Law and Municipal Law: Development of International Public Interests* (n 12).

46 MURASE Shinya and OKUWAKI Naoya (eds), *Kokka Kankatsuken: Kokusaiho to Kokunaiho: Yamamoto Soji Sensei Koki Kinen* (*State Jurisdiction: International Law and Domestic Law: In Commemoration of Professor Yamamoto Soji's 70th Anniversary*) (Keiso Shobo 1998) vii, 708. A book review of this can be found in (1998) 41 *Japanese Annual of International Law* 65–69 (ANDO Nisuke).

# 9

# ISHIMOTO Yasuo: the 'structural transformation' of international law

*WANI Kentaro*

## Introduction

ISHIMOTO Yasuo (1924–2015), who was of the same age as Shigeru Oda (1924–),[1] belonged to the first generation of post-war international law scholars in Japan, together with scholars such as TERASAWA Hajime (1925–2003), UCHIDA Hisashi (1926–2016) and YAMAMOTO Soji (1928–2013).[2] Their predecessors included SOGAWA Takeo (1911–1996)[3] and TABATA Shigejiro (1911–2001).[4] Ishimoto was greatly influenced by their work.[5] Ishimoto graduated from the University of Tokyo, Faculty of Law in 1948 and was appointed as an assistant at the same university (1948–1952). He subsequently held the positions of assistant, lecturer, associate professor and professor at Osaka City University (1952–1981) and professor at Sophia University (1982–1995).

Ishimoto commenced his research career with a historical study of the law of neutrality[6] and subsequently shifted his focus to the legal status of war in international law.[7] Based on these studies, he developed the thesis of the 'structural transformation' of international law, according to which international law is undergoing a transformation from classical international law to modern international law. In Ishimoto's terminology, the term 'classical

1 The former judge of the International Court of Justice (1976–2003).
2 See Chapter 8.
3 See Chapter 7.
4 See Chapter 6.
5 See 'Ishimoto's perspective and methods' and note 16 of this chapter.
6 ISHIMOTO Yasuo, *A Historical Study of the Law of Neutrality* (*Churituseido no Shitekikenkyu*) (Yuhikaku 1958) (in Japanese).
7 ISHIMOTO Yasuo, 'So-called "*de facto* War" (Iwayuru "Jijitsujo no Senso" ni tsuite)' in *Problems of Contemporary International Law* (*Gendai Kokusaiho no Kadai*) (Yuhikaku 1958) 279–325 (in Japanese); ISHIMOTO Yasuo, 'War and Contemporary International Law' in TAKANO Yuichi (ed.), *Modern Law and International Society* (*Gendaiho to Kokusai Syakai*) (Iwanamishoten 1965) 71–108 (in Japanese).

international law' refers to international law prior to the First World War. In contrast, the term 'modern international law' refers to international law after the First World War.

Ishimoto's thesis of the 'structural transformation' of international law and his argument about the legal status of war in classical international law are among the most successful arguments in post-war international law scholarship in Japan.[8] This chapter, therefore, examines Ishimoto's research with a focus on his thesis of the 'structural transformation' of international law, thereby showing one of the defining characteristics of Japanese international law scholarship. Ishimoto's thesis of the 'structural transformation' of international law, which was completed in his 1988 article,[9] is based on the idea of the 'transformation of the conception of war' as one of the *axes* of the 'structural transformation' of international law. His research on the law of neutrality is informed by his awareness that historically the 'regulation of neutral commerce' has 'supported the transformation of the conception of war' in a 'socioeconomic manner'.[10] Therefore, in order to comprehend Ishimoto's thesis of the 'structural transformation of international law', it is essential to return to his historical analysis of the law of neutrality and his subsequent studies on the legal status of war.

## A historical study on the law of neutrality

### *Ishimoto's perspective and methods*

Ishimoto's choice of the law of neutrality as his first research topic was based on his intention to elucidate the structural features of classical international law in relation to its socioeconomic foundations by examining the historical development of the law of neutrality, which is inextricably linked to the status of war in international law. Ishimoto observes:

8 MATSUI Yoshiro, 'International Law Scholarship as Social Science: Its Formation and Development in Japan (Shakai Kagaku to shite no Kokusaiho Gaku: Nihon ni okeru sono Keisei to Tenkai)' in YAMATE Naoyuki and KOZAI Shigeru (eds), *The Legal Structure of International Society: Its History and the Present* (*Kokusai Shakai no Hokozo: sono Rekishi to Genjo*) (Toshindo 2003) 19–26 (in Japanese).

9 ISHIMOTO Yasuo, 'The Structural Transformation of International Law (Kokusaiho no Kozotenkan)' in TAKANO Yuichi (ed.), *Problems of International Relations Law* (*Kokusai Kankeiho no Kadai*) (Yuhikaku 1988) (in Japanese).

10 ISHIMOTO Yasuo, *Gleanings of My Studies on International Law* (*Kokusaiho Kenkyu Yoteki*) (Toshindo 2005) iii (in Japanese).

> Generally speaking, the structural characteristic of the legal order depends upon what forms of power are permitted in that legal order. In other words, the criterion for the respective particularities of the legal order can be found in how it regulates and tolerates violence in general. Consequently, the transformation of the legal status of war in international law is not merely a matter of changes of each rule of international law, but rather, is a question relating to a structural change of the international legal order.[11]

As there is a 'structural connection' between the status of war and the law of neutrality in international law:

> the historical development of the law of neutrality is not only inextricably linked to the transformation of the legal status of war, but also the key to the understanding of the structure of the international legal order. It provides one of the most effective clues for those seeking to comprehend the evolution of the international legal order in relation to its social foundations, rather than in the abstract.[12]

Ishimoto adds a note to this sentence, in which he states that

> the historical character of international law cannot be understood simply by pointing out the primitive character of international law, as Kelsen did. It is beyond doubt that international law was formed as the law of the modern international society, that is to say, as modern law. [The character of international law] can only be understood precisely through an examination of the historical circumstances leading to the formation of each rule [of international law].[13]

In this context, Yoshiro Matsui, citing the names of Japanese international lawyers from the interwar to post-war period, such as Shigejiro Tabata, Takeo Sogawa and Yasuo Ishimoto, observes that 'while their approaches differed, they all shared a common objective of overcoming the pure theory of law [as represented by Kelsen]'.[14] As Matsui notes, while those scholars highly appreciated the rigorous logical analysis of law and the sharp distinction between law and politics offered by the pure theory of law, they also emphasised that such an approach would fail to take into account the actual functions of various institutions of international law and the specific socioeconomic foundations under which those institutions historically

11 ISHIMOTO, *A Historical Study of the Law of Neutrality* 8 (n 6).
12 Ibid.
13 Ibid 11 (n 18).
14 MATSUI, 'International Law Scholarship as Social Science' 13 (n 8).

emerged. In his book *A Historical Study of the Law of Neutrality* (1958), Ishimoto emphasised that the basic character of international law should be defined by historical understanding rather than by an abstract understanding of rules. As Matsui notes, the research method of elucidating the socioeconomic foundations of international law institutions through historical research on them became a clear trend in Japanese international law academia in the 1950s.[15]

In light of this perspective, Ishimoto undertook a historical investigation into the genesis and subsequent evolution of the law of neutrality, drawing on and utilising the most advanced economic historiography at the time, as represented by Hisao Otsuka (1906–1996).[16]

## *The emergence of the law of neutrality as an international law institution*

According to Ishimoto, a decisive factor in the historical development of the law of neutrality was the issue of 'neutral commerce' or the 'pursuit of economic gain in wartime' by neutrals. Maritime commerce to or from belligerent states in wartime was not merely a continuation of peacetime commerce; it often brought even greater economic gains than in peacetime. This was because, in wartime, the number of belligerent vessels was reduced, shipping rates soared and trade that would be monopolised by the belligerents in peacetime (e.g. colonial trade) was sometimes opened to

15 For example, TAKABAYASHI Hideo, *A Study of the Law of the Territorial Sea* (*Ryokai Seido no Kenkyu*) (Yushindo, 1968) (in Japanese); TAIJUDO Kanae, 'Occupation in International Law: A Historical Study (Kokusaiho Jo no Sensen Nitsuite)' (1955) 61 *Hogaku Ronso* 36–99 (in Japanese); KOZAI Shigeru, 'Expropriation of Foreign Property and International Law (Gaikokujin Zaisan no Shuyo to Kokusaiho)' (1955) 61 *Hogaku Ronso* (in Japanese); TAKEMOTO Masayuki, 'The Principle of Respect for Private Property in Land Warfare: Its Formation (Rikusen niokeru Shiyu Zaisan Soncho no Gensoku)' (1957) 63 *Hogaku Ronso* 73–115 (in Japanese). Matsui himself has conducted historical research on various fields of international law. For example, MATSUI Yoshiro, 'The Character of the Law of State Responsibility in Classical International Law: The Transformation of the Law of State Responsibility (Dentoteki Kokusaiho niokeru Kokkasekininho no Seikaku: Kokkasekininho no Tenkann (1))' (1990) 89 *Kokusaiho Gaiko Zassi* 1–52 (in Japanese).

16 In the afterword to his collected papers published in 1998, ISHIMOTO recalls that 'the need for a *historical* study of international law had already been convinced by Shigejiro Tabata's epoch-making masterpiece, *The Transformation of the Idea of Equality of States* (Akitaya 1946), and that Hisao Otsuka's economic historiography was an eye-washing guide for me'. ISHIMOTO Yasuo, *The Structural Transformation of International Law* (*Kokusai ho Kozo Tenkan*) (Yushindo 1998) 313 (in Japanese; emphasis in the original).

neutral merchants.[17] He also points out that maritime commerce in wartime was a way of gaining greater profits at greater risk. The law of neutrality could be established where neutral states perceived national interests in their own merchants benefiting from engaging in maritime commerce with belligerents, and there was an economic basis on the part of belligerents under which belligerents could recognise in principle the freedom of neutral commerce.[18]

Such conditions did not exist in medieval Europe. In European societies at the time of the feudal subsistence economy, 'each feudal state or region could exist in isolation and there was very little need to have an active relationship to war between other states'. 'Neutrality' and 'irrelevance' are not synonymous; rather, the law of neutrality cannot be established without some connection to war.[19]

Even in the Middle Ages, a feudal subsistence economy was not the only type of economy. Indeed, from around the eleventh century onwards, trade in remote areas, including the East, flourished, commonly known as the 'revival of commerce'. As Ishimoto notes, the *Consolato del Mare*, which represented the autonomous practices of the Mediterranean merchants, contained provisions that corresponded to the later rules of the law of neutrality.[20] However, at that time, the merchant class was not yet linked to state power, and the protection of neutral commerce had not yet become a demand at the state level. Therefore, Ishimoto assesses that there was no room for the establishment of the law of neutrality as an institution of international law, and that at best there was only a 'budding form' of such an institution.[21]

It was not until the sixteenth century that neutral states began to recognise a national interest in their own merchants engaging in maritime commerce with belligerents and in demanding protection from them. This period saw the development of world commerce, against the backdrop of the discovery of the New World and the development of the East India route, as well as the association of commercial capital, which had previously been independent of feudal power, with absolutist state power. Consequently, demands for

17 ISHIMOTO, *A Historical Study of the Law of Neutrality* 69–70 (n 6).
18 Ibid 58, 62–63, 65–67.
19 Ibid 58.
20 Section 276 of the *Consolato del mare* provides that enemy cargo on the ships belonging to 'friends' may be captured, whereas friends' cargo on enemy ships may not be captured. For the *Consolato del mare* and the later development of the law regulating neutral commerce, see Kentaro Wani, *Neutrality in International Law: From the Sixteenth Century to 1945* (Routledge 2017) 40–42.
21 ISHIMOTO, *A Historical Study of the Law of Neutrality* 62 (n 6).

freedom of neutral commerce originated not from the merchant class but from neutral states. Concurrently, however, belligerents enacted legislation to prohibit trade with the enemy entirely during this period. This resulted in conflicts of interest at the national level, a prerequisite for the establishment of neutrality in the sixteenth century, which were so intense and uncompromising that the law of neutrality could not be established to regulate them.[22]

Ishimoto attributes this to the character of commercial capital at the time, namely, the violent character of early capital. 'Early capital' is a central concept in Hisao Otsuka's economic historiography and refers to capital – commercial capital and loan shark capital – that existed before the establishment of capitalist society.[23] Early capital existed on the premise of the immaturity of equivalent exchange relations, the underdevelopment of commodity production and the underdevelopment of transport and transportation technology. Profits were extracted not from the production process but within the distribution process, specifically by exploiting price differences between regions (inequivalent exchange).[24] Otsuka points out that the creation of profit by early period capital was accidental, non-routine and speculative, and from this, the 'powerful and plundering character' of early capital. 'Peaceful trade can suddenly turn into violent plunder, depending on objective circumstances'.[25] As examples, Otsuka cites the case of Venetian merchants participating in the Fourth Crusade (1202–1204), who brought back numerous captures from Constantinople, and Hanseatic merchants raiding English and Flemish ships in the fourteenth century.[26] Ishimoto, referring to this argument by Otsuka, observes: 'The maritime unrest of the period was without precedent, and trade, whether in peacetime or wartime, was conducted by armed ships that repeatedly engaged in plunder and combat. ... In such a situation, it was extremely difficult for maritime commerce to be respected solely by third states in wartime'.[27]

Subsequently, from the mid-seventeenth century to the eighteenth century, a number of treaties were concluded between European states which recognised the principle of freedom of neutral commerce. In light of this development, Ishimoto observes that 'the substantial core of the law of neutrality

22 Ibid 65–73.

23 OTSUKA Hisao, *Collected Papers of Hisao Otsuka*, vol. 3, *The Genealogy of the Modern Capitalism* (*OTSUKA Hisao Chosakusyu*, vol. 3, *Kindai Shihonsyugi no Keihu*) (Iwanamishoten 1969) 27 (in Japanese).

24 Ibid 29–30, 37.

25 Ibid 38.

26 Ibid 37–38.

27 ISHIMOTO, *A Historical Study of the Law of Neutrality* 58 (n 6).

was established during this period'.[28] Ishimoto attributes this development to the fact that the major belligerents at the time, Britain and France, each had colonies abroad and had established productive foundations domestically. In such circumstances, they were less dependent on neutral states for wartime supplies, thereby allowing them to engage in neutral commerce. Furthermore, he notes that the strengthening of the belligerents' domestic productive foundations mitigated the 'violent character of early capital' and afforded room for the freedom of neutral commerce to be recognised.[29]

The law of neutrality was subsequently developed to achieve wider acceptance of the freedom of neutral commerce by the First Armed Neutrality (1780–1783), the Second Armed Neutrality (1800–1801) and the 1856 Paris Declaration.[30] He describes the economic basis for the formation of the Paris Declaration as follows:

> The British national economy has now reached a point where a policy of free trade can be justified on the grounds of increasing national wealth. The fact that Britain was able to embrace a far wider acceptance of neutral commercial freedom than during the period of armed neutrality can only be understood in the context of such a development of the British economy. It is therefore evident that the stability of international commerce, centred on Britain, constituted the fundamental basis for the development of international legislation on the law of neutrality [namely the Paris Declaration].[31]

## *The decline of the law of neutrality after the First World War*

Ishimoto assesses the subsequent development of the law of neutrality as having reached its 'climax' or 'completion' when it was codified at the 1907 Second Hague Peace Conference. He further states that it entered a 'process of decline' shortly after that.[32] The decline of the law of neutrality was precipitated by the mounting pressure exerted on neutral maritime commerce by the belligerents in the First and Second World Wars, and the outlawry of war and the introduction of a collective security system in the Covenant of the League of Nations.[33]

Regarding the economic and political background to the decline of the law of neutrality, Ishimoto observes:

28 Ibid 87.
29 Ibid 81.
30 For this development, see Wani, *Neutrality in International Law*, 41–42.
31 ISHIMOTO, *A Historical Study of the Law of Neutrality* 125.
32 Ibid 145, 154.
33 Ibid 154–214.

> In the long term, the decline of the function of the law of neutrality was undeniable. During the imperialist phase [of capitalism], the respect for the sovereignty of neutral states was not a concern for the belligerent powers. In the context of total war, the necessity of suppressing neutral commerce and utilising neutral territory intensified. Concurrently, the neutral powers were no longer able to be 'neutral' in the absolute sense, given that they were no longer solely driven by the pursuit of wartime gain and that the war had a direct impact on the international system, affecting their own prosperity. The decline of the function of the law of neutrality was an expression of this, and the 'theory of the war of aggression' was an ideology in response to precisely such a phase. The Second World War demonstrated this.[34]

As stated earlier in this chapter, Ishimoto has pointed out that the historical development of the law of neutrality was primarily defined by neutral commerce, namely, the pursuit of economic gain by neutrals in wartime. The law of neutrality was established as an institution of international law when neutral states found it in their interest to remain neutral and allow their nationals to engage in maritime commerce with belligerents, and when the belligerents made concessions to this. Such a condition existed in Europe between the seventeenth and nineteenth centuries, but not during the First and Second World Wars. To illustrate, the United States was not in a position to pursue economic gains by remaining neutral during the Second World War. Rather, in order to avert a military, economic and ideological crisis for the United States that would result from the victory of Nazi Germany, the United States provided military assistance to Britain. This included the 1940 destroyers-for-bases agreement with Great Britain and the enactment of the 1941 Lend-Lease Act. This ultimately resulted in the United States entering the war on the side of Great Britain on 11 December 1941.[35] Ishimoto states that 'the Great Powers were no longer able to pursue wartime economic gain in isolation, and as long as the war affected the international system itself for their own prosperity, they could no longer be "neutral" in the absolute sense'.[36]

34 Ibid 210.

35 For the neutrality policy of the United States during the Second World War, see Wani, *Neutrality in International Law* 161–162 (n 20).

36 ISHIMOTO, *A Historical Study of the Law of Neutrality* 210 (n 6).

## A study on the legal status of war

### *The relationship between the historical study of the law of neutrality and the legal status of war*

As seen previously, Ishimoto has identified the socioeconomic foundations of the development of the law of neutrality through historical research. Ishimoto links the historical development of the law of neutrality to the development of theories on the legal status of war. The just war theory, which had a tradition in Europe since the Middle Ages, became a 'fetter' in the seventeenth and eighteenth centuries, when the freedom of neutral commerce was recognised. This is because, 'as long as the just war theory was maintained, it would be difficult to grasp the concept of the law of neutrality, the basic principle of which is the impartiality towards all belligerents'.[37] Consequently, 'the influence of the medieval fetters of the just war theory, which were still deeply embedded in the conceptual framework, remained strong among international lawyers of the time. However, they gradually relaxed or overcame the just war theory in response to the demands of the rising bourgeoisie'.[38] As a result, the 'non-discriminatory conception of war' was more compatible with the structure of classical international law than the just war theory. Consequently, international legal doctrine shifted towards rejecting the just war theory and adopting a non-discriminatory conception of war. The term 'non-discriminatory conception of war', commonly used in Japan but scarcely used outside Japan, refers to a notion that the act of states to resort to war is not regulated by international law and that all belligerents are treated equally.[39]

Having identified the socioeconomic foundations of the law of neutrality and the conception of war, which was compatible with the law of neutrality, namely, the non-discriminatory conception of war, Ishimoto proceeded to address the question of how the structure of classical international law, which adopted the non-discriminatory conception of war, should be understood. In his articles of 1958, entitled 'The So-called *de facto* War', and of 1964, entitled 'War and Contemporary International Law', Ishimoto addressed this issue.

37 Ibid 89–90.

38 Ibid.

39 For the 'non-discriminatory conception of war', see YANAGIHARA Masaharu, 'The So-called "Non-Discriminatory Conception of War" and the Outlawry of War: With Particular Reference to Carl Schmitt's Theories (Iwayuru "Musabetsu Sensokan" to Senso no Ihoka: Carl Schmitt no Gakusetsu wo Tegakari to Shite)' (2000) 20 *Sekaiho Nenpo* 3–29 (in Japanese).

### *The 'war as a state' theory and the 'dualistic structure' of classical international law*

Ishimoto notes that war was regarded as a 'state' – a 'state of war' – in classical international law, despite the fact that war is actually waged through concrete acts such as attacks on enemy armies, the capture and detention of enemy combatants as prisoners of war and the occupation of enemy territories.[40] The fact that war was understood as a 'state' in classical international law does not simply mean that war involves a certain temporal duration. This is because any act cannot be terminated instantaneously. Rather, in classical international law, war was understood to exist in opposition to peace. This implies that war and peace were regarded as dualistic 'times' within the structure of international law. Ishimoto posits that peace and war must be regarded as 'dualistic' or 'valid with an interdimensional relationship' because the same act is evaluated in completely different ways depending on whether it occurs in peacetime or wartime. To illustrate, Ishimoto cites the deployment of armed troops into the territory of another state. Such an act is clearly contrary to international law in peacetime without that state's consent, whereas it is permitted during wartime. Another example is the termination or suspension of treaties between belligerents. While such termination or suspension is not permitted during peacetime, the outbreak of war automatically terminates or suspends treaties between belligerents.[41]

The central proposition of Ishimoto's international law scholarship is thus presented: classical international law was international law with a dualistic structure of peace and war. However, Ishimoto's examination of the status of war in classical international law, and the structure of classical international law as defined by it, does not end there. War could be understood as a 'state' only when the act of states to resort to war was not regulated by international law. If the act of states to resort to war was regulated in classical international law, war should have been regarded as an *act* because the concept of resorting to a *state* is nonsensical. Indeed, Kelsen, who believes that even in international law prior to the First World War, war was legal only as a sanction against illegal acts, argues that 'war is a specific action, not a status. From the point of view of international law, the most important fact is the resort to war, and that means resort to an action, not resort to a status'.[42] According to Ishimoto, therefore, 'in order to substantiate the "war as a state" theory, it is an essential prerequisite to

40 ISHIMOTO, 'So-called "*de facto* War"' 291–292 (n 7).
41 Ibid 292–294.
42 Hans Kelsen, *Principles of International Law* (Rinehart & Company Inc. 1952) 27.

examine whether the act of states to resort to war was regulated in classical international law'.[43]

## *Was the act of states to resort to war regulated in classical international law?*

The question of the legal status of war in classical international law remains a subject of much debate, and even within Japan, scholars' views are surprisingly varied. As we shall see later, Ishimoto believed that classical international law did not regulate the act of states resorting to war at all. In contrast, Ryoichi Taoka (1898–1985) maintained that even prior to the First World War, war was permitted only as a means of self-help, namely, only as a reaction to a violation of international law.[44] Shigejiro Tabata also argued that even prior to the First World War, 'the notion of war as a means of self-help remained a fundamental tenet of international law'.[45] In practice, however, almost all wars, which each state considered and asserted as a means of self-help, were deemed to be legal in international society, where there was no superior organ of judgement beyond states. Conversely, as with Ishimoto, other scholars who espouse the view that resort to war was completely unregulated in international law prior to the First World War include Yoshiro Matsui (1941–)[46] and Yasuaki Onuma (1946–2018).[47]

Ishimoto attempts to demonstrate that resort to war was unregulated in classical international law by examining and refuting Kelsen's theory of just war (*bellum justum*), according to which war was permitted only as a means of sanctioning violations of international law. Kelsen argues that the just war theory can be demonstrated by examining 'the historical manifestations of the will of the states – diplomatic documents, especially declarations of war and treaties between states'.[48] According to Kelsen, 'the governments of states resorting to war always try to justify so doing to their own people as

43 ISHIMOTO, 'War and Contemporary International Law' 75 (n 7).

44 TAOKA Ryoichi, *Outline of International Law* (*Kokusaiho Taiko*), vol. 2 (Yushodo 1939) 117–118 (in Japanese).

45 TABATA Shigejiro Tabata, *International Law* (*Kokusaiho*), 2nd edn (Yuhikaku 1965) 367–368 (in Japanese).

46 MATSUI Yoshiro, *The Principle of the Prohibition of the Use of Force: Its History and the Present* (*Buryoku Koshi Kinshi Gensoku no Rekishi to Genjo*) (Nihonhyoronsya 2018) 6–11 (in Japanese). For Matsui, see Chapter 10 of this book.

47 ONUMA Yasuaki, *International Law* (*Kokusaiho*), revised edn (Toshindo 2005) 470–471 (in Japanese). For Onuma, see Chapter 12 of this book.

48 Hans Kelsen, *Law and Peace in International Relations* (Harvard University Press 1942) 36.

well as to the world at large. There is hardly an instance on record in which a state has not tried to proclaim its own cause just and righteous'.[49] However, when Kelsen states the aforementioned passage, he does not cite any single specific document or case. Moreover, even if it is true that states resorting to war always attempt to justify their actions, it is not clear whether these justifications are legal; they may be political justifications.

It is this point that Ishimoto raises when he refutes Kelsen's theory of just war. Although Ishimoto does not provide an exhaustive examination of state practice, it is relatively easy to identify instances in which a state that resorted to war did not even allege that another state violated international law, i.e. that its own actions constituted self-help. In his 1958 article, Ishimoto notes that in the Japanese declaration of war in the Russo-Japanese War (1904–1905), Japan justified its war against Russia but did not claim that Russia had violated international law against Japan.[50] Building on Ishimoto's observations, Yoshiro Matsui delves deeper into the question of whether the 'juridical theory of just war'[51] as represented by Kelsen reflected a principle of positive international law before the First World War.[52] To do so, he draws upon the modern Japanese experience of war as an illustrative example. Matsui commences by noting that at the outbreak of the Sino-Japanese War in 1894, Japan asserted that China had infringed 'rights and interests of this Empire [Japan]' by disregarding the independence of Korea.[53] Indeed, the 1876 Japan-Korea Treaty of Friendship stipulated that 'Chosen [Korea], being an independent state, enjoys the same sovereign rights as does Japan' (Article 1).[54] Consequently, respecting the independence of Korea was a treaty obligation for Japan and a treaty right for Korea. However, since China was not a party to this treaty, it was not bound by it. Therefore, China's disregard for Korea's independence did not constitute an infringement of Japan's rights under international law. Moreover, even assuming that China's respect for Korea's independence was a right for Japan under international law, in the peace treaty between Japan and

49 Ibid 37.

50 ISHIMOTO, 'So-called "*de facto* War"' 304 (n 7).

51 The term 'juridical' here means 'not theological'. The 'theological' theory of just war was developed by theologians such as Thomas Aquinas in medieval and early modern Europe. In contrast, the 'juridical' theory of just war was advocated by positive international lawyers such as Kelsen.

52 MATSUI, *The Principle of the Prohibition of the Use of Force* 6–11 (n 46).

53 Proclamation of Emperor of Japan, declaring war against China, 1 August 1894, in *British and Foreign State Papers*, vol. 86 (William Ridgway 1899) 303–304.

54 Treaty of Peace and Friendship between Japan and Korea, 26 February 1876, in *British and Foreign State Papers*, vol. 67 (William Ridgway 1883) 530–534.

China (the Shimonoseki Peace Treaty),[55] Japan not only compelled China to recognise the full and complete independence of Korea (Article 1) but also acquired many new rights – such as the cession of Taiwan and the Pescadores Islands (Article 2) and the conclusion of new commercial treaties (Article 6) – which had nothing to do with pre-existing rights under international law. If war were a means of self-help, namely, a means of restoring violated rights, Japan's acquisition of these *new* rights would be inexplicable. Matsui also refers to the Japanese declaration of war in the Russo-Japanese War (1904–1905), in which the Japanese Government, while insisting that the occupation and the possible future annexation of Manchuria by Russia would threaten the integrity of Korea and the security of the region, did not insist that Russia had violated Japan's rights under international law.[56] According to Matsui, this justification by Japan 'was not a legal justification but a political one'. He concludes: 'It must be said that it is clear that the war of this period was fought not only for the restoration of violated rights, as 'the juridical theory of just war' argues, but also for the acquisition of new rights'.[57]

While an exhaustive study of diplomatic documents, including declarations of war, is necessary to definitively clarify the legal status of war in classical international law, the cases cited by Ishimoto and Matsui alone seem sufficient to demonstrate that war was waged not only to implement international law, i.e. as a means of self-help, but also to change international law, i.e. to acquire new rights. There are cases in which the declaration of war does not even mention the violation of international law by the opposing state as a justification, which means that states in this period did not consider that war was legal only as a means of self-help. In short, Kelsen's theory of just war did not reflect the positive international law of the period.

### *A response to Kelsen's argument: the legal character of classical international law*

Kelsen points out that if international law did not regulate war, which is unrestricted intervention in the sphere of interests of another state, then states would have no protected sphere of interests under international law, and international law would lose its legal character.[58] This view

55 Treaty between China and Japan, Signed at Shimonoseki, 17 April 1895, in *British and Foreign State Papers*, vol. 87 (William Ridgway, 1900) 799–805.

56 Text of the Imperial Proclamation, issued on 10 February 1904, in Ministry of Foreign Affairs, *The Documents on Japanese Foreign Policy*, vols 37 and 38, *Supplement:* (1958) *The Russo-Japanese War I* 143–145 (in Japanese).

57 MATSUI, *The Principle of the Prohibition of the Use of Force* 10 (n 46).

58 Kelsen, *Law and Peace* 52–53.

was shared by Taoka and Tabata, who believed that war was permitted only as a means of self-help in international law prior to the First World War.[59]

How did Ishimoto, who believed that classical international law did not regulate the act of states to resort to war at all, respond to Kelsen's argument? In his 1958 article, in a note rather than in the text, therefore, it does not appear to be a very upfront response, he states:

> He [Kelsen] astutely condemns the shortcomings of numerous scholars who affirm the legal nature of international law while avoiding addressing the status of violence (namely war) in international law. ... For those of us who specialise in international law and make our living from it, this is generally a rather shocking statement. This psychological threat can be avoided by recalling the empirical fact that international law is not law in the same way that domestic law is law. What a fragile normative structure! This was the defining characteristic of classical international law.[60]

He made a very different observation in his 1988 article:

> War was distinguished from peace as a 'special time' or as an 'anomalous state' and was expelled outside the law. Contrary to the common sense of lawyers, international law could only maintain its legal character through the extra-legality of war. The dualistic structure of war and peace thus became the foundation of classical international law. This enabled the establishment of the normative character of peacetime international law as a system of substantive law.[61]

While this explanation by Ishimoto may be difficult to understand at first sight, he argues that the legal character of *peacetime* international law was maintained by separating peace and war as distinct categories, or by excluding war from the system of peacetime international law.

## The 'structural transformation' of international law

### *The meaning of 'structural transformation'*

Ishimoto's thesis of the 'structural transformation of international law', according to which international law is undergoing a 'structural

59 See note 43 and accompanying texts.
60 ISHIMOTO, 'So-called "*de facto* War"' (n 7).
61 ISHIMOTO, 'The Structural Transformation of International Law' 9 (n 9).

transformation' from classical international law to modern international law, is an argument fully developed in a 1988 article,[62] but it already appeared in Ishimoto's earlier articles.[63] In this sense, the thesis of the 'structural transformation of international law' was a preoccupation throughout Ishimoto's scholarly life.

According to Ishimoto, a 'transformation' is not a mere 'change' but a '180-degree turn', or 'die Wendung' in German. Of course, in law, 'a 180-degree turn' is only a metaphor, but 'a turn means a change that upsets the existing system and requires a new foundation'.[64]

From this explanation, it is clear that the 'structural transformation of international law' is not merely a change in various rules or institutions of classical international law, but a fundamental upheaval of the institutions and concepts that were at the very foundation of the classical international legal order. For Ishimoto, the axes of the 'structural transformation of international law' were twofold: first, war, which was left 'outside the law' and unregulated in classical international law, is brought 'within the law' and regulated or prohibited in modern international law; second, as regards the incorporation of principles of private law into international law, which was the basic momentum that made classical international law conceivable as 'law', such principles are undergoing a transformation in modern international law.

### *Outlawry of war*

The first axis of the structural transformation of international law is the change in the legal status of war. As seen earlier, Ishimoto understands that classical international law did not regulate the act of states resorting to war and war was placed 'outside the law'. In this sense, classical international law was international law with a dualistic structure of peace and war. In modern international law, on the other hand, the dualistic structure of peace and war has collapsed, with the limitation and prohibition of war since the Covenant of the League of Nations to the United Nations Charter, and 'the act of resorting to war, which was previously outside the law, is now, so

62 ISHIMOTO, 'The Structural Transformation of International Law' (n 9).

63 ISHIMOTO, *A Historical Study on the Law of Neutrality* 5, 13 (n 6); ISHIMOTO, 'So-called "*de facto* War"' 287, 290 (n 7); ISHIMOTO, 'War and Contemporary International Law' 91 (n 7).

64 ISHIMOTO Yasuo, 'The Structural Transformation of International Law: A Dialogue for a General Theory' (1986), reproduced in ISHIMOTO, *Gleanings of My Studies on International Law* 57–58.

to speak, inside the law'.[65] This led to a shift in international law from the traditional dualistic structure to a monistic structure.

According to Ishimoto, the outlawry of war 'is not merely a new prohibition of certain state acts by international law', but 'represents a change in the entire structure of international law'.[66] The outlawry of war does not only mean that the act of states to resort to war has become subject to legal regulation, but also that it has implications for the entire structure of international law, in that it requires a re-examination of various traditional concepts of international law, such as the law of war, the right of self-defence, reprisals, the law of treaties and the acquisition of territorry.[67]

Furthermore, according to Ishimoto, modern international law 'even has the task of transforming the legal order itself, which has been constructed by force'. The outlawry of war does not mean reviving the just war theory. The just war theory identifies the causes that justify resorting to war (just causes) and distinguishes between just and unjust wars based on the legitimacy of those causes. In other words, according to the just war theory, a state may use violence – i.e. resort to war – if it has a just cause. In contrast, the outlawry of war, which denies the very idea of realising rights or state policies by force, regardless of whether the causes are just or not, is a completely different conception from the just war theory. Thus, the outlawry of war 'leads to the elimination of violence from the international community, regardless of its cause or reason'. 'The principle of eliminating violence from international society was conceived, at least in its original form, as applied only between states. However, its development would lead to the rejection of colonial and racist regimes. This is because such regimes have been established and maintained more or less by the use of force'.[68] This takes the form of the prohibition of forcible action which deprives peoples of their right to self-determination[69] and the recognition of the right of peoples to receive assistance in their resistance to such forcible action.[70]

65 Ibid 58.

66 ISHIMOTO, 'The Structural Transformation of International Law' 19 (n 9).

67 Ibid.

68 Ibid 23.

69 Declaration on the granting of independence to colonial countries and peoples (A/RES/1514(XV), 12 December 1960), paragraph 4; Declaration on Principles of International Law Concerning Friendly Relations and Co-operation Among States in Accordance with the Charter of the United Nations (A/RES/2625(XXV), 24 October 1970), the Fifth Principle, paragraph 5.

70 Declaration on Principles of International Law Concerning Friendly Relations and Co-operation Among States in Accordance with the Charter of the United Nations, the Fifth Principle, paragraph 5; Definition of Aggression (A/RES/3314 (XXIX), 14 December 1974), Article 7.

Ishimoto concludes: 'the transformation of the concept of war in contemporary international law, which disrupts the dualistic structure of classical international law, leads not only to the unconditional elimination of violence between states, but also to the dismantling of regimes constructed by violence in general'. He characterises modern international law as an order negating the 'violent order' created in the past.[71]

### *Principles of private law incorporated into international law and changes in these principles*

The second axis of the structural transformation of international law is the transformation of domestic private law principles which were incorporated into classical international law. Ishimoto describes how principles of domestic private law have been incorporated into classical international law. He states that 'peacetime international law has developed its normative content through the medium of domestic private law'.[72] In the formative period of international law, Roman law was first perceived as directly valid as international law (e.g. Genlitis), and later as a source or proof of natural law (e.g. Grotius). Even modern legal positivists, who strictly rejected the idea of natural law, did not completely exclude principles of private law from the sphere of international law. For example, von Liszt (1851–1919) stated that when the rich ideas of private law are used in international law, 'the general concepts and fundamental principles common to all law, namely the general theory of law (allgemeine Rechtslehre), are invoked'.[73] Moreover, Article 38(1)(c) of the Statute of the Permanent Court of International Justice lists, in addition to treaties and international custom, 'general principles of law recognised by civilised nations' to be applied by the Court.

According to Ishimoto, the normative structure of classical international law is fundamentally similar to that of modern domestic private law, and three basic principles of modern private law – legal personality of all persons, private ownership of property and the binding force of contracts – have been transposed into classical international law. When the principles of modern private law were incorporated into international law, they were 'refined' or 'modified' to suit the society of states. First, whereas domestic private law recognises the legal personality of all persons, classical international law recognises the legal personality of all states. Second, while private

71 ISHIMOTO, 'The Structural Transformation of International Law' 17, 24.

72 Ibid 10.

73 Franz von Liszt, *Das Völkerrecht: systematisch dargestellt*, 11th edn (Springer 1918) 38 (author's translation).

law recognises the private ownership of all goods, classical international law recognises states' sovereignty over all territory. Third, while private law recognises the binding force of contracts between individuals, classical international law recognises the binding force of treaties between states.[74]

Ishimoto observes that these principles of modern private law, which were 'refined' and transplanted into classical international law, serve as the normative basis of the capitalist economy, in particular its fundamental element, the exchange of goods. In contrast to the law of kinship and inheritance, these principles have a universal content that is common to the national laws of all countries.[75] Ishimoto explains the impact of this universality on classical international law as follows.[76]

> Thus, a common normative consciousness of nations has been cultivated through the legal norms of the domestic law of the capitalist economy. ... It is the normative consciousness inhabited in our human bodies that has created and maintained the law within the international community. This is the ultimate in international law and the fundamental element that makes international law law.
>
> This is a kind of fetishism. International law lacks a central authority comparable to that of domestic law. International law lacks law-enforcement authority, such as courts, police and armed forces. In this sense, international law is a social norm, as close as possible to a moral code. Nevertheless, international law can only be understood as 'law' because the normative consciousness of domestic society, which is enforced by the apparatus of power, has been 'empathised' in the international community.

Classical international law thus became a 'fairly self-contained legal system', despite its extremely weak legal structure and the lack of regulation regarding the conduct of states that resort to war.[77] 'It was and has always been impossible for international law to find its ultimate basis as law in coercion or sanctions' and that 'what gives international law its legal character is, in the end, the legal consciousness of the peoples of the world'.[78]

Ishimoto observes that international law has now entered a period of transition.[79] First, whereas classical international law recognised the legal personality of states and only states, modern international law, by recognising the right of peoples to self-determination, 'recognises legal personality

74 ISHIMOTO, 'The Structural Transformation of International Law' 10–13.
75 Ibid 13.
76 Ibid 13–14.
77 Ibid 4, 16.
78 ISHIMOTO, 'A Dialogue for a General Theory' 66.
79 ISHIMOTO, 'The Structural Transformation of International Law' 25–33.

to all national entities, namely peoples'. Second, with respect to the right of states to govern their national territory, modern international law, by promoting the international guarantee of human rights, 'limits the exercise of the right to govern from a human rights perspective more generally and to a greater extent' than the limitations on the right to govern in classical international law. Third, with respect to treaties between states, which were recognised as binding under classical international law, modern international law now invalidates treaties concluded as a result of the use of force in violation of international law or in conflict with peremptory norms (Articles 52 and 53 of the Vienna Convention on the Law of Treaties).

These three changes are related to the rejection of the colonial regime. With regard to the second change, 'apart from external matters [such as the treatment of foreigners and their property], the "state" as an entity capable of free rule, including colonial rule and racial discrimination, was never questioned'. However, 'the legal consciousness that underpinned this normative structure is now collapsing'. 'It is now inevitable that the repudiation of colonial and racist regimes, hitherto a domestic matter, will become one of the central issues in the weaving of an international bill of human rights'.[80] With respect to the third change, Ishimoto notes: 'In the past, all treaties were valid as "freely made agreements [between States]". Whether they were unequal treaties or subordinate treaties, [all parties to] the treaties were treated as free and equal at the time of conclusion. According to this idea, even treaties denying the right to self-determination of peoples would be valid'.[81] Although the 1969 Vienna Convention on the Law of Treaties does not specify what exactly constitutes peremptory norms of international law and leaves it open to interpretation, 'it is clear, however, that treaties which, for example, deny the right to self-determination and impose subordination, may be interpreted as violating peremptory norms'.[82] Furthermore, with regard to the first change, the right to self-determination does not end with the achievement of external self-determination, i.e. independence, but 'in view of the long period of violent deprivation of the right to self-determination, the right to "restoration" and "reparation" is naturally derived as a corollary'.[83] Examples of such thinking include paragraphs 4(f) and 4(h) of the 1974 Declaration on the Establishment of a New International Economic Order,[84] as well as new concepts such as 'permanent sovereignty

80 ISHIMOTO, 'The Structural Transformation of International Law' 31.
81 ISHIMOTO, 'A Dialogue for a General Theory' 84.
82 ISHIMOTO, 'The Structural Transformation of International Law' 32.
83 Ibid 28.
84 A/RES/3201(S-VI).

over natural resources', 'the right to development' or 'the common heritage of mankind'. Thus, in modern international law, two categories of norms coexist: one is a category of 'norms of international law based on the concept of equivalent exchange that characterised classical international law', and another is a category of 'norms of international law based on the concept of compensatory inequality that sublates the principle of private law'.[85]

## Conclusion

Ishimoto was one of the scholars who set the direction and basic framework of post-war Japanese international law scholarship. In particular, his thesis on the 'structural transformation of international law' is often cited when discussing the history and present of international law. An accurate understanding of the characteristics and structure of modern international law, compared with classical international law, is essential for both interpreting and making international law. Some of Ishimoto's arguments may now appear to require revision,86 but in any case, his most significant contribution was to present a deep analysis of fundamental issues of international law, including the question of the legal status of war in classical international law and to encourage a subsequent debate within Japanese international law academia.

85 ISHIMOTO, 'The Structural Transformation of International Law' 29, 35.

86 See, for example, WANI Kentaro, 'The "State of War" Doctrine Reconsidered: Was Traditional International Law Divided into the Law of Peace and the Law of War? ("Senso Jotai" Riron no Saikento: Dentoteki Kokusaiho ha Heiji-Senji no Nigenteki Kozo no Kokusaiho dattanoka?)' in IWASAWA Yuji et al. (eds), *The Dynamism of International Law* (*Kokusaiho no Dainamizum*) (Yuhikaku 2019) 627–650 (in Japanese).

# 10

# MATSUI Yoshiro: the social science of international law

*KODERA Satoshi*

## Introduction

This chapter focuses on the work of MATSUI Yoshiro (1941–) and analyses his theoretical features. Matsui is one of Japan's leading international law scholars and served as President of the Japan Society of International Law from 2000 to 2003. Matsui continues to critically analyse the relationship between international law and society today through numerous books and articles.

Although Matsui is positioned within the Kyoto School, whose founder is TABATA Shigejiro (1911–2001),[1] his position within the school is distinct. This is demonstrated in the Marxist approach he adopts. Although Tabata stressed the necessity of analysing the socioeconomic foundations of international law, he kept a certain distance from Marxism. In contrast, Matsui consciously adopted a Marxist approach and applied it to the analysis of international law. As such, Matsui's theory of international law is unique among Japanese international jurisprudence.

The period during which Matsui developed his theory of international law coincides with the 'post-war' period in Japanese society following Japan's defeat in the Second World War and its occupation by the Allied Powers. Matsui's theory of international law has evolved in line with Japan's international problems after the Second World War. For example, the revision of the Japan–US Security Treaty in 1960 and 1970, the reversion of Okinawa to Japan in 1972, the Gulf War in 1990, the Iraq War in 2003 and the Afghanistan War in 2011. As one of Japan's leading international legal scholars, Matsui has tackled these international issues while developing his theory of international law. In this sense, Matsui's theory of international law itself represents an essential aspect of post-war Japanese society.

1 See Chapter 7.

The discussion below proceeds as follows. First, Matsui's academic foundation will be examined by placing his academic career in the historical context of Japan. Then, the characteristics of Matsui's theory of international law will be clarified. Finally, the significance of Matsui's theory of international law will be discussed from the perspectives of Japanese and global international law jurisprudence.

## Formation of academic foundations

### *Undergraduate years (1959–1963)*

Born in Kyoto in 1941, Matsui entered the Faculty of Law at Kyoto University in 1959. In 1951, Japan concluded a security treaty with the United States, which allowed the stationing of US troops in Japan. Around 1958, negotiations began between Japan and the United States over revisions to the Japan–US Security Treaty. On 19 January 1960, Japan and the United States signed the new Japan–US Security Treaty. The treaty inserted a provision requiring joint defence by Japan and the United States.[2] After the treaty was signed, deliberations were held in the Diet in Japan. At the same time, numerous demonstrations and opposition movements took place in Japan over the new Japan–US Security Treaty.

The struggle over the Japan-US Security Treaty in 1960 profoundly influenced the subsequent development of Matsui's theory of international law. For example, although Matsui was not directly involved in this struggle, he pointed out that it gave him 'an awareness that legal matters must be considered in connection with the social issues surrounding them'.[3] It can be said that Matsui's methodology of analysing law in

2 Article 5 of the 1960 US–Japan Security Treaty provides that 'Each Party recognizes that an armed attack against either Party in the territories under the administration of Japan would be dangerous to its own peace and safety and declares that it would act to meet the common danger in accordance with its constitutional provisions and processes. Any such armed attack and all measures taken as a result thereof shall be immediately reported to the Security Council of the United Nations in accordance with the provisions of Article 51 of the Charter. Such measures shall be terminated when the Security Council has taken the measures necessary to restore and maintain international peace and security'.

3 MATSUI Yoshiro, YAKUSHIJI Kimio, TOKUGAWA Shinji and NISHIMURA Tomoaki, 'Professor MATSUI's Biographical Interview (MATSUI Yoshiro Kyoju Oral History)' (2010) 333–334 *Ritsumeikan Hogaku* 1872 (in Japanese).

relation to society was nurtured in the political environment of Japan during this period.

### *Graduate period (1963–1967)*

Matsui then entered the seminar of TABATA Shigejiro, a professor of international law at Kyoto University, and began his research in international law.[4] At that time, Kyoto University had two international law scholars, TAOKA Ryoichi (1898–1985)[5] and TABATA Shigejiro. Although they differed in their approaches, both emphasised the historical element in their research on international law. Of the two, Tabata especially developed an approach that analysed the socioeconomic foundations of international law. This approach later gave rise to a research trend known as the 'Kyoto School' among Tabata's disciples. However, when Matsui entered graduate school, it was still in the process of being formed.[6]

In 1963, Matsui entered graduate school at Kyoto University and began exploring his research theme under the guidance of Tabata. Ultimately, Matsui chose permanent sovereignty over natural resources as his first research subject. Matsui entered graduate school in the 1960s when decolonisation was at its peak. In a paper published while still a graduate student, Matsui carefully analysed the process of formation and development of the concept of permanent sovereignty over natural resources and depicted the background of conflicts among countries over this concept.[7] In the same paper, Matsui discussed permanent sovereignty over natural resources in relation to the right to self-determination, pointing out that the former can be regarded as a 'natural corollary' of the latter.[8] This perspective led to Matsui's later research on the right to self-determination.

4 Ibid 1871–1900.
5 See Chapter 5.
6 MATSUI Yoshiro and ASADA Masahiko, 'Dialogue: International Law in Kyoto (1) (2) (Taidan: Kyoto no Kokusaihogaku)' (2019) 64 *Hougaku Seminar* 62–67; (2020) 65 *Hougaku Seminar* 44–50 (in Japanese).
7 MATSUI Yoshiro, 'Permanent Sovereignty over Natural Wealth and Resources (1) (2) (Tennen no Tomi to Shigen nitaisuru Eikyuteki Shuken)' (1966) 79(3) *Kyoto Law Review* 35–71; (1966) 79(4) *Kyoto Law Review* 45–68 (in Japanese).
8 MATSUI, 'Permanent Sovereignty over Natural Wealth and Resources (2)' 51 (n 7).

## Nagoya University (1967–2004)

Matsui began working at Nagoya University in 1967 as an assistant professor. The following year, in 1968, he became an associate professor, and in 1976, he became a professor at Nagoya University. He continued to work at Nagoya University and trained many of his students until 2004, when he moved to Ritsumeikan University.

Matsui started his career at Nagoya University, where he first researched the Vietnam War. Matsui viewed the Vietnam War as an issue of the Vietnamese people's right to self-determination.[9] He argued that the US legal justification for the Vietnam War, the claim of South Vietnam's statehood, was, in fact, unsupportable under international law.[10] Matsui subsequently published a series of studies on the right to self-determination, and from the 1970s through the 1980s,[11] the right to self-determination formed one of the mainstays of his international law research.

One of Matsui's most essential studies in the 1970s was a legal analysis of post-war Japan's international relations, as highlighted by the struggle over the Japan–US Security Treaty from the late 1960s to 1970. The Japan–US Security Treaty, revised in 1960, had a ten-year term.[12] Various demon-

9 MATSUI Yoshiro, 'The Logic of 'Intervention' in the Vietnam War (Vietnam Senso niokeru 'Kainyu' no Ronri)' (1968) 40 *Horitsu Jiho* 84–90 (in Japanese).

10 MATSUI Yoshiro, 'International Legal Problems Concerning the 'Divided' State in Vietnam (1)(2) (Vietnam niokeru 'Bunretsu' Kokka no Kokusaihojo no Syomondai)' (1973) 72 *Kokusaiho Gaiko Zassi* 299–334; (1974) 73 *Kokusaiho Gaiko Zassi* 46–73 (in Japanese).

11 See, for example, MATSUI Yoshiro, *Contemporary International Relations and the Right to Self-Determination* (Shinnihon Shuppansha 1981) (in Japanese); MATSUI Yoshiro, 'Legal Status of National Liberation Movements (Minzoku Kaiho Dantai no Kokusaihojo no Chii)' (1982) 81 *Kokusaiho Gaiko Zassi* 523–579 (in Japanese); MATSUI Yoshiro, 'New Developments in the Theory of the Right of Peoples to Self-Determination: is the Right to Self-Determination *Jus Cogens*? (Minzoku Jiketsu Ron no Shintenkai: Jiketsuken wa Kyoko Kihan ka)' in TERASAWA Hajime and UCHIDA Hisashi (eds), *Basis Issues of International Law* (*Kokusaiho no Kihon Mondai*) (Yuhikaku 1986) 95–102 (in Japanese); MATSUI Yoshiro, 'The Right to Self-Determination on Trial: with a Focus on the Post-Cold War Situation in Europe (Shiren ni Tatsu Jiketsuken: Reisengo no Europe no Jokyo wo Chushin ni)' in KIRIYAMA Takanobu, SUGISHIMA Masaaki and FUNAO Akiko (eds), *International Law in Transition* (*Tenkanki Kokusaiho no Kozo to Kino*) (Kokusai Shoin 2000) 461–515 (in Japanese).

12 Article 10 of the 1960 US–Japan Security Treaty provides that 'This Treaty shall remain in force until in the opinion of the Governments of Japan and the United States of America there shall have come into force such United Nations arrangements as will satisfactorily provide for the maintenance of international peace and security in the Japan area. However, after the Treaty has been in force for ten years, either

strations and opposition movements took place in Japan over whether to extend the Treaty. Finally, while the treaty was automatically extended in June 1970, this struggle provided an opportunity to rethink Japan's position in international relations, which had been built around the Japan–US relationship.

In 1968, a year after Matsui took a job at Nagoya University, the Association of Democratic Scientists (*Minka*) began joint research on extending the Japan–US Security Treaty.[13] It was founded on 12 January 1946 by a group of Japanese Marxists and had various subcommittees, including the law section, where experts from different fields discussed the issues.[14] Matsui was actively involved in its law section and published a number of articles analysing Japan's post-war Japan–US security system based on Marxist jurisprudence.[15] It can be said that Matsui's Marxist approach was shaped by his legal analysis of the Security Treaty during this period.

## Characteristics of Matsui's theory of international law

### *From reality to theory*

A broad interest in all areas of international law characterises Matsui's theory of international law. As already noted, Matsui has published an enormous number of papers on permanent sovereignty over natural resources, the right to self-determination and the legal analysis of Japan's security

---

Party may give notice to the other Party of its intention to terminate the Treaty, in which case the Treaty shall terminate one year after such notice has been given'.

13 MATSUI, YAKUSHIJI, TOKUGAWA and NISHIMURA 1881 (n 3).

14 For the history of the Law Section of *Minka*, see, for example, The Law Section of the Association of Democratic Scientists (ed.), *Fifty Years of Minka's Law Section* (*Minka Horitsu Bukai no 50 Nen*) (Nihon Hyoronsha 1996) (in Japanese).

15 See, for example, MATSUI Yoshiro, 'The San Francisco Regime and Marxist jurisprudence (San Francisco Taisei to Marx Shugi Hogaku)', in AMANO Kazuo et al. (eds), *Establishment and Development of Marxist Jurisprudence in Japan: Courses of Marxist Jurisprudence*, vol. 1 (*Marx Syugi Hogaku Koza vol I: Marx Shugi Hogaku no Seiritsu to Hatten*) (Nihon Hyoronsha 1976) 258–289 (in Japanese); MATSUI Yoshiro, 'Contemporary Japanese Law and International Relations (Gendai Nihonho to Kokusai Kankei)' in AMANO Kazuo et al. (eds), *Analysis of Contemporary Japanese Law: Courses of Marxist Jurisprudence*, vol. 4 (*Marx Shugi Hogaku Koza vol IV: Gendai Nihonho Bunseki*) (Nihon Hyoronsha 1976) 23–77 (in Japanese).

regime, as well as on collective security,[16] state responsibility,[17] sources of law,[18] history,[19] international environmental law[20] and many other areas.

Besides establishing his methodology throughout the 1970s, Matsui's academic attitude may explain the vast number of his works on various areas of international law. Matsui pointed out two of his own academic characteristics. The first is the importance of looking at the historical context of the establishment and development of international law.[21] The second is Matsui's academic tendency to go 'from reality to theory'. Matsui described his academic attitude as 'a stance of taking up theoretical issues

16 See, for example, MATSUI Yoshiro, *The Gulf War and the United Nations* (*Wangan Senso to Kokusai Rengo*) (Nihon Hyoronsha 1993) (in Japanese); MATSUI Yoshiro, *Terrorism, War and Self-Defence: the US and Other Countries' Attacks in Afghanistan* (*Tero, Senso, Jiei: Beikokuto no Afghanistan Kogeki wo Kangaeru*) (Toshindo 2002) (in Japanese).

17 MATSUI Yoshiro, 'The Nature of the Law of State Responsibility under Traditional International Law: The Transformation of the Law of State Responsibility (1) (Kokka Sekininho no Tenkan: Dentoteki Kokusaiho niokeru Kokka Sekininho no Seikaku)' (1990) 89 *Kokusaiho Gaiko Zassi* 1–52 (in Japanese); MATSUI Yoshiro, 'The Transformation of the Law of State Responsibility at the United Nations: The Transformation of the Law of State Responsibility (2) (Kokka Sekininho no Tenkan: Kokusai Rengo niokeru Kokka Sekininho no Tenkan)' (1992) 91 *Kokusaiho Gaiko Zassi* 419–461 (in Japanese).

18 MATSUI Yoshiro, 'Can Customary International Law Theory Contribute to the Project of Social Progress? Towards a Reconstruction of Voluntarism (Kanshu Kokusaiho Ron wa Shakai Shinpo no Project ni Koken Dekiruka: Ishi Shugi no Saikosei wo Mezashite)' in MATSUI Yoshiro et al. (eds), *International law and the Challenges of the Law of the Sea in the 21st Century* (*21 Seiki no Kokusaiho to Kaiyoho no Kadai*) (Toshindo 2016) 5–43 (in Japanese); MATSUI Yoshiro, 'By Whom and How International Law is Generated (Darega Donoyoni Kokusaiho wo Tsukuru noka)' (2020) 39 *Yearbook of World Law* 1–33. Both papers are included in the following book: MATSUI Yoshiro, *Towards the Rule of Law in International Society* (*Kokusai Shakai niokeru Ho no Shihai wo Mezashite*) (Shinzansha 2021) (in Japanese).

19 MATSUI Yoshiro, 'Japanese Militarism's Theory of International Law: its Formation in "Manchurian Incident"' (Nihon Gunkoku Syugi no Kokusaiho Ron: 'Manshu Jihen' niokeru sono Keisei)' in Institute of Social Science, The University of Tokyo (ed.), *The Legal System of Post-War Japan: State and Society in the Period of Fascism 4* (*Senji Nihon no Ho Taisei: Fascism Ki no Kokka to Shakai 4*) (University of Tokyo Press 1979) 361–405 (in Japanese); MATSUI Yoshiro, 'The East Asian Community and the "Greater East Asia Co-prosperity Sphere": from a Historical Perspective (Higashi Asia Kyodotai to 'Daitoa Kyoeiken': Rekishiteki Shiten kara)' in NISHIGUCHI Kiyokatsu and KA Go (eds), *Building the East Asian Community* (*Higashi Asia Kyodotai no Kochiku*) (Minerva Shobo 2006) 280–299 (in Japanese).

20 MATSUI Yoshiro, *International Law of the Environment: its Fundamental Principles* (*Kokusai Kankyoho no Kihon Gensoku*) (Toshindo 2010) (in Japanese).

21 MATSUI and ASADA, 'Dialogue: International Law in Kyoto (2)' 47 (n 6).

in relation to incidents and events that occur in international society',[22] 'pulling the awareness of problems out of actual incidents'[23] and 'when a major incident occurs, I wonder how to think about it from the perspective of international law'.[24]

Matsui's academic topics are diverse, but they are always based on an extremely detailed analysis of the practices and theories of states and international organisations. This is derived from Matsui's academic attitude of first analysing reality rather than starting from theory.

This tendency to move from reality to theory has made it impossible for Matsui to ignore the phenomena occurring in international society. As a result, from decolonisation and the Vietnam War comes the study of the right to self-determination; from the Gulf War, Iraq War and Afghanistan War comes the study of collective security under the UN Charter;[25] and from the aerial bombardment of Kosovo comes the study of humanitarian intervention.[26] Matsui's prolific output reflects his sense of responsibility as an international lawyer to commit himself to the real world.

## *International law as a social science*

To understand Matsui's theory of international law, it is interesting to see how he positions it. In an article published in 2002, Matsui considered his international law theory to be in the lineage of 'international law as a social science'.

According to Matsui:

> the social science of international law means a method of international legal studies to see international law as an objective social phenomenon and from that basis to treat the science of international law as a part of social science,

22 Ibid.
23 Ibid 48.
24 MATSUI, YAKUSHIJI, TOKUGAWA and NISHIMURA (n 3) 1874.
25 See, for example, MATSUI, *The Gulf War and the United Nations* (n 16); MATSUI, *Terrorism, War and Self-Defence* (n 16).
26 See, for example, MATSUI Yoshiro, 'Humanitarian Intervention in Contemporary International Law (Gendai Kokusaiho niokeru Jindoteki Kansho)' in FUJITA Hisakazu, MATSUI Yoshiro and SAKAMOTO Shigeki (eds), *A New Century of Human Rights and Humanitarian Law* (*Jinkenho to Jindoho no Shin Seiki*) (Toshindo 2001) 5–63 (in Japanese).

> seeking to elucidate the social background and actual role played in international relations of international law.[27]

Matsui evaluated that the foundation of Japanese international law as a social science was laid by YOKOTA Kisaburo (1896–1993)[28] and his precise analysis of the normative and logical structure of international law, and TAOKA Ryoichi and his method of social and historical foundations of international law. On this foundation, TABATA Shigejiro, SOGAWA Takeo (1911–1996),[29] ISHIMOTO Yasuo (1924–2015)[30] and others established contemporary international law. Matsui paid particular attention to Tabata's research on the socioeconomic foundations of international law.[31] Matsui credited Tabata's clarification of 'the effects of the socioeconomic bases on the institutions and ideologies of international law'[32] with having a profound impact on later generations.

Matsui's theory of international law can be said to view the works of Sogawa, Tabata, Ishimoto and others as social science, to identify a Marxist methodology at their foundation and to consciously and explicitly apply it to international law. This is evident from Matsui's statement.

> Furthermore, in considering the analysis of the socioeconomic bases of international law, we cannot neglect the theory of Marxism...Such a Marxist method of analysis, although not always self-proclaimed to be so, was much more widely utilized in the works of Tabata, Sogawa and Ishimoto.[33]

To properly understand Matsui's self-evaluation of international law as a social science, it is necessary to understand the implications of the concept of 'social science' in the post-war Japanese context. Social science in post-war Japan developed mainly under the influence of Marxism. As INOKI Masamichi (1914–2012) indicated, 'In Japan, which had no social science tradition until the Meiji Restoration, Marxism served as an alternative to

27 MATSUI Yoshiro, 'The Social Science of International Law: Its Evolution in Japan' (2002) 45 *The Japanese Annual of International Law* 2.
28 See Chapter 2.
29 See Chapter 7.
30 See Chapter 9.
31 TABATA Shigejiro, 'Functional Changes in Diplomatic Protection (1) (2) (*Gaikoteki Hogo no Kino Henka*)' (1946) 52 *Kyoto Law Review* 193–217; (1947) 53 *Kyoto Law Review* 393–414 (in Japanese).
32 MATSUI 13 (n 27).
33 Ibid 15.

all social sciences'.[34] In the 1930s, the 'Japanese capitalism debate' developed among Japanese Marxists. This controversy, which addressed Japan's stage of capitalism, was inherited by Japanese social science in the post-war period. In this sense, social science in Japan has always developed with Marxism as its axis of reference.[35] Matsui's argument for international law as a social science must be understood in this post-war Japanese context.

### *Marxist approach*

As mentioned, Matsui acquired the methodology of Marxist legal theories in the struggle over the Japan-US Security Treaty in 1970 and applied it to international law. In doing so, Matsui actively referred to Soviet international law. Matsui, together with FUJITA Hisakazu (1937–2012),[36] has actively introduced Soviet international law to Japanese jurisprudence of international law, for instance, by translating a book by Grigory Ivanovich TUNKIN into Japanese.[37]

Regarding the relationship with Soviet international law, Matsui noted the following in an article evaluating Soviet international law, published in 1994 after the collapse of the Soviet Union.

> However, I have neither fully accepted the position of 'Soviet international law' nor argued that its claims are always correct. Nevertheless, as one who has positively evaluated the basic ideas of 'Soviet international law' and has endeavoured to adopt scientific socialism as my methodology, I consider it my unavoidable academic duty to catalogue the positive and negative legacies of 'Soviet international law'.[38]

Matsui noted that the Soviets have exerted a great influence on the establishment of various principles of international law, such as the prohibition of the use of force and the right to self-determination. However, he criticised

34 INOKI Masamichi, *Genealogy of Communism* (*Kyosan Shugi no Keihu*), new and enlarged edn (Kadokawa 2018) 387 (in Japanese).

35 UNO Shigeki, 'Transformation of Japanese Social Sciences in the 1990s (1990 Nendai Nihon no Shakai Kagaku)' (2006) 58 *The Journal of Social Science* 99–123 (in Japanese).

36 FUJITA Hisakazu is a Japanese international law scholar who has served as a professor at Kansai University, the University of Tokyo and Kobe University, and was appointed a member of Institut de Droit International (IDI) in 2007. Like Matsui, Fujita was also a student of TABATA Shigejiro.

37 Grigory Ivanovich Tunkin, *Law and Force in the International System* (*Kokusai Shisutemu ni okeru Ho to Chikara*), translated by FUJITA Hisakazu and MATSUI Yoshiro (Horitsu Bunkasha 1990) (in Japanese).

38 MATSUI Yoshiro, 'The Last Moments of the "Soviet International Law" ('Soviet Kokusaiho' no Shuen)' (1994) 157 *Nagoya University Journal of Law and Politics* 21–65 (in Japanese).

that, despite such contributions, the Soviets acted contrary to the principles they advocated.[39] At the same time, while appreciating the theoretical contributions of Soviet international law to international law as a social science, Matsui criticises the fact that it has not applied the theory of scientific socialism to international law in a sufficiently creative manner.[40]

Thus, Matsui's assessment of Soviet international law is ambivalent. It should be emphasised that Matsui does not deny the validity of Marxism or social science as methodologies.[41] Although Soviet international law played a significant role in the theory of scientific socialism in international law, the two are not identical for Matsui. Scientific socialism remains central to Matsui's theory of international law.

### *State sovereignty and the right to self-determination*

Another characteristic of Matsui's theory of international law is its position on non-state actors. This feature is demonstrated in Matsui's theory of sources of law, which he actively engaged in after moving from Nagoya University to Ritsumeikan University in 2004.[42]

Although Matsui acknowledges that non-state actors contribute to the formation and development of international law in various ways,[43] he is cautious about their direct involvement. For example, Matsui argues that non-state actors play only an indirect role in forming customary international law through states.[44] Such a view of non-state actors indicates Matsui's realist position that international society is still constituted primarily by states.

39 Ibid 52.

40 Ibid 55.

41 In 1976, at the 13th Extraordinary Party Congress, the Japanese Communist Party changed the term 'Marxism-Leninism' to 'scientific socialism'. The reason was that Marxism-Leninism was post-Stalin and contained many things that deviated from the original position of scientific socialism.

42 However, Matsui's theory of sources of law, particularly his awareness of the problems related to the formation process of the state's will, had already been presented in the 1970s. See, for example, MATSUI Yoshiro, 'Critique of the Theories of Interpretation of International Law (*Kokusaiho Kaishaku Ron Hihan*)' in AMANO Kazuo et al. (eds), *A Critique of Contemporary Jurisprudence: Courses of Marxist Jurisprudence*, vol. 7 (*Marx Shugi Hogaku Koza vol VII: Gendai Hogaku Hihan*) (Nihon Hyoronsha 1977) 210–236 (in Japanese). The revised version of this paper is included in MATSUI, *Towards the Rule of Law in International Society* (n 18).

43 See, for example, MATSUI, 'By Whom and How International Law is Generated?' (n 18).

44 MATSUI, 'Can Customary International Law Theory Contribute to the Project of Social Progress?' 39–40 (n 18).

At the same time, however, Matsui focuses on the significance of non-state actors as self-determining entities. For example, Matsui pointed out the formation of customary international law as follows.

> If customary law theory is based on the existing will of states, it ends up being an apology for the status quo of the international society. But the state is, at the same time, a 'self-determining entity', within whose framework peoples have the possibility of reflecting their will in their national practices and *opinio juris*, and through them in customary international law.[45]

In other words, Matsui does not view the state as a black box but instead actively positions the people and other non-state actors as constituting the state's inner reality. Furthermore, Matsui hopes that changes in the consciousness and involvement of these non-state actors are possible, leading to changes in the state and progress in international society.[46]

Matsui's academic position is deeply intertwined with his practice. In 2001, Matsui published a book entitled *Looking at the World Through International Law: An Introduction to International Law for Citizens*.[47] Matsui wrote this textbook of international law for citizens in a conversational style. As a background to the publication of this book, Matsui noted that 'citizens can have a correct understanding of international issues and consciously lobby their countries, or they can form NGOs and take an active role in international society'.[48] Thus, Matsui hopes that the people and citizens, as subjects of self-determination, will have a correct understanding of international law and international society and that this will lead to changes in the state and international society.

Matsui's position corresponds to the problem of the 'bearer of sovereignty' raised by Tabata. Tabata argued that the issue of sovereignty had been discussed abstractly in international relations and international law and stressed the necessity of examining the domestic structure of states and the question of 'What or who is actually the bearer of sovereignty in the

45 Ibid 43.

46 MATSUI, YAKUSHIJI, TOKUGAWA and NISHIMURA 1879 (n 3). Matsui's expectations of citizens have remained unchanged in the wake of the war in Ukraine and the conflict in Gaza. See MATSUI Yoshiro, 'How Have International Law and International Society Regulated the Use of Force? (Kokusaiho to Kokusaishakai wa Buryoku Koshi wo Donoyoni Kisei Shitekitaka?)' (2024) 1042 *Zenei* 66–67 (in Japanese).

47 MATSUI Yoshiro, *Looking at the World through International Law: An Introduction to International Law for Citizens* (*Kokusaiho kara Sekai wo Miru: Shimin notameno Kokusaiho Nyumon*) (Toshindo 2001) (in Japanese). The book has been published in its third edition (2011).

48 MATSUI, YAKUSHIJI, TOKUGAWA and NISHIMURA 1898 (n 3).

name of the state?'[49] Inheriting Tabata's argument, the Kyoto School sought to sublimate the conflict between sovereignty and human rights through the right to self-determination. Matsui stated as follows.

> (Thus, Tabata and Japanese) international law scholars that followed him have tried to settle the contradiction between human rights and sovereignty by relying on the right of peoples to self-determination. They have also stressed the importance of sovereignty buttressed with human rights and self-determination to be the ordering principle of the international legal order. In this way, they have aimed at placing individuals in the international legal order. This tendency seems to be theoretically indispensable for international legal studies as a branch of social science, as well as being of practical significance for the task of democratically transforming the international community.[50]

## Significance of Matsui's theory of international law

### *Succession and development of the Kyoto School*

The primary significance of Matsui's theory of international law in Japanese international law is that it succeeded and developed the Kyoto School, whose founder was TABATA Shigejiro. Of course, it should be noted that the Kyoto School has been viewed differently by various theorists. In this regard, it is important to confirm Matsui's evaluation of Tabata's theory of international law.

Matsui pointed out three characteristics of Tabata's theory of international law.[51] First, international law is understood as a social phenomenon in international society rather than as a general set of norms. This leads to the importance of studying the historical aspect of international law. Second, international law must be viewed in relation to the structure of international society, which is the basis of its validity. Therefore, the structural changes in international society that accompanied the emergence of socialist and emerging countries were crucial to analysing the development of international law. Third, the domestic structure of states is also included in the scope of international law jurisprudence. The aforementioned 'bearer of sovereignty' is a clear example of this point.

49 TABATA Shigejiro, 'Sovereignty of State in International Society (Kokusaishakai niokeru Kokka Shuken)' (1971) 33 *Koho Kenkyu* 1–16 (in Japanese).

50 MATSUI 31 (n 27).

51 MATSUI Yoshiro, 'International Law and Sociology of Law (Kokusaiho to Hoshakaigaku)' in The Japanese Association of Sociology of Law (ed.), *Japanese Sociology of Law* (*Nihon no Hoshakaigaku*) (Yuhikaku 1979) 186–187 (in Japanese).

Matsui attempted to overcome the challenges posed by Tabata's international law with Marxist methodology. As Matsui described,[52] the problem awareness of Tabata and the Kyoto School has not necessarily been inherited by Japanese international law. Rather, the issues and problems presented by Tabata and addressed by Matsui seem to align with global academic trends such as the Third World Approach to International Law (TWAIL)[53] and the Marxist approach.[54] Matsui has been actively referring to these works and incorporating them into his international law theory in recent years.[55] In this sense, Matsui's theory of international law may be said to bridge the gap between 'Kyoto' and the rest of the world.

## *Origin of critical streams*

One reason why the Kyoto School's awareness and methodology have not been fully inherited is the trend towards a positivist approach in Japanese international law. This trend can be seen in 'Tokyo' international law, which was strongly influenced by YAMAMOTO Soji (1928–2013)[56] and in Kyoto international law today. In this legal positivist approach, international law is seen as a set of norms, and the main task of international law studies is to analyse the interpretation of those norms in light of state practice. The history and social structure behind the phenomenon of international law are

52 MATSUI and ASADA, 'Dialogue: International Law in Kyoto (2)' 47 (n 6).

53 Andrea Bianchi discussed the history of TWAIL in three phases: the first is from the mid-1950s to the mid-1980s, the second starts in the 1990s and the third is currently developing. Andrea Bianchi, *International Law Theories: An Inquiry into Different Ways of Thinking* (Oxford University Press 2016) 205–226. As discussed below, Japanese international law scholars actively embraced the first phase through the international law of development. However, the acceptance of the second and third phases of TWAIL has been very slow and inadequate under the dominant influence of legal positivism in Japan.

54 See, for example, China Miéville, *Between Equal Rights: A Marxist Theory of International Law* (Pluto Press 2005); Susan Marks, *The Riddle of All Constitutions: International Law, Democracy, and the Critique of Ideology* (Oxford University Press 2000); Susan Marks (ed.), *International Law on the Left: Re-Examining Marxist Legacies* (Cambridge University Press 2008).

55 See, for example, MATSUI Yoshiro, 'Searching Legitimacy in International Law: with a Focus on Procedural Legitimacy (Kokusaiho niokeru Seitosei towa Nanika: Tetsuzukiteki Seitosei wo Chushin ni)' in IWASAWA Yuji and OKANO Masataka (eds), *International Relations and the Rule of Law* (*Kokusai Kankei to Ho no Shihai*) (Shinzansha 2021) 366–367 (in Japanese) (included in MATSUI, *Towards the Rule of Law in International Society* (n 18)); MATSUI, 'Can Customary International Law Theory Contribute to the Project of Social Progress?' 41–43 (n 18).

56 See Chapter 10.

outside the scope of international legal analysis. As a result, the structures that frame international law are not themselves critiqued.

However, even under the dominant influence of legal positivism, a critical stream of international law has persisted in Japanese international law.[57] The first is the acceptance of the international law of development that emerged in France in the 1960s. In accepting this theory, the works of Michel Virally, Guy Feuer, Maurice Flory, Hervé Cassin, Alain Pellet, Mohamed Bennouna, Mohammed Bejaoui and others were referenced, offering a critical perspective on the structure of international law that embraces injustice.[58] The other is the Marxist approach represented by Matsui. In Japan, 'Soviet international law' has been established as a field of study and mainly analysed by Matsui and his students.[59] Both have critically examined the existing international legal order using decolonisation as an impetus and Marxism as a common analytical method.

Since the late 1980s, the post-structuralist analysis by David Kennedy and Martti Koskenniemi has not been accepted contemporaneously in Japanese international law. It was not until the 2000s that Japanese international lawyers finally began to appreciate it.[60] One reason for this seems to be that the critical approach in Japanese international law was linked to Marxism. With the collapse of the Soviet Union, the momentum of the two origins of a critical scream, international law of development and Soviet international law, was lost.

However, some scholars in Japanese international law are now actively developing TWAIL and critical approaches. Matsui's theory of international law is one source of the current critical trend in Japanese international law.

57 See, for example, the special issue on 'Critical Perspectives in International Legal Studies' (2021) 40 *Sekaiho Nenpo* (in Japanese).

58 On the reception and evolution of international law of development in Japan, *see generally* KODERA Satoshi 'The Future of International Law of Development: Towards a New "New International Economic Order" (Kaihatsu no Kokusaiho no Yukue: Aratana "Shin Kokusai Keizai Chitsujo" emukete)' (2014) 120 *The Chuo Law Review* 261–290 (in Japanese).

59 Every year in Japan, the December issue of the journal *Horitsu Jiho* has an 'academic review (*Gakkai Kaiko*)', in which the year's leading achievements in various fields are reviewed. Interestingly, 'Soviet international law' was included as an area for academic review in 1995. OBATA Kaoru and YAMAGATA Hideo, 'Academic Review (Gakkai Kaiko)' (1995) 67 *Horitsu Jiho* 162–167 (in Japanese). See also MATSUDA Takeo, 'The Challenge and Decline of the Soviet International Law: In Reference to the Theories of Grigory I. Tunkin (*Soviet Kokusaiho no Chosen to Zasetsu: G. Tunkin no Gakusetsu wo Tegakari ni*)' (2001) 20 *Sekaiho Nenpo* 131–150 (in Japanese).

60 See, for example, SAKAI Hironobu, 'The Challenge of Critical Legal Studies and its Significance in International Law (*Hihan Hogaku no Kokusaiho Discourse*)' (2003) 22 *Sekaiho Nenpo* 107–135 (in Japanese).

### Overcoming state-centrism

The Kyoto School emphasised the importance of analysing the internal structure of states based on the concept of 'bearer of sovereignty', a concept Tabata had raised. Although it was not visibly realised at that time due to language barriers and the lack of communication, Japanese international law had a contemporaneous response to the global awareness of the problem of state-centrism in international law.

Overcoming state-centrism in Japan revolved around the study of human rights and the right to self-determination after the Second World War. Subsequently, it led to theoretical achievements such as 'international law participant' theory which was developed by ONUMA Yasuaki (1946–2018).[61] Matsui's theory of international law led the study of the right to self-determination in Japan and, at the same time, contributed greatly to overcoming state-centredness in Japanese international law.

Attempts to overcome state-centrism through human rights and the right to self-determination can take two directions: one that dissolves all rights to the individual and the other that finds particular significance in the collective, the people. Matsui consistently supports the latter position. Matsui noted that 'the right to self-determination will not lose its unique significance as long as the group as a collective continues to be subject to discrimination, oppression, and exploitation'.[62]

The issue for the study of the right to self-determination, as well as for Matsui, is how to construct 'the people' after decolonisation. For example, the Reims School, founded by Charles Chaumont and others, emphasised the significance of 'peoples' in international law. Still, the people it envisioned have been identified with the subjects of national liberation struggles.[63] In this respect, Matsui, based on a Marxist approach in the 1970s and 1980s, emphasised the class nature of peoples as subjects of self-determination[64] and defined them as peoples under colonial rule in a broad sense.[65] Later,

61 ONUMA Yasuaki, *A Transcivilizational Perspective on International Law* (Martinus Nijhoff Publishers 2010) 77–80. See also Chapter 12.

62 MATSUI, 'The Right to Self-Determination on Trial' 501 (n 11). See also MATSUI, YAKUSHIJI, TOKUGAWA and NISHIMURA 1877 (n 3).

63 Monique Chemillier-Gendreau, 'Contribution of the Reims School to the Debate on the Critical Analysis of International Law: Assessment and Limits' (2011) 22 *European Journal of International Law* 655–659; KODERA Satoshi, 'A Critical Stream in the French Doctrine of International Law: Charles Chaumont and the Reims School (France Kokusaihogaku niokeru Hihante teki Choryu: Charles Chaumont to Reims Gakuha)' (2021) 40 *Sekaiho Nenpo* 11 (in Japanese).

64 MATSUI 235 (n 42).

65 MATSUI, 'Legal Status of National Liberation Movements' 46–49 (n 11).

however, based on the transition of state practice after the Cold War, Matsui redefined it as a universal right that applies to people other than colonial peoples.[66] He expected the people to be subjects of self-determination to provide an opportunity to transform the state and international society.

## Conclusion

This chapter has examined the academic foundation, characteristics and significance of Matsui's theory of international law. Matsui formed his academic foundation within the Kyoto School, founded by Tabata, and developed his theory of international law in response to the international events Japan faced in the post-war period. Matsui identified the foundation of Marxist social science in the Kyoto School and consciously and explicitly applied its methodology to international law. In this sense, Matsui's international law theory can be said to have been constructed at the intersection of three contexts: the Japanese international context of the two Security Treaty struggles, the Japanese international law context of the Kyoto School and the post-war Japanese historical context of the Marxist social sciences.

Matsui's theory of international law has played a significant role in Japanese international law. It has carried on the problem awareness of the Kyoto School and continues to flow as one of the water veins of the critical currents in Japan. In addition, leading the study of the right to self-determination became an opportunity for Japanese international law to overcome state-centrism.

Finally, it must be noted that Matsui's theory of international law is always ongoing. Matsui's academic trajectory and enthusiasm for 'from reality to theory' have never wavered, and he continues to publish critical analyses of the Russian-Ukrainian conflict, initiated by Russia's 2022 invasion of Ukraine, from the standpoint of international law.[67] In addition,

66 MATSUI, 'The Right to Self-Determination on Trial' (n 11). However, Matsui does not seem to have lost the Marxist perspective of class struggle. For example, regarding the internal structure of the state, Matsui noticed that 'the state must thus be seen not as an entity whose interior is kept in a black box and whose outward face can only be seen, as generally assumed in international law, but as a framework within which various social struggles take place among the members of the state'. MATSUI, 'By Whom and How International Law is Generated?' 27 (n 18).

67 MATSUI Yoshiro, 'The War in Ukraine and the Future of the International Order: The Potential of Multilateralism (Ukraine Senso to Kokusai Shakai no Shorai: Takokukan Shugi no Kanosei)' (2023) 333 *Keizai* 91–103 (in Japanese).

on 14 February 2024, he made a statement as a witness before the House of Councillors' Foreign Affairs and Security Committee, strongly criticising Israel's attack on Gaza as a violation of international humanitarian law. As the reality of international society changes, Matsui's theory of international law also constantly evolves.

# 11

# KOTERA Akira: struggle of international legal scholars living on the 'periphery' of international law

*MEGURO Maiko*

## Introduction

KOTERA Akira (1952–2014) was a professor at the University of Tokyo's Graduate School of Arts and Sciences. He was known for a broad array of research subjects in international law and was an influential figure in both the academic and practical fields of public international law in Japan. He served as an expert member of the Sports Arbitration Tribunal and a legal adviser to various government departments, including the Ministry of Foreign Affairs, the Ministry of Economy, Trade and Industry, the Ministry of Finance, the Ministry of the Environment and the Cabinet Office.

Many readers might think that Kotera is an unusual subject to be treated in this compilation. Much of his writing is aimed at practitioners, and he is generally viewed as a scholar with an interpretive jurisprudence stance. His research and publications cover a wide range of issues in international law, while his most well-known academic theme was international economic law, including trade law and investment law, especially since his appointment as a professor at the University of Tokyo. Beyond his academic journey as a scholar of interpretative jurisprudence, this chapter also sheds light on his role as a scholar who struggled to be a 'peripheral' jurist in the face of the embedded Western structures of domination in the mainstream of international law. Unlike his contemporaries, who participated in variants of critical jurisprudence, including the Third World approach, he continued to seek interpretive jurisprudence in international law and believed this would eventually strengthen Japanese international jurisprudence and Japanese jurists and practitioners in the given structure.

The struggles of scholars who are aware that they are 'living on the periphery' are evident in the other scholars in this book, but Kotera is unique among them in that he did not make the theoretical framework of international law the core of his activities. With the recent upsurge of multi-perspectivism in Europe and the United States, theoretical currents from non-Western countries that have challenged the orthodoxy of public international law are occasionally taken up by Western authors. Some of the names in this edited volume draw new attention for those who want to collect the necessary colour for their pieces. However, in keeping with the force of conversation proposed by this edited volume and to present a more complete picture of the Japanese tradition of international law, the chapter considers it necessary to bring up the anecdotes of peripheral scholars who have been quietly reflecting on the state of international law.

Unlike ONUMA Yasuaki, who joined the theorists of the Third World approach and pointed out in his writings in English the West-centric bias that undermined non-Western cultures in the very fundamental norms of human rights,[1] Kotera did not engage with the Eurocentrism of the basic principles of international law or the very meta-rules that define the framework of international law. Kotera, from beginning to end, contended that international law should be constructed as objective rules in application. Instead, Kotera sought to build an interpretative basis for reflecting respective national circumstances, such as Japan's commercial practices under the conditions of its application, by pointing out the ambiguity of the boundary between international and domestic law in economic law.

In addition, Kotera was a scholar who was particularly warned of the self-reflexive and facile pluralist and multiculturalist tendencies of the Western academic world towards the end of his life. His academic journey was also a struggle for necessary objectivity in law while seeking ways for peripheral Japanese lawyers to engage with the international legal order and reflect diversity. The 'conversation' framework proposed in the Introduction does not assume the possibility of theoretical convergence on the various currents of international law, but Kotera's pragmatic approach to reach empirical objectivity through interpretative jurisprudence, as will be illustrated in the following, may provide some inspiration to the new era of Kyosei (co-habitation)[2] through conversation.

In the following, Kotera's footprints are analysed chronologically, in line with the book's overall structure. In doing so, two substantial axes of analysis will be established. The first is 'the state of Japanese interpretative jurisprudence for Japan's proactive involvement in the international (economic) order' and the second, is 'the awareness reform and education of domestic legal professionals who have been involved in international law as unilateral

1 Refer also to Chapter 12.

2 *Kyosei* 共生 is a concept which is hard to translate. The previous literature also translates the concept as co-existence, yet the current chapter uses co-habitation based on the advice by KAKU Shun.

recipients'. In so doing, it also considers the coexistence and conversation between different legal traditions, a theme that runs through this book.

## Early ambition on an international legal order: the 1990s

### *The vanishing divide in an emerging international order as an opportunity for the periphery*

Kotera began his academic career as an assistant professor at the University of Tokyo in 1976. Kotera was by no means a prolific scholar in the 1970s and 1980s, as he was known to be in the more recent decade, and his research was largely hermeneutic studies of the legal character of international organisations. Unlike some of the other scholars discussed in this chapter, who articulated their academic stance and main themes early in their careers, Kotera's stance may have developed and been refined over time. But in the 1990s, through his research on trade law and international control, Kotera became increasingly interested in the formation of an international legal order in international economics, such as trade and investment. The following explains Kotera's understanding of the nature of the international legal order that the WTO regime was shaping, and how he thought Japanese international lawyers should utilise this to engage with this emerging order.

Kotera had been highly engaged in the WTO regime since its establishment in 1995. In light of his enthusiasm for international legal order, he argued that the legal interests protected by the GATT/WTO are of an objective nature.[3] However, he did not project a vision of 'progress of international law' towards the natural legal order or any legal order similar to domestic law onto the development of the WTO regime. Rather, Kotera attached great importance to the politics and deals between sovereign states embedded in the dispute settlement process (DSP) and evaluated it as the mechanism underpinning the objective interests protected by the international economic law order under development.

Kotera argues, among other things, that the dispute settlement procedure (the DSP) in the GATT/WTO should not be seen as a system of simple mutuality about the subjective interests of the parties to the treaties, but as

3 KOTERA Akira, 'The Function and Limitations of International Control: The Legal Nature of WTO/GATT Dispute Settlement Procedures' (1996) 95(2) *Journal of International Law and Diplomacy*; KOTERA Akira, 'The Legal Structure of the International Economic Regime: WTO's Success and MAI's Stagnation' in *Trust Future Forum 'Akira Kotera Memorial Papers'* (2014).

one of international control, i.e. a system whose purpose is 'to maintain an objective legal system'.[4] In his view, the structure of Article 3 of the Dispute Settlement Understanding (DSU) established under the WTO indicates that the purpose of the dispute settlement procedure is 'to maintain the WTO treaty regime and that the remedy for the aggrieved party is secondary'.[5] In so arguing, he states that the provisions of the DSU define the DSP as a central element in providing security and predictability to the multilateral trading system, and such defined function is to clarify the systematic content of provisions of the WTO agreements in accordance with customary rules of interpretation of public international law, besides serving to preserve the rights and obligations of Members under the agreements.

With regard to execution, he supported Judge Fitzmaurice's restrained position in his dissenting opinion in the Namibia case before the International Court of Justice.[6] Kotera considered that there was only a flimsy basis in international law for arguing that the legal status of an organisation asserting international control was comparable to that of a contracting party to a treaty: unless the WTO Agreement provided for a recommendation or ruling adopted by the DSU as an official interpretation, it would co-exist with the independent interpretations of members other than the disputing parties, concluding that 'the competition would only be based on the quality of the interpretation'.[7]

Compared with other areas of international law, trade law's normative content is more directly related to the nature of domestic regulation. Given this nature, Kotera considered that a more flexible approach is needed that takes into account the circumstances of individual states that shape domestic measures, such as the nature of their economy and society, their industrial structure and the culture that shapes consumer life in their respective societies. In this context, Kotera often spoke of the success of the WTO regime in contrast to the stagnation of the OECD's multilateral investment agreements. In his view, the key was that even in the event of a finding of non-compliance, there was 'room for negotiation and deal among the countries concerned/parties on the outcome of dispute settlement procedures' under the WTO regime.[8] The OECD MAI, despite dealing with investment, an area

4 KOTERA, 'The Function and Limitations of International Control' 147 (n 3).
5 Simultaneously, Kotera also states that there is room for this to be understood narrowly as a 'dispute settlement procedure between member states' based on some provisions under GATT/WTO Agreements such as Article 23 of GATT providing that 'benefit accruing to a contracting party directly or indirectly under this Agreement is being nullified or impaired' in order for the party to be eligible for the DSU. See 'The Function and Limitations of International Control' 152.
6 KOTERA, 'The Function and Limitations of International Control' 168 (n 86).
7 Ibid 169
8 KOTERA, 'The Legal Structure of the International Economic Regime' 136 (n 86).

that goes further into individual domestic measures than trade, only allowed a narrower margin of discretion for sovereign states to determine the relative relationship between investors' interests and other various legal values.[9]

Kotera's pragmatic approach – accepting the objectivity of international legal order, but also assenting to the flexibility of sovereign states in its specific interpretative application as an integrated part of the international legal order – was a very important suggestion for Japanese lawyers, especially those within the Government of Japan, who struggled with the various value norms and principles inserted in the preamble and purpose and scope provisions during treaty negotiations. In many treaty negotiations, there is a practice of referring to universal values and institutions in preambles and purpose norms, which can be said to be the premises of international law, and these principles are inserted into both bilateral and multilateral treaties to establish an 'objective' legal order. It must be noted that the establishment of an international legal order and, what is more, supporting the 'objectiveness' of international law would strengthen Japan's shield in tough international politics. However, it must also be noted that Japan, as the latecomer and the only non-Western country among the leading countries, had to adopt a passive stance, accepting the already established concepts, principles and rules of international law built upon a Western legacy, choosing to benefit from international law rather than challenge it.

Kotera's pragmatism, if compared within this book, may be similar to Senga's, which creatively interprets and defends its own interests within the framework of order and international law created by the Western powers. Both chose positivism as a strategic instrument. As Chapter 1 illustrates, Senga saw positivism as 'a strategically optimal choice' that gave priority to the sources expressing the will of the sovereign; Kotera, similarly, chose to work within the given framework, but sought to strengthen Japan's position through the 'objectiveness' of its rules. International economic law, as a branch of international law, cannot compete with the structures embedded in the basic framework of international law itself, but at the same time, Kotera sees an opportunity in the peculiarity of international economic law and has actively argued since the mid-1990s that Japanese lawyers should be actively involved there.

Of course, the above argument does not prejudge the claims of recent critical jurisprudence regarding the linear understanding of history, which describes the periphery as unilateral receptors.[10] Here it is noted that even if we support previous works that argue that transplanted laws and ideas

9 Ibid 137; KOTERA Akira, *The Legal Structure of the WTO Regime* (Tokyo University Press 2000) 162, 177, 195–196.

10 Arnulf Becker Lorca, 'Universal International Law: Nineteenth-Century Histories of Imposition and Appropriation' (2010) 51 *Harvard International Law Journal*; Mohammad Shahabuddin, 'The "Standard of Civilization" in International

inevitably evolve in response to local needs and cultures,[11] this is not to say that there are no struggles for non-orthodox. Daily, international jurists from non-Western peripheral countries struggle to fit 'our ideas' into the mould of 'their ideas' if they want to make a valid and qualified argument for international law. In the case of Japan, however, Kotera's concern is that the Japanese lawyer no longer even struggles.

Kotera believed that even if the very foundations of international law were not supported by Japanese law, it should still be possible to engage with the nature of international law through interpretation. It was not until the 2000s, which will be discussed in the next section, that his interpretative jurisprudence clearly began to take shape, but his ambition to help shape the international order is already evident in his writings from the mid-1990s. It is not a coincidence that the WTO was established in 1995, and his first major advisory role with the Japanese government came in 1996. This role as an adviser to practitioners seems to have had a synergistic effect on Kotera's interest in and influence on order formation. From 1996 until shortly before his death, Kotera served on various expert committees at the Ministry of Foreign Affairs. He also served as an adviser to various ministries and agencies involved in international economic order, including the Ministry of Foreign Affairs, the Ministry of Economy, Trade and Industry, the Ministry of Finance, the Ministry of the Environment and the Cabinet Office, in addition to his professorship at the University of Tokyo and other key positions in academia.

### *Attempts to educate domestic legal professionals and improve understanding of international law*

In several works from this period, Kotera argues that the increase of treaties and agreements in the economic field, including WTO treaties, indicated that a new international legal order was emerging, with international law disciplines entering into matters that had previously been established solely by domestic law. On such a particular character of the emerging international

---

Law: Intellectual Perspectives from Pre-War Japan' (2019) 32 *Leiden Journal of International Law* 13.

11 On the notion of 'transplantation', see Otto Kahn-Freund, 'On Uses and Misuses of Comparative Law' (1974) 37 *Modern Law Review* 1; also, Maiko Meguro, 'Appraisal of Diversity in International Law' in 'Appraisal of Diversity in International Law: A Note on Self-Serving Biases and Interdisciplinarity' in P. Westerman, K. Gorobets and A. Hadjigeorgiou (eds), *Conceptual (De)Constructions of International Law* (Edward Elgar 2022) section 3.

economic law order, Kotera explained that, unlike in the traditional fields of international law, economic law matters, such as GATT and WTO disputes, have come to require not only elaborate interpretative theory but also detailed fact-finding, including each country's commercial practices. It was against this backdrop that Kotera insisted that it was essential for Japan to assert its legal position in light of its national circumstances.[12] Although it was a common practice for the Japanese Government to contract specialist lawyers from Europe and the US to handle disputes under international law at the time, Kotera expressed the view that, in light of this reality of economic order formation, 'it is necessary for [domestic legal experts] to work with the relevant ministries and agencies familiar with the domestic situation in Japan on a daily basis in order to legally assert the Japanese position'.[13] Kotera's strong engagement with departments and agencies of the Government of Japan could be the materialisation of such a view.

For legal scholars and practitioners outside certain institutions, such as the Ministry of Foreign Affairs or the Ministry of Economy, Trade and Industry, international law, which has a clearly different discipline from domestic law, tended to be perceived as 'Western diplomatic rhetoric' that had little relevance to Japan's national circumstances and legal practice. Of course, international law, particularly with regard to fundamental human rights, was sometimes referred to in Japanese domestic courts, but the courts 'rejected the plaintiffs' arguments without developing substantive interpretative arguments' and also the plaintiffs only additionally referred to international human rights law when listing their arguments. In sum, the interpretation of international law rarely influenced the outcome of the trial.

However, according to Kotera, in response to globalisation and an emerging international economic legal order, the recognition of rights and obligations in accordance with international law was becoming more familiar in legal practice. In addition, since the beginning of the Heisei era, the interpretation of treaties and customary law has become a major point of contention at the High Court and District Court levels.[14] In response to this situation, Kotera points out that when international law-specific legal doctrines 'are attempted to be dealt with by domestic legal thinking without a full understanding … inappropriate international law arguments have been

12 KOTERA Akira, 'Legal Training and International Law: The Meaning of International Law in Contemporary Society' (1998) (1131) *Jurist* 56–8.

13 Ibid 57.

14 For example, Judgment on the Siberian Internment Case (5 March 1993/Heisei 3), Tokyo High Court; Judgement on Nibutani Dam (27 March 1997/Heisei 9), Sapporo District Court.

extensively developed in courts and other legal practice'.[15] This recognition led to Kotera's insistence on the need to strengthen international law subjects in the education of legal practitioners in Japan.

In relation to this, when the amendment to the Bar Examination Act was proposed to Parliament to exclude international law from the subjects of the exam, Kotera argued thoroughly against this, and in various places appealed for the just treatment of international law in legal practice and litigation practice, while educating about the expansion of international disciplines in various fields and their penetration into the country.[16] At the same time, he appealed to international law scholars to get involved in the 'practice' of confronting the realities of day-to-day international transactions and international governance of global issues, and to work together with the practitioners, especially policymakers, on a daily basis.

## Shaping Kotera's interpretational jurisprudence: 2000s

### *Kotera's interpretative jurisprudence: debate with Onuma*

In his monograph *Paradigms in International Law*,[17] Kotera attempts to give a general explanation of the basic structure of international law. Kotera explains that his intention in writing *Paradigms in International Law* is to 'explicitly provide a basis for interpretative argumentation for Japanese international lawyers' as is done in Western jurisprudence and International Court of Justice cases. He is concerned that 'in Japan, there are scattered discussions in jurisprudence (for doctrinal stances) that do not provide a basis for interpretation of international law'.[18] The book indeed goes into details that provide the tools of interpretation, such as the different categories of legal interests and corresponding normative categories of rules in international law, the principles and rules and the relationship between the law and sources of international law (doctrine of sources). According

15 KOTERA, 'Legal Training and International Law' 58 (n 12).

16 The new bar examination system began in 2006, and it eventually included international law as a selective subject. Kotera was selected from the international law field as a member of the bar examination panel alongside KANEHARA Atsuko (Professor, Faculty of Law, Rikkyo University).

17 KOTERA Akira, *Paradigms in International Law: Basic Structure of International Law* (Yuhikaku 2004), based on a compilation of a series of articles (January 2001 to October 2002) in the journal *Law School* (*Hogaku Kyoshitsu*).

18 'Law Class: International Society and Law in the 21st Century (11): International Law in Japanese Society (with ONUMA Yasuaki)' (2008) 53(10) *The Law Seminar* (*Hogaku-Kyoshitsu*) 76.

to his positivist perspective, the legal order is defined by the different categories of interests to be protected by international law, broadly classified as 'national interests', 'common interests of peoples' and 'general interests of the international community'. In other words, insofar as these interests are embodied in substantive international legal rules and precedents, they are given an interpretive status and become the subject of scholarship and practice. He explained that the nature of interests plays an essential role in determining the nature of rules (contractual or legislative) formed under the international legal order and can give rise to different consequences in the operation and interpretation of the rules.[19]

Interpretive jurisprudence, in the opinion of Kotera, as already mentioned in the introduction, is not merely observing it but a mastery of international law as 'a grammar for developing one's own arguments internationally'.[20] Accepting much of international law remains 'Western law' for the Japanese jurisprudential tradition, it is to be an actor and player in interpretive practice rather than just introducing or citing Western theories and precedents.[21] At the same time, however, he saw that international law was a set of norms of adjudication. Hence, objectivity had to be ensured in the interpretation of international law, as long as the rules of international law are the evaluative framework for judging international cases. In this respect, he also attached great importance to the role of the Court.

This stands in sharp contrast to ONUMA Yasuaki, who saw Western-centrism and modern bias, under the guise of neutrality and objectivity, embedded in the creation and application of international law. Therefore, Onuma viewed the courts that apply such international law as merely one of the devices for generating social debate. For Onuma, international law is not a set of adjudicatory norms, as in domestic law, but rather a code of conduct, approved rather than objectively established through legal sources. In a 2008 dialogue with Kotera published in *Jurist*, the discussion ended on a parallel line on this point. Onuma fluffed the issue by saying that the objectivity of legal interpretation is, after all, only a matter of degree of persuasiveness. At the same time, Kotera maintained his position that certain entities should be called objective in everyone's eyes, such as the legal system of the continental shelf. He used the term 'objectiveness' in explaining his doctrinal standpoint. Kotera strongly insisted that the practice of law must

19 Chapter 1, *Paradigms in International Law.*
20 Ibid 72.
21 Ibid.

always be based on 'grounds and reasons' that are clear for everyone to see.[22]

Kotera was not a scholar who blindly accepted the assumed objectivity of law or the objective decisions of the International Court of Justice, but he clearly criticised the critical jurisprudential perspective raised by Onuma from his own position of constructing international law as a legal system. For Kotera, the boundary between law and non-law must be clearly distinguished. In contrast, Onuma's argument, if fully developed, could lead to relativism that international law is a product of perception and therefore differs from subject to subject, destroying the premise on which international law can be called law and undermining the benefits Japan has gained from the rule of international law. Onuma himself sought a kind of transnational 'commonality' in international law's codes of conduct, yet in a way that blurred the distinction between codes of conduct in general and those given the status of law, such as treaties and customary international law. At least that is what Kotera thought.

What, then, is Kotera's own view on the interpretative theory that should exist? As already mentioned, Kotera strongly insisted that international law functions as law in the narrow sense, specifically as an adjudicatory norm. From that standpoint, it is essential that the validity of legal propositions can be identified by certain common recognition, i.e. objectivity, and the most extensive way of doing this is, for him, reference to the sources of international law. Kotera criticised Onuma's departure from the sources of international law, arguing that even if the concept of sources is rejected, alternative ways of identifying general legal propositions must be articulated.[23] Kotera's core claim on the objectivity in the interpretation of international law is often expressed as requiring a 'verbalised basis of argument' (rather than an assumed basis) since his early writings.

With regard to the argument required for interpretation, Kotera repeatedly refers to the need to identify the purpose and nature of a system/instrument/institution (制度 – seido) as the basis of the argument. *Seido*, to which he refers, is a bundle of legal rules and principles which constitute the normative type of a particular act by subjects. In his resume for a workshop on international legal interpretation organised in 2009, Kotera stated that 'we should question the nature of *seido* in international law, such as states, oceans, continental shelves, space, etc., to reveal legal interpretations that cannot be derived from a mere literal interpretation'. Kotera cites the North

22 Ibid 77.

23 The résumé was provided by Professor WANI Kentaro, contributing to Chapter 9 on ISHIMOTO.

Sea Continental Shelf case as an example of how the ICJ identified the *seido* of the continental shelf as a precondition for and also as the act of legal interpretation, as to whether the continental shelf is a 'system pertaining to the topography of the seabed' or a 'system dependent on the distance from the coast'. In this case by the ICJ, the continental shelf up to 200 nautical miles under international law was understood as the latter.

In short, his view on interpretation does not end up with a literal interpretation at the superficial levels, nor does it fall into a political balancing of interests expressed in the guise of legal interpretation. Kotera focuses on the nature of *seido* as a totality of rules and principles and emphasises whether the identification (or construction) of its nature is convincing in relation to the problem before the court. For him, this is the essence of interpretation in international law. And this focus on *seido* did not exceptionalise the system of legal interpretation. Article 31 of the Vienna Convention on the Law of Treaties (VCLT) materialises the basic rules of treaty interpretation in international law.[24] The rules of VCLT themselves constitute an integral part of the legal system – or *seido* of interpretation – and are subject to interpretation. Kotera states that it is commonly accepted that the purpose of the 'seido of interpretation' in the VCLT is to 'understand the treaty text as the intention of the parties and to do so correctly'.

Yet it seems that Kotera's own theory of interpretation did not necessarily rely on VCLT, as he had in mind the PCIJ and ICJ's theory of interpretation until around the 1980s. A glimpse into Kotera's thinking comes from his argument about how the 'unity of the WTO regime' should be positioned in the interpretation of law in the WTO treaty regime. In Kotera's view, under the system of interpretation provided for by Article 31(3)(c) of the VCLT,[25] the 'relevant rules of international law' used for interpretation can include even bilateral and multilateral treaties to which not all the WTO parties are members.[26] Kotera then held that treating the unitary nature of the WTO regime as a central consideration in interpretation is an act of interpretation from a 'legitimate policy objective', which the treaty law convention avoided, and does not arise univocally from an understanding of the *seido*

24 '1. A treaty shall be interpreted in good faith in accordance with the ordinary meaning to be given to the terms of the treaty in their context and in the light of its object and purpose'.

25 '3. There shall be taken into account, together with the context: (c) any relevant rules of international law applicable in the relations between the parties'.

26 In his view, it is understood from the ordinary context that all members are understood to be intended to harmonise with existing international law and rules, even if they are not parties to the treaty when concluding a multilateral agreement like the WTO, unless otherwise stated.

of interpretation under the VCLT. Although Kotera himself had not published any systematic interpretive works, his assessment of the regimented nature of the WTO regime suggests he would allow for policy-theoretical interpretations that deviate from the traditional interpretation of the VCLT.

Incidentally, the ICJ has not been very clear that the rules of interpretation themselves are subject to interpretation. In addition, although Kotera stated that his focus on *seido* followed the ICJ and others, the ICJ *in recent years* seems to align more closely with the VCLT approach. For example, the ICJ in the Territorial Dispute case (*Libya v. Chad*) in 1994 stated that 'in accordance with customary international law, reflected in Article 31 of the 1969 Vienna Convention on the Law of Treaties ... Interpretation must be based above all upon the text of the treaty'.[27] In the next year, the ICJ reaffirmed the judgment and clarified its VCLT-based interpretation.[28] The ICJ seems to go even further from the VCLT, such as in the Raglan case, where a robust interpretation of the text without any consideration of the drafting process led to the interpretation that Article 36(1)(b) of the Consular Relations Convention conferred rights on individuals.

## *The WTO as a system and a regime*

As noted above, supporting the 'objectiveness' of international law would, in Kotera's view, strengthen Japan's shield in tough international politics. One of the consequences of Kotera's interpretive jurisprudence was that he construed the WTO as an objective legal system maintained through interpretive practices that reflect the politics and deals among sovereign nations. Kotera believed that Japan should be actively involved in shaping the international economic law order through this interpretive practice, and in the 2000s, he became increasingly absorbed in defining the nature of the regime.

In the 2000s, Kotera's interest in the international economic order remained strong, and he published a series of publications on the WTO and other issues in economic law. Among these, his monograph in 2000, *The Legal Structure of the WTO Regime*, discussed how the WTO should be regarded in relation to the general international legal order, based on the dual aspects of the WTO as an interest balancer among sovereign states and as a system whose institution is not reduced to serving the subjective interests of member states alone. The argument presented in the book represents

27 Territorial Dispute case (*Libyan Arab Jamahiriya v. Chad*), Judgment, I.C.J. Reports 1994, para. 41.

28 'It is accordingly incumbent upon the Court to decide the meaning of the text in question by applying the rules of interpretation that it recently had occasion to recall in the case concerning the Territorial Dispute (Libyan Arab Jamahiriya/Chad)'.

the arrival point of his thinking on the international economic law order and the system that supports it.

Kotera indicated that the nature of the WTO is that of a regime, an order in which the application of general international law is limited for the sake of protecting the common interests of members.[29] In this book, Kotera finds in the WTO regime an emerging international economic law order – thus, a publicness in which the fulfilment of obligations relates equally to all recipients within the discipline, not just subjective rights of members, and is shaped by the needs of basic economic principles.

In his assessment, there is no significant legal value added in the transition from the GATT to the WTO in terms of several key institutional changes, such as the WTO's explicit status as an international organisation.[30] From Kotera's perspective, it is more significant that the WTO system has become a legally systematic mechanism with an integral character, abolishing the former system of respective subsidiary agreements and the multiple steering committees that coexisted in the GATT era.[31] This integral and systematic character is inextricably linked to the legal nature of the WTO regime as discussed by Kotera. This includes limiting the application of general international treaty law and customary international law, and prohibiting individual states from taking countermeasures under international law against the suspension of concessions and other obligations under WTO agreements. Alternatively, if the respondent does not implement the recommendation, a retaliatory measure[32] can be invoked by the complaining state after completing the necessary steps under the DSP.

According to Kotera, WTO dispute settlement is still based on the need to restore the balance of rights and obligations between the complainant and respondent countries. At the same time, it is strongly based on the aspect of embodying international control to maintain the integrity of the WTO legal system by suspending rights and obligations under general international law.[33]

Unlike the International Court of Justice, the WTO dispute settlement procedure is not explicitly recognised as having a legally binding nature for

29 KOTERA, *Legal Structure of the WTO Regime* 80–81 (n 9).

30 Ibid 25. Here, KOTERA also expresses his view that GATT would meet the requirements of an international organisation with juridical personality by applying the requirements set out in the 1949 ICJ judgment (in the case of Reparation for Injuries Suffered in the Service of the United Nations).

31 KOTERA, *Legal Structure of the WTO Regime* 27 (n 9).

32 KOTERA states that he does not evaluate whether this constitutes countermeasures or sanctions under international law in this book. Ibid 42.

33 Ibid 133, see also 'The Function and Limitations of International Control' (n 3).

the decisions of the Panel and the Appellate Body.[34] Furthermore, according to Kotera, the specific content of the implementation is 'primarily determined by the respondent state on the basis of the grounds for the finding of violation',[35] which is clearly different from the performance of a judgment in the domestic legal system. Nevertheless, Kotera argued that there is now a strong argument for interpreting the outcome of dispute settlement procedures in the WTO regime as legally binding,[36] 'binding Member States to implement the decisions prospectively'[37] based on the past rulings of the Panels and Appellate Body, while recognising that there have been swings in the stance of past rulings. Furthermore, Kotera argues that the WTO regime should be recognised as an objective discipline, which arose with the strengthening of the discipline of trade in goods and the expansion of discipline beyond trade in goods in the Uruguay Round, which has manifested itself in a major change in WTO dispute settlement: the adoption of the negative consensus approach and the establishment of the Appellate Body.[38] In other words, these changes have encouraged the rapid accumulation of precedents and the formation of case law, and the emergence of a new approach that allows even different disputes to be dealt with consistent legal principles through the elaboration and formulation of legal interpretations. Here, his understanding of the WTO dispute settlement as 'international control' seems to be taking on a further regime character than his own view, analysed in Chapter 10.[39]

However, the inclusion of non-trade concerns exposed a structural tension in Kotera's regime theory. To give an example, Kotera draws on the reasoning of the Appellate Body decision in *United States: Import Prohibition of Certain Shrimp and Shrimp Products*[40] regarding the relationship between trade and the environment, arguing in particular that the reference to 'environmental protection' in the chapeau of Article 20 'allows an interpretation that if a multilateral agreement aimed at protecting marine turtles is made, it is to be read into the requirements of the chapeau. On the one hand, this

34 In 1996, the AB ruled, without stating any particular rationale, that the Panel's decision was binding on the disputants in *Japan – Alcoholic Beverages II:* Appellate Body Report WT/DS8/AB/R, WT/DS10/AB/R, WT/DS11/AB/R, DSR 1996:I.

35 KOTERA, *Legal Structure of the WTO Regime* 40, 112 (n 9).

36 Ibid 58.

37 Ibid 59.

38 KOTERA, *Legal Structure of the WTO Regime* 152 (n 9).

39 In his 1996 article on international control, Kotera based his argument on the dissenting opinion of Fitzmaurice in the Namibia case, i.e. he did not recognise the primacy of the interpretation of the controlling actor (DSP).

40 WT/DS58/RW (the Panel report), WT/DS58/AB/RW (the Appellate Body Report).

would also allow such a treaty to effectively supersede the GATT, although the WTO dispute settlement procedure cannot treat the treaty as its applicable law'.[41] On the other hand, Kotera also states that this possible outcome brings 'the environment into the WTO regime and allows for a more comprehensive legal assessment of disputes over the environment'.[42] But there appears to be a contradiction between the assessment that multilateral provisions on environmental protection can take precedence over WTO provisions and its self-containment as a regime.

The inclusion of non-trade concerns seems to have continued troubling Kotera. He launched an edited volume project[43] on non-trade concerns at the Research Institute of Economy, Trade and Industry (RIETI),[44] concluding that while the argument that non-trade concerns should be brought under the WTO umbrella is inherent in the political dynamics surrounding the WTO regime, the substantial need to bring such arguments within the WTO regime is not self-evident from a legal or economic perspective. The project was published around the time Japan began to steer towards FTA/EPAs and WTO negotiations. Even at this point, however, Kotera believed that FTAs can only play a complementary role to the WTO, and the WTO remains, and will remain, a strong determinant of the global economic order and of Japan's trade policy. Although Kotera maintained that relying solely on the WTO for Japan's international trade policy is excessive, the WTO's role in Japan's international trade policy should not be underestimated. As such, he was concerned that non-trade matters would be discussed at the behest of politics and that their inclusion would lead to a deadlock or a transformation in the nature of the regime of the WTO.[45]

### *Stagnation of the WTO negotiations and the formation of international investment law in its infancy*

In previous chapters, Kotera's approach to the international economic order and his jurisprudence of interpretation were explained. Kotera believed that

41 *Legal Structure of the WTO Regime*, 139. For this, Kotera refers to Joel Trachtman, 'Domain of WTO Dispute Resolution' (1999) 40 *Harvard International Law Journal* 363–364.

42 Ibid 142.

43 It was later published as the edited volume, 'WTO in Transition: Analysis of Issues of Non-Trade Interest' (Toyo Keizai Shinposha 2003).

44 See https://www.rieti.go.jp/en/ (accessed 31 May 2024).

45 *WTO in Transition*, also see 'The Nature of the WTO Regime: Its Impact on the International Legal Order' (2004) (281) *The Law Seminar* 41.

by clarifying the *seido* of the WTO regime through detailed analysis of the evolution of the WTO articles and DSP precedents, and by incorporating this into daily interpretive practices, Japanese international law practitioners and researchers could contribute to making the international economic order more viable and objective. In other words, he envisioned participating in the construction of the international economic order through a strategic interpretation based on the needs of Japanese society and market realities. However, the systematic and objective WTO legal order envisioned by Kotera began to crumble for several reasons. One was that, as depicted in Chapter 10, Kotera himself assessed the relationship with non-trade interests as 'a glimmer of tension between the partial discipline of the WTO regime and the objectivity of WTO discipline'.[46] The other was the expansion of bilateral and minority country initiatives, such as economic partnership agreements/free trade agreements, that covered a broader scope than traditional investment agreements.

As the conclusion of FTA/EPAs accelerates worldwide, they are becoming broader and more sophisticated commitments aimed at further strengthening intra-regional economic relations and optimising supply chain efficiency. This overlap in the substantive norms of FTA/EPAs and the WTO, as well as jurisdictional conflict over the forum for dispute settlement, was viewed as increasing the risk of 'fragmentation' in international economic law.

Since concluding an Economic Partnership Agreement (EPA) with Singapore in 2002, Japan has been at the forefront of FTA/EPA promotion. The government's official position is that 'FTA/EPAs complement the WTO-centred international economic system and will be promoted in a manner consistent with the GATT'. This understanding is based on GATT Article 24. In reality, however, Kotera believed that any regional trade agreements, such as FTA/EPA, violate the MFN principle, a fundamental principle of the WTO Agreement, and that Article 24 is rarely observed in its original meaning. According to Kotera, the Japanese government has been forced to change its policy in order to use them as 'tools for Japan's East and Southeast Asian diplomacy' and to 'deal with the disadvantages that Japanese companies suffer in countries with FTA/EPAs with other countries'.[47] In the acute need to respond to the reality of international politics, Kotera strongly argued for taking the leadership in systematisation and judicialisation of the Eastern Asian economic order as Japan's priority. Yet Kotera argued

46 Legal Structure 155 (n 9).

47 KOTERA Akira, 'Significance and Challenges of Economic Partnership Agreements: Has Japan's Trade Policy Changed? Is the Formation of an East Asian Community Imminent?' (2005) 77(6) *The Law Review* (*Horitsu Jiho*) 27–32.

that the APEC regional economic order has been blocked by ASEAN, which sees the move as the US using APEC regional frameworks to sway Europe in response to the impasse in WTO/GATT negotiations, and hence, as Asia caught in a confrontation between Western nations.[48] Perhaps for this reason, he insisted on Japan's participation in the Trans-Pacific Partnership (TPP) with a smaller and effective membership size from its inception, and strongly supported the enhancement of the dispute settlement system tied to the investment chapter of the TPP.

In parallel with this policy debate on the formation of a systematic Asian economic order, Kotera initiated a study analysing the legal doctrine of a growing number of investment treaties (including the investment chapter of EPA/FTAs) and investment treaty arbitration to guide the interpretation of agreements on the legal protection of outward investment. Regarding the fragmentation, while WTO agreements partially regulate investment-related disciplines, there are no unified, comprehensive investment rules. The results of this research, conducted primarily with the support of RIETI, have become the standard reference for international investment law research in Japan, and an edited version involving key researchers in the project was published in 2010.[49]

According to Kotera, investment treaties have the dual functions of protecting and liberalising investment. They can take the form of bilateral investment treaties (BITs), investment chapters of free trade agreements (FTAs) or multilateral treaties in specific areas, depending on their purpose.[50] When Kotera began his research on investment law, there was still much uncertainty regarding the determination of the procedural and substantive nature of investment arbitration. Kotera not only analysed precedents and articles, but also called for a comprehensive examination of how investment treaties should function, and advocated the construction of an investment treaty system based on an interpretation that integrated policy theory and interpretive theory in arbitration, as he did for the WTO.[51]

However, it is unclear whether Kotera was trying to construct international investment law as a body of law, or whether he envisioned an international investment court beyond the systematisation of arbitration outcomes.

48 KOTERA Akira, 'International Economic Law and Order in Asia' (2002) 74(4) *The Law Review* (*Horitsu Jiho*) 37–41.

49 KOTERA Akira (ed.), *International Investment Agreements: Legal Protection Through Arbitration* (Sanseido 2010).

50 KOTERA Akira, 'The Contemporary Significance of Investment Agreements: Strengthening Their Functions Through Arbitration' in Kotera (ed.), *International Investment Agreements: Legal Protection Through Arbitration* (Sanseido 2010) 3.

51 Ibid., 14–16.

It seems that Kotera's mission was to make international law more objective and judicial through interactive interpretation by lawyers worldwide, but by the time the 2010 edition on international investment law was published, Kotera was already suffering from cancer; he passed away in February 2012.

### *The melancholic international law scholar from the periphery*

Critical legal approaches in international law have revealed the Western-centric hegemony hidden behind the assumption of the neutrality and objectivity of international law. Yet, simultaneously, we cannot ignore that it is extremely difficult to overcome the 'Western-centricity' of the very frameworks, concepts, standards and other basic expertise that define the international legal system and the ideas that underlie it. It is a structure embedded in the very patterns of common legal language and specific legal reasoning that maintain the integrity and coherence of international law in the practice and training of professionals. Many of the scholars who remained on the 'periphery' of international law after drinking the 'red pill' accepted this Western centrality and the fact that they could not destroy international law, which, at least, plays a certain role in the current international order, and many sought a way out in the tactics of practice or in the education of practitioners. Kotera was one of them.

To sum up first, it seems that Kotera had reached a kind of resignation in his later years. No matter how Western-centric the framework of thought that defined international law as international law may be, to deny it would be to deny international law as a whole. To remain an international jurist, one must learn the framework of thought and apply the rules more wisely for one's own ends than such 'others', even if the rules were set by them. It was with this view that Kotera remained involved in practice and the education of younger generations for many years.

For Kotera, interpretive jurisprudence, in his view, was not about successfully organising European and US theories around precedents or explaining the law in a scholarly manner. Although he trained his students to thoroughly study the thinking of Western legal thought that constitutes the reasoning of the jurisprudence of international law, interpretative jurisprudence for him was 'to offer an interpretation that can appropriately cut against the reality that confronts us'. It was against this backdrop that he cynically stated that if the role of Japanese international law scholars 'is to propagate European doctrines, international precedents and WTO dispute settlement reports in Japan, they certainly do not need to publish research results in English or to confront actual international law practice'.[52] Despite

52 KOTERA Akira, 'International Law (11): The Melancholy of International Legal Scholars' (2011) 606 *Window on the Study (Shosai-no-mado)* 13–18.

the fact that international law has become a major industry in Japan, he wrote that Japanese scholars 'write much of their work in Japanese' in his 2011 article, and criticised this as only encouraging Western-centricity and Japanese peripherality. Lamenting that he himself should have also recognised this earlier, but said that 'it was now behind me'.

Perhaps Kotera's academic difficulty and notable uniqueness is that, even though he accepts that the rationale of international law is Western-centric, he does not argue from a critical perspective like Onuma,[53] nor does he regard 'objectivity' as metaphysical, as in the context of natural law traditions in Western jurisprudence. What Kotera means by 'objectivity' is, according to the author's view, that jurists elaborate '*seido*' by means of universally trained patterns of legal reasoning, and he regards this method as interpretive jurisprudence. Of course, from the perspective of critical jurisprudence, the specific argumentative pattern itself enforces the hegemony embedded in professional knowledge. But for Kotera, 'the objectivity' that we international lawyers can have in common is a method of legal reasoning, and *seido*, a kind of empirical existence that is confirmed by it.

As alluded to at the beginning of this chapter, Kotera was a scholar who was particularly wary of the self-reflexive, pluralist and multiculturalist tendencies of the Western academic world, as they did not provide an alternative to the necessary universal or objective ground that the discipline of law requires. The 'conversation' framework proposed at the beginning of this chapter does not assume the possibility of theoretical convergence on the various currents of international law. Continuing the conversation may begin to relativise the 'orthodox genealogy' in the interpretation of international law, but it will require a reasonable amount of time and investment.

Readers may feel short-changed. They think that we are human beings; we should be able to dialogue, discuss and reach a conclusion. The author of the chapter is slightly more pessimistic because no communication, including conversation, can take place between a man and a dog. It is this very incommensurability that makes 'conversation', the continuation of a relationship without expecting mutual understanding, viable. The man-and-dog comparison is just an analogy. There is no end to the number of people who claim that they have a heart-to-heart with dogs, but it is a pernicious joke. People who have no way to understand the world from the dog's point of view will never have a heart-to-heart or communicate with them. In multi-cultural communication of international law, if one's perspective is that of a person, whether orthodox or periphery, the other is a dog. Because we understand this so painfully, many scholars in the past have sought to explain international law and the world as seen from the periphery in a way that is understandable to those with different lenses and languages. But the very framework of international law, international justice and international politics that is the

53 ONUMA himself did not define himself as being a critic.

premise for understanding these things is 'not ours', which is a problem for the periphery and others, where the distance from the Western world is great in every sense of the word, including religion, culture and race.

From the perspective of the author of this chapter, Kotera was a jurist who, in the light of the reality of the international order and international jurisprudence, understood well that dogs and people were incompatible, and that peripheral jurists were locked into the dog position. Against his recognition of reality, Kotera would use interpretation as its own battlefield and argued that, by learning and internalising the thoughts and thinking patterns of 'people', he could strategically use them to interpret the law in realising the interests of the client. He also insisted that Japan's international jurisprudence should actively continue to engage with the shaping of the international economic law order by connecting to the daily practice of international politics and administrations, even if engaging with the interpretation of international law may fix the status quo and put us permanently in a 'dog's' place. Regrettably, in contrast to Onuma, Kotera's limited English-language publication in his later years and his early death from illness may have made his aspirations and vision less accessible to others. After Kotera's death, the Government of Japan shifted its diplomatic stance, becoming actively involved in shaping the regional and international systems on different issues, and an increasing number of scholars began to publish in English. I wonder what Kotera would have written if he had lived to see that new reality.

# 12

# ONUMA Yasuaki: a transcivilisationalist international lawyer

*KAKU Shun*

## Introduction

ONUMA Yasuaki (1946–2018) is perhaps best known for his transcivilisational approach to international law. While the idea certainly captures his distinguished scholarly contribution to international law, the achievements of this extraordinary individual can hardly be depicted by a single notion. Being both a scholar and activist, universalist and nationalist, idealist and pragmatist, egalitarian and elitist, democrat and conservative at the same time, Onuma had a personality with many shades, though this did not mean he lacked personal integrity. Rather, the apparent contradictions reflect a deeper level of consistency in his personality. To understand Onuma more fully as an international legal scholar, it may be helpful at the outset to outline some aspects of his personality related to the latter two sets of contrasts, as they may be less perceivable than the former three in the following sections.

He was born into a prestigious sake-brewery family in Yamagata and was proud to be affiliated with the nation's top university, the University of Tokyo, throughout his academic career. He was none other than an elite. Nonetheless, he always saw reality from the perspective of those marginalised in society and deemed it his responsibility to alleviate their plight. Perhaps this perspective was grounded in his personal experiences as a person from Yamagata, an area that has been somewhat left behind in the modernisation process since the late nineteenth century. Once, with some sarcasm, he offered his visiting disciples dried kaki (Japanese persimmons) he had sent from Yamagata, saying they were a treat when Japan had been poor.[1] For Onuma, the Japanese success in economic development was a living memory, and he appeared to never forget what society had been like

1 Dried kaki was a traditional preserved food that farm households commonly made during the winter low season. It is still popular in Japan and is sometimes only obtainable

before, nor the shadows of development. While there was an undeniably elitist tone when he spoke of his students at the University of Tokyo as elites, it was, for him, inseparable from what they owed to society.

In contrast, as was common among his generation, Onuma did not hide his admiration for the society and culture of the United States, which he saw as democratic, morally driven and egalitarian. Although the US has made many grave mistakes in foreign and domestic policy, he saw the virtue of its democracy and idealist self-identification that it was capable of learning lessons from its past wrongs. Nevertheless, Onuma retained a conservative posture in his life. He was always dressed in a bespoke suit (he maintained that ready-made clothes did not fit his thin body), holding his back straight (he was a university ballroom dancing club alumnus). In the classroom, he emphasised discipline and politeness, though he would never forget to encourage students to speak up: 'You may think it shameful to make a mistake in front of your classmates. You should be ashamed, however, if you have survived a class without being ashamed', Onuma said to his students. An Americanised world was the last thing he wanted – Onuma loathed students taking drinks or wearing hats in his class. His conservatism reflects a kind of value pluralism in approval of the plurality of values embedded in diverse cultural or civilisational traditions, which would later materialise in his transcivilisational approach to international law.

## By 1990: confronting the past

### *A post-war generation in a post-war society*

Born in February 1946, Onuma was the first generation born after the Second World War. Though the country was covered in rubble and chaos from war, he grew up inhaling the liberated air of post-war society in Japan. He was very much a product of the era, in the sense that he was deeply engaged both as an academic and an activist in the international issues confronting post-war/post-imperial Japan, while also enjoying freedom within and beyond academia. When he started his academic career in the Faculty of Law at the University of Tokyo, Onuma greatly enjoyed the liberal stance of his mentor, Yuichi Takano, who, his traditional, positivist orientation notwithstanding, allowed his disciple to adopt a more sociological cum aspirational approach towards international law.

at a handsome price. Presumably, Onuma's point was that there was not a good variety of food or sweets when he was young.

That fostered Onuma's first major scholarly work, *Senso Sekininron Josetsu*,[2] published in 1975, which illustrated the emerging norms of individual war crimes under international law by following their development between and after the two World Wars. The book was originally completed as a dissertation research that he, as a research associate, had to submit by the end of their three-year term. In those days, research associates were selected from the undergraduate students with top marks and employed immediately after graduation from the law faculty at major universities. (Before he was appointed as a research associate, Onuma had spent an extra year in the Politics Course at the Faculty of Law at the University of Tokyo after he graduated from the Private Law Course.) In this earliest work, Onuma already exhibits, albeit in a fledgling form, most of the main academic themes he pursues throughout his entire academic career.

The book was an attempt by a scholar of the post-war generation, born into a society shattered by a war for which they were not individually responsible, yet who nonetheless had to bear the burden of its guilt as part of the nation. By the early 1970s, memories of the Second World War appeared to be fading rapidly as a new international political landscape in East Asia emerged. Japan had already proclaimed its resuscitation and rapid economic growth by successfully hosting the first Tokyo Olympics in 1964 and the Japan World Exposition in Osaka in 1970. The Agreement Between Japan and the Republic of Korea Concerning the Settlement of Problems in Regard to Property and Claims and Economic Cooperation had concluded in 1965, providing a comprehensive solution to the issues of the former Japanese imperial rule on the Korean Peninsula, at least about the southern half, which was, and still is, under the government of the Republic of Korea. In 1972, Japan normalised its relationship with the People's Republic of China and recognised the latter as the 'sole legal Government of China' in the Joint Communiqué of the Government of Japan and the Government of the People's Republic of China. Although the Cold War cast a dark shadow over the Far East, Japan appeared to have finally settled the major post-war issues with its neighbouring countries. Japanese society may have been in a mood of being liberated from the memories of colonisation and militarism.

This was, of course, wrong. Or, at least so believed Onuma. The book was dedicated to the two scholars who had once studied in Japan and were executed by the South Korean military regime. Onuma had actively supported them until it became impossible because of his focus on the dissertation required for a research associate. In a suppressed tone, he,

2 ONUMA Yasuaki, *An Introduction to War Responsibility* (*Senso Sekininron Josetsu*) (Tokyo Daigaku Shuppankai 1975).

in expressing regret for his withdrawal from the movement, condemns the Japanese people for being complicit in the atrocity by providing economic assistance for the military regime in South Korea. Onuma did not realise that Japan's post-war years had ended. While Japanese colonialism as a social system may have collapsed with the war, its remnants still haunted Japanese society and elsewhere. The Korean people, after being momentarily liberated from Japanese rule, were de facto divided into two states, both ruled by military dictators and harbouring animosity towards the other. The people from the former colonial territories were not only deprived of Japanese nationality but also confronted by incessant formal and informal discrimination in post-war Japan. The Cold War environment was favourable for Japan, as the United States, faced with the threat of the Socialist bloc, which eventually materialised as the Korean War, reversed its occupation policy in Japan, supporting its reindustrialisation and even the establishment of defence forces. In the same circumstances, however, Japan's former imperial subjects were in predicaments, and Japanese society did not just look the other way but was deeply involved.

In Onuma's view, Japan had failed to take full responsibility for the victims of its colonial rule and aggressive war. One lesson Onuma learned from the Anti-Vietnam War movement of his time was that, when faced with such deep-rooted societal issues, one cannot remain neutral by not acting. By doing nothing, one sides with the establishment.[3] Once in a class, Onuma explained his conviction that he must act as rooted in his nationalist pride. He thought it shameful that his nation had not faced its past directly. As mentioned above, in undertaking the task of confronting historical injustice as a scholar, he had to relinquish his role as an activist, but throughout his life, he sought to reconcile the two roles.

## *The question of war responsibility*

The main purpose of *Senso Sekininron Josetsu* was to delineate the origin and development of the crime against peace provided for in Article 6 of the Charter of the International Military Tribunal (IMT). In Onuma's view, the crime against peace is grounded in two distinct ideals: the illegality of war and the war responsibility of political leaders. He accounts for the former as the continuation of the legal thought of the interwar period while

3 ONUMA Zemi, 20 Shunen Kinen Jigyo Jikko Iinkai, *Between 'Postwar' and 'Cohabitation': Twenty Years of Onuma Zemi at the University of Tokyo ('Sengo' to 'Kyosei' no Aida: Todai Onuma Zemi no 20 Nen)* (Onuma Zemi Dosokai 1994) 13.

reaching the conclusion that the latter was a novel invention rather than an established rule or principle of international law. Strange as it may appear, little mention is made in the book of the Japanese case. The appraisal of the Japanese war responsibility, however, is no doubt the underlying theme, as is hinted at by his remarks on the executed Korean scholars in the afterword and the repeatedly raised question of the ideological nature of the war crimes.

In his analysis, Onuma apparently confined himself to what could be strictly said on the basis of historical materials and doctrinal writings. By doing so, he wanted to identify the scope of the crimes of war in international law as it existed during the Second World War, by demarcating what could legitimately be regarded as an application of the established laws and the manifestation of the victor's justice in the jurisprudence of the IMT. In need of firm evidentiary facts, the young scholar vigorously accumulated as broad a range of materials as he could obtain, both primary and secondary, written in various languages. The extensive analysis of the development of legal discussions during the interwar period led him to the conclusion that crimes against peace were yet to be established at the time German war criminals were prosecuted at the IMT. In this sense, the criminal procedure of the Tribunal was at odds with the *nulla poena sine lege* principle, which lay at the heart of the criminal law.

However, Onuma did not stop there. He then went on to pose a question, 'Was it not a development in a desired direction?' This question was a precursor to his later analysis of various 'functions' of law in international society.[4] Despite a tendency, especially among positivist doctrines, to identify the law with what is applied as international legal rules and principles by the international courts and tribunals, adjudication is only a portion of the vast area in which law operates. As Onuma later vehemently emphasises, the distinction between norms of adjudication and norms of conduct is more pertinent in international society, where, due to the lack of mandatory jurisdiction in international adjudication, far fewer disputes are brought to a court than in domestic society.[5] We must not lose sight of international

4 ONUMA Yasuaki, 'Law and Politics in International Society: Overcoming the Curse of "Legal Positivism" in International Legal Scholarship and 'Realism' in International Political Studies (Kokusai Shakai no Ho to Seiji, Kokusai Hogaku no "Jitteiho Shugi" to Kokusai Seijigaku no "Genjitsu Shugi" no Jubaku wo Koete)' in Japanese Society of International Law (ed.), *Law and Politics in International Society* (*Kokusai Shakai no Ho to Seiji*) (Sanseido 2001).

5 ONUMA Yasuaki, 'The ICJ: Emperor without Clothes? International Conflict Resolution, Article 38 of the ICJ Statute and the Sources of International Law' in

law's dynamics as 'living law' by focusing exclusively on its operation in the judicial process.

Onuma did not see the judgments of the IMT simply as 'the victor's justice' as they are often criticised. For him, both the ideas of the illegality of war and of the war responsibility of political leaders in international law had an 'ideological' aspect as well as 'bindingness'. Since their introduction in the aftermath of the First World War, the two-fold ideas of the illegality of war and the war responsibility of political leaders have had an ideological character, as their deployment and subsequent development in the diplomatic discourse among Allied political leaders was undoubtedly politically driven. The United States was conscious that a defence must be given to its breach of traditional rules of neutrality in support of the United Kingdom before its participation in the war. For the UK, separating German political leaders from other members of the nation and limiting war responsibilities to the former was necessary to avoid any excessive loss of soldiers due to the Germans' desperate resistance. The US also saw this as a means of gaining support from domestic public opinion, showing a distaste for pursuing the collective responsibility of the entire German nation.

This did not mean, however, that the adoption of the two principles was completely arbitrary, for once they were recognised as law, states could not escape from their regulatory force. To be sure, the outbreak of the war itself demonstrated the failed attempt to outlaw war by the Kellogg–Briand Pact in 1928. Nonetheless, under the pressure of public opinion, states no longer saw themselves as free to wage war. States tended to play down military conflict as being short of war in the formal sense, employing the term 'incident' instead. When circumstances did not allow that option, states invoked self-defence to defend their moral and legal high ground. Meanwhile, the idea of the war responsibility of political leaders also restricted the US policy against Germany, as once it had been introduced and gained popular support, President Franklin Roosevelt, despite his preference, was no longer able to push through the so-called 'Morgenthau plan', the idea proposed by Henry Morgenthau Jr, then Secretary of the Treasury, of pursuing the war responsibility of the entire German nation.

In hindsight, two themes that will be developed through Onuma's subsequent works appear to be already present in *Senso Sekininron Josetsu*. One is that, in order to fully understand law's function, one must not focus exclusively on law's bindingness or obligatory force upon legal subjects. Put more positively, law's functions are far broader and extend to shaping ideas

Ando Nisuke et al. (eds), *Liber Amicorum Judge Shigeru Oda*, vol. 1 (Kluwer Law International 2002).

and perceptions of, and channelling communications among, various players involved in international relations. The other related theme might be less conspicuous, but nonetheless recognisable when read in conjunction with Onuma's later criticisms of the domestic law analogy prevalent in international legal scholarship or, more specifically, of the positivist preoccupation with the jurisprudence of international courts and tribunals.[6] The decentralised structure and the lack of compulsory jurisdiction in international society make the focus on international judicial procedure less obvious. The book's focus on state policymaking, diplomatic negotiations, public reactions and so on is, in a sense, a performative vindication of 'living' international law.

### *Rectifying the past wrongs of colonialism*

The second theme that characterised Onuma's earlier works was the rectification of Japan's past wrongs of colonial rule and its aftermath. His special focus was on the rights of the Koreans and their descendants living in post-war Japanese society. As mentioned above, Onuma regretted that he could not prevent the two former Korean students of the University of Tokyo from being executed by the South Korean military regime. With this bitter experience, his scholarly conscience was directed to a broader perspective on the predicament of the Korean diaspora. Since the Korean Empire was annexed by the Japanese Empire in 1910, a large number of Koreans migrated to the suzerain's territory. At the time the Second World War finally ended for Japan, what would later be defined as the territory of post-war Japan was the base and centre of life of more than 500,000 Koreans. Despite the fact that for a great number of Koreans (and Taiwanese), it is unimaginable to lead a life with their social ties severed from Japanese society, when Japan regained its independence in 1952, with the Treaty of San Francisco coming into effect, they were deprived of Japanese nationality,[7] and left only with a precarious legal status as special permanent residents in Japan.

6 See n 5 above.

7 No Diet legislation has ever been made to determine the nationality of the former Japanese colonial subjects. The Alien Registration Ordinance, the last Imperial Edict 207, issued just one day before the new Japanese Constitution came into effect, provides 'Those among Taiwanese determined by the Interior Minister and Koreans [*Chosenjin*], with regard to the application of this Edict, shall for the present be *deemed* as Aliens' (Art. 11) (emphasis added). On 19 April 1952, a few days before Japan recovered its independence with the Treaty of Peace with Japan coming into force on 28 April, the Director-General of the Civil Affairs Bureau at the Attorney General's Office (later the Ministry of Justice) issued a circular notice stating 'All

His second monograph, *Tan'itsu Minzoku Shakai no Shinwa wo Koete* (1986),[8] is a compilation of his essays on nationality and border control in postcolonial Japan. Included in the book are not only scholarly articles but also pieces from popular periodicals, which exemplify how Onuma's academic work and advocacy role are intertwined. Indeed, his writings, regardless of who the reader may be, share the same tenet. As the title indicates, the book's main purpose was to overcome the implacable myth of Japanese society as monoethnic. This convenient neglect of Japan's colonial history created institutionalised discrimination against Koreans in Japan who did not have Japanese nationality. In several chapters, Onuma repeatedly emphasises that the second and later generations of ethnic Koreans, born and raised in Japan, did not enter the country as other foreign nationals typically did. Typically, they are more fluent in Japanese than in Korean. In one chapter, Onuma points out that Korean residents in Japan are nevertheless treated categorically as foreign nationals and unfairly refused the protection of the law compared with Japanese nationals.[9]

Onuma enumerates four such areas of law: immigration control, occupation, social security and education. His point is that the indiscriminate designation of the Koreans as foreign nationals has made it possible to similarly restrict the rights of Korean residents in Japan as other foreign nationals, without paying due regard to the historical origin of the very presence of the Korean ethnic minority in Japan. Most Korean residents in Japan had been living in the country and were part of society well before the post-war constitutional regime was established.[10]

Moreover, the Immigration Control Act of 1951 (originally a Cabinet Order mandated by an Imperial Edict upon the acceptance of the Potsdam Declaration) and its 1981 amendment left broad discretion to the administrative branch to decide whether to order the deportation of foreign nationals, with ambiguous criteria. This was enabled by subsuming all foreign nationals into the same indiscriminate category, especially in disregard of the historical circumstances of ethnic Koreans who had Japanese nationality before the end of the war as resident foreign nationals. But how could a person be thrown out of the country who retained Japanese nationality until

---

Koreans and Taiwanese [...] will lose the nationality of Japan' by that date. Although, as a circular notice, this should technically have had no effect on the legal status of individuals, Koreans and Taiwanese were effectively excluded from Japanese family register affairs and, thereby, from Japanese nationality.

8 ONUMA Yasuaki, *Beyond the Myth of the Monoethnic Society* (Toshindo 1986).

9 Ibid 161ff.

10 Ibid 162–170. Although Onuma's primary focus is on the Koreans, similar considerations also apply to the Taiwanese.

he had been deprived of it by the government he was under, and who had had the base of life there only because he or she was now a foreign national? Onuma suggests that the administration and the court should adopt a negative application. The grounds for deportation should be such that it is absolutely necessary, and the burden of proof rests with the government.[11]

In another chapter, Onuma makes an interesting argument that while the Korean ethnic minority are believed to be holding (South or North) Korean nationality only, in fact, they should be regarded as at least potential Japanese nationals.[12] Even if we dare deny such a view, there are a considerable number (more than one hundred thousand at that time) of ethnic Koreans who have acquired Japanese nationality through naturalisation. There are also children who are ethnically half Korean but inherited Japanese nationality from either parent as a result of interethnic marriage. Japan should not be regarded as a monoethnic society, nor should the issues of the Koreans and their descendants in Japan be regarded as concerning foreigners only. Here, we might notice another aspect of the relationship between Onuma's academic work and his role as an advocate. This line of argument that ethnic Korean residents retain potential Japanese nationality, which appeared in a popular essay, would later be elaborated in his monograph, as will be seen later.

## By 2000: a turning point

### *The repatriation of the Koreans left behind in Sakhalin and the Asian Women's Fund*

Onuma became involved in the civic campaign to repatriate Korean workers who, despite their wishes, had been unable to return from the former Japanese territory of Sakhalin after the Second World War. The book *Saharin Kimin* (1992)[13] was a compilation of a detailed study of the historical origin of the issue and the historical background and legal situation of the Korean workers, combined with what he had experienced throughout the campaign for their return.

Despite its composed tone, the book shows Onuma's sympathy for the plight of individuals entangled in politics between states. His conviction was that the primary responsibility should be borne by the Japanese

11 Ibid 218–225.

12 Ibid 160.

13 ONUMA Yasuaki, *The Abandoned in Sakhalin* (*Saharin Kimin*) (Chuo Koron Shinsha 1992).

government for the repatriation of the Korean workers, for they had been sent to Sakhalin as imperial subjects in the name of the former Japanese Empire. The Japanese government was of the view that, because they were no longer Japanese nationals, they had no right to enter, let alone reside in, Japan if they were rejected by the South Korean government. For the South Korean government, it was not their business to bring them home, not only because Japan was to blame, but also because not returning their nationals conveniently testifies to the Soviets' evil. During the Cold War, the Soviet Union adopted a restrictive policy on emigration and departure, which limited the scope for repatriation. As the leader of the communist bloc, it also had to avoid any misunderstandings of communist North Korea of showing favour to Japan and South Korea.

Domestic circumstances were not favourable, either. In the early stages, the repatriation campaign was a solitary struggle led by a Korean man, Park Nohak, who returned from Sakhalin with other Japanese workers in 1958 with the help of the Japanese government, as he was married to a Japanese woman. Soon after settling in Japan, he started the campaign but suffered from a lack of funds, expertise and popular understanding. Almost a decade later, with a growing consciousness of war responsibility in Japanese society through the turbulent 1960s, support for the campaign gradually widened. A notable development was made by a group of campaigners who brought the case to court and fought a battle that would last fourteen years. While the lawsuit attracted public attention and pressured the Japanese government, the initial enthusiasm waned in the course of the prolonged court procedure, and the campaign reached an impasse.

In 1981, Onuma founded an association (Ajia niokeru Sengo Sekinin wo Kangaeru Kai) with a group of eight scholars and law practitioners and was elected its chair. The association reported the situation of the Koreans to the Human Rights Commission, but this proved counterproductive, as it faced strong opposition from the Soviet Union. This bitter experience made Onuma painfully aware of how closely intertwined human rights issues and politics are. The next move was to organise an international symposium that included participants from Japan and South Korea, which seemed a success. Onuma further explored different channels to prompt the Soviets' action, and one day, the then-Soviet foreign minister announced a policy change in the treatment of Koreans in Sakhalin, or that was what he took it to be. Nothing followed.

Feelings of frustration overwhelmed Onuma, but after a while, he came to feel undaunted, in part thanks to other campaigners. In 1986, Onuma, albeit grudgingly, took the issue to politicians, whom he regarded as rather impure and antithetical to the academic world, as a last resort. It brought a major breakthrough. Hearing the plea, two members of the Diet moved to form an all-party-affiliated group within the Diet. One was HARA Bunbei, an influential Liberal Democrat with strong ties to the Soviets, and the other was IGARASHI Kozo, a motivated Socialist with pragmatic skills. The earnest push of the Diet members' group prompted renewed negotiations between Japan, Korea and the Soviet Union, and in 1988, fifteen Koreans visited Korea with special permission from the Soviet government. Since then, hundreds of Koreans have been able to temporarily visit home via Japan at the expense of the Japanese government, some of whom permanently returned there. The South Korea-Russia relations were also alleviated. The book concludes with the return of 120 Koreans with a direct flight from Yuzhno-Sakhalinsk to Seoul.

In 1995, the Asian Women's Fund was established to resolve the issue of comfort women in the countries and regions occupied by the Japanese military during the Second World War. The issue came to the fore in the 1990s. The fund was supported by donations from the Japanese people, with the Japanese government only subsidising its operational costs, as it took the view that the issue of wartime compensation had been settled by the respective peace treaties. Nevertheless, payments to victims was delivered with a letter from the then-Prime Minister MURAYAMA Tomiichi, who was personally supportive of the fund. Onuma was one of the fund's proposers and played a major role in materialising it.

These commitments to civic movements, which he appeared to personally find fulfilling, albeit at times not without remorse, as well as the publications as byproducts, added a distinctive colour to Onuma's academic career. His stance was pragmatic rather than idealistic, notwithstanding his sympathies for human suffering. As a legal scholar, he was always cautious about the textual and legal basis of his arguments, which defined what could plausibly be argued. He was also aware that governmental policies are made on a delicate balance between competing political forces, which sometimes made it necessary to seize the moment to take a step forward. He later recalled that the campaign for Koreans in Sakhalin was the most successful of his experiences.[14] As mentioned earlier, he met two politicians through campaigning. Their support was essential to overcoming resistance from right-wing politicians who opposed any move to settle post-war issues as a compromise with the opposing states. A lesson Onuma learned from these two respected politicians was that, instead of accusing and criticising those with opposing views, it is important to build an alliance to advance a

14 UTSUMI Aiko et al., *Postwar Responsibilities: Meeting the Eyes from Asia* (*Sengo Sekin, Ajia no Manazashi ni Kotaete*) (Iwanami Shoten 2014).

common cause by combining the merits of those with competing interests and opinions, thereby creating a force to change a government policy.

This lesson was well learned and practised, as Onuma deliberately published in a right-wing magazine during the campaign for a fund for wartime reparations. It was part of a strategy for persuading the opposing faction to gain the necessary support.[15] After the establishment of the Asian Women's Fund was decided with a more limited focus than was originally intended, Onuma also travelled to Korea several times to talk to the intellectuals and NGOs pertinaciously opposing the fund because it was not an official apology by the Japanese government. Through such experiences, as he later recalled, he kept company not only with campaigners on the left wing, but also with critics on the right.

## *The re-reading of the history of international law*

While Onuma's earlier writings focused on particular historical events, such as the Nuremberg trial or the predicament of ethnic Korean residents brought about by the Japanese immigration control regime, his thought, over time, was directed towards a more general analysis of international law from both historical and theoretical perspectives.

Onuma's interest in the history of legal thought, partly manifested in his first book, fully materialised in *A Normative Approach to War, Peace, War and Justice in Hugo Grotius* (1993).[16] It is a translation with supplements of a preceding book published in Japanese, *Senso to Heiwa no Ho* (1987). A revised edition was later published in 1995,[17] an extensive study on Hugo Grotius's *De jure belli ac pacis* by six ambitious Japanese legal scholars. Published in English, it soon attracted the attention of scholars across disciplines worldwide, as evidenced by the number of positive reviews in major international journals.

As its editor, he exhibits three motives that animated the book in the introduction. To take up the third one first, this might be a natural extension of his first book on war responsibility, that is, a criticism of the apparent passivity of international legal scholarship in its treatment of war and peace. While the period immediately prior to the two world wars did not distinguish between just and unjust wars, the purpose of international law,

15 Ibid 206.

16 ONUMA Yasuaki (ed.), *A Normative Approach to War, Peace: War, and Justice in Hugo Grotius* (Clarendon Press 1993).

17 ONUMA Yasuaki (ed.), *The Law of War and Peace* (*Senso to Heiwa no Ho*) (Toshindo 1987/1995).

at its origin, was to prevent unjust wars and defend peace. For Grotius, living in the era of the Thirty Years' War, this was an urgent practical problem that had to be solved, and he ventured to respond to it by vindicating the independence of international law from religious doctrine.

The other two motives appear, albeit arguably discernible in previous works, to be a rather novel development in Onuma's thought. First, the book is critical of the methodology of prior works in the history (and the history of ideas) of international law, concentrating almost exclusively on thinkers' works and ideas on international law with little attention to either the more comprehensive theoretical framework or the contemporaneous social context which defined it. In particular, Grotius must be understood not only in the genealogy of international legal scholarship represented by Suarez, Gentilis, Pufendorf and Wolff, but also in juxtaposition with social contract theorists such as Hobbes, Locke and Rousseau. Neither should Grotius' broader theoretical framework be viewed as lacking consistency when modern ideas are projected onto it without reflecting on differences in social structures and frames of reference.

Second, it must be borne in mind that neither international law as delineated by Grotius nor the Westphalian system, which it allegedly governed, could be universal without the subsequent history of domination by European powers. Not only did individual rules and principles of international law lay grounds for colonialism, but the international legal system as a whole, while claiming universality, served to sustain European – and later also American – domination, founded on the exclusion of non-Western peoples. In this light, the 'naturalness' of natural law as depicted by Grotius is to be more carefully scrutinised, and a more nuanced approach taken to Grotius as the 'father of international law'. This point is further elaborated in the Appendix, newly written for the English version.

It appears that, especially with regard to these two motives, *A Normative Approach to War* succeeded in achieving its objectives. Indeed, the book caught the attention of several reviewers in Western countries. Even those reviewers who made a more acerbic appraisal of the book might be seen as proving the legitimacy of these motives, for there seemed to be a felt necessity for a detailed response, if not rebuttal, as one of them made in his lengthy article, to this 'anti-Festschrift' dedicated to Grotius.[18] By casting a distanced, non-European light on the Grotian tradition, and instigating

18 Anthony Carty, 'Japanese Deconstructions of the Grotian Tradition in International Law: *A Normative Approach to War: Peace, War and Justice in Hugo Grotius*. Edited by Yasuaki Onuma. Oxford: Clarendon Press, 1993. xvi + 421 pp. £40' (1999) 66 *British Yearbook of International Law* 477–490.

debate surrounding it, the book marked 'their [the outsiders'] ... arrival at the centre'.[19] It was an arrival at the centre because it was not only an objection to the power structure of the mainstream narrative but also an internal critique based on a robust, academically sustained reading of texts. In this sense, the authors of the book should not be seen as 'outsiders', though their scepticism of the Grotian tradition in international law was presented physically and culturally outside Europe or the West. This point is implicit in one reviewer's appraisal of the book as 'the most careful, sustained reading of JBP [De jure belli ac pacis] in English'.[20]

### *Inter-/transcivilisational perspective on international law*

*Jinken, Kokka, Bunmei* (1998)[21] was, in a sense, a synthesis of Onuma's practical inclination, on the one hand, and his theoretical interest in international law, on the other. As mentioned previously, he had the bitter memory of having failed to rescue Korean academics from being executed by the military regime in South Korea and had since published quite a few articles on the issues of Korean minorities in Japan to be read within and outside the academic circle. In so doing, Onuma found the language of human rights to be the most effective practical instrument for challenging and reforming the law to alleviate the plight of minorities.

Onuma's espousal of human rights as a pragmatic tool is not without tension. The idea of human rights originates in natural law theory, which also founded modern international law. An idea was later accepted that states are in the state of nature just as individuals are in their relations with one another prior to the social contract. Insofar as this idea still has a grip on present-day international law thinking, human rights as fundamental rights of individuals are often at odds with the equally fundamental, or so it is alleged, rights of states. In practice, this means that while human rights are a powerful tool for protecting the interests of individuals as the weak at the national level, they may work against them at the international level by eroding the claims of sovereignty of weaker states. Thus, the task of international lawyers is to strike a balance in specific cases.

Neither did the structural bias towards the West in the human rights discourse escape Onuma's critical eye. Although the widespread acceptance of the idea of human rights in international society is undoubtedly a great

19 Robert Chu, 'Grotian Encounters' (1994) 35 *Harvard ILR* 596.
20 Nicholas Onuf, 'A Normative Approach to War: Peace, War, and Justice in Hugo Grotius by Onuma Yasuaki' (1994) 88 *American Political Science Review* 3.
21 ONUMA Yasuaki, *Human Rights, the State and Civilisation* (Chikuma Shobo 1998).

achievement in modern international law, the discursive space is dominated by major international NGOs based in Western countries, such as Amnesty International, Human Rights Watch, Freedom House and Oxfam. By adopting human rights standards that are contentious, they often give poor marks to non-Western societies, which ignites antipathy and resistance among the latter.

Onuma's responsiveness to the antagonisms of governments and peoples, especially those in the Third World, towards the Western-biased 'global standards' might be predictable in light of his previous writings. When he wrote about the plight of Korean minorities, Onuma was particularly receptive to unfairness within society and the international environment that contributed to it. As a scholar from a non-Western society writing on Grotius, he himself was also acutely aware that international law is predominated by Eurocentrism or West-centrism. For Onuma, however, his sympathies towards those who are marginalised posed no barrier to supporting and strengthening the legitimacy of international law. The challenge for Onuma was to defend the universality of human rights while rectifying the Western bias in the human rights discourse.

It was for this purpose that Onuma introduced what he called an 'intercivilizational' perspective on, or approach to, international law to explore viable grounds for its legitimacy. Although subsequently a slight change in the wording would be made from intercivilisational to transcivilisational[22] – in English, whereas in Japanese, the expression *bunsaiteki* was adhered to – that was the core idea that would become the hallmark of Onuma's subsequent works. In the present context, Onuma's point is that human rights norms should not be a device with which 'they' measure 'us' only, or vice versa. There is a tendency among Western societies to see that other societies and they only are at fault for human rights violations, while non-Western societies defend themselves on particularist grounds that they have a different cultural tradition. However, this curbs the potency of human rights. Instead, culturally unbiased standards should be established that are universally shared and by which the conventions of all societies, regardless of cultural tradition, are assessed. An intercivilisational perspective is a way to construct such common ground through a dynamic process of mutual transformation of multiple traditions.

22 The reason for the change in terminology is explained in Onuma, *A Transcivilizational Perspective on International Law: Questioning Prevalent Cognitive Frameworks in the Emerging Multi-Polar and Multi-Civilizational World of the Twenty-First Century* (Martinus Nijhoff 2010) 131–132. In sum, his intention was to avoid unfortunate confusion with Samuel Huntington's provocative idea, the 'clash of civilizations', which was publicised afterwards.

From a practical point of view, Onuma's intercivilisational perspective could be persuasive on several points. First, the notion of civilisation is found in positive rules in certain fields of international law, which would justify recourse to it more generally. For those who feel they are treated unfairly in international relations, an intercivilisational perspective could also be a useful strategy for regaining balance in the debate. Moreover, there is a truth in the claim that international law has an unreflective bias towards non-Western societies on human rights and other issues. Those with a conscience may, confronted with a protest from an intercivilisational perspective, at least pause for a while. On the other hand, from a theoretical point of view, the idea of an intercivilisational perspective appears to have several shortcomings, which will be considered in the next section.

## After 2000

### *The Asian Society of International Law*

For Onuma, promoting a transcivilisational perspective on international law was not only a matter of scholarly theory but also of a practical commitment, as epitomised by his dedication to founding the Asian Society of International Law.[23] OWADA Hisashi, the then-President of the International Court of Justice, when he suggested in a private conversation with Onuma in late summer 2003 the establishment of an association of international lawyers in Asia, found the right person who could instantly see its importance and would eventually bring it to fruition. Onuma had a genuine motivation as he was keenly aware of the international legal discourse dominated by doctrines, practices, languages, judges and so on of the West, and the breadth of his scholarly interests, as well as his assertive character and experience, had equipped him with the necessary connections with international legal scholars, diplomats and other practitioners.

This came to fruition with the inauguration conference of the Asian Society of International Law in Singapore in the spring of 2003 and the second conference in Tokyo in 2009. Onuma recalls how rapidly – it took only four years or less – the steps of founding the Society were taken since it had first been discussed. The Society now has four national chapters in Japan, Bangladesh, Iran and Korea, and holds international conferences in various Asian countries biennially, providing a rare opportunity for scholars and practitioners from across Asia and beyond.

23 Onuma recalls his experiences during the process in 'The Asian Society of International Law: Its Birth and Significance' (2011) *Asian Journal of International Law* 1.

In a sense, the establishment of the Asian Society emanated from his aspiration and realism combined. On the one hand, his patriotic wish was for Japan to take a more active role in the international sphere academically as well as politically. This is connected to his view on law. For Onuma, law is inseparably intertwined with politics, as he contended in 'International Law in and with International Politics' (2003).[24] He was thus acerbic about the positivist tendency in Japanese international legal scholarship, viewing it as submissive and complicit in sustaining the status quo unawares, which is, in effect, to the advantage of the West. Whether this view was correct is debatable, as there were Japanese international lawyers, such as KOTERA Akira, who consciously adopted a positivist methodology as a strategy for gaining discursive parity with Western international lawyers. Still, a regional society outside America or Europe would serve as political leverage to rectify the bias in international legal discourse, and, if one were to be established in Asia, it would be unimaginable without Japan, with its hefty tradition of international legal scholarship as well as its economic power, playing a major role.

On the other hand, Onuma was mindful through his association with victims of Japanese imperialism that a Japan-predominated society would not be hugely popular in the region, deflecting potential entrants. As governmental involvement must be kept out, other ways to secure the Society's financial basis were necessary. This was especially true, as the annual individual member fee was kept low to account for economic disparities within the region. Not only was the participation of law firms and practising lawyers in itself an essential part of the Society's activities, but their financial contribution was also vital in establishing a truly regional organisation. Singapore, both as the location of the secretariat and the venue of the inauguration conference, was also a deliberate choice. Onuma was also realistic about who would be elected president. Although his initiative and devotion throughout the preparatory phase were undeniable, and his personality was not short of self-confidence, he considered it necessary for this newborn Society to have a prominent public figure as its head to attract as much attention as possible. Thus, the honour was accorded to Judge Owada to become the first President of the Society.

24 ONUMA Yasuaki, 'International Law in and with International Politics: The Functions of International Law in International Society' (2003) 14 *Journal of International Law* 1.

### *Reaching a wider audience*

In the period after 2000, Onuma worked to consolidate his previous academic achievements and accelerated his efforts to reach the general public and university students, as well as a global audience. One such product was his first textbook, *Kokusaiho:: Hajimete Manabu Hito no Tameni* (2005),[25] the second edition of which was published in 2008. Its idiosyncratic character came not only from its attentiveness to politics in the background of law but also from the cover graphic of the Church of the Light by ANDO Tadao and a number of illustrations by OTOMO Hiroshi, both of whom were Onuma's acquaintances. What made it also distinctive was the extensive list of references for readers, a manifestation of the author's academic conscience and educational considerations.

He also published *Zainichi Chosen-Kankokujin no Kokuseki to Jinken* (2004),[26] an expanded version of his previous work published in a university periodical in 1979–1980. Though the theme reiterated what motivated the 1986 book, it provided a more systematic and comprehensive analysis at the national and international levels of the legal status of Korean residents in Japan.

In 2007, Onuma delivered a lecture at the Hague Academy of International Law, the substance of which was later published as *A Transcivilisational Perspective on International Law* in 2010.[27] This provided Onuma with an opportunity to further develop his transcivilisational approach to international law by linking to his earlier achievements. By around this point, Onuma had already published articles in several international English-language journals, such as *The European Journal of International Law*[28] and *International Legal Theory*,[29] including an article, 'When was the Law of International Society Born?' (2000),[30] which has become, according to

25 ONUMA Yasuaki, *International Law: For the First-Time Learner* (*Kokusaiho: Hajimete Manabu Hito no Tameno*) (Toshindo 2005).

26 ONUMA Yasuaki, *The Nationality and Human Rights of Korean Residents in Japan* (*Zainichi Kankoku- Chosen Jin no Kokuseki to Jinken*) (Toshindo 2004).

27 ONUMA, *A Transcivilizational Perspective on International Law* (n 22).

28 ONUMA, 'International Law in and with International Politics' (n 24).

29 Onuma, 'Is the International Court of Justice an Emperor Without Clothes?' (2002) 8 *International Legal Theory* 1.

30 ONUMA Yasuaki, 'When was the Law of International Society Born? An Inquiry of the History of International Law from an Intercivilizational Perspective' (2000) 2 *Journal of History of International Law* 1–66.

one reviewer,[31] influential, as it provides an alternative, less European narrative of history.

In the 2010 book, Onuma made it more explicit that constructivism, which recognises the role of values and ideals in international politics, laid the foundation of his approach. Onuma put much emphasis on the power of international law, not only the material power of the state. From a transcivilisational perspective, less emphasis was put on the role of the court in international society in favour of multilateral fora such as the United Nations General Assembly. This, combined with the criticism of the domestic law analogy, led to his scepticism of counting the judicialisation or legalisation of international law as progress. Onuma stressed that international law, as it was, must not be seen as 'one of the Europeans' making', for it had undergone a radical transformation through globalising, i.e. the acceptance of non-European states as members of international society in the late nineteenth century and the process of decolonisation in the late twentieth century. He also provided a defence of the universality of human rights from a transcivilisational perspective by rectifying the excessive focus on individual liberty rights. The main thrust was that, at their core, international law and human rights must be such that people in different religions, cultures and civilisations could see them as legitimate.

## *Towards a transcivilisational world*

These themes were revisited in his colossal English textbook on international law, *International Law in a Transcivilizational World* (2017).[32] Although the basic tenets remained unchanged, the book was not a simple reproduction in a different language of the preceding Japanese textbook. Reflecting the subsequent development of his ideas and his attunement to global readers, it represented a consummation of his scholarly achievements.

As various reviewers concur, the book is unlike a conventional textbook in either its approach or its composition. This is evident in the first three chapters. The first chapter, entitled 'International Law in a Multi-civilizational World', sets the book's general framework based on a transcivilisational approach, followed by the second, which critiques the source-based doctrine of international law and adopts a process-oriented approach. The notion of 'participants' of international law introduced in Chapter 3 resonates with

31 Lauri Mälksoo, 'ONUMA Yasuaki (1946–2018)' (2019) 21 *Journal of History of International Law* 2.

32 Onuma, *International Law in a Transcivilizational World* (Cambridge University Press 2017).

this. In Onuma's view, various non-state actors are involved in 'international legal processes', not limited to inter-state diplomatic relations.

Overall, Onuma focuses on the various functions of international law in social reality, not merely its textual expressions and scholarly interpretations. In international legal processes, diverse individuals play roles in different capacities in different settings. Thus, it is not a matter of accommodating non-state actors as secondary subjects, but rather of perceiving states, international organisations, companies, non-governmental organisations and so on as non-unitary groups of individuals, and of how international law works in the complex relations within and between them. Only in this way is the power of international law fully appreciated. Furthermore, if international law holds sway globally over many aspects of social relations, it should, again, become legitimate in the sense that it is accepted as the law for all humans and not merely for Europeans and Americans.

## Towards true universality

In a sense, Onuma passed away at the pinnacle of his career. Onuma's family recalls he was a scholar until the very end of his life. While terminally ill in hospital, he was making his final efforts to finalise a book to be published posthumously, *Kokusaiho* (2018),[33] another attempt to reach novice students and the general public. He might have been, as one of his colleagues uttered, demanding, but he was also demanding no less of himself.

Onuma was arguably the first Japanese international legal scholar with worldwide fame. However, Onuma perhaps did not give outright approval of his fame. His transcivilisational approach might be well received because it offered a convenient alternative to mainstream international legal scholarship. It is hardly deniable that there was an Orientalist mentality. Alternative discourses are welcomed as long as they remain at the margins and do not pose a serious threat to mainstream, allegedly universal, discourse. Apart from his close friends, the majority of those who come from outside East Asia might find enigmatic Onuma's insistence on the way he was named by his foreign colleagues, 'Onuma-san' rather than 'Yasuaki' (his first name), or the name order (putting family name first and given name thereafter). It is easy to attribute it to his peculiar personality and take it as a plea for an exception, dismissing the issue of cultural and intellectual hegemony,

33 ONUMA Yasuaki, *International Law* (*Kokusaiho*) (Chikuma Shobo 2018).

something Onuma, in fact, wanted to problematise.[34] Although there may be many legitimate objections to Onuma's transcivilisational approach to international law, his diagnosis of international law lamentably remains valid. There is a great disparity in political, economic and social power between states and peoples, which inhibits international law from becoming a true law of the global community. Those who disagree with Onuma's approach have yet to respond to the challenge of establishing the legitimacy of international law in a globalised world.

34 Richard Falk, 'International Law in a Transcivilizational World by ONUMA Yasuaki', *Yale Journal of International Law Forum*, https://www.yjil.yale.edu/book-rcview-international-law-in-a-transcivilizational-world/. Being a friend of Onuma's, Falk certainly does not adopt such a dismissive attitude.

# 13

# MOGAMI Toshiki: an unfrenzied normative realist

*NEGISHI Yota*

## Introduction

MOGAMI Toshiki (1950–), featured in this chapter, is a figure in the history of Japanese international legal theories who clearly and consciously set out his normative position. Mogami's academic career began at the University of Tokyo, where he earned a BA in law in 1974 and completed his PhD in 1980 at the University of Tokyo's Graduate School of Law and Politics. He then took a lecturer position at the International Christian University, where he primarily taught international law and international organisation theory, while also serving as Director of the Peace Research Institute at the university. He was subsequently made Professor Emeritus in 2011 and moved to Waseda University, where he taught international law and international organisation theory. In terms of academic activities, he not only served at the domestic level as President of the Japan Association for Peace Studies from 1999 to 2001, but also as President of the Japanese Association of the Asian Society of International Law from 2017.

His academic contributions have reached beyond international law to international relations and peace studies, influencing many future generations. In the recently published edition titled *International Law as Constructive Resistance toward Peace and Justice*, scholars of international law and international politics influenced by Mogami draw on and develop his theories from their own perspectives.[1] In this chapter, we trace how Mogami's own academic attitude has been formed through human interaction. Next, we summarise Mogami's views on international organisations, which he chose when he began his research and has been consistently interested in since then. Then, in the two sections that follow, we follow

1 Makoto Seta and Yota Negishi (eds), *International Law as Constructive Resistance Towards Peace and Justice* (Brill 2024). This chapter builds on the book's Introduction but expands it to include more varied perspectives.

what Mogami presents as his own view of international law, *just contra anarchiam* and *jus contra oligarchiam*, in turn. The final section presents Mogami's critical analysis of international law and its scholarship in his recently published book, *After International Law*.

## Scholarly attitudes shaped through intellectual interactions

### *Law and politics: unfrenzied normative realism*

Although many people have influenced his research style, we will limit ourselves to the two he specifically mentions in his memoirs. The first was his supervisor, SAKAMOTO Yoshikazu. Mogami recalls his high school days, when he aspired to become a doctor but decided to go to law school after coming across a book. He was fascinated by the logical writing style presented in the book *International Politics in the Nuclear Age*. The writer was Professor Sakamoto, who later became Mogami's mentor. Professor Sakamoto studied under the supervision of Professor Maruyama Masao, who had a major influence on post-war politics in Japan. Sakamoto calls Maruyama's attitude 'unfrenzied normative realism' and describes Maruyama as 'realistic' in the sense that he saw world politics as moving with complex and contradictory elements, and 'normative' in the sense that he focused on extending these trends. While agreeing with Maruyama's theory, Mogami also describes Sakamoto himself as having inherited his 'unfrenzied normative realism'. Naturally, this attitude was also inherited by Mogami himself.[2]

Another strong influence on the academic stream at the top was Richard Falk. The American legal scholar, together with colleagues including Sakamoto, organised the World Order Models Project (WOMP) and worked to develop an alternative vision of world-building under the constrained conditions of the Cold War era. Mogami himself participated in the movement and was greatly inspired by it. However, Mogami sees the most potential in Falk's theory, which he presented before he started the WOMP. Falk attempted to take an 'intermediate' position between Hans Kelsen, who sought to construct a system of restraints to control state action through international law, and Myres McDougal, who led the New Haven school of legal policy and saw international law as a process of authoritative

2 MOGAMI Toshiki, 'On "Unfrenzied Normative Realism" ("Sameta Kihanteki Riarizum" ni Yosete)' (2014) 863 *Sekai* 64–70 (in Japanese).

decision-making.[3] The intermediate position presents a theory of international law as a means of 'communication' between states and policymakers in order to meet the 'living needs of the international community'. Falk expected that the communicative function of international law would curb state overreaction and quell unbounded emotional reactions. Being aware of the indeterminacy of international law, Falk attempted to somehow resuscitate it without abandoning its existence by incorporating politics, an external factor of international law, into his theory.[4] In this sense, Falk was probably also one of those who took the position of 'unfrenzied normative realism', although Mogami does not explicitly describe Falk as such.

These academic edicts of 'unfrenzied normative realism' provided the methodological basis for Mogami to develop his own theories. In fact, Mogami attempted to conceive of a normative, value-based world order that incorporated the harsh realities of international politics, as Sakamoto and Falk had sought to do. They discussed in earnest the issues of peace and violence on a global scale as well as international organisations such as the UN. As will be explained later, these issues are often overlooked in a similar strand of global constitutionalism that later emerged from Europe. On the other hand, the WOMP took an all-inclusive approach to incorporate various values in envisioning an alternative world order to the Cold War structure. Similarly, global constitutionalism left room for all groups of issues under the trinitarian formula (human rights, democracy and the rule of law). On the contrary, Mogami consciously narrowed down his theory to the following two principles: *jus contra anarchiam et oligarchiam*, namely, international law against (principally) inter-state violence and oligarchically institutionalised power exercised in the name of justice.

### *Law and Christianity: anonymous sacrifice*

As well as being strictly aware of his duties as a researcher, Mogami has continued to confront how he lives his life as a Christian. As he left a caution in a lecture record, when writing books and articles on international law and international organisations, he did his utmost to refrain from saying that he was writing such content because of his faith. At the same time, however, he did not have the deception that his own research was completely divorced

3 Richard A. Falk, *Status of Law in International Society* (Princeton University Press 1970) Chapter 2: 'The Relevance of Political Context to the Nature and Functioning of International Law: An Intermediate View'.

4 MOGAMI Toshiki, *After International Law* (Misuzu Shobo 2024) 242–247 (in Japanese).

from his faith. Rather, he was aware of the inseparable link between the two. Indeed, he stated the linkage between his own professional findings and his faith in Christ as follows:[5]

> We must be peaceful. And we must be humane to the fullest extent. This is a matter of course. The important thing in this, I think, is whether or not we have in our hearts the principle of restraining our own righteousness. If you talk about being humane without the principle of restraining justice, it often leads to violence. Instead, what is most important when trying to be humane and just is how to restrain it. This restraining principle will vary from person to person, but I believe that for a Christian, the faith of Christianity can be the restraining principle for justice. Or perhaps, I should say that it must be.

It was the influence of two great Christians that led the Mogami to have such a restraining Christian faith in justice and peace. The first was Dag Hammerskjöld, who served as the second Secretary-General of the United Nations. Mogami recalls buying Hammerskjöld's famous diary, *Vägmärken* (translated as *Michi-Shirube* in Japanese),[6] when he was in high school and reading it over and over again on various occasions since then. One of Hammerskjöld's favourite verses was Matthew 6:5, where Jesus Christ admonishes us not to pray like hypocrites, which was also important for Mogami to develop his above-mentioned humble attitude. Against the background of this verse, Hammerskjöld worked on the creation of the United Nations Peacekeeping Force in 1956, which represents the idea of 'non-violence' as an antithesis to individual and collective violence within international organisations. The attempt also required 'anonymous sacrifice', such as lightly armed surveillance operations in dangerous areas. Hammerskjöld's diary entries at the time left a lasting impression, in which he warned against making anonymous sacrifices and asking for nothing in return.[7]

Another Christian devoted to anonymous sacrifice and who had a profound influence on Mogami was Dietrich Bonhoeffer. He was a German pastor and theologian, an absolute pacifist in his youth. Nonetheless, Bonhoeffer was arrested and executed for his part in a failed assassination plot against Hitler during the Second World War. His faithfulness to Christ led him to make such a harsh decision, as he believed that his homeland invaded neighbouring countries and slaughtered Jews, contrary to God's

5 MOGAMI Toshiki, 'To Be Humane, and to Be Peaceful (Jindoteki de Arukoto to Heiwateki de Arukoto)' in *Peace Without Borders* (*Kokkyo Naki Heiwa Ni*) (Misuzu Shobo 2005) 222–223 (in Japanese).

6 Dag Hammarskjöld, *Vägmärken*, Albert Bonniers förlag AB. 1 uppl. 1963.

7 MOGAMI, 'To Be Humane, and to Be Peaceful' 208–213 (n).

great commandments. However, this was done without glorifying his actions in the context of religious tension, but rather by undertaking to bear alone and unnoticed in sin.[8] Bonhoeffer's self-controlled attitude had a certain influence on Mogami's research stance, especially in the ultimate dilemma of humanitarian intervention discussed below.

Against the background of Christianity, Mogami's understanding of peace extends from direct state use of force to the *indirect* form of violence caused by the distortion of social structures. The paper on the *right to peace* in the early stage of his career, for example, shrewdly detected its emerging character to challenge the structural barriers preventing 'a social and international order in which the rights and freedoms [...] can be fully realised' as promulgated in Article 28 of the Universal Declaration of Human Rights.[9] In the textbook of his lectures concerning human rights and humanity carried by Japan's public broadcaster NHK (Japan Broadcasting Corporation), Mogami redefined the concept of peace through the lens of *structural* violence coined by Johan Galtung, from the absence of inter-state violence (negative peace) to that of any type of violence (positive peace).[10] The need to overcome the structural obstacles is of particular weight, as Mogami warns, for vulnerable and marginalised peoples whose suffering is continuing under the structure of international law,[11] including the Palestinian people under Israeli occupation,[12] *hibakusha* (victims of nuclear bombs) in Hiroshima and Nagasaki,[13] the population of Okinawa/Ryukyu, which remained under

8 Ibid.

9 MOGAMI Toshiki, 'The Right to Peace (Heiwa ni taisuru Kenri)' (1989) 40 *Freedom and Justice* 33–39, included in *The Era of International Constitutionalism* (*Kokusai Rikken Syugi no Jidai*) (Iwanami Shoten 2007) (in Japanese). To succeed this paper in terms of the contemporary developments, see Yasue Mochizuki, 'The Right to Peace Revisited: beyond an Aspiring Norm' in Seta and Negishi 80–110 (n 1).

10 MOGAMI Toshiki, 'Redefining Peace: Peace for Humanity (Heiwa wo Saiteigi Suru: Nngen no Tame no Heiwa)' in *What is Peace Now? Nine Stories Around Human Rights and Humanity* (*Ima Heiwa toha: Jinken to Jindo wo Meguru 9 Wa*) (Iwanami Shoten 2006) 89–108 (in Japanese). See also, Johan Galtung, 'Violence, Peace, Peace Research' (1969) 6 *Journal of Peace Research* 167–191.

11 Mogami Toshiki, 'Japan' in Simon Chesterman, Hisashi Owada and Ben Saul (eds), The *Oxford Handbook of International Law in Asia and the Pacific* (Oxford University Press 2019) 320–340.

12 Kyo Arai, 'Enemy or Disobedience? Paradigm Crisis on the Use of Lethal Force in Occupied Territory' in Seta and Negishi 142–162 (n 1).

13 Masashi Nakayama, 'Treaty on the Prohibition of Nuclear Weapons as Legal Correction of International Injustice: Issues of Normalization of "Human Security" and Creation of World Law' in Seta and Negishi 113–141 (n 1).

US military presence even after the occupation ended in 1972[14] and so-called comfort women in East Asia during the Second World War.[15]

## *Law and critique: indeterminacy and deconstruction*

Among Japanese international scholars, Onuma Yasuaki has mutually influenced Mogami in the same generation. As discussed in the chapter, Onuma was a rare figure in Japanese international legal scholarship in the post-war era who pursued a critical perspective. In a roundtable discussion with Onuma, Mogami pointed out the following three points in common between the two scholars: First, while there is a strong tendency in international legal scholarship to assume the objectivity of norms as given, both scholars question this perception. Second, neither of them completes their research by focusing on the rules themselves, but rather on the theoretical background behind the rules. Third, despite the difference that Onuma is involved in various civic movements and Mogami in the world of discourse, both have faced reality. In addition, they agreed on the potential of critical legal studies to emancipate international law from the mainstream positivist mindset.

In this sense, Martti Koskenniemi should be mentioned as someone who shares a critical mindset at the same age as Mogami, even though they have not had direct contact in shaping their theories. In *From Apology to Utopia*, Koskenniemi famously demonstrates a battle of legal minds on two fronts in examining the objectivity of international law: on the one hand, the 'concreteness' of the law by distancing it from theories of natural justice and, on the other hand, the normativity of the law by creating distance between it and actual state behaviour, will or interest.[16] According to Mogami, the indeterminacy theory of international law had already been problematised by him before Koskenniemi pointed it out and made it famous worldwide. Although they share the same critical mindset, a difference is pointed out. Koskenniemi's discussion of indeterminacy is more in the nature of individual epistemology, emphasising the doctrines and arguments of international jurists. In contrast, Mogami derives indeterminacy in terms of the structure

14 Kohki Abe, 'For Belated Justice in International Law: Righting Historical Wrongs in East Asia' in Seta and Negishi 36–56 (n).

15 To inherit the feminist perspective implied in Mogami's achievements, see Miho Omi, 'Gender-Based Violence against Women in International Law: Transformative Possibility of International Law' in Seta and Negishi 59–79 (n 1).

16 Martti Koskenniemi, *From Apology to Utopia: The Structure of International Legal Argument, Reissue with a New Epilogue* (Cambridge University Press 2006) 17–23.

of international law, which presupposes a system of sovereign nation-states, and from the provisional nature of all norms.

## International organisation as a catalyst for international ordering

### *In-organisational (counter-)hegemony: political organs*

Throughout his academic life, Mogami has engaged in theorising the dynamic phenomenon of international organisations as a focal point of international law and politics.[17] In contrast to the existing literature that descriptively explicates the authorities and functions of international organisations that actually exist, Mogami's analysis is normative and critically addresses the conceptualised phenomena of utilising international organisations and/or multilateralism for the international order.[18] Among his original conceptual inventions, the term *in-organisational counter-hegemony* proved useful to describe a revolutionary momentum that occurred within the United Nations during the Cold War.[19] In fact, the newly independent states, less powerful outside the United Nations, gained more influence within the organisation. It can be compared to those who maintained their oligarchical hegemony in the Security Council. If we call the latter the first type of multilateralism, the former can be labelled the second. This counter-hegemonic action stemmed not from hard military or economic power but from the normative and democratic legitimacy conferred by the principle of sovereign equality.

To describe such an overturn of the hegemonic structure with normative power, Mogami published a book titled *The Crisis of UNESCO and the World Order: International Organisation as Non-Violent Revolution* in 1987. The main title refers to the financial difficulties caused by the United

17 Mogami finished his doctoral thesis in 1980 on the dynamic regional integration of the European Community. His theory on international organisation is summarised in the textbook *Kokusai Kiko Ron Kogi* (*Lecture on International Organisation*) (Iwanami Shoten 2016).

18 Toshiki Mogami, 'On the Concept of International Organization: Centralization, Hegemonism, and Constitutionalism' in Madeleine Herren (ed.), *Networking the International System: Global Histories of International Organizations* (Springer 2014) 43–52.

19 Toshiki Mogami, 'The United Nations System as an Unfinished Revolution' (1990) 15 *Alternatives: Global, Local, Political* 177–197; Toshiki Mogami, 'Grafting the Past onto the Future of the United Nations System' in Richard A Falk, Robert C Johansen and Samuel S Kim (eds), *The Constitutional Foundations of World Peace* (SUNY Press 1993) 129–146.

States' withdrawal from the international organisation and, more generally, to the crisis of multilateralism. Behind this trend was the 'politicisation' by the newly independent states, which problematised sensitive issues such as disarmament studies, guarantees of collective rights and support for Palestinian refugees. The sub-title concerns the seemingly contradictory concepts of revolution and non-violence, for which Mogami drew inspiration from the terms 'creative destruction' coined by Joseph Schumpeter and 'creative anarchy' by Rajni Kothari.[20] The first aspect of revolution refers to the counter-hegemonic actions against the inter-organisational hegemonic power of the United States, based on the one-country, one-vote system. The second aspect of non-violence means that such a reversal was realised by discussions within the international organisation in pursuit of community interests on a global scale, which is differentiated from the superficially common benefits among hegemonies.

The idea of linking non-violence and resistance was continued in the next monograph, *Beyond the United Nations System*, published in 1995. In the United Nations, the Super Power, a collective security regime, has been positioned as the antithesis of Single Violence by individual states.[21] The cycle of violence has not been stopped, but it has the risk of getting worse. Mogami then presents another dialectic between the Single/Super Violence thesis versus the Non-Violence antithesis, as represented by peacekeeping operations and peaceful dispute settlements.[22] This circumstance could equally be described as a form of 'anarchic structuring'. Unlike Hedley Bull's assertion of anarchy that permits inter-state conflicts, it instead facilitates a pursuit of 'universality from below' by various stakeholders attentive to mutual considerations.[23]

### *Touchable and visible organisation: secretariat and special organs*

The UN's functions are not exhausted by the Security Council and the General Assembly. The former is mobile but lacks legitimacy due to its oligarchy, while the latter ensures sovereign equality and has legitimacy but

20 MOGAMI Toshiki, *The Crisis of UNESCO and the World Order: International Organisation as Non-Violent Revolution* (*Yunesuko no Kiki to Sekai Chitsujo: Hi Boryoku Kakumei to Shiteno Kokusai Kiko*) (Token Syuppan 1987) 169–198 (in Japanese).

21 MOGAMI Toshiki, *Beyond the United Nations System* (*Kokuren Sisutemu wo Koete*) (Iwanami Shoten 1995) 95–107 (in Japanese).

22 Ibid 107–125.

23 Ibid 177, 185–186.

is less effective. Such shortcomings are, in fact, compensated for by civilian, humanitarian and field-based organs that underpin human life on the ground. Mogami calls such organs 'the touchable and visible UN', including the World Food Programme (WFP), the UN Children's Fund (UNICEF), the World Health Organization (WHO), the UN Development Programme (UNDP), the Office for the Coordination of Humanitarian Affairs (OCHA) and the UN High Commissioner for Human Rights (OHCHR). They represent the third type of multilateralism, non-state in character, unlike the interstate multilateralism of the Security Council and the General Assembly.

Another embodiment of the third type of multilateralism is the Secretariat. As mentioned above, the foremost credit goes particularly to Hammerskjöld, who, as the second UN Secretary-General, presented the role of international law as a *dam*. In the Last Words to the Staff, Hammerskjöld called for his colleagues to 'reduce the dangers' not by 'waging a war for peace' but through 'effective work for building dams against the floods of disintegration and violence'.[24] This conception of a dam was represented by the UN Peacekeeping Force, which the Secretariat, under his leadership, worked hard to provide to prevent a total collapse of the world order. Although it is 'extremely modest', Mogami appreciates such an action to 'explore the conditions under which legal norms that cannot work automatically can function' and to create 'a mechanism to prevent outbursts of political assertions and intersections from breaking out' by 'assembling small parts and preventing outbursts at different stages'.[25]

In this context, non-governmental organisations (NGOs) and civil society organisations (CSOs) must also be mentioned as actors working closely with the aforementioned 'touchable and visible' intergovernmental organisations (IGOs). Mogami notes that NGOs and CSOs in the public sphere, such as human rights and development, work with UN civilian, humanitarian and field-based organs to 'restore deprived humanity' or 'de-victimisation'.[26] Examples include Amnesty International, Human Rights Watch (HRW), International Committee of the Red Cross (ICRC) and Médecins Sans Frontières (MSF). These non-state actors are increasingly participating in the process of making and implementing international legal norms, either formally or informally.

24 https://www.un.org/depts/dhl/dag/time1961.htm

25 MOGAMI, *After International Law* 254 (n).

26 MOGAMI Toshiki, 'Peace, Human Rights and Citizens: Toward Globalisation of Civil Society (Heiwa to Jinken to Shimintachi: Shimin Syakai no Sekaika he)' in *Peace Without Borders* 132–133 (n).

## *Jus contra anarchiam*

### *Normative multilateralism against anarchical unilateralism*

Drawing on his observations in the study of international organisations, Mogami embarked on elaborating an original concept of *normative multilateralism*. For him, multilateralism has, by nature, a normative agenda that designates certain fundamental modes of action, namely, collective making of decisions and actions based on common norms. This normative aspect of multilateralism is thus essentially tied to several different components of *the rule of law*. Its multilateral character should not be equated with multi-state but rather encompass the roles of non-state actors that challenge the state-centric idea under international law and politics.[27]

Applying this concept to the various aspects of *violence* at the international level, the first aspect of Mogami's analytical framework, *jus contra anarchiam*, gradually emerged. It criticises the direct form of violence, namely, the use and threat of force between states. He particularly directed his criticism at the unilateral use of force by the US and its allies without clear legal bases: one against Afghanistan after the 9/11 terrorist attacks in 2001 based on the right to self-defence against non-state actors;[28] and another against Iraq for the allegations of weapons of mass destruction (WMDs) in 2003 based on the prior authorisation from the Security Council.[29] The idea of normative multilateralism can be applied in the contemporary era where China rises as a new power, and Russia launches aggression against Ukraine.[30]

Concurrent with his research on the use of force by the hegemonic actor, Mogami consistently pays careful attention to the interaction between the UN Charter (Article 2(4)) and the Constitution of Japan (Article 9), the

27 MOGAMI Toshiki, 'Non-State Actors and International Law: A Tentative Theorisation on the Conversion of the Principle of the Legal Order (Hi Kokka Syutai to Kokusaiho: Hochitsujo no Tenkan ni Kansuru Shiron)' (2009) 108 *Journal of International Law and Diplomacy* (*Kokusaiho Gaiko Zasshi*) 117–143 (in Japanese).

28 MOGAMI Toshiki, 'The Legal Structure of Justice and Humanity: What Determines the Legal Justness? (Seigi to Jindo no Hokozo: Nani ga Hotekina Tadashisa wo Kimeruka)' (2002) 74(6) *Horitsu Jiho* 5–10, included in *The Era of International Constitutionalism* (n).

29 MOGAMI Toshiki, 'Multilateralism and the Rule of Law: A Reflection on the Position of the Norm on the Prohibition of Use of Force (Takokukan Syugi to Ho no Shihai: Buryoku Fukoshi Kihan no Teii ni Kansuru Ichi Kosatsu)' (2004) 23 *Yearbook of World Law* (*Sekaiho Nenpo*) 93–123, included in *The Era of International Constitutionalism* (n).

30 Tetsuya Yamada, 'The United Nations and the Big Powers at a Time of 'Patriotic Unilateralism' and 'Global Governance' in Seta and Negishi 217–229 (n).

amalgam of which he labels as 'the norms of common destiny'.[31] In the case of the Gulf Crisis, in which Security Council Resolution 678 '[a]uthorise[d] Member States to use all necessary means [...] to restore international peace and security in the area', Mogami lamented the Japanese Government's involvement in a coalition and proposed it to be a *conscientious objector state*.[32] When the administration of Shinzo Abe assertively promoted what was alleged to be an unconstitutional reinterpretation of the constitution through interpretation for collective self-defence in 2014, Mogami asserted that the right to collective self-defence under international law cannot be invoked to justify such a political decision.[33]

### *Humanitarian intervention*

Mogami's *Jus contra anarchiam* was also developed in a more complex issue of humanitarian intervention. When facing the NATO bombing of Kosovo in 1999, which provoked the oft-repeated 'illegal but legitimate' argument in the name of humanity, Mogami published a booklet titled *Humanitarian Intervention: Is There a Just Use of Force?* In this book, having traced the history of humanitarian intervention, Mogami suggests that the concept has been abused in doubtful and ambiguous situations.[34] Even in the case of NATO's intervention in Kosovo, he questions whether it satisfied the requirements of legality and legitimacy which many countries and people would accept.[35] Against his Christian insight, Mogami names the situation of humanitarian intervention as the Bonhoefferian situation, which needs to be done anonymously and sacrificially on its own. It should be differentiated from the narcissistically righteous attitude, which easily falls into the just war doctrine.[36]

31 Toshiki Mogami, 'Normativity: Domestic and International Dimensions' (1987) 12 *Peace and Change: A Journal of Peace Research* 39–50.
32 MOGAMI Toshiki, 'For a Testimony of Conscientious Objector State: Seeking the Cornerstone of Post-Cold War Security (Ryoshinteki Heieki Kyohi Koku no Akashi no Tameni: Posuto Reisen no Anzen Hosyo no Soseki wo Motomete)' (1990) 547 *Sekai* 23–34 (in Japanese).
33 MOGAMI Toshiki, 'International Law Is Not the Imperial Standard (Kokusaiho ha Nishiki no Mihata deha Nai)' (2015) 873 *Sekai* 62–70 (in Japanese).
34 MOGAMI Toshiki, *Humanitarian Intervention: Is There a Just Use of Force? (Jindoteki Kainyu: Seigi no Buryoku Koshi ha Aruka)* (Iwanami Shoten 2001) 19–41 (in Japanese).
35 Ibid 96–128.
36 Ibid 190–195.

While most studies on humanitarian intervention tend to focus on the (uppercase) *Humanitarian Intervention* involving intra-state violence, Mogami emphasises the (lowercase) *humanitarian intervention* undertaken by IGOs, NGOs and CSOs to provide humanitarian relief.[37] The latter is also paraphrased as *humble activism*, whose interventions are made out of empathy for the persecuted, not imposition.[38] He particularly appreciates the anonymous sacrifice of civilians who are sympathetic to the suffering of others and rescue others across national borders and without regard for the danger involved.[39] This type of non-violent intervention ranges not only from *reactive* relief in emergency situations but also *preventive* measures in everyday missions: to pictorialise the latter, Mogami borrows the words '*Intervenir oui, mais en amont*' (intervene, yes, but upstream) by Ignacio Ramonet, the editor-in-chief of Le Monde diplomatique.[40] This corresponds to the third type of multilateralism described above, complementing the first (the Security Council) and second (the General Assembly) types thereof, all of which constrain unilateral military action in the guise of humanity.

## *Jus contra oligarchiam*

### *International constitutionalism against oligarchical hegemony*

In pursuing normative multilateralism, Mogami explicates the essence of *international constitutionalism*.[41] An outline of international constitutionalism was already presented in 1995, celebrating the fiftieth anniversary of the UN and the bicentenary of Immanuel Kant's *Zum Ewigen Frieden*.[42] Mogami refined his theoretical position of international constitutionalism in light of previous studies. Although evaluating the visions of world government advocated by Tabata Shigejiro,[43] Mogami admits that it has not been realised and rather focuses on the world organisation represented

37 Ibid 207–210.
38 Ibid.
39 Ibid 164–188.
40 Ignacio Ramonet, 'Intervenir', *Le Monde diplomatique*, January 1993.
41 Akihiko Kimijima, 'Japan's Contribution to Global Constitutionalism' (2009) 4 *Societies Without Borders* 105–116.
42 MOGAMI Toshiki, '"Two Hundred Years" of the United Nations: A Memorandum on International Constitutionalism (Kokuren no "200 Nen": Kokusai Rikken Syugi ni tsuite no Oboegaki)' (1995) 67(6) *Horitsu Jiho* 44–50, included in *The Era of International Constitutionalism* (Iwanami Shoten 2007) (in Japanese).
43 TABATA Shigejiro, *The Thought of World Government* (*Sekai Seihu no Shiso*) (Iwanami Shoten 1950) (in Japanese).

by the United Nations. It does not mean, however, that Mogami accepts Bardo Fassbender's idea of equating *The United Nations Charter as the Constitution of the International Community*.[44] While Fassbender has optimistic expectations on the constitutional frameworks built on the founding document, Mogami retains unfrenzied normative realism to acknowledge a diversity of problems which cannot be solved by the constitutional characterisation.[45]

A less ambitious project of global constitutionalism, mainly launched by German public scholars such as Anne Peters and Mathias Kumm, was more acceptable to Mogami. Although he later adds critical insights to the project, Mogami appreciates Peters' framework to the extent that it concerns the (re-)ordering of the international order, departs from individuals (rather than sovereign states) and shares a value-oriented, normative foundation of humanity. Basically, in a similar fashion to global constitutionalism, Mogami criticised the illegitimate exercise of international public power within the realm of international constitutionalism. It is the second aspect of his analytical framework, *jus contra oligarchiam*.[46]

The law against oligarchy is primarily directed at the unrestricted legislative power of the Security Council, represented by its Resolutions 1373 on counter-terrorism and 1540 on counter-WMD proliferation.[47] In the particular case of targeted sanctions, the European Court of Human Rights (e.g. *Behrami and Saramati*) and the European Court of Justice (e.g. *Kadi*) revealed a certain kind of disobedience to put limits on the Security Council's public authority.[48] Even though these judicial reactions originated primarily from Europe, Mogami argues that such disobediences imply the legitimacy for seeking a constitutional system of international law based on universal human rights principles.[49] In other words, such challenges represent a form of *constructive resistance* that relativises the established hierarchical

44 Bardo Fassbender, *The United Nations Charter as the Constitution of the International Community* (Martinus Nijhoff 2009).

45 MOGAMI, *After International Law* 137–146 (n).

46 Toshiki Mogami, 'Towards *Jus Contra Oligarchiam*: A Note on Critical Constitutionalism' (2012) 55 *Japanese Yearbook of International Law* 371–402.

47 Masami Maruyama, 'Legal Control for the UN Security Council: toward jus contra oligarchiam as Critical Global Constitutionalism' in Seta and Negishi 186–214 (n 1).

48 Ryuya Daidouji, 'International Organisations and Contestation: Reconsidering Democratic Control in Global Constitutionalism' in Seta and Negishi 165–185 (n 1).

49 MOGAMI Toshiki, 'Universal Public Power and Universal Legal Order: On the Judicial Review of the Resolutions and Actions of the United Nations Security Council (Fuhenteki Kokenryoku to Fuhenteki Hochitsujo: Kokuren Anzen Hosyo Rijikai no Ketsugi oyobi Kodo ni Taisuru Shiho Sinsa ni tsuite)' in MATSUDA Takeo, TANAKA Norio, YAKUSHIJI Kimio and SAKAMOTO Sigeki (eds), *Thoughts and Structure of*

structure of power 'from above', and thereafter seeks to establish alternative universal principles 'from below'.[50]

## *Critical constitutionalism*

In his recent works, Mogami has chosen a more explicit notion of *critical constitutionalism* to examine the existing literature of international or global constitutionalism. Behind the emergence of critical constitutionalism, there already existed epistemic and methodological diversity and norm proliferation around the notion of international constitutionalism, thereby making its conceptual framework seriously ambiguous. More seriously, the 'trinitarian mantra of the constitutionalist faith' has limits to be criticised from Mogami's eyes.[51] In spite of 'globality' in its naming, the Eurocentric project has uncritically presupposed the universalist 'trinity' of human rights, democracy and the rule of law, which are 'historically contingent' and 'deeply contextual' in the local history.[52] Mogami suggests that the Eurocentric bias causes the dual problem of normativity: deflation and inflation.

As regards normative deflation, on the one hand, Mogami points out that peace and security, the most important foundations in ordering the international community, have been neglected in the trinitarian formula of global constitutionalism. The historical conditions that made it possible to consecrate the holy grail were the end of the Cold War, or more precisely, of the 'European Civil War', against the background of the integrated EU system.[53] Put differently, if the project seeks to be truly global, the sacred formula should incorporate the peaceful value, which is central for most of the rest of the world. Even in the camp of global constitutionalism, some started to reflect 'how poorly [trinitarian] norms represent the real, grim

*Contemporary International Law*, vol. II: *Environment, Sea, Criminal, Dispute and Foresight* (Toshindo 2012) 371–404 (in Japanese).

50 MOGAMI Toshiki, 'A New Horizon of International Constitutionalism: Hierarchy, Heterarchy, De-Europeanisation (Kokusai Rikken Syugi no Aratana Chihei: Hieraruki, Heteraruki, Datsu Yoroppa)' (2013) 85(11) *Horitsu Jiho* 6–12 (in Japanese).

51 Mattias Kumm, Anthony F. Lang, Jr, James Tully and Antje Wiener, 'Editorial: How Large is the World of Global Constitutionalism?' (2014) 3 *Global Constitutionalism* 1–8, 3–4.

52 Jefferey L. Dunoff, Antje Wiener, Mattias Kumm, Anthony F. Lang, Jr and James Tully, 'Editorial: Hard Times: Progress Narratives, Historical Contingency and the Fate of Global Constitutionalism' (2015) 4 *Global Constitutionalism* 1–17.

53 MOGAMI, *After International Law* (n).

and violent world of contemporary globalisation'.[54] In this respect, Mogami reflects that the WOMP, which preceded contemporary debates on global constitutionalism, first and foremost envisioned a world order with the goal of minimising violence (preventing and deterring war).[55]

The normative inflation, on the other hand, can be observed in both the WOMP and the project of global constitutionalism. The WOMP's interdisciplinary nature 'tended to include many political ideals and societal aspirations, regardless of whether they could legitimately be part of legal discourse'.[56] The same criticism is directed at the project of global constitutionalism. In fact, Anne Peters examines the imbalance between *first* generation (civil and political) rights and *second* generation (economic, social and cultural) rights, and proposes a remarkable transformation that 'the traditional trinity of global constitutionalism can and should be extended to cover a fourth aspect, a social limb'.[57] Against this background, Mogami consciously disciplines his own position not to envision an all-encompassing order construction but to zero in on the legal rectification of allegedly illegal actions and illegitimate institutions according to constitutional principles (regarding *jus contra anarchiam* and *jus contra oligarchiam*).[58]

## After international law

### *Deconstructing international law (scholarship)*

In his latest book, *After International Law*, Mogami's critical perspective is ultimately directed at both international law itself and the scholarship in this field. Published after the Russian aggression against Ukraine, the book begins by citing a challenge to international law and the UN by President

54 James Tully, Jefferey L. Dunoff, Anthony F. Lang, Jr, Mattias Kumm and Antje Wiener, 'Editorial: Introducing Global Integral Constitutionalism' (2016) 5 *Global Constitutionalism* 1–15.

55 Toshiki Mogami, '*Perpetuum Mobile*: Before and After Global Constitutionalism' in Takao Suami, Anne Peters, Mattias Kumm and Dimitri Vanoverbeke (eds), *Global Constitutionalism from European and East Asian Perspectives* (Cambridge University Press 2018) 29–57.

56 Ibid 36.

57 Anne Peters, 'Global Constitutionalism: The Social Dimension' in Suami and Others 277–350 (n).

58 Mogami Toshiki, 'Criticism of International Constitutionalism and Critical International Constitutionalism (Kokusai Rikken Syugi Hihan to Hihanteki Kokusai Rikken Syugi)' (2014) 33 *Yearbook of World Law* (*Sekaiho Nenpo*) 1–32 (in Japanese).

Volodymyr Zelensky. In a speech on 5 April 2022 at the Security Council, the President of the invaded state gave an ultimatum to Member States: 'Are you going to dissolve the UN? Do you think that the era of international law has passed?'[59] This warning from Kyiv provoked further discussion of international law through the media, and a discourse even emerged that argued for the 'death' of the rules-based international order.[60] As Mogami acknowledges, it is not right to say that international law 'is coming to an end' following this incident, but it 'has been coming to an end' for some time, and can be understood as President Zelensky beginning to speak of the final death sentence.[61] According to Mogami, as the current situation regarding the prohibition of the use of force has shown, a significant part of what is called international law remains 'ineffective'.

As a diagnosis of ineffectiveness, Mogami regards international law as 'heterogeneous', comprising combinations of multilateral and bilateral treaties, general and special international law, lex lata and lex ferenda. A more serious problem underlying the heterogeneity is the unorganised mix of effective and ineffective law, which is uniformly referred to as international law. This point may remind us of the famous proposition advocated by Louis Henkin: 'almost all nations observe almost all principles of international law and almost all of their obligations almost all the time'.[62] Mogami criticises that this proposition creates 'invisible ineffectiveness' on two occasions: when the infringements of international law are of such gravity that they lead to major upheavals in the international order, and when there is no international law to regulate the situation, which results in the obstruction of international relations.[63] As represented by the Henkin proposition, the majority of international legal scholars have not faced such ineffectiveness head-on by covering international law with a veil of objectivity.[64]

However, as deconstructed by Koskenniemi in *From Apology to Utopia*, international law is destined to be indeterminate in the language of international lawyers. This indeterminate nature is labelled 'general hypothetical hypothesis' by Mogami, which stems from the structure and function of international law. While appreciating Koskenniemi's deconstructive analysis in *From Apology to Utopia*, Mogami notes that it seems to fall into

59 Speech by the President of Ukraine at a Meeting of the UN Security Council, 5 April 2022.

60 The Washington Times, *Death of International Law: Flouted by Despots and Weaponized Against Small Nations*, 14 June 2022.

61 MOGAMI, *After International Law* 1–7 (n).

62 Louis Henkin, *How Nations Behave*, 2nd edn (1979) 47.

63 MOGAMI, *After International Law* 35 (n).

64 Ibid 48–76.

agnosticism. He rather seeks a normative solution from a different angle: 'To put a stop to the argument that calling what exists as definite as if it were imbued with immutable objectivity, and to recognise that legality in the present is not legality in eternity, leaving room for the search for new universals'.[65] However, Koskenniemi in the book's new epilogue also envisioned the normative project to 'provide resources for the use of international law's professional vocabulary for critical or emancipatory causes'.[66]

### *What only theory can do*

After deconstructing international law (scholarship), Mogami envisions its aftermath. In the academia of international law, legal positivism has been mainstreamed and even mystified. According to Andrea Bianchi, '[b]y interpreting judgments and other legal materials, and by administering their interpretations as initiation rites, scholars collectively participate in the rituals and practices that reproduce a logic of domination'.[67] In referring to Bianchi's critical insight, Mogami demystifies and diversifies the theory of international law. The gospel of 'binding, universal norms', and the oneness of theory, sanctified by priest-like legal positivists, shall be disenchanted. Mogami notes:

> If we abandon our attachment to binding legal norms, we will be able to envision a different role for international law in the international community. Rather than establishing a body of law that compels states to obey even against their will, international law will be given a completely different function. Of course, as researchers, we can only speak theoretically about what that function could be. It is those who can exercise political power, including the elite of the international law industry, who will put it into practice. It will be the task of those who belong to this new world of international law to persuasively demonstrate to them what the necessary law of the world is.

As a concrete potential of the necessary law mobilising the politics, Mogami finally attempts to 'rewind the time'. He takes the example of mass killings of Indigenous peoples in the German colony of Southwest Africa (now Namibia) between 1904 and 1908. In this past injustice, some 65,000 Herero (Ova Herero) and 10,000 Nama people, corresponding to 80 and

65 Ibid 112.
66 Koskenniemi, *From Apology to Utopia* 589–590 (n).
67 Andrea Bianchi, *International Law Theories: An Inquiry Into Different Ways of Thinking* (Oxford University Press 2016) 34.

50 per cent, respectively, were executed by the German colonial ruler. On 29 June 2017, the German federal parliament rejected a motion whose statement of motion said: 'The murders of the German groups [sic] meet *today's criteria* for genocide, as defined in the United Nations Convention of 1948 on the prevention and punishment of the crime of genocide and, for that reason, must be recognized by the German government as such'.[68] To reflect the present-centred concept of time, both governments made the Joint Declaration, by which Germany confirms 'a special historical and moral responsibility towards Namibia'.[69] The wording of 'historical and moral responsibility', reversely speaking, is criticised for lacking the recognition of Germany's legal obligation to provide reparation to affected communities.

The conflict of views stems from differing understandings of intertemporal law. In the *Palmas* arbitration, Max Huber famously addressed the question of which of the different legal systems prevailing at successive periods is to be applied in a particular case. To answer this conundrum, he made the distinction between the *creation* and *existence* of rights: 'The same principle which subjects the act creative of a right to the law in force at the time the right arises, demands that the existence of the right, in other words its continued manifestation, shall follow the conditions required by the evolution of law'.[70] According to the first part of this passage, the German government's claim that the massacres were not prohibited under international law 'in force at the time' may be justified. While it might be useful for 'legal certainty' for the traditional powerful (colonial and imperial states), it can never be 'certainty' in the sense that objections remain in terms of justice and risk inviting further coercion and violence.[71]

Instead, Mogami underscores the second part of Huber's statement, according to which 'the conditions required by the evolution of law' concerning genocide until the contemporary era may rewind time on past injustice. The second principle of intertemporal law is certainly invoked by the dissenting opinion of Judge Tanaka Kotaro in the second phase of the *South West Africa* (Namibia) case in 1966.[72] More recently, the rewinding

68 Stefan Talmon, 'The Genocide in Namibia: Genocide in a Historical-Political or in a Legal Sense?' *German Practice of International Law*, 23 September 2017 (emphasis added).

69 Joint Declaration by the Federal Republic of Germany and the Republic of Namibia 'United in Remembrance of Our Colonial Past, United in Our Will to Reconcile, United in Our Vision of the Future' (2021).

70 Reports of International Arbitral Awards, vol. II, 829–871.

71 MOGAMI, *After International Law* 294–295 (n).

72 *South West Africa*, Second Phase, Judgment, ICJ Reports 1966, 6, Dissenting Opinion of Judge Tanaka, Reports, 250, 293.

time approach is taken by the Allegation Letters by the mandate holders of the special procedures under the UN Human Rights Council regarding the Herero and Nama genocide in Namibia.[73] A similar reparation claim is made by the Caribbean Community (CARICOM) Reparation Commission regarding the tragic human legacy of slavery and colonisation by European countries.[74]

In an attempt to correct these past injustices, Mogami coined the term *jus coactum* (compelled law) as a twist on the term *jus cogens* (compelling law).[75] *Jus coactum* is not an individual, forced treaty, but a historical concept that refers to the totality of so-called 'international law' in a given period of time. This so-called 'international law' was devised by dominant countries to subjugate other countries, and it 'was not the law of the international community'. At such an 'in-between, unclear stage', the powerful nations may say that it was 'legal', but for the countries and people that were invaded and forced, it was simply 'illegal'. If it is affirmed that even at that time it was 'illegal', time will move backwards and we will return to the 'original state of humanity'. Mogami is not making a radical proposal to rehash all past injustices to the point of destabilising the international community. However, he argues that if reconciliation between the nations cannot be achieved without acknowledging the illegality of the past in this way, then the 'reversibility of time for the future' is necessary.[76]

## Conclusion

Mogami's unique theory of international law has been formed by intellectual interaction that features politics, Christianity and critique. Starting with the dynamism of international organisations, his research interests extended to the restraint of inter-state and institutionalised violence (*jus contra anarchiam et oligarchiam*). Mogami has a never-stopping spirit of inquiry and is further expanding on the prolegomena on normative multilateralism he

73 United Nations Human Rights Council Special Procedures, AL DEU 1/2023 and AL NAM 1/2023, 23 February 2023.

74 CARICOM Ten Point Plan for Reparatory Justice. See also, Report of the Special Rapporteur on Contemporary Forms of Racism, Racial Discrimination, Xenophobia and Racial Intolerance, A/74/321, 21 August 2019.

75 MOGAMI Toshiki, 'El Sol Del Membrillo, Inter-Temporal Law, and *Jus Coactum* (Marumero no Yoko, Jisaiho, *Jus Coactum*)' (2014) 43 *UP* (University of Tokyo) 28–33 (in Japanese). Mogami's doctrine of intertemporal law is succeeded by Abe 36–56 (n).

76 Ibid 32.

wrote earlier, with global history[77] and the punitive character of universal jurisidciton.[78] All the way through, his theory is based on 'a social science sensibility based on empathy with others'.[79]

Mogami's sensibility of seeking encounters with others leads to the 'conversation with the incommensurable' raised in the Introduction of this book. As is explained in the context of *After International Law*, Mogami decisively supports the legality of international law to denounce Russia's aggression against Ukraine. Meanwhile, he is critical of Western countries' double standards that defend their own violence but exert the politics of ostracisation and isolation of Russia from multilateralism.[80] Even though, in the short term, some aspects were unavoidable in order to express firm solidarity, in the long term, they would make it impossible to resolve complex political tensions.[81] To avoid such euphoric reactions overemphasising justice, Mogami's critical mindset again exhibits 'unfrenzied normative realism':

> As well as dealing with the difficulties [of rescuing lives and refugees and of holding accountable and making reparations], we must also review the weaknesses of international law and the international organisational system that allowed such barbarism to take place. It will be an endless task, but it does not seem an impossible task when one looks at the solidarity of people around the world crying out against this aggression. If grassroots solidarity already exists on the prohibition of aggression and respect for international humanitarian

77 MOGAMI Toshiki, 'The Relocation of Multilateralism: Prolegomenon (Multilateralism no Saiteii: Josetsu)' in Noboru Kashiwagi and Others (eds), *Comparative Law Seen from Japan and Brazil: Festschrift in Honour of Professor Masato Ninomiya's 70th birthday (Nihon to Brazil kara Mita Hikakuho)* (Shinzansya 2019) (in Japanese).

78 MOGAMI Toshiki, 'Prolegomenon of Theory of Universal Jurisdiction: The Structure of Confluence and Renovation (Fuhenteki Kankatsuken Ron Josetsu: Sakuso to Kakushin no Kozo)' in Sakamoto Shigeki (ed.), *The Frontier of International Law-Making (Kokusai Rippo no Saizensen)* (Yushindo Kobunsha 2009) 3–28. On this point, see also Makoto Seta, 'The Role of Universal Jurisdiction in Achieving International Legal Justice: a Global Constitutionalism Perspective' in Seta and Negishi 230–250 (n 1).

79 MOGAMI Toshiki, 'In This Corner of the Beautiful World (1): The Gaze at the Beauty of the World' (2012) 41 *UP* (University of Tokyo) 22–27 (in Japanese). On this point, see also Yota Negishi, 'The Phenomenological Embodiment of International Lawyers: The Gaze at People Living "In This Corner of the Beautiful World"' in Seta and Negishi (n).

80 Martina Buscemi, 'Outcasting the Aggressor: The Deployment of the Sanction of "Non-Participation"' (2022) 116 *American Journal of International Law* 764–774.

81 Fionnuala Ní Aoláin, 'Why Pushing Russia Out of Multilateral Institutions is Not a Solution to the War', *Just Security*, 22 March 2022.

> law, there is no other way but to walk the long road of nurturing and strengthening it. At the same time, we must live 'post-Ukraine' not without, but with, Russia.[82]

This passage doubts the imposition of *dialogue* (*Taiwa*) to achieve the one-sided, ostensible truth by excluding the incommensurable; it rather invites even incommensurable others to *conversation* (*Kaiwa*) for the sake of conviviality within normative multilateralism.[83]

82 MOGAMI Toshiki, 'Straining to Hear Ukraine: The Last War of Conquest (2)' (2022) 715 *Misuzu* 11.

83 As a writing inspired by Mogami's idea, see Yota Negishi, 'Postscript: International Legal Discourse in the Russia-Ukraine Crisis: Defence, Critique and Renewal of "the Rules-Based International Order"' in Jean d'Aspremont, *International Law as a Belief System* (*Shinten Taikei to shite no Kokusaiho*), translated by Yota Negishi (Shinzansya 2023).

# Index

EU authorised representative for GPSR:
Easy Access System Europe, Mustamäe tee 50,
10621 Tallinn, Estonia
gpsr.requests@easproject.com

www.ingramcontent.com/pod-product-compliance
Ingram Content Group UK Ltd.
Pitfield, Milton Keynes, MK11 3LW, UK
UKHW021010120926
8556IPUK00029B/463
*9781526174949*